EXPOSURE

SELF EXPOSURE

Human-Interest Journalism and the Emergence of Celebrity in America, 1890–1940

Charles L. Ponce de Leon

The University of North Carolina Press

Chapel Hill and London

© 2002

The University of North Carolina Press

All rights reserved

Manufactured in the United States of America

Designed by Richard Hendel

Set in Scotch Roman and Bahnhof Ultra

by Tseng Information Systems, Inc.

The paper in this book meets the guidelines for

permanence and durability of the Committee on

Production Guidelines for Book Longevity of the

Council on Library Resources.

Library of Congress Cataloging-in-Publication Data

Ponce de Leon, Charles L. (Charles Leonard)

Self-exposure: human-interest journalism and the

emergence of celebrity in America, 1890–1940 /

Charles L. Ponce de Leon.

p. cm.

Includes bibliographical references and index.

ISBN 0-8078-2729-0 (alk. paper)—

ISBN 0-8078-5403-4 (pbk.: alk. paper)

1. Sensationalism in journalism—United States.

2. Celebrities—Press coverage—United States.   I. Title.

PN4888.S46 P66   2002

302.23—dc21   2002002099

cloth   06 05 04 03 02   5 4 3 2 1

paper 06 05 04 03 02   5 4 3 2 1

For my mother

and the memory of

my father

CONTENTS

A section of illustrations follows page 140.

. . . .
ACKNOWLEDGMENTS

This book has been many years in the making, and in the course of seeing it to completion I have received plenty of encouragement and support. Many of the ideas that appear here were first developed in graduate school at Rutgers, where I had the good fortune to study and earn
my Ph.D. The training I received there from Jackson Lears, John Gillis,
Thomas Slaughter, Richard L. McCormick, and others, and the stimulus
and fellowship provided by my fellow graduate students, were vital to
my development as a scholar, teacher, and intellectual. After graduate
school, I had the pleasure of teaching full-time in the history department at Princeton, a tremendously enriching experience that sparked
new interests and eventually compelled me to rethink the trajectory of
my research. I want to thank Daniel T. Rodgers and Christine Stansell,
in particular, for their advice and moral support during my two years
there.

Though these experiences were essential in providing me with the
intellectual foundation that enabled me to produce this book, it was
not until I came to Purchase College and spent several years teaching
that I actually conceived and wrote it. Indeed, it is Purchase, more than
any other institution, that is responsible for influencing the content and
point of view expressed here. Besides granting me much-needed financial support, a semester off from teaching, and the luxury of extra time
in order to write an entirely new book, the administration, faculty, and
staff at Purchase have been incredibly nurturing, offering me the freedom to teach widely and cultivate the outlook of a generalist, an ideal
to which I still aspire. Perhaps most important has been the example
offered by my wonderful friends and colleagues in the Division of Humanities, many of whom remain true intellectuals despite the pressures
of academic specialization. I also want to extend a special thank you
to Angela Messina of the Purchase College Library, who expertly and
cheerfully handled my innumerable requests for interlibrary loan material.

The bulk of the research that went into this book was conducted at the New York Public Library and Firestone Library at Princeton, stellar institutions where I was always treated with respect and courtesy. I also want to acknowledge the efforts of the staff in the Photoduplication Department at the Library of Congress, who were responsible for providing me with the book's illustrations. A special thanks to David Perry, Pam Upton, and the staff at the University of North Carolina Press. Though David inherited this project, he was shrewd and farsighted about how to make it the best possible book. He and I also received excellent advice from the anonymous readers who so graciously agreed to evaluate an early version of the manuscript. In addition, I want to thank my friend Chris Rasmussen for offering advice on this early version and Michael Kazin for commenting thoughtfully on the chapter on political celebrity. Many other friends and colleagues, too numerous to mention, have also enriched my thinking about the subject, and for this I am extremely grateful.

Finally, I want to acknowledge the contributions of my family: my wife, Lynn, and my children, Caroline and Christopher. I could never have written this book without the love and emotional support they constantly provide me, and I want to thank them for helping me keep my sense of perspective and reminding me of the truly important things in life.

SELF EXPOSURE

INTRODUCTION

At first he was simply the "dark horse," the shy, obscure Midwesterner determined to fly solo, the least publicized of the aviators seeking to win the "race" and become the first to complete the dangerous flight across the Atlantic. Because he avoided reporters and the media circus that had developed around the other teams of aviators, little was known about Charles A. Lindbergh. Indeed, until his arrival on Long Island in May 1927 he was nobody. And though his backers in St. Louis had hired two press agents to accompany him, during the week he was in New York Lindbergh remained aloof from the publicity mongering in which rivals engaged. Instead he obsessed over the condition of his plane and the vagaries of the weather. When the press referred to him it was often as the "Flying Fool," a moniker that reflected his obsessiveness and the widespread belief that a solo flight was almost certainly suicidal.

All of this changed on May 22, when seemingly against the odds Lindbergh reached the European continent and landed at an airfield outside Paris. Suddenly Lindbergh became the hottest name in the newspaper business. Reams of material about him appeared in the press, detailing every angle of his flight and seeking to illuminate the man who had performed this spectacular feat. The torrent of publicity continued for days, as reporters scurried to learn about Lindbergh's background and personality. Within a week of his flight he had become the most highly publicized person in the world, the subject of an unprecedented outpouring of news and human-interest journalism. Recast by the press as "Lucky Lindy," he was now instantly recognizable, the details of his life well known to millions of people who two weeks before had never heard of Lindbergh or met him in person. To Lindbergh's dismay, many of these details were spurious, the products of rumor and gossip that newspaper editors were willing to publish to satisfy the enormous public demand for information about him. Even worse, much of the information published focused not on aviation, as Lindbergh had hoped, but on his personality and private life, offering the public a seemingly intimate glimpse of the "real" Lindbergh.

These developments caught Lindbergh by surprise. He had expected his flight to attract press attention, but he had naively assumed that newspapers would respect his privacy and emphasize his contribution to the field of aviation. This was why he had avoided most reporters after his arrival in New York and shown so little interest in making use of his press agents. Thus Lindbergh was ill prepared for the volume of publicity that his flight would spark and aghast at the *kinds* of news stories that the press published after his triumph, most of which focused on "Lindbergh the man" rather than "Lindbergh and the cause of aviation."

To rectify this, when Lindbergh returned from Europe and embarked on a career as a spokesman for the fledgling aviation industry, he sought to place strict limits on press access to his private life, refusing to answer "personal" questions and cultivating close relations with a few reporters who specialized in the aviation beat and could be trusted to depict him as a serious aviator. Lindbergh's determination to control his media image was reinforced by the powerful businessmen who became his mentors and confidantes in the months after his return to the United States and who saw Lindbergh as the ideal spokesman for a controversial new industry in which they had a large financial stake. Instead of encouraging him to develop better relations with the press, they supported his efforts to draw a line around his personal life, believing that this would make him—and the industry that he embodied—appear more serious and "scientific." In short, while Lindbergh was disdainful of human-interest reporting and sought to restrict the press's ability to depict him in this light, he was quite willing to capitalize on his celebrity to promote the aviation industry and the enterprises in which he and his colleagues were investing. For the next few years he waged a fierce campaign to set the terms of his representation in the press.

This campaign was largely a failure. Rather than respect Lindbergh's wishes and steer clear of his private life, many reporters became more assertive in their determination to acquire information about it, bribing servants to get "inside dope" about his home life and stalking Lindbergh and his wife so that they could take candid, unauthorized photographs. By 1930 these efforts had escalated dramatically, infuriating Lindbergh and prompting him to reinforce his defenses against reporters' zealous, ingenious, and often unscrupulous assaults. But in the end, no matter how hard Lindbergh tried to keep the press at bay, he could not prevent reporters from writing human-interest stories about him. And as he became more obstinate about protecting his privacy, his reluctance to "open up" itself became the focus of news stories, drawing attention to Lindbergh's interest in manipulating the press.

Lindbergh's peculiar fate—the sudden notoriety, the relentless invasion of his privacy, the superficial and occasionally spurious information that the press published about him, his dogged efforts to control his image and cash in on his fame—was not unusual. It was a common experience for those thrust from obscurity into the spotlight of celebrity. And though no previous figure may have experienced quite the level of press scrutiny and harassment that Lindbergh did, many celebrities in later years found themselves in a similar situation, torn between a desire to exploit their fame and an equally powerful one to retreat from the glare of publicity and limit the ways in which the press could portray them. Lindbergh's case was among the first to inspire journalistic introspection about America's culture of celebrity, as editors and feature writers debated whether some members of the profession had gone too far. This sort of soul searching would accompany virtually every celebrity scandal of the twentieth century, from the hue and cry over the morality of movie stars in the 1920s to the media's hysterical response to the affair involving President Clinton and Monica Lewinsky in the late 1990s. By Lindbergh's day it had become clear to journalists and many of their readers that celebrity was an acute cultural problem with important cultural repercussions.

Indeed, perhaps no feature of the contemporary American scene inspires so much anguish among pundits and social critics as the American public's obsession with celebrity. It is an obsession, they contend, that exerts a pernicious influence on the news media, the major culture industries, business, politics, sports, even the world of high culture. Contempt for the culture of celebrity cuts across ideological lines, uniting liberals and conservatives who can agree on little else. Much of this criticism is perceptive and well intentioned, revealing disturbing trends that should alarm anyone concerned about the future and unsatisfied with the glib celebration of the ephemeral that many advertisers, designers, artists, and self-styled postmodernist scholars have been engaged in for the past twenty or so years. But much criticism of celebrity is also vague or simple-minded about the causes and historical antecedents of this undeniably important phenomenon.[1]

The aim of this book is to deepen our understanding of the place of celebrity in modern American culture, providing its critics—and I count myself among them—with more solid footing from which to assail it, but also enabling us to appreciate some of its features that from the conventional vantage point appear perverse or simply bizarre. For example, critics must accept that celebrity is intimately related to modernity—that this unique way of thinking about public figures, which differs so dramatically from the hagiographic discourse of fame, is a direct outgrowth of developments that most of us regard as progressive: the spread of a market economy and the rise of democratic, individualistic values. Throughout modern history these developments have steadily eroded all sources of authority, including the aura that formerly surrounded the "great." The culture of celebrity is not some grotesque mutation afflicting an otherwise healthy organism, but one of its central features, a condition arising directly from the encouragement that modern societies provide for social mobility and self-invention. Acknowledging this need not dispirit critics or swell the ranks of the postmodern chorus who are loath to criticize anything from which consumers derive a modicum of pleasure; if anything, it can make our criticism more penetrating, allowing us to direct our guns not at surface phenomena but at the deeper forces that corrode faith in authenticity and fuel the public curiosity about celebrities that can only be satisfied by invading their privacy or compelling them to engage in degrading rituals of self-exposure.

When I first began this project I was as hostile to the culture of celebrity as its fiercest critics, and I fully expected to produce a book that would contribute to their often distinguished literature. Yet over time, as I immersed myself in the sources on which the book is based, I became increasingly surprised by the complexity of the culture of celebrity—by ambiguities and contradictions that did not fit the pattern established by leading scholars and critics. This discovery was affirmed when I familiarized myself with developments in the growing field of cultural studies and came to recognize the usefulness of some of its methods and assumptions, particularly its insistence that mass-produced popular culture is Janus-faced, a repository of utopian hopes as well as a vehicle encouraging acceptance of the status quo. I have tried to keep these complexities uppermost in my mind; at the same time, I have tried not to lose sight of the broader concerns that drew me to this project in the first place and inspire many critics of the culture of celebrity. The result, I hope, works as criticism and also as scholarship.

But first, a few caveats. This book is not a comprehensive history of celebrity; nor is it about celebrities and the experience of being famous. Rather, it is concerned with the role of the mass-circulation press in the development of celebrity as a particular kind of public visibility, and focuses on human-interest journalism *about* celebrities. In other words, this is a book about representations of celebrities in the mass media—media images, not the people behind them. Rather than dismiss such images, as the vast majority of debunking biographers do, I take them seriously and use them to explore the larger symbolic role of celebrity in modern America. There is good reason for this. In the course of my research, I became convinced that the news media—defined broadly to include publications and programs that many professional journalists revile—are the most important institutions that sustain the culture of celebrity. By virtue of their ability to make public figures visible and familiar to millions of people who have never encountered them in the flesh, it is the news media that literally create celebrities.

This is not to say that other institutions play no role. For example, as scholars in cinema studies have demonstrated, the motion pictures and television programs that actors appear in are important in shaping seductive "star images" that cut across various media and can have tremendous iconographic power. But as we shall see, the culture of celebrity operates according to different principles and is geared toward the exposure of the "real selves" that are presumed to lie behind these images—a project in which the news media, because of their association with facts, play the central role. Indeed, a major theme of celebrity journalism is that movie roles, professional activities, and public appearances are unreliable as guides to the nature of such selves and must be supplemented with "inside dope"—preferably about a celebrity's private life, packaged as human-interest feature material—that is more accurate and thus revealing. Of course, this inside dope itself may not be real—it can be, in fact, yet another image—but its packaging as news gives it more authority than other forms of visibility and makes it the best place to begin in our effort to understand the phenomenon of celebrity.[2]

My belief that the news media are the most important institutions responsible for creating celebrities does not mean that I believe celebrities themselves to be mere pawns of the press. Most of them are active in fashioning their media images, and some of the best historical work in recent years has examined how individuals in the past—from the eighteenth-century evangelist George Whitefield to the aviator Amelia Earhart—brought themselves to the attention of their countrymen through the strategic presentation of personas. To do so, however, they had to be conscious of the mechanisms by which people in their time became visible and had to tailor their efforts in order to take advantage of these mechanisms. Since the early nineteenth century this has meant familiarizing themselves with the conventions of newsgathering and subjects of interest to the press. To be lifted to the status of a celebrity, one must be newsworthy or interesting in the eyes of the news media, a person whom journalists think their readers or viewers want to know about. More often than not, people achieve this status not by accident but through conscious effort, by following a carefully mapped out plan for attracting publicity and projecting an image that will make them interesting and attractive to the media—the essential conduits through which individuals are made visible to the public. Even those who become celebrities through no efforts of their own quickly learn how to use the media to make the best of the situation.[3]

This book, as the title suggests, also has chronological limits of which the reader should be aware. Aside from a brief epilogue, I do not examine contemporary celebrity journalism; instead, I focus on its manifestations between 1890 and the early 1940s. Here too I was motivated by a logic that did not become apparent until I was well into my research. Though the origins of celebrity journalism can be traced to the mid-nineteenth century, and I could have devoted the entire book to this fascinating and important moment, I soon discovered that the various forms of reportage that make up the genre did not mature until early in the twentieth century, when most newspapers and magazines, in their efforts to meet the needs of new kinds of readers, increased their commitment to the publication of feature stories and developed the narrative themes that still dominate the genre. A crucial turning point, I came to see, occurred in the 1890s, when journalists began crafting new techniques and rhetorical strategies for depicting celebrities, innovations that contributed to the creation of a new representational mold that was firmly in place by the 1920s. As we shall see, in the press of the early twentieth century celebrities were portrayed as "human beings," an angle expressly designed to make them seem more "real." Shaped by transformations in the social order and intellectual currents that encouraged a revised estimate of selfhood, this new mold that journalists employed to depict celebrities eventually spread to virtually every kind of publication—from sensational tabloids to slick, general-interest monthlies to the sober and respectable *New York Times*. Despite the introduction of new technologies like television and substantial changes in American culture as whole, there has been relatively little change in how celebrities are represented in the media. Conventions established during the early twentieth century remain paradigmatic, making it all the more important that they be examined and understood.[4]

A major goal of this book, then, is to redirect the attention of critics toward the institutions that are most responsible for the rise of celebrity and toward the period when the culture of celebrity acquired the unique features that make it so distressing in the eyes of its detractors today. I can understand the concern that many critics express about television and new visual media that are integral to the contemporary culture of celebrity. Television newsmagazines and Barbara Walters specials, tabloid TV programs, new cable channels like E!, Internet gossip columns, official as well as fan-produced celebrity websites—all of these have dramatically increased the power of the spotlight that has been directed at public figures since the mid-nineteenth century. Yet with a few notable exceptions, they have not fundamentally altered the mission that has inspired celebrity journalism since its maturation around 1900—the illumination and exposure of the subject's "real self."

I came to these conclusions after exhaustive research in both newspapers and mass-circulation magazines going all the way back to the 1830s. Throughout this process I was careful to make sure that I had read enough to have a good grasp of major trends in the development of celebrity journalism as a specific genre, and that my reading was wide enough to warrant the broad claims I wanted to make. For example, to compensate for an early middle-class bias in my choice of sources, I spent a summer immersed in newspapers catering to working-class readers. Fearful of relying too heavily on the New York press, I also sampled celebrity journalism in publications from cities in other parts of the country. These forays confirmed my belief that in the years after 1890, celebrity journalism became remarkably uniform in form and content, a trend encouraged by new conventions in the business of newsgathering and feature-writing, a growing reliance on wire services and feature syndicates, and the emergence of newspaper chains and media empires like those of Frank Munsey, William Randolph Hearst, and Henry Luce. By the early 1900s this new kind of reportage had also become a staple of new-style mass-circulation magazines, which were deeply influenced by metropolitan journalism and the growing emphasis on human-interest features.

However, while I read broadly and judiciously from a range of publications directed at both working-class and middle-class Americans, I did not read everything—and not just because it would have taken me decades to do so. My sample of sources was confined to what one might call "mainstream" journalism and did not include reportage from the foreign-language press, the labor and socialist press, small provincial newspapers, and specialized publications. I did take a close look at newspapers directed at African American readers, but only to compare their coverage of notable blacks with coverage of the same figures in the white press. My sample was also confined mostly to material—disseminated through wire services, feature syndicates, and magazines—with national reach, produced and distributed by an emerging national media culture that began in the years after 1890 and reached full bloom in the 1920s and 1930s. Conceivably, a book that eschewed such material might look different and be more interesting to some readers, particularly professional historians who are fascinated by the diversity of the American past and "subaltern" cultures. But examining mainstream journalism and the national media culture that emerged in the twentieth century is absolutely vital to understanding our recent history and the forces that have conspired to obscure our diversity in the name of creating a common national identity and experience. For better or worse, mainstream institutions continue to occupy a central place in contemporary America, and to dismiss studies of them as "elite history" is woefully misguided. In my view, understanding how the mainstream media operate is essential if we are to encourage real media literacy and a revival of democratic politics.

This is the primary reason why I have framed this book around the production of celebrity journalism and not its consumption by audiences. One of the most exciting developments in cultural studies has been the appearance of research focusing on the consumption of popular culture by ordinary consumers, usually contemporary audiences whom scholars have been able to interview systematically. These are enormously interesting and important works. Joshua Gamson's interviews with focus groups about their engagement with the culture of celebrity, for example, have deeply influenced my own views and the argument of this book. But such an approach works best when dealing with contemporary popular culture. Historians, with limited access to sources that would illuminate the uses made of popular culture by consumers in the past, have not employed it very often. And when they have, the results have been mostly speculative.[5]

But it was not just the difficulty of knowing how consumers responded to celebrity journalism that led me to shy away from this enterprise. My experience with students at Rutgers, Princeton, and SUNY-Purchase has convinced me that while many consumers are indeed skeptical of popular culture and inclined to refashion it to suit their own needs—the principal argument of scholars who study audiences—this skepticism is largely uninformed, a kind of reflex. It is not based on knowledge of how the popular culture industries actually work or how the products they disseminate are related to larger ideological agendas. Moreover, it coexists with a tendency to view popular culture as mere entertainment, to put aside one's skepticism in order to better enjoy the show. To be truly media-literate—to read against the grain in the manner celebrated by cultural studies scholars—one must be more than simply skeptical. One must understand the forces that contribute to the production of media images and be a sophisticated reader of these images, refusing to be seduced by their claim to be just entertainment and thus unworthy of serious scrutiny.

This brings me to my final caveat. Though my reading and interpretation of the sources was informed by the latest professional scholarship in a number of different fields, and though I tried to maintain a reasonably balanced perspective, this book was also influenced by my own situation and circumstances as a relatively young, progressive academic in fin-de-siècle America. It could not be otherwise. I do not doubt that years from now, if another scholar immersed in a different milieu examined the very same sources that I did, he or she would arrive at different conclusions—just as my generation has come to different conclusions about historical issues that previous generations had regarded as settled. Nevertheless, I stand by my interpretations and conclusions, even while recognizing the constraints under which all of us in academia—and those in the humanities and social sciences in particular—labor. There is power in such recognition, allowing us to see how works of scholarship, even those assessing the distant, seemingly exotic past, speak to our collective needs and concerns as members of communities, cultures, and nations.

The book's chapters are arranged thematically, beginning with an Olympian perspective of celebrity and then descending slowly so that the reader can take in and appreciate more detail. The first chapter broadly surveys the development of celebrity as a new form of public visibility made possible by social, economic, and political change—a visibility increasingly mediated by the mass-circulation press. The second chapter examines the specific forms of reportage that came to define celebrity journalism as it matured in the late nineteenth century and the early twentieth, paying close attention to the new rhetorical strategies journalists developed when writing about famous people. Here I also identify important changes in the press's criterion for newsworthiness that increased the range of people who were elevated to celebrity status. In chapter 3 I explore the conventions of newsgathering that lay behind these articles and assess the role of celebrities and their publicists in the production of celebrity journalism. Chapter 4 illuminates the major themes and "master plot" of celebrity journalism, revealing their links to larger developments within American culture as a whole. In the four subsequent chapters I demonstrate how this master plot was applied to celebrities from distinct professional and occupational worlds —business and "society," politics, show business, sports—and identify widely publicized archetypes around which reportage about them revolved. Though more specific, these chapters are vitally important and are the heart of the book. They shed light on the ways in which journalists used a seemingly trivial form of reportage to address serious issues that often extended beyond their specialized beats. In the epilogue I make a case for the continued relevance of narrative themes and rhetorical strategies that were first developed in the early twentieth century, and discuss some of the broader implications suggested by the book.

My hope is that readers will come away from this book with a greater appreciation of the central place that celebrity occupies in modern American culture—and never be able to look at a celebrity profile or a Barbara Walters interview quite the same way again.

1

BECOMING VISIBLE
FAME AND CELEBRITY IN
THE MODERN AGE

Published in 1959 to considerable fanfare, Earl Blackwell's and Cleveland Amory's *International Celebrity Register*, a massive volume offering readers capsule biographies of 2,200 public figures, arrived on the American cultural scene with an aura of importance that was not uncommon among works published during the 1950s. This was a time when authors, publishers, and most Americans were acutely conscious of living amid new circumstances, in a society that was the quintessence of the modern. And what could be more modern than this new reference work, bringing together figures from a variety of backgrounds and occupations under a new rubric, which made a mockery of the old distinctions of lineage and class that had marked its precursor, the notoriously elitist *Social Register*?

As Blackwell and Amory noted, the *Celebrity Register* covered "a multitude of fields" and included baseball players as well as businessmen, starlets as well as scientists, comedians as well as Supreme Court justices. What united these disparate figures was not accomplishment "in the sense of true or lasting worth" but rather visibility. All of them, to one degree or another, had seen their activities publicized, and this treatment, in turn, had lifted them into the company of other celebrities. "We think we have a better yardstick than the *Social Register*, or *Who's Who*, or any such book," Blackwell and Amory asserted in a triumphalist tone that echoed the confidence and democratic spirit of the era. Rather than argue over the merits of achievements in widely divergent fields, a course that over the years had penalized entertainers, athletes, and other figures whose work was not considered serious, Blackwell and Amory had identified a new means of comparison: "all you have to do," they suggested, "is weigh . . . press clippings."[1]

Yet for some commentators this seemingly logical innovation was another sign that American culture had reached a new level of banality. Not long after the appearance of the *Celebrity Register*, the historian Daniel J. Boorstin delivered a searing indictment of the culture of celebrity and the "big names" who dominated the media and the public's consciousness, an indictment that pointed to Blackwell's and Amory's reference book as a prime example of a widespread tendency to embrace the vacuous and the ephemeral. "The celebrity," Boorstin argued, "is a person who is known for his well-knownness." His fame bore no relation to achievements; manufactured by press agents adept at exploiting the conventions of newsgathering, often it was not even deserved. Yet there he stood, ensconced in a pantheon in which the starlet Anita Ekberg appeared alongside President Eisenhower, the subject of television interviews, magazine profiles, and regular items in syndicated gossip columns, his face instantly recognizable, his name a household word.

According to Boorstin, the celebrity was a "human pseudo-event," one of countless pseudo-events that clamored for the public's attention. Bearing an ambiguous relationship to reality, pseudo-events were conceived to be newsworthy and thus attract the press. Their rise was attributable to what Boorstin called the "Graphic Revolution": the spread of new technologies—printing, telegraphy, photography, moving pictures, television—that allowed for the preservation, transmission, and widespread diffusion of information and images. The application of these technologies to newsgathering, Boorstin contended, had increased public demand for such information and images; the demand exceeded the supply of legitimate events, resulting in the manufacture of contrived events that were more interesting to the public. The public appeal of pseudo-events had further encouraged the press and the publicity industries to rely on them. By the middle of the twentieth century they had crowded out legitimate events and assumed center stage in public discourse.

Even worse, the rise of pseudo-events and the new culture of celebrity posed a dire threat to heroism. Boorstin conceded that acts of heroism remained common in modern America, and that some of the men and women responsible for them occasionally gained public recognition for their deeds. But these heroes were now dwarfed by celebrities. "All older forms of greatness now survive only in the shadow of this new form," he noted ruefully. And when an authentic hero—Boorstin's example was the aviator Charles Lindbergh—appeared on the scene, he was inexorably drawn into the maw of the celebrity-making machinery and reduced to the trivialized stature of less deserving figures. The well-knownness of the celebrity, in short, was a condition fostered by the mass media, which cheapened the substantive achievements of people deserving fame by placing them alongside people whose fame was undeserved, a process made possible by the media's propensity for focusing the spotlight not on achievements but on "personalities."[2]

Recognizing the pivotal role played by the media is the essential starting point for any analysis of celebrity. What distinguishes celebrities from the anonymous masses is visibility, a kind of visibility made possible by the media and shaped by journalistic conventions that make celebrities seem at once extraordinary and real: complex, interesting "human beings" whose unique talents and gifts are accompanied by traits that are commonplace and familiar to ordinary people.[3] Viewed from this angle, as a peculiar state to which some people are elevated by the media, celebrity is more easily understood as a historical phenomenon. It appears not as some degraded product of technological innovation and its mind-numbing effects on the public, but as a modern, mass-mediated incarnation of a much older and venerable concept. The appropriate distinction is not between celebrity and heroism, as Boorstin would have it, but between celebrity and its premodern antecedent, fame.

This is the conclusion of Leo Braudy's magisterial history of fame from antiquity to the present, *The Frenzy of Renown*. For Braudy, celebrity represents the most recent stage of a sweeping "democratization of fame" that began with the development of printing and the spread of literacy, and accelerated when the new technologies of Boorstin's Graphic Revolution were introduced. But as even Boorstin recognized, not just technology was at work here. The emergence of celebrity was inspired even more by the social, economic, and political transformations that have remade the world since the sixteenth century, and by new values and beliefs that were integral to this process of "modernization." Thus celebrity is fame not just democratized but *modernized*—a fame informed by values that have fundamentally altered the ways we think about individuals and the social order.[4]

* * *

Fame, Braudy reminds us, was rare and highly valued. People did not become famous overnight; in most cases, it took many years, sometimes even generations, for a person to achieve wide renown. Fame was also reserved for those who performed, or were said to have performed, heroic or miraculous deeds, and was transmitted through folklore. These tales, embellished and revised over the years, stressed the qualities that made famous people extraordinary and enabled them to perform their feats, qualities that lifted them far above the common rung of humanity and brought them close to the realm of the divine. Indeed, fame was intimately related to hagiography, a mode of literature that was overtly religious or supernatural in inspiration. It was their connection to the supernatural that made the famous "great."

But as Braudy also reminds us, from the outset fame was vulnerable to a kind of corruption that is widely associated with celebrity. Vain and ambitious leaders like Alexander the Great built elaborate monuments to their achievements to ensure that their fame extended into posterity. Other rulers had scribes write flattering official biographies, or commissioned artists to produce portraits and sculptures depicting them in a heroic, often exaggerated light. Around the sixteenth century such self-promotion was greatly facilitated by the development of new media. Printing and engraving allowed biographies and images of the famous and soon-to-be famous to reach a wider audience than in the past, an audience that would continue to grow with the expansion of literacy and the invention of technologies of mass reproduction. Portraits, statues, and manuscripts had been the property of elites or confined to locales that precluded their viewing by a large number of people. Public monuments had reached a wider audience, but one composed primarily of persons who lived nearby. Printing and engraving changed all of this, creating new modes of communication that enabled those seeking fame to spread their names and countenances across vast expanses of space. Quickly recognizing the utility of these new media, rulers such as Elizabeth I and Louis XIV directed their scribes and artists to create materials expressly designed to be disseminated among their subjects. At stake here, as Louis XIV revealed when he addressed an assembly of writers commissioned to be his official historians, was something quite valuable—"the most precious thing in the world to me"—the persona that would be visible to his subjects and remembered over time.[5]

By the seventeenth century these efforts were inspired not just by vanity but by the desire of elites to bolster their rule. They were especially important for monarchical regimes committed to economic modernization. As many nobles and aristocrats discovered, campaigns devised to centralize authority, encourage new forms of economic activity, raise more revenue from their subjects, and exploit new opportunities abroad often produced unanticipated consequences. Groups who had been content and deferential became angry when new policies affected them adversely. And in many countries new classes emerged, eager for a share of power and determined to use any means—including mobilizing the common folk—to acquire it. The result, as historians of the early modern period have noted, was an upsurge in protest and political activity among groups previously noted for their quiescence. It is therefore not surprising that many monarchial regimes eagerly embraced the self-promotional opportunities afforded by the new media of printing and engraving, for they appeared as a tool for managing conflicts and regaining the loyalty of newly restive groups. For example, by shrewdly manipulating these new cultural forms, Elizabeth I fashioned a persona that allowed her to embody a unified, imperial England, a strategy that was widely imitated, with varying degrees of success, by nobles on the Continent.[6]

These new media could also be used by the opposition, however. By the mid-eighteenth century a vast underground literature attacking the prerogatives and pretensions of monarchs, aristocrats, and the church had emerged, particularly in France, where one of the regimes most strongly committed to modernization refused to share power with an increasingly assertive bourgeoisie. This literature, as the historian Robert Darnton has shown, included not only the writings of the philosophes but also vitriolic diatribes and exposés like *The Private Life of Louis XV*. Written in a style that "anticipated the gossip columnists of the yellow press," these *chroniques scandaleuses* revealed the corrupt and decadent behavior of the nobility and its lackeys, information allegedly gathered through an elaborate network of snoops and gossips. The authors of these books and pamphlets were aware of the role that imagery and symbolism had come to play in buttressing the nobility's authority. And so rather than address substantive issues that divided the regime and its critics, they expressed their contempt for it by "desanctifying its symbols, destroying the myths that gave it legitimacy in the eyes of the public, and perpetuating the countermyth of degenerate despotism."[7]

The appearance of this literature marked a watershed in the democratization of fame and the emergence of celebrity. Rulers had always been the subjects of gossip that circulated by word of mouth among their subjects—gossip that no doubt contradicted the hagiographic imagery and stories promulgated by their hired flacks. Yet the gossip had circulated informally, and it had never been visible to the same degree as official representations of the regime.[8] It is likely, however, that the strains created by the new policies of modernization increased the quantity and virulence of orally transmitted gossip and, with the development of printing, transformed it into a genuinely subversive force. Thus the *chroniques scandaleuses* gave new form and a potent political edge to a discourse—unflattering gossip—that had long existed under the *ancien régime* and may well have been as old as antiquity. Now in print and mobilized for political and commercial ends, this subterranean counterpoint to the hagiographic discourse of fame achieved a new level of visibility and made the public images of elites increasingly contested.

By the late eighteenth century printed gossip challenging the official personas of elites had spread beyond France to other nations on the Continent, in England, and in the fledgling United States. Such material was part of a proliferation of broadsheets, pamphlets, newspapers, and books, most of them unremarkable in every way. Yet combined they came to constitute the outlines of what Jürgen Habermas has called the "bourgeois public sphere," a realm apart from the state where individuals—at this point only propertied, educated men—could express their views and debate issues of common concern. Though rooted in new institutions and physical spaces like voluntary associations, debating societies, and coffeehouses, the public sphere was essentially a discursive space, linked by new forms of printed material, where all sorts of claims and arguments were made and contested. By the mid-nineteenth century public spheres had developed within virtually every Western nation-state, and over the course of the nineteenth century, as literacy rates increased and communications technology improved, these national public spheres came to influence one another and coalesced into a larger, overlapping sphere of transatlantic dimensions.[9]

As Habermas's critics have noted, from the start the exclusivity of the bourgeois public sphere was assailed by a host of counterpublics, composed of women, peasants, workers, and peoples of color, demanding inclusion and forcing bourgeois men to address issues that they would have preferred to ignore. Thus the bourgeois public sphere was never the only the public sphere, and during the course of the nineteenth century, as it grew in order to accommodate these counterpublics, it assumed a different shape, becoming a site of conflict and negotiation between dominant groups and the often discontented groups that they presumed to lead. Moreover, from the start the public sphere was a realm tainted by the pursuit of private interests, despite conventions that seemed to prohibit this. Celebrated as an arena where rational discussion prevailed, the public sphere was equally open to polemics, propaganda, and self-promotion—much of it crafted to arouse an emotional response, be it sympathy, contempt, or outrage. The public sphere was as accessible to the muckraking authors of the *chroniques scandaleuses* as it was to the philosophes. And in the nineteenth century, as it was enlarged and influenced by commercial values, the public sphere became even more strongly dominated by material that was self-promotional, sensational, or produced for a specific effect.[10]

The emergence of public spheres within large cities and nation-states, and the gradual linking of those spheres to a larger transatlantic sphere, had a tremendous effect on the ways in which individuals fashioned their public personas. Now the subjects or potential subjects of widely disseminated printed exposés, traditional elites redoubled their efforts to exploit the opportunities for publicity created by the public sphere, so as to regain legitimacy and secure a place in a society increasingly dominated by bourgeois values. This was particularly true in nations like the United States and England, where democratic currents were stronger than on the Continent and the upper classes were more likely to be subjected to criticism. In the early nineteenth century, for example, many members of the educated gentry in the United States sought to advertise their commitment to democracy and "producer" values, a trend that inspired Theodore Sedgwick, the son of an archconservative Federalist, to attack the ideal of leisure that had long shaped the lives of men in his circle. "[T]o live without some regular employment," Sedgwick proclaimed, "is not reputable." Sedgwick was not alone in expressing such views. Beginning in the 1790s they were common among educated, well-to-do American men, especially those who identified with Jeffersonian values but even, after 1810, among men like Sedgwick and the rising Massachusetts politician Daniel Webster, whose political views were far more conservative.[11]

The public sphere's influence on ambitious men from humble backgrounds was even greater. The new avenues for visibility that it offered were ideally suited to individuals eager to promote themselves or build support for causes to which they were devoted, ranging from republicanism to phrenology. And to gain visibility it was not always necessary to write material for publication. As commoners discovered, visibility could be acquired through other means, such as by striking the right poses at public events or making an impression on the streets. Benjamin Franklin was one of the early masters of this peculiar new game: his skill was integral to his rise to prominence in eighteenth-century Philadelphia, and he later employed it quite successfully while serving as a diplomat in Europe. Eager to distinguish the United States from the Old World, Franklin created a sensation by dressing in animal skins at public functions and allowing himself to become an icon of republican simplicity—even while, behind the scenes, he immersed himself in sybaritic pleasures provided by his aristocratic hosts. These public appearances, as we shall see, became all the more important as the mass-circulation press expanded its coverage of urban life and made it possible for individuals to enhance their visibility by becoming the subjects of reportage. In short, the development of the public sphere created a new sort of visibility that was inextricably tied to self-promotion and the advancement of causes—a visibility largely mediated through the press. Within the public sphere individuals became "public figures," a category that owed more to their visibility and ability to attract publicity than to their achievements or pedigree.[12]

* * *

For most commoners, gaining visibility was only the beginning. It was equally important for them to ensure that they were linked to the right values—"modern" values that distinguished them from representatives of the old regime. For example, many merchants and entrepreneurs joined churches and voluntary associations that advertised their dedication to the work ethic and the values of worldly asceticism. Franklin's Junto, a literary club that he and other young men-on-the-make established in the 1720s, was an important antecedent of these groups, which proliferated in the nineteenth century. Other ambitious men wrapped themselves in the mantle of republicanism. Rejecting the fashions, demeanor, and political views of the upper classes, men like Samuel Adams and Patrick Henry adopted modes of self-presentation that made them appear "common," in touch with the people and thus more entitled to lead them. Quite a few writers and intellectuals, increasingly attuned to the expanding literary marketplace, adopted the role of "illustrious moderns" committed to the Enlightenment. As the writings of such figures as Jean-Jacques Rousseau, Denis Diderot, Thomas Jefferson, and David Hume gained a wider audience, their names and reputations spread beyond the circles where their books were read, thanks to the assiduous labors of admiring entrepreneurs like Josiah Wedgwood, who produced portrait-medallions, plates, and flatware displaying their faces. Equally important were the contributions of biographers and literary critics who championed the work of these intellectuals, introduced them to a wider audience, and confirmed their status as representatives of the modern age. Inexpensive popular biographies of Enlightenment luminaries that began to appear in the 1790s and early 1800s were more widely read. The quintessential American work of this kind was Mason L. Weems's *Life of Washington*, first published in 1800.[13]

The heightened visibility of these businessmen, politicians, and intellectuals signaled the dawn of a new era. With the emergence and steady expansion of the public sphere, virtually any man could be famous—could become a public figure known to a large number of people. It was no longer necessary to be a member of the nobility or aristocracy; nor was it even necessary to be rich, though having money and the social position that came with it was certainly an asset. Those aspiring to fame, moreover, could "author" themselves, creating public personas that rejected aristocratic models of achievement in favor of an emerging democratic model that would steadily evolve in tandem with changes in values. In fact, the visibility offered by the public sphere also created an opening for women to become public figures, as the widespread notoriety of Mary Wollstonecraft in the 1790s demonstrated. But the real importance of the public sphere lay not so much in the opportunities that it created to achieve visibility, but rather in the ways in which it led men and women alike to rethink how they presented themselves in public, a process that sparked a new self-consciousness about appearances.[14]

This self-consciousness was not confined to dress, demeanor, and choice of public association. It also affected how people presented and came to understand their life stories. By locating their origins and measuring the distance they had traversed since birth and childhood, the life stories that people told about themselves and sometimes published were deeply implicated in their quests for social mobility and vital to establishing a reputation in the public sphere.[15] Sometimes this agenda was overt, as in Benjamin Franklin's widely read autobiography, in which he stressed the importance of cultivating a public persona to win the respect and trust of business associates. "In order to secure my Credit and Character as a Tradesman," he wrote, "I took care not only to be in *Reality* Industrious & frugal, but to avoid all *Appearances* of the Contrary."[16] Indeed, Franklin's highly selective account of his life was itself a tool in his lifelong project of strategic self-presentation. Ironically, so too was Rousseau's *Confessions,* a milestone in autobiography in which the renowned yet reclusive philosophe, dissatisfied with how others had depicted him, claimed to be presenting his "real" self. In its own way, and in spite of its seeming candor, Rousseau's autobiography was as selective and self-serving as Franklin's. Both authors displayed a new concern for reputation and performance, though in Rousseau's case this objective was cloaked by a rhetorical strategy that emphasized intimate revelation. Rousseau's innovation set the genre of autobiography on a new course, as authors followed his lead in seeking to make the versions of themselves that they wished to promote seem more authentic to readers.[17]

The same conventions also influenced the evolving genre of biography. Inspired by the Enlightenment project of telling the truth, biographers like James Boswell employed a new sophistication and scrupulousness in depicting their subjects, in some cases diverging from the portraits that the subjects desired. It was such misrepresentation that led Rousseau to write his *Confessions.* "[S]ince my name is fated to live," he observed, "I must endeavor to transmit with it the memory of that unfortunate man who bore it, as he actually was and not as his unjust enemies unremittingly endeavor to paint him." Biographers also employed techniques derived from drama and the novel to make their work more vivid and entertaining to readers. All sorts of subjects, including notorious ones like criminals, became suitable for the biographical mill. And in keeping with the new interest in authenticity kindled by the claims and counter-claims that echoed within the public sphere, the most ambitious biographers sought to illumine their subject's real self through anecdotes, dialogue, and extensive description of the subject and his surroundings—often culled from extensive observation and acquaintance. The most illustrious example of this new approach was, of course, Boswell's detailed and engrossing life of the writer Samuel Johnson.[18]

Yet as literary critics have noted, the use of these techniques, which were applied to give works authenticity, was no guarantee that the resulting portrait was any more authentic than a run-of-the-mill hagiography. While Boswell and his followers posed as "insiders" who thoroughly understood their subjects, the depictions that they crafted remained selective and often biased. In some cases, the bias was inadvertent, a result of the limited or skewed sources that the biographer chose to rely on; in other cases, it was inspired by the ideological commitments of the author and his determination to use his work to promote some larger cause. Boswell's biographies, for example, were indelibly shaped by his aversion to the secular rationalism associated with Rousseau.[19] Thus the maturation of biography in the eighteenth century not only moved the genre away from the conventions of hagiography and toward a more nuanced depiction of its subjects; it also created a new species of writer whose relationship to his subject was more ambivalent than a hagiographer's or a muckraker's. Aiming his work toward the literary marketplace, where readers were as eager to be entertained as they were to know the truth, the modern biographer assumed an important new role within the public sphere as a largely independent, though not unbiased, arbiter of the claims made by public figures. This role would be adopted later by the reporter for the mass-circulation press.

No matter what strategy they employed, the personas that ambitious commoners fashioned, or had fashioned for them by their biographers, were often deeply influenced by new ideals of selfhood that emerged during the eighteenth century. Rather than appear as supernatural or akin to the divine—as was standard hagiographic practice before the Enlightenment—they appeared as exemplary human beings, models of possibility suggesting the heights that men could reach if they adopted an "enlightened" model of self-development allowing for the complete unfolding of their potential. By the late eighteenth century the most widely hailed model of self-development stressed the role of reason and enlightened self-interest in directing human behavior. According to the conventional wisdom, if a man followed a systematic program of self-control and self-improvement, he could ensure that these "rational" faculties maintained supremacy over unruly passions that could lead him astray and thwart the full development of his innate talents. One of the most articulate statements endorsing this project was written by the Unitarian clergymen William Ellery Channing in 1838. Addressing a gathering of young workingmen, Channing asserted, "We have the power not only of tracing our powers, but of guiding and impelling them; not only of watching our passions, but of controlling them;

not only of seeing our faculties grow, but of applying to them means and influences to aid their growth."[20]

The aim of this program was attainment of "character," an ideal widely associated with successful businessmen and political figures in the eighteenth and nineteenth centuries and central to the ideology of republicanism. The man of character—and he was always a man, for character was a rigidly gendered ideal—was noted for his "virtue," his ability to put the commonweal ahead of self-interest when the two came into conflict. This ability, in turn, rested on his devotion to habits of industry, piety, thrift, sobriety, and self-improvement, which enabled his rational faculties to control the penchant for self-interested behavior— associated with the "passions"—that lay within every human being. In their struggle against the passions, the rational faculties also received vital assistance from the "benevolent affections," emotions like love and sympathy that ranked below reason and enlightened self-interest yet were essential to the complete development of the self, making men truly well-rounded, paragons of sensibility as well as self-discipline.

The man of character was the antithesis of the dissolute nobleman or aristocrat. He embodied the bourgeois challenge to monarchial society—and to the principles of ascription and deference that restricted social mobility and the complete development of the individual's potential. As originally conceived by eighteenth-century intellectuals, the ideal of character was viewed as difficult to achieve and thus exclusive, accessible only to men who were learned and well-to-do, Thomas Jefferson's "natural aristocracy." This formulation made it compatible with the relatively elitist version of republicanism held by most of the Founding Fathers and political moderates in England and on the European continent, who sought to restrict the political participation of common people on the grounds that they lacked the ability to become men of character and acquire the dispassionate outlook of their betters. By the 1830s, however, the character ideal had been appropriated by petit-bourgeois and plebeian interests committed to a more democratic variant of republicanism. In the hands of men like the radical Jacksonian editor William Leggett and the abolitionist Frederick Douglass, the ideal became more inclusive, open to any man willing to submit to its regimen. Inspired by a belief in the free will of individuals—a belief fueled by evangelical Protestantism and other more liberal religious faiths—its champions made character the defining quality of the upwardly mobile. In doing so, however, they also made lack of character the all-purpose rationale for a man's failure to rise in status and enabled successful men to derive an often undeserved sense of moral superiority from their achievements.[21]

The dominance of the character ideal was readily evident in nineteenth-century biographies of "self-made men," especially the short biographies and character sketches appearing in inexpensive books bearing titles such as *Lives of Eminent Businessmen* and in new publications like *Hunt's Merchant Magazine*. Eschewing the ambivalent perspective of the most sophisticated eighteenth-century biographers, the authors of these didactic pieces downplayed the idiosyncratic traits of their subjects, instead stressing common features that revealed them to be men of character. Their objective was made plain by the genre's most illustrious practitioner, the Englishman Samuel Smiles, who wrote: "Biographies of great, but especially good men are . . . most instructive and useful, as helps, guides, and incentives to others. Some of the best are almost equivalent to Gospels—teaching high living, high thinking, and energetic action for their own and the world's good."[22] Smiles's preference for biographies of the "good" as opposed to the "great" is telling, enabling us to recognize his books, and the entire genre of didactic biography, as part of a broader strategy: according to this strategy, middle-class writers sought to encourage commitment to bourgeois values among newly literate readers from the lower classes and legitimize the recently gained social status of the entrepreneurs and engineers whom their writings celebrated.

Less numerous but equally important were short biographies of prominent English and American women that began to appear in the mid-nineteenth century. Despite being closed out of politics and most occupations and confined to the home and other spaces that came to be viewed as the "private sphere," elite and middle-class women found a variety of ways—as novelists, reformers, educators, even consumers—to enter and influence the public sphere. And once visible, some of these women became public figures, suitable subjects for newspaper profiles and short biographies, particularly in publications aimed at women. Focusing on exemplary figures like Florence Nightingale and Harriet Beecher Stowe, these works extolled the virtues of piety, selflessness, and moral purity—values that were thought to distinguish women from men and made them well-fitted to nurture others and serve as moral guardians of society. Women who possessed these values were "true women" whose activities in the public sphere in no way detracted from their femininity; indeed, the common feature that united them was their sincere devotion to the ideal of true womanhood. Unlike ordinary women, however, they had found public outlets for their mission, and this made them worthy subjects for biographers.[23]

Thus whether depicting men or women, the widely read short biographies of the Victorian era championed values that were central to the bourgeois worldview. And considering their popularity among people from virtually all classes of American and English society, the genre of short biography may have been as instrumental as prescriptive literature in spreading these values beyond the middle classes and encouraging a large number of people to regard them as the foundation of "respectability." But there was a downside. Mobilized for new ends, the hagiographic tradition was detached from its original source of inspiration and reduced to a more conventional variety of moralism. Samuel Smiles and his comrades, recognizing the potential for biographical subjects to serve as role models, took pains to make their subjects' achievements appear attainable to readers. The shift in focus from the "great" to the "good" was a calculated strategy to make biography a more useful tool in the project of winning followers and achieving cultural hegemony. Yet Smiles and the others failed to recognize that reducing the stature of their subjects would shatter the sense of awe that "great" figures had customarily inspired among common people. In the hands of the moralists, the subjects of hagiographic profiles were praised—but also drained of their mystery. This not only resulted in their being brought down a few notches. It made their personas more vulnerable to questioning and more likely to be dismissed as self-promotion.

To understand why this was so we need to view the emergence of the public sphere and the new opportunities that it provided for self-fashioning as part of a much larger process that cast all forms of self-promotion and publicity in a different light. This process was what many scholars call "modernization," the rise of an urban-industrial society in Western Europe and the United States, a process that inspired new values, beliefs, and commitments—a whole new way of life. The roots of modernization can be traced to the Renaissance, but what really set it in motion was a dramatic increase in long-distance trade and a quickening of the pace of economic development that began in the seventeenth century. The first country affected by these trends was England. By the early nineteenth century, however, they had appeared in the United States and most of Europe. A key element of modernization was the spread of market exchange beyond the physical spaces— squares, marketplaces, fairs—to which it had been largely confined before the seventeenth century. This encouraged the transformation of virtually all goods and services into commodities whose prices fluctuated according to supply and demand, and created new opportunities to buy, sell, earn profits, and accumulate capital. Such capital, when invested in new enterprises and techniques for producing and marketing commodities, was the wellspring of economic development. Once unleashed, these forces produced changes that were truly epochal.[24]

Indeed, they completely unsettled traditional ways of life. The spread of market exchange resulted in the commercialization of agriculture, as small farmers and large landowners alike switched to the production of cash crops. This development hurt marginal producers who could not effectively compete, and reduced many yeomen to tenants or agricultural wage-laborers. It also encouraged a gradual depopulation of the countryside and the dramatic growth of towns and cities, where migrants from rural areas usually moved and competed with one another for work. It was in these cities, where a large number of propertyless and often desperate men and women were clustered, that new industries emerged. These industries, employing new technologies as well as countless wage-laborers, began producing goods on a scale previously unimaginable, and as people from various classes came to rely on these goods, a new urban, consumer-oriented way of life was born. To be sure, for most of the nineteenth century the standard of living of the working-class majority was too low to allow its members to embrace this predominantly bourgeois way of life. But over time, as new production processes lowered the price of goods, and as workers were able to use their collective power to secure higher wages from employers, the working classes in the United States and many nations in Europe were able to adopt peculiarly working-class versions of it. Nevertheless, the new goods and opportunities offered by industrial capitalism could never banish the competition and insecurity that were, and remain, its essential features.[25]

The changes were particularly dramatic in the burgeoning cities of England, Western Europe, and the United States. Compared to rural villages and small towns, the city was a world of strangers, where ties that bound newcomers to their families and communities back home were strained by a cultural as well as physical distance. And though migrants struggled to set down roots and establish new networks of kin and community, their urban enclaves could never be as isolated or self-sufficient as the communities they had left behind. The tenor of urban life was simply too different, and the myriad sights and sounds of the city invariably drew people out of their enclaves and into contact with a much wider range of people. For newcomers in particular, the anonymity of urban life offered new and often welcome opportunities for self-creation, a chance to cast aside one's old identity and assume an entirely new one. These opportunities were amplified by changes in the economy that encouraged new forms of entrepreneurial activity and made it possible for some men to rise dramatically in economic and social status. The city was the setting where the modern project of creating an individual identity was born, and where a large number of people—now free from the expectations and constraints imposed by families, communities, and traditions of ascribed status—came to view themselves as architects of their own self-making.[26]

The sense of empowerment provided by this new setting, however, was offset by new anxieties peculiar to urban life, anxieties that would eventually come to pervade all modern societies. By the middle of the eighteenth century many of the rituals and conventions that had circumscribed economic life—laws regulating the sites of trade, notions of "just prices" for many goods, "customs of the craft" establishing common prices and wages among artisans and guild members, religious injunctions against usury and speculation—were being swept aside by the principles of market exchange. Freed from these restrictions, men displayed a new boldness in their business dealings. Not surprisingly, this boldness was accompanied by a growing mistrust of others, a fear of being duped or exploited—symbolized by the principle of *caveat emptor*, or "let the buyer beware." Given the new conditions of economic life, the mistrust was entirely justified. Without the customary rituals to ensure that both parties were on the level, and as commerce began to be conducted over longer distances among businessmen who were not personally acquainted, opportunities for deceit and exploitation had multiplied—and an increasing number of men seemed eager to embrace them. In response, many entrepreneurs began to place a new premium on performance, on presenting manipulable "fronts," as men hid their real intentions from those who might use knowledge of them to gain advantage. As for the more assertive and unscrupulous, they cynically employed fronts to engage in the new kinds of behavior that market exchange seemed to allow.[27]

In this new economic milieu, as Benjamin Franklin and a host of other advice writers observed, success came to men who could win the confidence of others and overcome the suspicions intrinsic to market exchange. This meant making good on promises and developing a reputation for honesty. But it also meant advertising that reputation in order to put business associates at ease, making it possible to gain a strategic advantage and drive the kinds of hard bargains that were now essential to achieve success. The trick was to do so without angering others and tarnishing one's laboriously crafted reputation for honesty. As Franklin's example demonstrated, an ambitious man could enhance his reputation, and potentially compensate for bad publicity, by maintaining a high profile in civic and philanthropic affairs, and by cultivating a public persona that exuded propriety. Success in the city, in other words, rested as much on appearances as on accomplishments. The lesson of Franklin's widely read and discussed *Autobiography* was that the two were intertwined. Urbanization and the spread of market exchange had made economic relations distinctly theatrical, inspiring the new concern with appearances and fronts in the public sphere.

But this phenomenon was not confined to the world of business. Numerous historians have noted that the imperative to "perform" quickly spread to other areas of life, inducing both men and women to pay more attention to their public personas and to view these as tools in their efforts to achieve upward mobility. The result was a virtual epidemic of people—mostly from the middle classes—seeking to pass as higher in status than they actually were, hoping that if they appeared to belong to the social circle to which they aspired they would eventually gain admission to it. The subject of countless novels, this widely practiced confidence game was encouraged by the demise of sumptuary laws and the proliferation of advice books and mass-produced commodities that promised to make a person appear "respectable" or even "refined."[28]

Yet like the new economic opportunities created by the spread of the market, the ability of the aspiring to acquire the visible trappings of status was a hollow victory. Suspicions that shaped economic relations began to infect social life, inspiring elaborate codes of etiquette designed to unmask pretenders. By the middle of the nineteenth century the new opportunities for self-creation and success sparked by economic development had generated a widespread suspicion of appearances, a sense, as a writer in *Godey's Ladies Book* put it in 1839, that "[t]he exterior of life is but a masquerade." Though initially an urban phenomenon, in the twentieth century this belief would spread beyond cities to affect all of American and European society, as the individualistic values encouraged by the market worked their way into every realm of social life and transformed virtually everyone into a self-interested "player" pursuing the main chance.[29]

The repercussions of this mistrust of appearances were sweeping, inspiring new rationalizations of duplicitous, self-interested behavior, yet also prompting efforts to contain it. This was the context that produced the ideal of character, which was devised as an antidote to the potential for chaos unleashed by the market. Exercising control over his passions, the man of character could resist the new opportunities for deceit and self-aggrandizement that market relations appeared to allow. He competed vigorously yet fairly, employing fronts only in self-defense, to protect himself from men lacking character who would exploit him. His ability to do so depended in part on the efforts of others, however, a fact obscured by the myth of the self-made man but made quite clear when we direct our attention to novels and advice literature directed at middle-class women.[30]

Recognizing the chaotic, volatile nature of the new social order emerging in their midst, the authors of these works encouraged women to transform their households into "homes": tranquil, morally uplifting havens to which their embattled husbands could retire at the end of the business day and within which they could raise their sons to be honest as well as enterprising. Within the home, Sarah J. Hale, the longtime editor of *Godey's*, suggested in 1830, men could find "reciprocated humanity . . . unmixed with hate or the cunning of deceit." By reconceptualizing the household in this fashion, middle-class writers like Hale were attempting to set it apart from the market and the public sphere, to establish a distinct *private* sphere where different values might prevail: love, sincerity, benevolence, selflessness. The role of women in this scheme—a role to which they were believed naturally suited—was to use their "influence" within the home to promote these values, and to endow their men with the moral ballast necessary to act honestly when they ventured forth in public.[31]

What emerged from this literature was the modern understanding of public and private, a development that rationalized the aggressive spirit of men-on-the-make by establishing a realm presumably governed by values at odds with those of the market. In the view of ministers, advice writers, novelists, and reformers, the public sphere was competitive, strife-ridden, and dangerous, a realm where fronts were essential for defending oneself against unscrupulous people, who would eagerly take advantage of those who revealed too much. The locus of the private sphere was the home, where the acquisitive and potentially antisocial instincts of men, unleashed by the new opportunities of the era, could be tamed and directed toward socially responsible behavior. More important, the private sphere was the realm where a man could let down his guard and reveal his true self among family and the trusted friends admitted there, and where that real self would be loved and accepted. The private sphere made it possible to enjoy a private life—a life sheltered from the pressures and anxieties of urban-industrial society. In fact, the elite and middle-class people who embraced these views found it difficult to keep artifice and theatricality outside the home. And over the course of the nineteenth century, as many scholars have observed, interaction within the homes of these people became increasingly ritualized and governed by formal codes of propriety. Yet the belief that private life was the realm of the natural persisted. It eventually encouraged a more informal mode of family life and socializing in the early twentieth century and became the foundation of a new estimate of selfhood.[32]

By the mid-nineteenth century the residents of cities in the United States, England, and many areas of Western Europe had concluded that everyone employed fronts when in public, and that all self-presentation in the public sphere was, to one degree or another, artificial and unreliable as a guide to a person's real self. When one encountered a person in the public sphere it was safe to assume that she was acting, engaged in the perpetual confidence games that had come to shape social and economic relations in cities and would eventually become a salient feature of modern life. To glimpse a person's real self it was necessary to see her in private, when she dropped her front and refrained from the contrived, mannered self-presentation that she adopted in the public sphere—understood to be not just the workplace and the world of business but formal social gatherings outside the home where people interacted among strangers and mere acquaintances. It was also necessary to win her trust so that she fully revealed herself and did not hide behind a mask of formal manners. But even then one could never be entirely sure that the mask had been completely removed, that the self exposed was authentic. And so it was also necessary to learn to read body language and interpret the meaning of physical details, to be able to see how a person's self was revealed through the decor of her home and her relations with family and intimate friends—to discern things she might not willingly reveal. The real self, in short, was a private self, one that men and women protected from view and revealed only under special circumstances.[33]

This perception dramatically increased the doubts and suspicions that had always been aroused by self-promotion and publicity, and gave rise to a growing conviction that the personas of public figures, reiterated by sympathetic biographers or reporters, were contrived to make them appear virtuous. There were good reasons for believing this. Economic development during the first half of the nineteenth century, particularly in cities, produced new strains and conflicts that made it increasingly difficult for prominent businessmen, politicians, and civic leaders to cast themselves as disinterested elites looking out for the welfare of all. These conflicts produced events like the bloody Astor Place riots in 1849, which revealed the widespread contempt that working-class New Yorkers had come to feel toward the upper classes, and set the tone for class relations in many big cities for the rest of the century. Indeed, workers had first-hand knowledge of the cruelty and lack of benevolence that well-known "captains of industry" often showed their employees, while rivals and former associates could testify to their greed, ruthlessness, and duplicity. Similar evidence dogged well-known politicians, clergymen, and reformers, revealing them to be corrupt, self-interested, and hypocritical.

There had always been witnesses who could offer personal testimony contradicting the public claims and personas of elites. But in the nineteenth century, with the spread of literacy and the appearance of new forms of printed material, the audience for such testimony—now predisposed to distrust the claims of elites and all public figures—grew enormously, becoming an identifiable market. The appearance of this market inspired writers, reporters, and editors to investigate the claims made by public figures and to produce new varieties of muckraking, which made it even more difficult in the end to believe that anyone was truly good, much less "great."[34]

* * *

The institution that was most responsive to the growing interest in exposure was the mass-circulation press. First appearing in London in the late eighteenth century, then spreading to the United States and cities in Western Europe as the urban population swelled and censorship laws were relaxed, inexpensive newspapers directed at a broad, cross-class audience were the nucleus of the rapidly expanding public sphere and a primary form of communication among urban residents. "He who is without a newspaper is cut off from his species," P. T. Barnum, a frequent user of the press, insisted in his autobiography. Though a bewildering array of books, magazines, and pamphlets were published during the nineteenth century, the visibility and impact of such works, as entrepreneurs like Barnum recognized, often depended on publicity or advertising in newspapers. And as the scope of press coverage increased, so did the range of subjects and public figures that fell under its purview. More than in any other medium, it was in the pages of newspapers that claims and counter-claims were presented to the public, and it fell to editors and reporters to sort through this welter of competing appeals to determine which were authentic. This role was encouraged by the press's adoption of the Enlightenment project of revealing the "truth" and making it accessible to ordinary people, thereby spreading knowledge and the ability to be an informed citizen. It was reinforced when many newspapers distanced themselves from political parties and began to rely on advertising as their primary source of revenue. One of the first to chart such a course was James Gordon Bennett's *New York Herald*, a paper that explicitly sought to appeal to "the great masses of the community." Now committed to delivering consumers to advertisers, newspapers like the *Herald* expanded coverage to long-neglected areas of life and developed the modern concept of "news" — defined as anything of interest to readers.[35]

As self-styled arbiters of truth, reporters and editors were compelled to view public figures with a new skepticism that from the latter's perspective bordered on impudence. Yet this treatment was not reserved for elites and the upper classes alone. It was accorded to anyone who made claims in the public sphere, including men and women with unimpeachable democratic credentials. Usually the skepticism of the press was expressed when it reported the statements of men or women making counter-claims, disputing "facts" asserted by a first party. Among the most common examples were allegations of political corruption leveled against virtually every prominent politician or civic official, usually by an opponent. While partisan newspapers confined their attacks to figures from the opposing party, by the mid-nineteenth century papers like

Bennett's *Herald,* which took a more independent line, were likely to print critical stories about politicians from either of the major parties, especially if the stories arose from an independent investigation and could be framed as news and not simply partisan ravings. Sometimes, though, the skepticism of the press took a more aggressive form, as when crusading editors like Bennett and Horace Greeley of the *New York Tribune* instructed their reporters to seek out evidence of hypocrisy, a task made easier by the tendency of disputes to result in litigation that came to the attention of court reporters and made such cases matters of public record.[36]

Public figures, particularly businessmen and well-to-do civic leaders, remained the subjects of flattering reportage, including hagiographic character sketches that became more common after the 1850s, when big-city newspapers began adding pages of "feature" material. The appearance of these pieces, as we shall see in the next chapter, was a testament to the ability of public figures ranging from P. T. Barnum and Fanny Fern to Henry Ward Beecher and General George Armstrong Custer to exploit the new medium for their own advantage. But as Barnum and Beecher alike could attest, the new opportunities for self-promotion that the press offered were accompanied by new perils. Unlike hired scribes or sympathetic biographers, reporters and editors were more independent, and the conventions of journalism encouraged them to publish unflattering material inconsistent with the personas that public figures so assiduously cultivated.

These trends proceeded the furthest in the United States, which lagged behind other countries in the development of newspapers but quickly surpassed them in the degree to which its press embraced its democratic mission. In many European countries laws regulating the press limited the issues and range of opinion that could be expressed in newspapers throughout the nineteenth century. This was not so in the United States, where the relatively fluid, egalitarian society that emerged by the mid-nineteenth century was an ideal setting for the rise of an assertive, independent press—embodied by ambitious and influential editors and publishers like Bennett, Greeley, Charles A. Dana, and Joseph Pulitzer. Of course, a growing reliance on advertising created new constraints that by the early twentieth century made the American press relatively conservative. Yet these constraints were constantly challenged, and sometimes overcome, by the press's need to display its independence to readers, an audience that from the start included a substantial number of working-class people. Indeed, as industrialization and mass immigration enlarged the working-class population and made American society increasingly diverse, the most successful newspapers were those that were most proficient at attracting this audience by adopting a populist editorial voice: Pulitzer's *New York World*, the chain of papers owned by William Randolph Hearst, and the urban tabloids of the 1920s. On the whole, papers of this sort were more willing than conservative ones to criticize prominent public figures and engage in the business of exposure, particularly when several of them competed and sought to outdo each other in their pursuit of "scoops."

To cope with such an assertive press and the unflattering claims that its representatives were willing to publish, public figures gradually altered their strategies of self-promotion. By the end of the nineteenth century most allowed themselves to be interviewed and sought to appear natural and sincere in the presence of reporters. This was but one of several techniques that enabled them to use the press to gain favorable publicity. Equally significant were changes in how the authors of character sketches portrayed their subjects. As we have seen, since the early nineteenth century short biographies had become increasingly didactic, a weapon of an aggressive bourgeoisie determined to spread its values and way of life. To achieve this goal, the authors of these works had sought to make their subjects increasingly human, "good" rather than "great." The aim here was not only to celebrate a subject's achievements but to reveal how he or she exemplified traits that the middle classes viewed as virtuous. Prominent men—regardless of their field—were portrayed as embodiments of "character," while the few women who were celebrated appeared as icons of "true womanhood." But as readers became accustomed to a regular diet of exposés questioning these static, idealized depictions, the rhetorical strategy became more difficult to employ without undermining the credibility of the author and the publication in which the work appeared. The problem, as George William Curtis, the editor of *Harper's*, noted in 1884, was that subjects depicted along these lines did not seem "real." "[I]f a biographer assumes to tell us of a man," Curtis argued, "he must tell the truth." This might mean revealing that his subject's life was "loose, irregular, immoral, or noble, unselfish, and well-ordered." In the end, the job of the biographer was not to "smooth the wrinkles" but to give the reader a view of the real man.[37]

Accordingly, new strategies were devised to make the portraits crafted by biographers and sympathetic journalists more credible to the public. These techniques, first developed in the 1890s, were meant to illuminate the subject's "real self." Focusing on characteristics that made him interesting or unique, they shifted the spotlight away from traits that he shared with other prominent figures—and away from idealized portrayals in general. The result was profiles and sketches that presented their subjects as complex, even flawed "human beings." This was a far more effective strategy for depicting public figures, for it recognized the degree to which the public had become skeptical, even cynical, about appearances and self-promotion. Like the techniques of eighteenth-century biography, their precursor, these new techniques were no guarantee of authenticity; a profile that utilized them could be just as biased as a piece of hagiography. But their use certainly made profiles and biographies *seem* more trustworthy, and for writers whose reputations within the public sphere depended on appearing truthful, this was all-important.

Though shaped in large part by the problem of appearances that by the late nineteenth century had become a defining feature of life in the urban-industrial United States, the new stress on presenting public figures as complex human beings was also encouraged by other influences. One of these was Darwinism, which reshaped intellectual discourse and had a broad impact on the culture at large during the second half of the nineteenth century. The popularization of Darwin's theory of evolution led people to view humans as part of the natural world, pawns in a process over which they had relatively little control. Even when invoked by optimistic interpreters like Lester Frank Ward and William James, Darwinian theory emphasized the instrumental features of human nature and made it more difficult to believe in a person's nobility or virtue. This conclusion was given further impetus by developments in the new field of psychology, which promoted the belief that human behavior was motivated by unconscious instincts and drives. From this point of view, the drama of human existence was not so much the struggle of rational, self-directed individuals to discipline themselves and control their environment—the heroic mission celebrated by bourgeois moralists like Samuel Smiles—but a more prosaic struggle to adapt to that environment and make the best of it. Theories advanced by leading scholars in the fledgling social sciences echoed the same themes. According to Charles H. Cooley and George Herbert Mead, the self was shaped by the environment and external factors, particularly interpersonal relations.[38]

Over time, these theories fundamentally altered the worldview of the educated classes and many ordinary Americans. Ironically, this would never have occurred had it not been for the work of prominent Protestant ministers like Henry Ward Beecher and Washington Gladden, who struggled to reconcile the new findings of scientists with religious belief and thus paved the way for their broad acceptance by much of the public. The work of popularizers like Edwin Youmans, Richard T. Ely, and Ray Stannard Baker, who wrote countless articles on these subjects for newspapers and both popular and genteel magazines, was equally important in introducing the new theories to a wider reading public and transforming them into conventional wisdom within the public sphere. When combined with the tendency to distrust appearances, this new understanding of self and society had a powerful influence on the manner in which public figures were portrayed in the press and in many biographies.[39]

For a vivid illustration of their early influence, there is no better example than William Dean Howells's novel *The Rise of Silas Lapham*, published in 1884. Howells was a pioneering literary realist fascinated with journalism, and some of his novels feature characters who work in the field. One of these is Bartley Hubbard, the protagonist of *A Modern Instance* who also appears at the beginning of *Silas Lapham*. It is Hubbard who introduces the reader to Lapham, a wealthy mineral-paint magnate, when he visits him to write a newspaper profile. The piece that results from this encounter is cliché-ridden and formulaic, written in the inspirational mold perfected by Smiles. However, it is clear to the reader that Hubbard is contemptuous of his subject and cynically going through the motions of the interview just to get enough material to plug into the mold. Lapham goes along innocently, confirming Hubbard's dim view of him. But as the novel proceeds, and as we come to understand the forces that have shaped him, Lapham emerges as a complex and ambiguous character, and his rise to riches is revealed to be far more interesting and problematic than Hubbard's laudatory yet simplistic profile suggests. In this novel, Howells lampoons the didactic conventions of bourgeois hagiography, demonstrating how the techniques of realism could produce more truthful portraits—portraits focusing on private life and personal relationships, now viewed as constitutive elements of selfhood.[40]

By the 1890s most metropolitan newspapers had adopted some of the techniques of literary realism to make their reportage more credible among suspicious readers. And writers for new mass-circulation magazines like *Munsey's* and *McClure's,* now allowed more space and literary license, made ever greater use of them. Profiles and sketches of people in the news became more like the first chapter of *Silas Lapham,* accounts of reporters meeting and interacting with their subjects, and less like Hubbard's final product. But credibility was not the only concern that prompted this development. It was also inspired by a desire to make the journalists' products more interesting and appealing to readers, most of whom now had a variety of new leisure-time activities from which to choose. This imperative was especially strong for newspapers and magazines eager to attract women and working-class readers, two groups that had a marked preference for reportage resembling works of popular fiction or otherwise conforming to what Michael Schudson has called "story" journalism. As the pathbreaking press baron Joseph Pulitzer instructed a lieutenant, "Please impress on the men who write our interviews with prominent men the importance of giving a striking, vivid pen sketch of the subject: also a vivid picture of the domestic environment, his wife, his children, his animal pets, etc. Those are the things that will bring him more closely home to the average reader." Thus the turn toward realism in the depiction of public figures by the press was not a turn toward cold, clinical treatments. Realistic portraits were supposed to make subjects more interesting and lifelike as well as more credible.[41]

* * *

This departure shifted the focus of profiles, sketches, and biographies away from project of character building and toward a new concern, the state of the self in an increasingly complex, highly organized society. Inspired by the findings of naturalists, psychologists, and social scientists, who challenged the ideal of autonomous selfhood, writers began to shape their work around new questions that seemed to intrigue an increasing number of Americans. In a society where a host of external forces impinged on the autonomy of the individual, how could a person maintain a measure of control over his life and realize his full potential? To what degree was his potential constrained by heredity and native endowment? Was it possible to overcome the limitations of such an endowment? If so, how? And if not, how could one learn to be content with one's lot in life? Given the growth of cities and the impersonality of the new urban-industrial social order, how could an individual distinguish himself from the crowd and have his unique attributes recognized by others?

These questions were fueled by a widespread recognition that the social and economic changes of the nineteenth century had dramatically altered the setting where individual men and women were supposed to shape their own destinies. In the view of many Americans, the emergence of an urban-industrial society had undermined the autonomy of the self. While it was still possible for ambitious, enterprising men to rise in status, the most readily available avenues for doing so were now within large, hierarchical organizations. Successfully navigating these institutions required an ability to work with others and, more important, a willingness to conform to specialized functional roles that appeared to limit employees' creativity and individuality. Even more onerous were the constraints placed on workers at the lower levels, where scientific management and the introduction of new machinery were transforming many factory jobs into mindless, repetitive routines. After the turn of the century these innovations spread to the expanding white-collar sector of the economy and began to affect more and more middle-class men. And as an increasing number of women were drawn into the paid-labor force, they too were subjected to the new regime. The consequences of these trends, as scholars have demonstrated, were profound. With the world of work becoming increasingly complex and rule-bound, private life began to assume an even greater importance. It became the realm where, more than ever, many men and women invested their emotional energy and expected relief from the alienating demands of the modern workplace. Even more than in the nineteenth-century, time away from work came to be viewed as "free" time, when a person might pursue his true interests and express himself in ways that were impossible on the job.[42]

The increased value placed on free time and its association with self-expression led to a gradual waning of interest in "character" and the commensurate growth of a substantially new ideal that would play a central role in modern American culture, the ideal of "personality." First developed in the seventeenth century, the concept of personality referred to the peculiar array of faculties, instincts, and dispositions that made each man or woman unique. Most middle-class Victorians viewed individuality as problematic, however. Indeed, in a dynamic, competitive society where individuals had so much freedom, a commitment to personality could make them self-centered or antisocial and undermine the cohesiveness of the social order. Hence the celebration of character, which involved subordinating the lower passions and instincts to the higher faculties of reason and enlightened self-interest through a rigorous program of self-discipline. The objective of character was to contain the potentially unruly dimensions of an individual's personality so that the worthy dimensions could be fully developed and expressed—a project, Frederick Douglass asserted in an address entitled "Self-Made Men," that exemplified "the grandest possibilities of human nature." [43]

By the turn of the century, however, as many Americans began to chafe at the constraints of the modern, scientifically managed workplace, and with free time assuming greater importance as the locus of self-expression, even the middle-class people who had been the most committed devotees of character building began to question the need for such a regimen. Influenced by the insights of the new psychology, they began to view their passions and instincts more positively, as essential to selfhood and deserving of nurture and expression. To be sure, control over impulses and instincts that might produce antisocial behavior remained crucial. And people were still expected to pursue a program of self-improvement—beginning with early lessons learned as children and extending beyond formal schooling—that would enable them to develop fully their potential and play a constructive role in the world. But added to this was a new objective, the necessity of emotional development and self-expression. Combined, these imperatives were the essential ingredients of self-realization or personal "growth," a new therapeutic ideal that in the early twentieth century came to replace the ideal of character as the reigning model of self-development. [44]

Women, not surprisingly, were the first to embrace this ideal. Long encouraged to nurture and express their emotions, they were predisposed to place a high value on private life and regard it as the most conducive site for achieving fulfillment. The constraints that the vast majority of women faced when they were finally allowed into the workforce—whether as factory hands, clerical workers, or members of the expanding "pink-collar" professions—made this commitment to private life seem even more compelling. As numerous labor historians have shown, by the 1880s many working-class men had come to much the same conclusion. From their point of view, the modern industrial order provided few opportunities for ordinary workingmen to make an impact or express their individuality. They responded by displaying a growing interest in new forms of leisure and recreation, and by supporting the movement for higher wages and a shorter workday, which promised to make it easier for them to enjoy their time away from work. By the early twentieth century men and women from the working class and lower-middle class were devoted to a wide range of activities that stressed adventure, excitement, and opportunities for self-expression. The eagerness with which many upper-middle-class women plunged into some of these activities was important in encouraging men from such backgrounds to do so as well, leading even them to adopt the new view of leisure time that had become popular among their fellow Americans. Though for upper-middle-class men the workplace remained an arena where it was possible to earn a comfortable income and achieve a measure of self-fulfillment, the highly organized and collaborative nature of much corporate and professional work sometimes diluted its psychological rewards. According to historians, this realization may have induced many of them to join their wives in the quest for self-realization.[45]

This quest was not new. Belief in the redemptive nature of private life had been integral to the bourgeois worldview since the early nineteenth century. And its hold on the imagination of middle-class Americans had been strengthened by the influence of Romanticism and a growing interest in "culture" and "refinement," an interest that had spurred the sale of commodities thought to confer the desired attributes on their consumers. But it was not until the second half of the nineteenth century that this understanding of private life truly blossomed, as the public sphere came to appear not just strife-ridden but threatening to self-expression and individuality—a place where even the well-to-do could no longer make their individual mark. This perception led most Americans to reaffirm their commitment to private life, and encouraged visionary businessmen like the department-store magnate John Wanamaker and the vaudeville impresario Tony Pastor to promote new kinds of consumer goods and leisure-time activities as vehicles through which individuals could express themselves and achieve self-realization. By the early twentieth century a consumer-oriented private life was being promoted by advertisers, professionals, and reformers as an antidote to the impersonal, rule-bound world of work. As the economist Simon N. Patten noted in his prophetic book *The New Basis of Civilization* (1907), people would continue to work, despite the alienating conditions of modern labor, so that they could afford the goods and experiences that would make their private lives more satisfying. "Their zest for amusement urges them to submit to the discipline of work, and the habits formed for the sake of gratifying their tastes makes the regular life necessary in industry easier and more pleasant." However, as Patten made clear, for the great majority work would remain a means to an end, and in the modern age fulfillment would most likely occur in private life, through leisure and consumption.[46]

This new understanding of selfhood reinforced the tendency of reporters and biographers to focus on a subject's private life—now viewed not merely as the domain of the real self but as the realm where the subject was most likely to find fulfillment. Shifting attention to this realm enabled the press to construct portraits that were more interesting and relevant to the wide array of readers who made up the mass audience of the twentieth century. These readers might fantasize about duplicating the achievements of notable public figures, but they were likelier to draw inspiration from the more prosaic and accessible ways that these figures used to express their individuality and fulfill themselves. In adopting this new approach, reporters and biographers did not entirely abandon their interest in the achievements or the tangible lessons revealed by a prominent person's success. Yet this subject was treated in a new way, with achievements serving not as proof of a subject's virtuous character but as visible manifestations of his ability to express himself—the ultimate fantasy for people dwarfed by the size and complexity of the institutions that now dominated the public sphere and defined the nature of modernity.[47]

By the 1920s magazine profiles, newspaper sketches, and most biographies betrayed the signs of the new approach. No matter what area of a public figure's life a writer focused on, the emphasis remained the same: illuminating the real self and revealing how the subject, now viewed as a complex human being, nurtured and expressed his or her individuality. Often, self-expression was central to the subject's work or profession, providing rewards—money, power, recognition of the subject's uniqueness—that were beyond the reach of ordinary citizens. But in the end, the subject's ability to achieve personal growth and happiness rested on the quality of his or her private life, and the manner in which he or she managed the "art of living."

* * *

The emergence of celebrity was a result of more than simply the development of new media and the new opportunities for self-promotion offered by the public sphere. Visibility—the chance to become well-known through self-promotion and the stunts that Boorstin called pseudo-events—was certainly important. But as we have seen, underlying social and economic conditions exerted tremendous influence over how people used the new media and sought to present themselves in public, and this had momentous consequences. The freedom to fashion one's own identity and pursue the new economic and social opportunities made possible by modernization aroused a profound suspicion of appearances—including a suspicion of the personas that public figures projected in the public sphere. With the public sphere viewed as a realm where everyone was acting, people concluded that a person's real self could only be viewed in private, and only if the person wished it to be seen.

This belief, a cardinal principle of modernity, sparked a heightened interest in the private lives of public figures, and encouraged writers, reporters, and biographers to employ new techniques that made their subjects appear more realistic. Over time, the growing use of these techniques made hagiographic approaches—even the more modest hagiography practiced by bourgeois moralists like Samuel Smiles—unsatisfying to much of the public, especially as new intellectual currents made belief in the unmitigated virtue of human beings difficult to sustain. After the turn of the century, the tendency to portray prominent public figures as human beings was reinforced by a new interest in personality and the rewards of private life, a theme that diverted celebrity discourse even further from its antecedents.

Celebrities emerged when public figures—people visible in the public sphere—were subjected to this new mode of presentation, a process that began in the mid-nineteenth century but was not complete until the 1920s. It is pointless, therefore, to lament the failure of the media to celebrate the achievements of heroes, or their tendency to cheapen the few that they notice at all. By the mid-twentieth century there was no other way for the media to portray public figures except to present them as celebrities and endow them with all the features that so repulsed Boorstin and other intellectuals of his era, and still repulse many observers today. The irony is that this devaluation of "greatness" was a direct result of social and economic changes that most Americans regard as eminently progressive. Empowering common people required belittling the distinguished—and shattering the notion that a human being could ever be "great."

2
. . . .
THE RISE OF CELEBRITY
JOURNALISM

If media visibility was the distinguishing feature of the celebrity, no American of the late nineteenth century better epitomized this new condition than Chauncey M. Depew. As chairman of the New York Central Railroad, a leading figure in the Republican party and one of the "bosses" of its machine in New York State, an active member of numerous charitable organizations and social clubs, a frequent guest and speaker at lavish public banquets throughout the Gilded Age, Depew was well situated to attract the attention of the press. And unlike some other prominent men of the era—John D. Rockefeller, for example— who shrank from the increasingly bright spotlight directed at public figures, Depew relished the possibilities that it offered for publicity, becoming an expert at cultivating the friendship of reporters and providing them with a steady stream of quotes and inside dope. By the 1890s his opinions were solicited on issues that ranged far beyond business and politics, and he was the subject of articles in newspapers and magazines that were published throughout the country, not just in his native New York. While some of these stories focused on his activities as a railroad executive and politician, others sought to illuminate his "home life" and present him as a "human being." Depew, in short, was not merely a well-known public figure; he was a national celebrity.

And his celebrity hinged on his relationship with the press. Though Depew was conscious of the many ways a man could make himself visible in the public sphere, he recognized that the press was the pivotal institution that determined the degree and nature of his visibility, the institution through which other strategies of self-promotion were filtered and refracted. He was aware, for example, that the audience for his witty after-dinner speeches was not confined to the well-to-do men and women in attendance. It included the reporters who had been invited as guests, thousands of New Yorkers who would see accounts of the dinner in the next morning's papers, and millions of people outside New York who would read about it in wire-service accounts or national publications like *Harper's Weekly*. Depew's understanding of this reality profoundly shaped his interaction with the prominent reporters—men such as Julian Ralph, James Creelman, and Lincoln Steffens—who covered politics and business and regularly came to him for information. By drawing them into his confidence and making them feel like insiders, he turned them into allies who could be trusted to reveal only what he regarded as appropriate for public consumption. Reminiscing about his friendship with reporters in his autobiography, Depew noted, "No reporter has ever abused the confidence I reposed in him. He always appreciated what I told him . . . and knew what was proper for him to reveal and what was not for publication." This "cordial relationship," Depew conceded, was "of great value in getting our side before the public." With a few notable exceptions, press coverage of Depew was influenced by the conviction that he was a good, reliable, eminently quotable source whose willingness to cooperate with reporters deserved sympathy and in some cases protection.[1]

In Depew's case, this inclination to give him good press was reinforced by an even more powerful belief, one that Depew actively encouraged: that Depew, far more than many other public figures, was peculiarly interesting, a man whose opinions and activities were "colorful" and thus of intrinsic interest to the public and the press. This belief, widely held by newspaper and magazine journalists in the 1880s and 1890s, allowed Depew to become the subject of celebrity journalism, a new form of reportage that expressly focused on public figures, evoking interest in them as "personalities."

This new species of journalism merits close examination. Far more than the myriad news items in which public figures like Depew appeared, it was responsible for transforming them into celebrities occupying a new pantheon. As we shall see, the first forms of celebrity journalism began to appear in the mid-nineteenth century. It was not until the 1880s and especially the 1890s, however, that it became a staple of the metropolitan press, as entertainment values became increasingly emphasized and the press embraced new rhetorical strategies that dramatically altered the ways in which certain public figures were portrayed in newspapers and magazines. Depew was among the first to be cast in this new light, one of a relatively few celebrities who achieved national visibility during the late nineteenth century, when new institutions were forging the outlines of a truly national media culture. This new media culture would continue to grow during the first few decades of the twentieth century, becoming more centralized and making it possible for many more public figures to achieve the kind of visibility that Depew had enjoyed in the 1890s. By the 1940s hundreds of public figures were visible and well-known to the public, the inhabitants of a vastly enlarged mass-mediated community. Meanwhile, the biggest celebrities, an elite drawn from disparate worlds of business, politics, society, entertainment, and sports, were in another league altogether, the subjects of unprecedented publicity who often found themselves under the glare of a spotlight unfathomable in Depew's day.

* * *

Celebrity journalism emerged during the second half of the nineteenth century, a period of tremendous growth for the mass-circulation press. As the population of American cities increased, so did the number of newspapers that were directed toward this new urban audience. By 1900 there were well over a dozen daily papers in New York alone, and big cities like Chicago, Philadelphia, and Boston had nearly as many. Some of these newspapers boasted circulations that approached a million copies per day, reaching readers from a wide range of classes and ethnic groups—what enterprising publishers like James Gordon Bennett, Charles A. Dana, and Joseph Pulitzer regarded as the highly coveted "mass" audience. The appeal of metropolitan newspapers among these readers can be attributed to several factors. Hawked on the streets by newsboys, they were inexpensive and accessible to the vast majority of urban residents. Their prose was clear, free of jargon, their stories written in an engaging, often dramatic style tailor-made for readers who were literate and eager for knowledge but not especially learned. Urban newspapers were also useful, providing readers with a compelling vantage point from which to survey and make sense of the dynamic, bewildering urban environment. Newspapers illuminated vast expanses of the great, mysterious city, allowing readers to see things that would otherwise escape their view. By the 1890s newspapers had also begun to dispense advice on how best to navigate the city and make the most of its unique features. Directed at women as well as men, the mass-circulation press portrayed the city as spectacle, a fascinating tableau where individuals and groups struggled for recognition, material success, and public influence.[2]

This function stemmed from the newspaper's commitment to covering "news." Before the emergence of newspapers like Benjamin Day's *New York Sun* and Bennett's *New York Herald* in the 1830s, editors had a rather different understanding of their mission. They covered a very narrow range of events, and they did so haphazardly, without regard for timeliness or presentation. Their papers were sold by subscription to a small, select audience of elite merchants and civic leaders, a fact reflected not only in their limited coverage but in their high price—six cents—and lack of accessibility. The "penny press" pioneered by Day and Bennett dramatically expanded coverage to many different areas of urban life. By the 1840s reporters had been assigned to city hall, the courts, the police department, the mercantile district, the city's churches, high society, and the theater and other commercial amusements. And by the 1880s whole squads of reporters were responsible for reporting from each of these beats. The scope of newspaper coverage steadily expanded as papers grew in size, owing to improvements in technology and the willingness of businessmen to buy advertising space. This coverage, while predominantly local, was never provincial. From the beginning editors like Bennett and Dana published letters from "correspondents" in other cities, particularly state capitals and Washington. And coverage of developments outside the metropolis increased with the introduction of wire services, which allowed for reports about national and international events and greatly enlarged the spectacular vista covered by the press.[3]

Metropolitan newspapers like Bennett's *Herald* and its slew of imitators encouraged readers to assume the role of spectators and consumers of information provided by reporters. This mission was fueled by a belief in the importance of disseminating knowledge throughout society, to bolster republican citizenship and banish traditions that in the past had led common people to defer to elites. The expansion of news coverage, in other words, was inspired by a conviction that newspapers covered things that the public had a right to know.[4] But the mass-circulation press's commitment to revealing the truth and spreading knowledge coexisted with an equally compelling obligation to provide readers with good stories. It was this very different mission that led editors to appropriate vernacular forms that had long been a staple of broadsheets and ballads and make them the foundation for "human-interest" stories, which were central to the penny press and an increasingly important feature of all newspapers in the years after the Civil War.[5] The editors' reliance on such material derived from an important insight. Reading newspapers was not only inspired by a desire for knowledge and self-improvement; it was also an activity most likely to occur during a reader's leisure time, influenced by yearnings for diversion and escape from the daily routine of the urban-industrial workplace. And as publishers sought to expand their readership to include more women, workers, and immigrants, emphasis on making their stories entertaining as well as informative increased. By the early twentieth century it was conventional wisdom that readers, as the author of an early journalism handbook put it, wanted to be "informed in a way that interests them."[6]

To be sure, metropolitan newspapers were not identical. While Bennett's *Herald* established a new mold that was widely imitated, other publishers pursued a different course. Some papers, like Horace Greeley's *New York Tribune* and Henry Raymond's *New York Times,* were conceived in opposition to the insouciant, popular style developed by Bennett. Directed at an audience that regarded itself as serious and respectable, these newspapers adopted a more sober editorial voice, and they reaped significant financial rewards by convincing advertisers of the merits of their upscale approach. In the 1850s the success of these papers led publishers like Bennett to tone down their sensationalism in an effort to appeal to the coveted middle-class audience.[7] But the trend of the future was in the opposite direction. As the urban population expanded and economic development enlarged the ranks of the wage-earning class, a new generation of publishers and editors, led by Dana, Pulitzer, and E. W. Scripps, refined and expanded the formula conceived by Bennett, creating newspapers that were even more popular—and far more profitable than the self-styled "respectable" press. In the 1890s they were joined by an ambitious newcomer, William Randolph Hearst, who quickly assumed the role of trailblazer. The Hearst press set a new standard for sensationalism and entertainment values in journalism, forcing its competitors—notably Pulitzer and Scripps—to adopt similar practices, a development that exerted a broad influence on the content of all big-city papers during the first decade of the twentieth century.[8]

The appearance of these unabashedly sensationalistic newspapers

aroused anguished cries among more conservative publishers and inspired Adolph Ochs to transform the *Times* into an even more dour paragon of respectability. By the second decade of the century, however,
elements of the "story" journalism developed by Pulitzer and Hearst
had begun to appear in papers—even Ochs's *Times*—that professed contempt for "yellow journalism." The trend continued unabated into the
1920s and 1930s, when the appearance of urban tabloids like the *New
York Daily News* and Hearst's *New York Daily Mirror* made Hearst's
conventional-size papers appear tame in comparison.[9] Though differences among newspapers persisted, with the tabloids occupying the
most sensational and entertaining edge of the continuum and the *Times*
and *New York Herald-Tribune* the more sober and informative, all of
them, to one degree or another, were committed to entertaining as well
as informing their readers, particularly in their popular Sunday editions. They diverged chiefly in their interpretations of what constituted
entertainment. These interpretations were shaped in part by the kinds
of readers that editors viewed as their target audience—for the tabloids and the Hearst press, the urban, largely ethnic working class; for
the *Times*, the *Herald-Tribune*, and their respectable imitators, the more
educated and pretentious elite and upper-middle class; for the majority
of papers that sought to occupy a sensible middle ground, the more affluent upper ranks of the working class and the burgeoning lower-middle
class of clerks, salespeople, and small proprietors.[10]

In practice, this resulted in an abundance of sensational serial fiction and advice-oriented feature stories in the tabloids, and a reliance
on more high-toned fiction and features in the respectable press—often
written by well-known authors or about seemingly significant subjects
like, say, the "future of aviation" or the exploits of a noted explorer and
anthropologist. In the 1920s features assumed a new prominence in virtually all newspapers, and Sunday editions of the *Times* were chock full
of material that reflected a liberal view of Ochs's dictum "All the News
That's Fit to Print." A Sunday edition from March 1927, for example,
offered readers in-depth news stories on the Ruth Snyder murder case
and other scandals, feature stories on the First Lady and the legal travails of the Broadway producer Earl Carroll, lengthy gossip columns on
the literary world, the theater, and the movie industry, a whole section
devoted to "society," and a lavish photo supplement that included pictures of the exiled Russian leader Alexander Kerensky, the tennis champion Helen Wills, the poet Edna St. Vincent Millay, the Yankee owner

Jake Ruppert with his star slugger, Babe Ruth, the author of "Gentleman Prefer Blondes," Anita Loos, and an aging Chauncey M. Depew wintering in St. Augustine. Indeed, the sheer volume of features in the Sunday *Times* far exceeded the volume of features in the nation's most widely read tabloid, Joseph Medill Patterson's *New York Daily News*. Offset by sober news reports written in the colorless prose that had become the paper's most distinguishing characteristic, feature stories were a major staple of the *Times* under the pioneering managing editor Carr Van Anda and a big reason for its growing popularity among middle-class New Yorkers—a fact obscured by Ochs's and Van Anda's determination to associate their paper with objectivity and serious news. As the press critic Silas Bent noted, the aura of seriousness at the *Times* was in many ways misleading: "It outdistances all competitors in the space it accords to sensational events, and in the scope of its coverage." The presence of features in the *Times* was a testament to their importance to metropolitan journalism.[11]

One of the most remarkable traits of the mass-circulation press was its ability to make ordinary people visible at a time when urban growth appeared to be submerging individuals into an anonymous mass. Illuminated by the press, men and women gained a new kind of conspicuousness and were transformed into public figures. As we have seen, for this to occur they did not have to occupy a position of leadership or perform an extraordinary feat; all it took was for them to seem newsworthy. And as the press expanded its coverage to include new areas of social life, the criteria that journalists employed to determine newsworthiness expanded as well. By the mid-nineteenth century anybody involved or associated with a news story or an institution regularly covered by the press was a legitimate candidate for journalistic publicity and transformation into a public figure: the victims, perpetrators, and witnesses of crimes; those involved in scandals or noteworthy court cases; others whom reporters encountered in the course of covering their beats, especially people who ran important political, economic, and civic organizations; still others with expertise and inside dope on subjects reporters deemed interesting to the public; even obscure people whose travails, once brought to the attention of the press, became the grist for colorful, often poignant human-interest stories.[12]

During the early years of the penny press the visibility provided by newspapers was limited by meager resources and primitive technology. For example, in the pathbreaking coverage of the Robinson-

Jewett murder case by the *New York Herald* in 1836, the first event that was highly publicized by the mass-circulation press, the paper's editor James Gordon Bennett also served as a reporter, visiting the crime scene, questioning witnesses and other important parties, and writing accounts of the trial. There was only so much, however, that Bennett and his small staff could do in covering the case. Lacking extensive connections, he was forced to rely on hearsay and unreliable "correspondents" for information about the background of the victim, Helen Jewett, a prostitute who had moved to New York from Maine. This disadvantage was endemic in an era when big-city newspapers like the *Herald* were small enterprises employing no more than a handful of employees. More serious were technological limitations that made it impossible for Bennett to give the story all the attention he might have thought it deserved. Illustrations of the major players, for example, were few and extremely crude, and Bennett was further confined by his inability to produce a paper that exceeded four pages. Despite these constraints, the Robinson-Jewett murder case received an unprecedented degree of coverage in the *Herald* and other newspapers in New York, and a wide range of people involved in it were thrust into the public eye, including inhabitants of the demimonde like Jewett's fellow prostitutes and Rosina Townsend, the proprietor of the brothel in which she was killed.[13]

Gradually these constraints were overcome. For evidence of this, one need only compare coverage of the Robinson-Jewett case with press treatment of the murder trial in 1907 of Harry Thaw, a businessman convicted of murdering the renowned architect and bon vivant Stanford White. By this time newspapers had grown exponentially in size, offering readers multiple sections and updated editions three or four times a day. Many were lavishly illustrated with photographs and realistic drawings. Editorial departments had also grown. Big-city dailies employed dozens of staff writers and many more freelancers, and reporting had been divided into specific tasks overseen by editors, a process that tended to separate reporters into two main camps: "leg men," who were responsible for going out and getting news, and "rewrite men," who assembled this material into coherent stories. All these advances were on display in the coverage of White's murder. Teams of reporters were dispatched by editors of the New York press to cover every conceivable angle of the case. Wire-service reporters covered it for papers outside New York and provided reams of material on the backgrounds of Thaw, White, and Thaw's estranged wife, the model Evelyn Nesbit, with whom White had been having an affair. The trial produced even more copy, as a host of renowned feature writers—from Alfred Henry Lewis and Samuel Hopkins Adams, two journalists well known for muckraking, to Winifred Black, Dorothy Dix, and Nicola Greeley-Smith, the leading "sob sisters" of the American press—supplemented the lengthy dispatches of court reporters with commentary and observations, including detailed sketches of every witness who appeared. By the early twentieth century, therefore, people elevated to the status of public figures, even those whose relationship to news stories was peripheral, were subjected to a degree of exposure that far exceeded anything experienced by their predecessors during the heyday of the penny press. This development was a direct result of the press's steady expansion of coverage, and the new possibilities for exposure created by large reportorial staffs and new technologies, which increased the size of papers and the number of columns that could be devoted to newsworthy events and people.[14]

Of course, the great majority of people endowed with visibility by the press during such events were just as quickly returned to obscurity. The essence of news was timeliness, and when it seemed as if readers had grown tired of a story and its principals, editors had no compunction about shifting the spotlight elsewhere. Yet even in Bennett's day, some people became the subjects of regular publicity and remained visible for a much longer time, sometimes many years. Many of these people—the abolitionist William Lloyd Garrison and the health guru Sylvester Graham, for example—were the leaders of groups seeking public support or influence. Others, like Daniel Webster, Thurlow Weed, John Jacob Astor, and Henry Ward Beecher, occupied positions of political and cultural authority as elected officials, heads of political parties and machines, wealthy businessmen, ministers of prominent churches, or leaders of civic organizations. Their newsworthiness derived from the positions they occupied and their ability to shape urban life. Still others were savvy promoters like P. T. Barnum, Tony Pastor, Richard Kyle Fox, key figures in the emerging field of entertainment and popular culture, who recognized the importance of the press in publicizing their activities. Indeed, their adroitness in gaining publicity made possible the celebrity of the performers who appeared in their attractions. As a result, by the 1850s the ranks of well-known public figures—about whom the word "celebrity" was first employed—included the actor Edwin Forrest, the singer Jenny Lind, and the minstrel-show performer T. D. Rice.

By the late nineteenth century, however, the visibility offered by the mass-circulation press had produced a new class of public figures who were more than simply the subjects of regular publicity. Like Depew, they were celebrities. Though sometimes featured in news stories by virtue of their position or connection to an important event, most of them owed their visibility to their well-knownness, which, in the view of the press, gave them "news value" and ensured their continued visibility. They were drawn from a wide range of fields, reflecting the broadened scope of news coverage. The "big names" of the late nineteenth century, for example, included not just powerful and influential men like Depew, Beecher, James G. Blaine, and Andrew Carnegie—the kinds of figures who dominated press coverage in the 1840s and 1850s. They also included Frances Willard, head of the Women's Christian Temperance Union; the prizefighter John L. Sullivan; the English actress and "professional beauty" Lillie Langtry; "Diamond Jim" Brady, a raffish man-about-town known for his love affairs with actresses and regular feasts in New York at the glittering lobster palaces that lined Broadway; and William F. "Buffalo Bill" Cody, an ex-scout and the colorful star and promoter of Wild West shows.

* * *

To appreciate the novel position of celebrities, we need to look at the specific forms of reporting that made them visible. The most common were conventional news stories, usually short items about the profession or institution with which the celebrities were associated. Depew, for instance, was a recurrent character in stories about the railroad industry, especially the interests of the Vanderbilts that he oversaw and for which he was a spokesman, and the fortunes of the New York branch of the Republican party. Such stories were the primary means by which newspaper readers became aware of public figures and came to understand their place in the social dramas depicted by the press. Other stories focused on celebrities alone, noting their activities and revealing their commitments, associations, and beliefs. These could range from short items, two or three sentences in length, to extensive, illustrated profiles like "Home and Home Life of Chauncey M. Depew," which appeared in 1892 in *Munsey's*.[15] Such reporting was celebrity journalism, a new genre that encompassed a number of different forms but was united by the assumption that "names make news"—that readers were sufficiently interested in public figures like Depew to read both news and feature stories about them. In the 1880s and 1890s these forms were still in their early stages of development, and it was not until the 1920s that they matured. They were sufficiently developed, though, to lift Depew and his fellow celebrities to a new level of conspicuousness.

The first forms of celebrity journalism were gossip columns and short items of "local intelligence." These were fixtures of the antebellum penny press, the forum where the professional and private activities of public figures were reported. Among the activities noted by the press were speeches and appearances at banquets and public functions, involvement in civic and philanthropic causes, the inauguration of new business ventures, and personal milestones like marriages and the births or deaths of family members. For example, in a column titled "Movements of Distinguished People," the *Herald* regularly reported on the comings and goings of a host of well-known figures, information gathered by reporters assigned to train stations and leading hotels. Such items were often a prelude to more in-depth coverage. A short announcement of Daniel Webster's arrival in New York in April 1850, for instance, was followed the next day by a long, impressionistic account of his day in the city, gleaned largely from unnamed "friends" who dined with him after he delivered an important address on the political crisis that would soon result in the Compromise of 1850.[16]

By the end of the nineteenth century features of this sort had become more numerous and specialized, with distinct columns covering the activities of politicians, businessmen, society figures, writers and artists, theatrical folk, and athletes, along with the usual columns that ranged more widely. In 1890 Pulitzer's *New York World,* for example, offered readers information about celebrities in features like "Among the Players," a column focusing on Broadway stars; "In Millionaire Society," one of several gossip columns covering the antics of the so-called Four Hundred; "Doings of Women Folk," a more specialized feature on the activities of prominent members of women's clubs; and "People Often Talked Of," a more general column where readers might learn about the First Lady Frances Cleveland, Senator John J. Ingalls of Kansas, or Mark Twain. The appeal of this brand of reportage was not lost on magazine publishers, and in the 1890s more lengthy, illustrated gossip columns began to appear in new-style publications like *Munsey's, Cosmopolitan,* and *McClure's.* "In the Public Eye" was the title of the gossip feature in *Munsey's,* which provided readers with one- or two-paragraph accounts of the latest doings of a wide range of public figures. An issue in 1895, for example, illuminated the activities of Queen Victoria, police commissioner Theodore Roosevelt of New York, the suffragist Susan B. Anthony, the editor E. L. Godkin, and the writer and arts-and-crafts guru William Morris.[17]

In the 1920s an entirely new breed of gossip column emerged, covering public figures from an even wider array of fields, especially those who patronized elegant and often exclusive restaurants and nightclubs in New York, Los Angeles, and resort areas like Santa Barbara, Miami, and Palm Beach—the denizens of what came to be known as "cafe society." Made possible by the new eagerness of society figures and rich businessmen to consort in public places with entertainers, athletes, and other representatives from the world of popular culture, this new social group began to take shape in the early 1920s, when Prohibition led to the rise of new forms of nightlife where all of kinds people rubbed shoulders for the first time. The journalistic possibilities created by this development were first exploited by show-business reporters like Walter Winchell and Mark Hellinger, who wrote columns for the New York tabloids that often focused on members of this group. As Neal Gabler has noted, it was Winchell who made the most of it, dramatically expanding the kinds of information conveyed by gossip columns and creating a venue where the private affairs of public figures were more openly addressed— innovations that made his syndicated column one of the most popular features of the Hearst press from the 1930s through the 1950s. Basing his operations at Sherman Billingsley's Stork Club, where he took phone calls from celebrities and press agents and posed for photo opportunities with those in attendance, Winchell gathered and published material on all sorts of people—not just the show-business types who were the original subjects of his column. In the process, he and his imitators blurred the lines that had separated celebrities into occupational groups and made the pantheon of celebrity more inclusive—a place where, in terms of visibility, Jack Dempsey was the equal of Franklin D. Roosevelt.[18]

An even more important form of reporting was the interview. Though Bennett and reporters for the penny press asked their sources questions and, on occasion, the answers appeared in direct quotations, interviews did not become a regular feature of newspapers until the 1870s, and it was not until the turn of the century that the now common practice of interspersing quotations from sources was widely employed. A major reason for this delay was the reluctance of many public figures to speak directly for attribution. The information they revealed to reporters was usually paraphrased and attributed to "an informed source." By the 1880s, however, when it had become clear that being quoted directly was a good way to avoid being misunderstood, an increasing number of public figures were allowing reporters to interview them—though some demanded that reporters show them the copy before publishing it, a demand in which most reporters freely acquiesced. In a book entitled *Adventures in Interviewing* (1919), the veteran journalist Issac Marcosson endorsed this practice, recalling his first interview with Woodrow Wilson, then the governor of New Jersey, when Wilson had asked to see a copy of the article that Marcosson had produced from their long talk. "It was a wise precaution," Marcosson observed. "If more public men would examine and revise what they say for publication before it is printed they would save themselves and other people much trouble." By the early twentieth century, journalists like Marcosson had persuaded many celebrities—including the notorious "Wall Street sphinxes," a group of powerful businessmen who had long avoided the press—that opening up to reporters was the best strategy for ensuring favorable coverage. This, in turn, sparked a huge increase in the number of public figures willing to be interviewed and allowed editors to publish more of such material.[19]

Yet not all interviews were the same. The majority that appeared in the press after 1890 were related in some fashion to a pertinent news story, and were usually inspired by a desire for more information that could only be provided by the subject. It was their desire for information about the railroad industry or the New York State GOP, for example, that prompted reporters like Julian Ralph and James Creelman to seek out Depew. The same imperative led them to interview many other prominent figures, and over time these men and women gained a reputation with reporters and the public for being in the know about developments in their field. Meanwhile, a smaller number of public figures were becoming the subjects of a rather different kind of interview: one that purported to reveal the subjects' views on a wide range of topics, published because of their well-knownness, and not because of any special insight they might have on an issue or the news. Obviously, some celebrities were better suited than others to such treatment. Witty, opinionated, entertaining figures like Depew and Mark Twain were in high demand, encouraging reporters to return to them again and again for material. Equally attractive were celebrities like Thomas Edison and George Bernard Shaw, who eagerly assumed the role of public sage and could be counted on to produce interesting remarks on topics both serious and mundane. Shaw, Edison, Theodore Roosevelt, and the automaker Henry Ford were among the widely interviewed public figures of the early twentieth century, a select group to which Albert Einstein was added in the early 1920s, when Carr Van Anda, managing editor of the *New York Times*, began dispatching reporters to solicit the physicist's views on subjects such as Prohibition, religion, and the future of mankind.[20]

Celebrities were also the focus of new kinds of feature stories that became more common in newspapers during the 1880s and 1890s. Many articles about important, sometimes complex trends and developments highlighted public figures who were thought to epitomize them. The oil tycoon John D. Rockefeller, for instance, was often portrayed as embodying the movement toward "combination" in the field of business, and articles about the subject often cited his creation of Standard Oil as an example of this trend. The spirit of scientific invention was personified by Edison, who was regularly asked by reporters to explain how new technologies would change the lives of ordinary Americans. Theodore Roosevelt represented the growing influence of the "gentleman in politics," a trend that was highly touted by journalists at the turn of the century, while the actress Ethel Barrymore symbolized the importance of "personality" in the theater, another widely discussed trend. This tendency to "personalize" the news was inspired by the need to make stories vivid and accessible to readers, and was most widely employed in feature sections, Sunday supplements, and mass-circulation magazines that were influenced by metropolitan journalism. It was essential, the publisher S. S. McClure informed his staff in the 1890s, that articles about any subject contain "a realistic portrait of the human personalities involved."[21]

People were more likely to be the subjects of such reportage, however, if they seemed "interesting" to reporters. This could mean a number of things. In the 1880s interest in Rockefeller arose from his power over the oil industry, a power that reporters depicted as unprecedented, even awe-inspiring. By the turn of the century it was his staggering wealth that made him interesting to journalists. Rockefeller's dour private life, by contrast, inspired few articles, especially when compared to the private lives of flamboyant businessmen like J. P. Morgan, whose fondness for art, yachting, and others luxuries was as interesting to the press as his command over the nation's banking interests. More interesting still were figures like Depew and Andrew Carnegie, who shared Morgan's affinity for the good life but were much friendlier with reporters, often inviting them into their homes and sitting for lengthy interviews. Yet for the press, an interesting subject was not always someone who was powerful or rich. The most important prerequisite was that he or she be witty, colorful, and complex, possessing traits that were peculiar or seemingly incongruous—the prizefighter who was as "gentle as a woman" outside the ring, or the female reformer whose tiny, frail body belied the strength of her will. H. F. Harrington, the author of a textbook on feature writing, suggested in 1925 that an interesting subject was a person with a vivid personality, whose life was adventurous and whose opinions were "fresh and unfettered"—a person "who *does* things in a unique, original way." Here was the key that lifted some figures to a level enabling them to tower over their fellows, even those who occupied positions of similar or even greater power and influence.[22]

By the 1890s the press's commitment to publicizing such figures had given rise to perhaps the most important species of celebrity journalism—the profile or sketch. More often than not, newspaper profiles were short, inspired by an event thought to have kindled public interest in the subject. But the growth of Sunday papers, with sections exclusively devoted to features, made it possible for editors to publish longer profiles, including elaborate sketches that appeared in magazine-like supplements. An issue of the *New York World* in 1890, for example, included a long, illustrated profile of the head of the American branch of the Roman Catholic Church, offering readers a "GLIMPSE OF HIS DAILY LIFE" and an appraisal of his "personality" and "habits." The most highly developed profiles were published in mass-circulation magazines like *Munsey's* and *McClure's*. Fusing elements of the traditional hagiographic sketch, the newspaper interview, and the personalized feature story, magazine profiles established a new model for reporting on celebrities that was quickly adopted by newspaper editors and incorporated into their expanding feature sections.[23]

Celebrity profiles were not biographies, though biographical details were usually sprinkled throughout the text. Indeed, unlike the short biographies which had long appeared in genteel magazines like *Harper's*, *Scribner's*, and the *Century*, profiles in newspaper supplements and popular magazines were informed by a new agenda that diverged substantially from the didacticism of the conventional biographical sketch. Their objective, as would-be feature writers were advised in 1919 by

W. G. Bleyer, a veteran journalist and one of the founders of journalism education, was to allow readers to see celebrities "as they really are" — as "living men and women." The profile writer's task was to portray his subjects so vividly that "we shall feel as if we had actually met them face to face." Many profiles were also inspired by a belief that the subject was "misunderstood," his "real self" unknown to the public. By the turn of the century this assumption had become central to celebrity journalism and the opening gambit of many a profile. For example, as a writer for the *Saturday Evening Post* observed in 1903, very different estimates of J. P. Morgan could be cobbled together from the testimony of friends and press coverage of his activities, and there was some truth to all of them, for Morgan was "many-sided." The aim of the piece, however, was to assess the entire man and provide readers with an understanding of "The Unknown Morgan." In short, the *raison d'être* of the celebrity profile was to cut through the hagiographic claptrap and gossip that obscured the public's view of prominent figures like Morgan and reveal them as truthfully as possible, a process, journalists insisted, that made portraits more complex and realistic.[24]

* * *

Journalists employed a variety of rhetorical strategies to fulfill this mission. Some visited the offices of men of affairs, the places from which they directed their organizations and financial empires. Such visits gave readers a glimpse of the inner workings of important institutions, and allowed them to see men like Morgan or the meatpacking magnate Philip D. Armour handle the levers of power. When profiling entertainers such as Joseph Jefferson, Lillian Russell, and Maude Adams, reporters often journeyed backstage, circumventing the security guards that kept the public from seeing their favorites outside the footlights. Other sites where journalists encountered celebrities were hotel suites and secluded tables at restaurants and clubs—once again places to which public access was limited. But perhaps the most common strategy that reporters employed in their quest to reveal the "real selves" of celebrities was visiting their homes, and in the years after the turn of the century such visits became integral features of celebrity journalism, a practice that persists to this day. Interest in the "home lives" of the famous was encouraged by journalists' claims that it was perfectly natural to want to see celebrities at home, in an informal setting, for it was here that they let down their guard and that one could "get behind the veil with which everyone attempts to conceal his innermost thoughts and feelings." Access to the home was essential to apprehend the real self and form a complete picture of the subject's personality. As Mattie Sheridan, the author of the *Munsey's* profile of Depew put it, "Those who have known Mr. Depew at his desk or on the rostrum have but half known him." The other, more significant half, she suggested, was only visible at home, where he spent time with his family.[25]

These visits were often depicted in laborious detail, and provided considerable information about the subject's private life. Sheridan's profile of Depew, for example, offered readers vivid descriptions of his wife, son, and daily routine. Her account of his "handsome, substantial mansion" resembled the text of a tour guide specializing in interior decor, highlighting the furniture, the art, and the arrangement of bric-a-brac. It was also common for a profile to devote attention to the subject's hobbies and avocations; some profiles were framed around activities that reporters and their subjects engaged in together. Profiles of Theodore Roosevelt, for example, emphasized his love of outdoor activities like hunting, horseback riding, and chopping wood, while many articles about John D. Rockefeller discussed his devotion to golf and occasionally bore titles like "Playing a Round of Golf with John D." A profile of the veteran actress Sarah Bernhardt in *Ladies' Home Journal* in 1912 was entirely devoted to the recreations that she enjoyed while vacationing at her summer home on the coast of France—and that the reporter visiting her was induced to join in as well. This rhetorical strategy made the subjects of celebrity profiles all the more lifelike and familiar, and reinforced the notion that private life was a crucial site for self-expression and the display of a person's real self.[26]

Celebrity profiles also differed from conventional biographical sketches by acknowledging the presence and active mediation of the author. At first, in the 1880s and 1890s, newspaper reporters relied mostly on descriptions of the subject and his surroundings, supplementing this with a few quotations. For example, a profile of William Waldorf Astor that appeared in the *New York World* in 1890 was almost entirely descriptive, drawing on previously published material and information from unnamed "friends" to provide readers with a portrait of the young heir's background and personality. After the turn of the century journalists altered this formula, increasing their reliance on quotations and placing themselves at the center of narratives, now framed as "conversations" with celebrities. News of Theodore Roosevelt Jr.'s engagement in 1910 appeared in Hearst's *New York American* in the form of a jocular front-page interview between the subject and a reporter. Feature writers were most likely to resort to this practice. It was especially common among journalists who specialized in covering show-business figures. Alan Dale's profiles of Broadway stars for the Hearst press nearly always began with humorous accounts of their meetings, in which Dale's expectations were confounded when his subjects behaved quite differently from what he had anticipated. Invariably, the stars were revealed to be unlike their stage personas, and Dale's method of conveying this fact enabled readers to share his surprise in discovering it.[27]

Common in most newspapers by the 1890s, this more chatty style of profile was slow to spread to mass-circulation magazines. Not surprisingly, the first publications to feature them were the new-style magazines established by Frank Munsey, S. S. McClure, and Edward L. Bok, men eager to adapt the innovations of the daily press to the staid field of magazine journalism. "A successful magazine," Bok, the editorial genius behind *Ladies' Home Journal*, explained in his autobiography, "is exactly like a successful store; it must keep its wares constantly fresh and varied to attract the eye and hold the patronage of its customers."[28] In their effort to stock their new publications with "fresh wares," Bok and his fellow editors began to publish all kinds of material that was common in newspapers but unprecedented for magazines, including chatty celebrity profiles. But since most magazines at the turn of the century were still directed at middle-class and upper-middle-class readers, who remained interested in "serious" topics and disdainful of sensationalism, such profiles appeared mostly in publications— like *Munsey's* and *Everybody's*—that catered to the lower middle class and the more affluent segment of the working class. Not until 1910 did they become a regular feature in *McClure's*, *Collier's*, and the *Saturday Evening Post*. Once on the bandwagon, however, editors at these more respectable magazines embraced the form with relish. After 1910 the *American Magazine*, a slick monthly founded by a group of disgruntled writers at *McClure's*, became an important new venue for celebrity profiles, and its success with the genre led other publications to increase their use of them. By the 1930s state-of-the-art celebrity profiles were fixtures of virtually all mass-circulation magazines, and magazine journalists like John K. Winkler, Adela Rogers St. Johns, and Henry F. Pringle had become the new pioneers of celebrity journalism, perfecting techniques and rhetorical strategies first developed by newspaper writers at the turn of the century to produce profiles of considerable sophistication.[29]

Many profiles acknowledged the author's friendship with his subject. This gambit was first widely employed by magazine journalists like Ray Stannard Baker, William Allen White, and Lincoln Steffens in their coverage of Theodore Roosevelt. By the second decade of the twentieth century, however, it had become a favorite strategy of many different kinds of writers eager to appear as insiders and was especially common in profiles targeted at women—either in general-interest magazines or more specialized publications like *Woman's Home Companion* or Bok's *Ladies' Home Journal*. St. Johns's profiles for the Hearst syndicate, *Liberty*, and the movie magazine *Photoplay*, for example, nearly always stressed her friendship with her subjects and derived their authenticity from intimate revelations that, St. Johns suggested, her subjects were unlikely to divulge to anyone else. In these stories St. Johns often assumed the role of therapist as well as confidante, allowing readers to see the complex forces that shaped the lives of celebrities, who could thus be understood as "human beings." To shed further light on her subjects, St. Johns also devoted an unprecedented amount of attention to their private lives, establishing a new benchmark for intimacy that writers for other publications were compelled to match if they hoped to compete with her. For St. Johns and the many journalists who followed her lead, the private and the public were intimately connected. To explain the public behavior of Clara Bow, she noted in a classic profile in *Liberty* in 1929, you had to know something about Bow's background, the peculiar circumstances of her rise to stardom, and the off-screen pressures that had come with her fame. Yet even this was inadequate: "I think you could live with Clara Bow for years and never begin to fathom her strange and complex nature. For just as you begin to believe that you understand her, she slips through your fingers like quicksilver and comes out in some entirely new shape."[30]

Thus by the 1930s the range of topics addressed by the authors of celebrity profiles had widened dramatically, and the intimate knowledge of the subject that the writer often enjoyed—and rarely failed to advertise—allowed for profiles that were far more sophisticated and psychologically acute than biographical sketches in the nineteenth century or the more concise celebrity journalism that appeared in newspapers. Offering writers ample space and more freedom in how they might present their subjects, mass-circulation magazines were ideal venues for the genre to mature. Paradoxically, the publications that led the way in the 1920s and 1930s were not those that catered to a downscale clientele, reversing a trend that had prevailed since the 1880s, when Pulitzer's *World* and magazines like *Munsey's* were the trail-blazers. They were new publications like *Vanity Fair*, the *American Mercury*, and the *New Yorker*, magazines that specialized in a modern version of the "higher journalism." Dismissing conventional celebrity profiles as hagiographic mush, editors like Harold Ross at the *New Yorker* pushed his writers—a stellar cast that included Winkler, Pringle, and Alva Johnston—to produce profiles that displayed literary grace and analytic acuity. The idea here, as the magazine's managing editor Katherine Angell informed a contributor, was "to give . . . something more intimate and personal than the average Sunday magazine newspaper write-up."[31] In the 1930s the new standard established by these journalists began to influence writers for many other publications, including mainstream organs like *Collier's*, the *Saturday Evening Post*, and Henry Luce's *Life*. The result was a discernible shift in the tone and emphasis of most celebrity journalism—away from the didactic, hagiographical pieces which had served as a kind of bridge between the old journalism and the new, and toward an even greater interest in celebrities as unique, complex individuals.[32]

The new uses that writers made of anecdotes were equally path-breaking. Anecdotes had been central to biographical sketches since the era of Plutarch, a means by which authors revealed the character of their subjects, and the highly popular short biographies of the nineteenth century had made ample use of them. The authors of celebrity profiles continued this trend, gleaning anecdotes by interviewing relatives, friends, and business associates. But they also developed important new practices, such as allowing celebrities to define the most significant moments in their lives. This strategy gave many profiles a distinctly autobiographical tone, and enabled their subjects to assume greater control over their life stories—a feature, as we shall see, that was very attractive to celebrities interested in using the press to advance their careers and a major reason for their cooperation with prominent profile writers like St. Johns, Frederick L. Collins of *Liberty*, and the *American Magazine*'s Mary B. Mullett—journalists who specialized in writing puff pieces. Following the example of Alan Dale, many reporters also began providing readers with accounts of incidents they had witnessed while in the company of celebrities, incidents that illuminated their uniqueness and complexity—the very factors that made them interesting in the eyes of the press. The sportswriter W. O. McGeehan, for instance, informed readers of *Vanity Fair* of a peculiar meeting he had with the prizefighter Gene Tunney. Bundled in a huge overcoat that he had donned to obscure the formal wear he was wearing to attend a party at the home of a well-to-do friend, Tunney complained bitterly to McGeehan, one of his few supporters in the press, about the criticism leveled at him by many journalists—that the new champion was a prig with a "swelled head." His coat, he explained, was a disguise to keep other reporters from seeing the tuxedo and saying that he had gone "high hat" again. For McGeehan, though, the tuxedo was emblematic of the real Tunney, reflecting his sincere and laudable interest in the "nice people" and cultivated things that had become accessible to him since becoming the heavyweight champion.[33]

By the teens, celebrity profiles often featured detailed descriptions of the setting and circumstances that reporters had encountered when they met their subjects, whether at home or at their place of business. This material was often placed at the beginning of profiles, allowing the reader to see the subject in her milieu, immersed in the varied activities that occupied her time. For instance, in a profile of Mary Pickford in the *American Magazine* in 1923, the journalist Mary B. Mullett began with a lengthy description of the bustle that she encountered when she arrived at Pickford's suite at the Ritz-Carlton in New York—a bustle, Mullett suggested, that was at odds with the Ritz-Carlton's reputation as a "very aristocratic and dignified hotel" yet perfectly fitting for the assertive, earnest, unaffected Pickford, whom writers like Mullet depicted not merely as an actress but as one of the movie industry's most important entrepreneurs. Observing celebrities in such settings, journalists asserted, was more revealing than any anecdote about their past. Having been witnessed by reporters, accounts of these incidents were also more credible than stories about events that allegedly occurred years before and may have been spurious or exaggerated. As the veteran reporter Edwin Lefevre explained in an article on profile-writing in the *Saturday Evening Post* in 1914, "The worst thing about all anecdotes . . . is their doubtful authenticity. There is what one might almost call a regular anecdote industry in certain newspaper offices."[34]

Perhaps the most innovative feature of celebrity profiles was their use of visual materials. Before 1900 a newspaper profile was often accompanied by a drawing, usually an artist's rendition of a photographic portrait of the subject. On the whole, however, visuals played a relatively small role in the celebrity journalism of the late nineteenth century. It was only after the turn of the century that reproductions of photographs became widespread in newspapers. By 1905 drawings and photographs illustrating news and feature stories were central to the Hearst press and its sensational cousins, and by the teens they had been integrated into the layout of the self-styled respectable press as well. Mass-circulation magazines made even greater use of them, particularly during and after the 1890s, when magazine publishers like Frank Munsey and S. S. McClure began to employ the new halftone engraving process to illustrate their publications. Mattie Sheridan's profile of Depew in 1892, for example, included photographs and realistic drawings of his family and several rooms of his house. And "Human Documents," a regular feature in early issues of *McClure's,* displayed photos of prominent celebrities at various ages, revealing changes in their appearance over time. After the turn of century photographs also illustrated magazine gossip columns. Taking full advantage of their ability to labor painstakingly over an issue and publish articles far longer than those that appeared in newspapers, magazine editors made extensive use of illustrations depicting celebrities engaged in various forms of action—riding horses, playing tennis or golf, dining at a fashionable restaurant. By the teens the use of photographs in newspapers and magazines was so widespread that captions began to replace longer textual reportage. Whole pages showed the faces of "interesting people," while captions noted their recent activities or claims to distinction. This trend culminated in the 1920s, when prominent metropolitan newspapers like the *New York Times,* the *Chicago Tribune,* and the *Atlanta Constitution* began publishing thick rotogravure sections in their Sunday editions.[35]

It was also during the first two decades of the twentieth century that editors began to publish candid photographs of celebrities—photos taken by staff photographers or by freelancers who worked for newspapers and photo syndicates like the Bain News Service, a key source for editors. As public demand for candid photographs increased, editors began to move away from the use of posed portraits, the standard practice from 1880 to 1910, gradually replacing them with candid shots and informal portraits that appeared more lifelike. The increased use of candid photographs created problems for public figures who had accommodated themselves to the use of illustrations by supplying editors with copies of recent portraits. To the consternation of many celebrities, this practice, which had been greatly appreciated by reporters and editors, was no longer enough, and in the years after 1910 photographers began to badger celebrities for more informal shots. This inspired an important new ritual among celebrities and the press: the photo opportunity. Posing for photographers became an inescapable feature of life for most celebrities, and their willingness to play along with photographers was a key factor that determined their treatment by the press. During the 1920s posed photographs filled metropolitan newspapers, especially new tabloids like the *New York Daily News*. But they were also a staple of rotogravure sections in conservative papers and, in the 1930s, of a new weekly magazine that gave photographs even more prominence, Henry Luce's *Life*. These were crucial innovations, giving celebrity journalism the compelling visual dimension that remains one of its hallmarks today.

To be sure, not all articles about celebrities appeared under the bylines of journalists. By the 1920s many profiles were autobiographical —seemingly written by celebrities. This trend was most prevalent in newspaper features and magazines directed at women, and was clearly influenced by the phenomenal success of Bernarr Macfadden's *True Story Magazine*. The majority of these autobiographical profiles were "ghosted" by the subject's publicist or by a journalist with whom the subject was close. For example, Mary Pickford's reminiscences of her early years on the stage and in the fledgling motion picture industry, published as "My Story" in *Ladies' Home Journal* in 1923, were in fact written by her longtime publicist and advisor, the screenwriter Frances Marion. And many of Charlie Chaplin's frequent articles in magazines like *Collier's* were penned by Jim Tully, a press agent who later capitalized on his inside knowledge of the movie industry to became a novelist and well-paid writer specializing in the Hollywood beat.[36] Entertainers were not the only celebrities to employ ghostwriters; so did businessmen, politicians, and other prominent civic officials—from Henry Ford to Mayor Jimmy Walker of New York. Ford began using ghostwriters as early as 1906, and in the teens he hired a prominent journalist away from the *Detroit News* to head his company's publicity bureau and write articles and editorials in his name. Also common were articles written by close friends and business associates of celebrities: people, like Tully, with status as insiders. These pieces promised to present the subject in a different, more intimate light—as never seen previously. For example, to plug a "candid picture" of Wendell Willkie written by his secretary, the editors of the *American Magazine* noted, "Who, of all people . . . has the best front-row seat to the big show that is Willkie? Who but his private secretary? So we looked her up and, after much persuasion, got her to give us the low-down on her boss."[37]

Whether written by journalists, celebrities, ghostwriters, or self-styled insiders, the emphasis of celebrity journalism—especially long, copiously illustrated celebrity profiles like "Home and Home Life of Chauncey M. Depew" or "My Boss, Wendell Willkie"—was on exposure. Articles encouraged readers to believe they were glimpsing the subject's "real self," a self that under ordinary circumstances was inaccessible to ordinary citizens, but was now exposed thanks to the work of the press and the willingness of the subject to allow reporters into the private spaces that he or she inhabited. Belief in the authenticity of the reports was fostered by new rhetorical strategies, the creative use of illustrations, and the privileged status of the men and women who were identified as its authors. Written for readers who were skeptical of appearances and public posturing, celebrity journalism was crafted to mollify and reassure, banishing the specter of self-promotion and hagiography by directing a spotlight at the personal, the intimate, and the real.

* * *

By the 1920s celebrity journalism, like other forms of human-interest reporting, appeared in virtually every American newspaper and mass-circulation magazine—even conservative publications that professed outrage at the spread of entertainment values into journalism. The major difference between publications lay in the quantity and placement of the material. Sensational publications directed at the working class and lower middle class published a lot of it and put it front and center, while more conservative ones, which defined themselves in opposition to "sensationalism," published less and were more likely to put it inside, on the back pages, or in feature sections and supplements. Conservative publications, by and large, were also more reluctant to publicize the nonprofessional activities of show business and sports figures. Though celebrities such as George M. Cohan, Mary Pickford, and Babe Ruth were regularly featured in newspapers like the *New York Times* and in magazines like *Time* and the *Saturday Evening Post*, the editors of these publications preferred to lavish attention on politicians, businessmen, and society figures—or "authentic heroes" like Charles Lindbergh. Despite this relative lack of coverage in conservative organs, by the early 1930s entertainers and athletes had become every bit as visible and well-known as figures from more serious fields, and their comparative lack of visibility in some publications was offset by massive visibility in others, especially urban tabloids, the Hearst press, and unabashedly popular magazines like Bernarr Macfadden's *Liberty*.[38]

But the inclusiveness of the press in its choice of subjects went only so far. Journalistic conventions inherited from the nineteenth century created a peculiar gender bias in coverage of celebrities, a pattern of exclusion that was even more pronounced in the press's treatment of racial minorities. As we have seen, belief that the proper place of women was within the private sphere limited their opportunities to achieve public visibility. Yet during the second half of the nineteenth century women like Harriet Beecher Stowe, the actress Charlotte Cushman, and the reformer Frances Willard managed to attract the attention of the press, and as newspapers and magazines expanded their coverage and sought to make their products more interesting to women, particularly the burgeoning number of "working girls," the number and kinds of women who became the subjects of reportage gradually increased. Most were mentioned in news stories, but a few were given more publicity, becoming the subjects of celebrity journalism. A long feature in an issue of the *New York World* in 1890, for example, offered readers a glimpse of "Lillian Russell at Work." And by the 1890s interviews with and profiles of female reformers, activists, and entertainers were common in many newspapers, and the publicity accorded to the wives of presidents—especially the youthful, fashionable Frances Cleveland—and rich women like Consuelo Vanderbilt far exceeded the short notices that had constituted coverage of high society before the Civil War. Vanderbilt's marriage to the Duke of Marlborough in 1895 inspired a frenzy among reporters weeks before the event and culminated in a wave of publicity that was truly remarkable for the day, a wave that included detailed accounts of the new bride's activities and lavish, illustrated profiles like the *World*'s "Miss Vanderbilt—Our New Duchess."[39]

Around the turn of the century female celebrities achieved a new degree of visibility. Though still outnumbered by male celebrities, a small number of women had become nearly as visible as the most prominent men, and in the early 1900s celebrity profiles became vehicles for promoting a new understanding of womanhood. Actresses like Maude Adams and Ethel Barrymore led the way, serving as the subjects of countless gossip items, short notices, and lengthy profiles in magazines and Sunday supplements. Inspired by the new discourse of "personality" and a belief that much of the public was interested in the "new woman," journalists writing about such figures began to endow them with traits—independence, creativity, business sense—not previously attributed to women, but more likely to make female celebrities interesting to women readers. Profiles of Alice Roosevelt, TR's daughter, exhibited many of the same characteristics, and established a new precedent for reporting about society women. Writing about Roosevelt in *Munsey's* in 1905, the journalist Emma B. Kaufman asserted that the president's daughter was no anomaly but the quintessential "twentieth-century American girl." "In Alice Roosevelt," Kaufman wrote, "the power of the American girl, the character and the force that are her common inheritance, seem to have reached their height. She has not only the capacity to think, but the originality to act as she thinks."[40]

Increasingly portrayed as distinct, forceful individuals, female celebrities in Roosevelt's wake bore little relation to those who had been extolled in the pages of nineteenth-century newspapers. This was especially true of women involved in controversial political or social movements. For instance, the suffragist Alice Paul was noted for her "sound academic intelligence" and her advocacy of women's suffrage through complex legislative strategies that she developed by "accumulating facts." Yet her most compelling trait, a writer for *Everybody's* suggested in 1915, was the way that she galvanized her followers and inspired them to acts of protest—while remaining the strategist behind the scenes. Even more remarkable was the birth control advocate Margaret Sanger, whose defiance of the notorious Comstock Law made her a widely publicized figure during the late teens. Though Sanger's rabble-rousing was often denounced in newspaper editorials and her association with sexual emancipation during this period made her too controversial for most publications to profile, she nonetheless succeeded in becoming the subject of many news stories, and from these she emerged as a shrewd, courageous, and dedicated champion of women's reproductive rights, a foundation that would allow her to gain even more favorable coverage during the 1920s and 1930s.[41]

At the same time, one cannot help being impressed by the degree to which celebrity journalism about women continued to be shaped by conventional attitudes. The fact is that the most visible female public figures in the years between 1890 and 1940 were actresses and entertainers, and the publicity accorded them dwarfed that received by more serious figures like Jane Addams, Alice Paul, and Margaret Sanger. In addition, profiles of female celebrities were more likely to focus on their romantic lives, commitment to motherhood, and tastes in fashion and home decor. Female celebrities like Frances Perkins, the nation's first woman cabinet member, who were largely unwilling to discuss these issues with reporters, put themselves in a difficult position. By limiting the press's access to their private lives and traditionally "feminine" subjects, they often discouraged journalists from writing about them altogether. Far more effective was the course adopted by Eleanor Roosevelt, who shrewdly used material about her private life as an entree to the more serious subjects she was determined to publicize. While productive as a means of generating favorable press, this strategy was not without its perils. Indeed, one could easily conclude that female celebrities like Roosevelt who adopted the course of least resistance unwittingly contributed to the perpetuation of traditional views of women. With their aid, the new model of womanhood promoted by the authors of celebrity journalism retained key elements of the old model, including a belief that in the end, relationships and family life were more important to women—even highly successful and powerful women—than to men.[42]

This was not always their intention. In the 1920s and 1930s writers such as Adela Rogers St. Johns and Margaret Case Harriman often penned profiles that expressed a feminist perspective, even when covering actresses and entertainers. For example, in 1934 St. Johns praised the actress Katharine Hepburn for her "modern" marriage and commitment to "individualism" and her work. But as a writer for the Hearst press and popular magazines like *Liberty,* St. Johns was also aware that for every reader who was thrilled by Hepburn's iconoclasm, there were others who might regard it as unseemly, and so she immediately tempered her observation by insisting that Hepburn's "soul"—presumably, the deepest core of her self—was "as maternal as her mother's," thereby linking the old to the new. For writers with feminist commitments, mass-circulation journalism was an imperfect forum for promoting a new ideal of womanhood; it was far better suited to the promotion of incremental changes that appealed to liberal female readers but did not alienate the many readers who remained quite conservative when it came to women's roles in society. From this perspective, journalists' simultaneous embrace of novelty and tradition made perfect sense, allowing them to address an important issue without undermining their potential for enjoying mass appeal.[43]

The press's treatment of racial minorities was more conventional. African Americans had been the subjects of news stories since the antebellum era, when small populations of free blacks developed in many Northern cities, and African Americans became involved in the many activities that the press defined as news. Their visibility increased when some abolitionists—particularly prominent blacks like Frederick Douglass and Sojourner Truth—sought to publicize the injustices faced by free blacks in the North, a campaign that continued into the period of Reconstruction. From the end of the Civil War to his death in 1895, Douglass remained a tireless and highly effective spokesman for black rights in the North as well as the South, using his reputation to gain the attention of the press. But press coverage of Douglass—whose controversial views included support for interracial marriage, and who was himself married to a white woman—paled next to coverage of the prominent white men of the era.[44] And this was not only a result of Douglass's radical views and unorthodox lifestyle. When Booker T. Washington assumed the mantle of black leadership in the 1890s he was similarly marginalized, despite his professed admiration for upper-class whites, support for racial segregation, and strenuous efforts to present himself as a paragon of bourgeois respectability. Like Douglass, Washington was able to secure interviews and have his public appearances noted by the press. But the notices were short and relatively infrequent. More important, Washington was not made the subject of fawning celebrity profiles—at a time when such profiles were becoming a staple of mass-circulation journalism and even third-rate political hacks and inexperienced ingenues fresh from the chorus line could get this kind of publicity.[45]

Washington's marginalization from the world of celebrity is a curious phenomenon. Though he did everything that should have made him a worthy subject for celebrity treatment, editors and reporters for newspapers and magazines aimed at white readers refused to "humanize" him, perhaps recognizing the implications of such an angle during an era when white supremacy rested on the fundamental dehumanization of nonwhites. The whole point of celebrity journalism was to make its subjects familiar—on the assumption that the commonalities linking the great to the lowly were a universal source of "human interest" that would appeal to readers. The bonds that celebrity profiles were supposed to evoke, in other words, were bonds of sympathy and identification. For journalists concerned about class and ethnic divisions among whites, this was a useful strategy that could build circulation and potentially restore cohesiveness to the social order. Yet as a number of historians have recently noted, this project of transcending class and ethnic divisions during the Progressive era was premised on constructing a common "whiteness" that placed nonwhites outside the "imagined community" of America.[46] Here lay the obstacle in front of Booker T. Washington's celebrity—a racially exclusive understanding of "human nature" that made it virtually impossible for most whites to represent or even think of nonwhites as human beings. Even when influential white friends like Walter Hines Page, editor of the *Atlantic* and later of the *World's Work,* wrote about Washington, the results were awkward. A long article on Washington's "characteristics" that Page wrote for *Everybody's,* for example, completely ignored his personality and home life and instead focused on his educational philosophy.[47]

The field of entertainment, where blacks enjoyed more opportunities to work with whites and achieve distinction, offered African Americans somewhat better prospects for becoming celebrities. Black entertainers like the vaudevillian Bert Williams were very popular with white audiences and earned good money. But the financial rewards of show business were accompanied by persistent discrimination that dogged even the biggest stars. In Williams's case, the inability to stay at the best hotels or eat at many of the restaurants where his co-stars dined was only the beginning. Far worse was having his success as an entertainer to whites depend on his willingness to perform minstrel-derived songs and skits lampooning African Americans—the only roles in which whites audiences accepted blacks. Nor did his appeal translate into the publicity enjoyed by white stars like George M. Cohan. Williams's performances were often reviewed in the press, and he was one of the most highly praised entertainers of the era. Yet popular appeal and critical plaudits did not make him the subject of much celebrity journalism; most of what was written, as with Washington, steered clear of his personal life. Ironically, one of the few profiles of Williams in a national magazine was written by Washington—and it asserted, falsely, that Williams had never experienced racial discrimination.[48]

The situation for black athletes was equally bleak. On the one hand, as an arena where hard work and practice as well as innate talent were paramount, the world of sports was as close to a meritocracy as existed in late-nineteenth-century America. In such a realm, the success of black athletes was a direct affront to the ideology of white supremacy, particularly when blacks competed against whites. It was this that led officials in nearly all sports to draw the "color line" and prohibit blacks from competing against and potentially beating their "superiors." By the turn of the century only the disreputable sport of prizefighting had not completely segregated the races. This anomaly allowed Jack Johnson to become the first black man to win the heavyweight championship, a position that ordinarily allowed the titleholder abundant publicity and a chance, if he was "colorful," to become one of the nation's most visible celebrities. Unless, of course, he was a black man—especially one, like Johnson, who steadfastly refused to follow the path established by Booker T. Washington.[49]

Unlike Washington, Johnson openly flouted the racial etiquette and conventions of middle-class propriety. Using his winnings from the ring, he bought an expensive automobile and was regularly arrested for speeding, and he spent most of his time between fights fraternizing with urban "sports" and white prostitutes at the notorious "black-and-tan" nightclubs of Chicago and New York. In 1910, after defending his title against the ex-champion Jim Jeffries, he bought his own nightclub, which became the home base for his sybaritic pursuits, and he never missed an opportunity to be photographed with his white wife.[50] In fact, Johnson behaved no differently from past heavyweight champions like John L. Sullivan, who was famous for his dissolute lifestyle— behavior that inspired outrage among sportswriters but also made him "colorful" and a regular source of copy. Johnson expected to receive roughly the same degree of publicity. When he was ignored, he simply redoubled his efforts to attract attention. This tactic eventually succeeded in outraging journalists, yet it also ensured that Johnson had no allies in the press when federal prosecutors and police officials in Chicago began their persecution of him, which resulted in his conviction for violating the Mann Act. Admittedly, sportswriters praised Johnson's abilities as a fighter, and were hopeful when he was training for a bout and shunned his usual pastimes. But because he was black, they could not publicize his activities outside the ring as they had Sullivan's, for to do so would have reminded white readers of his transgressions. Only when Johnson was arrested and journalists were presented with an opportunity to moralize did they discuss his deeds in any detail—and then only to reaffirm the importance of keeping the races apart and cleaning up the urban demimonde of which Johnson was a product. In short, though Johnson was undoubtedly interesting, he was denied the kind of coverage accorded to white heavyweight champions. And there was but one reason for this—his race.[51]

Jack Johnson's marginalization from the world of celebrity paralleled Booker T. Washington's, revealing the influence of white supremacist assumptions on mass-circulation journalism during the late nineteenth and early twentieth centuries. It is important to stress, however, that the exclusion of African Americans and other nonwhites from celebrity status was not the result of a conspiracy. White editors may have acted from the prejudices noted above, but this was probably unconscious and entangled with a more pragmatic concern—the belief that white readers were not interested in black public figures and were likely to become angry if blacks were the subjects of celebrity profiles. In the end, prominent blacks were not the subjects of celebrity journalism because white editors were not interested in appealing to African American readers: since the 1870s, these readers were being served by black newspapers that had been established in virtually every city with a significant African American population. It was in the pages of the black press that Douglass, Washington, Williams, and even the notorious Johnson achieved celebrity status—despite their treatment by the white press. Indeed, in publications aimed at their own people they assumed the stature not just of celebrities but of "culture heroes," in whom the aspirations of the entire black community were invested.[52]

It was not until the late 1930s, when mass-circulation newspapers in major cities began to show an interest in the burgeoning black audience and liberal racial currents started to spread throughout the culture and undermine the white supremacist assumptions that had implicitly shaped press coverage of nonwhites, that the treatment of blacks and other racial minorities in the white press gradually improved. Black leaders such as Walter A. White, the eloquent and urbane head of the NAACP, began to receive more frequent and courteous notice, as did black entertainers and artists like Bill "Bojangles" Robinson, Louis Armstrong, and especially the gifted opera singer Marian Anderson.[53] But it was the celebrity of Joe Louis that finally broke the mold. To win the respect of white reporters, Louis made a point of contrasting himself with the disreputable Johnson, adopting a modest, deferential demeanor outside the ring, a tactic that made it much easier for sports-writers to promote him to white readers. By the early 1940s Louis was the most highly publicized athlete in the United States and the subject of the kinds of profiles and sketches that had eluded his bitter and frustrated predecessor. However, Louis's celebrity owed more to the times than to the man. Had he acted exactly the same in 1910 he might not have been vilified like Johnson, yet neither would he have become the celebrity that he was in the early 1940s, when it was finally possible to "humanize" an African American in publications aimed at whites. And as several historians have noted, Louis's humanization remained provisional and halfhearted, more a testament to his willingness to conform than a bellwether of racial tolerance. Ideologically, the United States in the 1940s was a more inclusive "imagined community," having found a place for nonwhites in response to the overt racialism of the Nazis. And while this inclusiveness was limited by residual white supremacist assumptions, it opened a door that had been firmly shut, and created the possibility for later, unprecedented developments—like the multiracial appeal of the iconoclastic Muhammad Ali.[54]

By the 1940s the kinds of journalism that sustained the modern culture of celebrity had fully matured. Journalistic trends that first emerged in the 1880s and 1890s, when an increasing number of newspapers and magazines reoriented themselves around entertainment values, had produced a broad variety of reporting, and this new celebrity journalism could be found in a majority of publications. Many of these pieces were inspired by an interest in exposure—enabling readers to see the subject as he or she really was, divorced from the puffery and moralism that were now associated with the discourse of fame. To fulfill this objective, journalists developed new rhetorical strategies that appeared to bring readers into more intimate contact with celebrities and gave the reporters who enjoyed regular access to famous people the highly esteemed status of insiders. As these changes were occurring, journalists also increased the range of public figures who were lifted to the ranks of celebrity, creating a more varied and inclusive roster that would be reflected in Blackwell's and Amory's *Celebrity Register.* By the 1940s this roster included not just prominent men of affairs—the era's equivalents of Chauncey Depew—but actors, entertainers, athletes, even journalists like Walter Winchell and the syndicated columnist Dorothy Thompson. It included women as well as men, blacks as well as whites—though, as we have seen, patterns of bias continued to shape journalism even as the press embraced more liberal values.

The new contours of celebrity journalism are readily visible when we examine the press's treatment of Louis, one of the most widely publicized figures of the early 1940s. Louis first became a celebrity in the mid-1930s, when leading sportswriters began writing about his exploits in the ring. By the late 1930s he had become the subject of sympathetic human-interest profiles in major newspapers and slick mass-circulation magazines like the *Saturday Evening Post,* and in the early 1940s, as he reached new levels of achievement as a fighter, a rising tide of favorable publicity lifted him to heights that no African American had ever reached. But with celebrity status came more penetrating and less flattering reportage, too. The imperative to illuminate the "real" Louis inspired some journalists to view him through the detached, often cynical lens that many writers by the 1930s regularly adopted in their efforts to produce complex and analytically acute portraits of celebrities. Curiously, perhaps the most widely read example of this more ambivalent reporting, a profile of Louis that appeared in 1940 in *Life,* was written by a black journalist, Earl Brown, a Harvard graduate and at the time the managing editor of the *Amsterdam News,* one of the nation's most prominent African American newspapers. Though sympathetic to Louis, Brown could not conceal his dismay that the most widely publicized black American was an uneducated, profligate lowbrow. "Serious thoughts about his position in the world do not bother the champion," Brown noted in the arch tone characteristic of writers influenced by the *New Yorker.*[55]

But Brown's cynicism went further. He suggested that Louis's wholesome image—which had enabled him to become popular with whites—had been carefully and laboriously crafted by the fighter's managers, two shady characters whom the press liked to portray as idealistic, college-educated advocates of racial uplift. With the aid of the promoter Mike Jacobs and sportswriters eager to improve the reputation of prizefighting, Louis's managers had succeeded in their quest to make their "investment" an authentic celebrity as well as a heavyweight champion, an achievement that allowed Louis myriad commercial opportunities and enabled his managers to become very rich—their real objective,

Brown implied. Here was the downside of the new rhetoric of exposure that had become a defining feature of celebrity journalism. The same devices that made it possible for readers to glimpse a celebrity's real self could also cast a more cynical light on him, calling into question the degree to which his or her mass-mediated image was real.

3

EXPOSURE OR PUBLICITY?
THE PARADOX OF
CELEBRITY JOURNALISM

The cynicism that Earl Brown expressed about Joe Louis's public image was not unusual. By the 1940s many journalists betrayed a similar attitude in profiles of celebrities, and while most of this reporting appeared in publications associated with the "higher journalism," its influence extended well into the mainstream. Often cynicism was built into a profile's frame, drawing the reader's attention to misinformation or falsehoods about the subject that made his real self unknown and the profile in question a valuable contribution to public knowledge about him. On some occasions, journalists attributed the spread of misinformation to a celebrity's unwillingness to open up to the press; on other occasions, writers noted the complicity of journalists in its dissemination. Also common were allusions to press agents and publicists, who were routinely cited as the Machiavellian masterminds responsible for creating the public images of celebrities. In Brown's view, for example, Louis's image as a symbol of Negro respectability was attributable to the combined efforts of journalists, his managers, Mike Jacobs, and Jacobs's canny press agent, Steve Hannagan—all whom stood to gain from its acceptance by the public.

These revelations made celebrity journalism paradoxical, a form that in seeking to establish authenticity drew attention to its regular trafficking in falsehoods. As early as the 1890s readers were being apprised of the possibility that much of what was being peddled as the "real story" might not be true at all, and by the 1940s this skepticism was firmly ingrained in the rhetorical strategies of the genre, no doubt influencing many readers and requiring most writers to distinguish their work from the norm. Because of the prominence of these revelations, readers of American newspapers and magazines could not help being aware that celebrity journalism was not simply a product of journalistic initiative—the writer's commitment to revealing the subject's "real self" for the benefit of a curious and appreciative public. It was also related, in one way or another, to the self-promotional stratagems of celebrities and their hired representatives, a situation that made celebrity journalism all the more complex and difficult to evaluate.

For this reason, to really understand celebrity, looking at reporting alone is not enough. We must also investigate the journalistic practices that influenced its production. By this I mean the routines and conventions that reporters followed in producing articles about celebrities, practices that were central to the business of newsgathering. From the start these practices were shaped—a more jaundiced person would say compromised—by contact with the subjects. In the early twentieth century, the nature of this contact changed, as the rise of human-interest journalism increased the press's interest in public figures as celebrities, and many of these figures began to rely on publicists to manage their relations with reporters, especially the relatively small group of insiders who produced the bulk of celebrity journalism. As we shall see, this sort of interaction made the production of celebrity journalism complicated, sometimes even messy. And the multiple influences and agendas that went into its making gave the genre an important tension between exposure and publicity—a tension that undermined the authority of every piece of reporting, but was also integral to its allure as a form of journalism and popular culture.

* * *

As we have seen, between the 1890s and the 1940s newspapers and magazines in the United States greatly expanded their coverage of celebrities, adding new forms of human-interest stories and publicizing the activities of figures from a wide range of fields. These trends gave celebrity journalism a high profile in specific publications and the industry at large. By the 1920s it had become virtually ubiquitous, one of the most commonly acknowledged features of a new journalism that had emerged since the 1890s—a journalism fixated on entertainment values, on presenting stories that "satisfy or stimulate primitive appetites," as the press critic and former journalist Silas Bent observed in 1927.[1]

But the ubiquity of celebrity journalism belied an important fact.

Though it might have seemed as if newspapers and magazines had re-assigned much of their staff to the coverage of celebrities, most celebrity journalism was produced by a comparatively small group of journalists, an elite of insiders who had special access to celebrities and connections within the industry that allowed their work to reach a broad audience. Indeed, like many other forms of popular culture, the production of celebrity journalism had become increasingly centralized, a process orchestrated from new centers of power and cultural authority that had arisen since the mid-nineteenth century. This process encouraged standardization, as many publications drew from the same sources of material. Even more important, the process contributed to the emergence of national celebrities and a new realm that these figures came to inhabit—a realm, from the perspective of readers, at once remote and familiar.

For much of the nineteenth century, celebrity journalism was produced in a haphazard fashion. Reporters working for newspapers did the bulk of the work, hunting down celebrities, interviewing them, and writing about their activities, and the resulting articles reached a local audience. Of course, for many big-city papers a local audience in the mid-nineteenth century was substantial, exceeding 100,000 for widely circulated publications like the *New York Herald.* And by the 1870s and 1880s, as urban centers like New York, Chicago, Philadelphia, and Atlanta gained greater influence over the rural hinterlands, and provincial newspapers began republishing stories that had appeared in leading metropolitan dailies, the audience for some of these stories became more widespread, extending far beyond the cities where they had originated. In the mid-nineteenth century the spread of this material was also encouraged by the publication of weekly editions of papers like the *Herald* and its chief rival, Horace Greeley's *New York Tribune,* which were expressly designed to be distributed in small towns and the countryside. A growing reliance on wire services, first established during the 1840s but not widely employed until after the Civil War, made it even easier for provincial newspapers to get information about celebrities who resided in big cities. They also created new opportunities for reporters. Though constrained by editorial dictates conceived to make copy concise and suitable for many kinds of papers, wire-service correspondents who covered Washington, state capitals, and important financial developments in New York developed important connections and became journalistic insiders, joining a small cadre that included leading reporters for prominent metropolitan newspapers. In the 1890s members of this select group, whose most illustrious members were Julian Ralph of the *New York Sun* and Richard Harding Davis of the *New York Herald*, found it possible to parlay their connections into work as freelance writers. In this capacity they wrote profiles and sketches of leading businessmen, politicians, and literary figures for older, genteel magazines like *Scribner's* as well as new-style ones like *McClure's*.[2]

One source to which well-connected reporters contributed articles was feature syndicates. First established in the 1880s by entrepreneurs like Irving Bachellor and S. S. McClure, these were clearinghouses that provided metropolitan newspapers with a wide array of feature stories, especially stories suitable for the new Sunday supplements that publishers had come to view as sure-fire circulation builders. Offering serial fiction, advice columns, comics, and breezy articles on scientific developments and exotic locales, feature syndicates played a crucial role in the maturation of the mass-circulation press, enabling newspapers in small cities to publish the same kinds of material as big-city papers— in many cases, the very same features. Limited by financial considerations and a lack of connections, editors of provincial newspapers ardently embraced these new institutions, which allowed them at relatively low cost to offer a more exciting, sophisticated product. And as an increasing number of papers displayed an interest in syndicated material, the number of feature syndicates steadily grew, as did the kinds of products they offered to newspapers. "The syndicates sell everything from a two-line filler at the bottom of a column to a twenty-two page magazine section or rotogravure supplements ready printed," Silas Bent noted in his review of the American press. Chief among these products were articles about celebrities.

For provincial newspapers, however, the consequences of this development were mixed. Relying on these institutions gave editors access to material that would otherwise be unavailable and made their papers more appealing to most readers. "The small-town newspaper, in particular, has been greatly enriched in its reading content by publication of syndicated material," H. F. Harrington, a veteran feature writer, opined in 1925. But syndication also made provincial editors dependent on the initiative and connections of reporters and editors over whom they had no control—and who quickly came to dominate access to information about prominent public figures.[3]

This process of centralization was also encouraged by the rise of newspaper chains. The key figures here were E. W. Scripps and William Randolph Hearst. Scripps's empire began in the Midwest in the late 1870s with papers in Detroit and Cleveland, and by 1911 had expanded to include eighteen papers in medium-sized cities in the Midwest and Upper South. Hearst's originated in 1895, when the pathbreaking publisher of the *San Francisco Examiner* moved to New York and bought the moribund *New York Journal*. By 1903 Hearst had added papers in Boston, Chicago, Los Angeles, and the morning *American* in New York, which became the flagship of his growing chain. To service their chains and fulfill their ambitions as crusaders, Scripps and Hearst established new wire services that became important rivals of the venerable Associated Press. Scripps's United Press, founded in 1907, was inspired in part by the belief that the publishers who dominated the AP were excessively conservative both politically and journalistically. Hearst's International News Service, which began operation in 1909, became an important conduit for news stories produced by his high-priced stable of feature writers, a group that by the mid-1920s included the novelist Rex Beach, the sportswriter and columnist Damon Runyon, and America's premier sob-sister, Adela Rogers St. Johns. Both Scripps and Hearst offered readers abundant feature stories that appeared in every paper they owned, enlarging the audience for specific items, including the celebrity profiles that were important features for both chains.[4]

New-style mass-circulation magazines served much the same function. Unlike older magazines like *Scribner's, Harper's,* and the *Century,* the new publications established by McClure, Frank Munsey, John Brisben Walker, and others were designed to be topical and entertaining. Among their regular features were profiles and sketches of leading national figures in business, politics, and high culture, written by journalists with acknowledged reputations as insiders. Drawing on revenues derived from lucrative agreements with national advertisers, the editors of these magazines paid their contributors handsomely, making their publications attractive to well-connected newspaper correspondents looking to supplement their salaries by doing freelance work. Not surprisingly, when editors such as McClure and George Horace Lorimer of the *Saturday Evening Post* hired staff writers to pen the bulk of their features, they drew heavily from the ranks of these veteran reporters, who had demonstrated hustle, good connections, and an ability to write features. Even more than newspapers, these magazines were instrumental in transforming men and women with local or regional reputations into nationally known figures. In their efforts to make their reportage interesting to readers across the country, the authors of celebrity profiles in magazines like *Munsey's* and *McClure's* often tried to link their subjects to national events and developments, establishing a cast of characters who were associated with these trends. Writing in *McClure's* in 1901, for example, Ray Stannard Baker portrayed the financier J. P. Morgan as "the most advanced expression of a new world movement," a commitment to consolidation and the fostering of a "community of interest" among leading businessmen.[5]

Together, wire services, feature syndicates, newspaper chains, and mass-circulation magazines formed the nucleus of a national mass culture that emerged in the 1890s and gradually supplanted the diverse urban "commercial cultures" that had existed in American cities since the mid-nineteenth century. Through these institutions, public figures like Morgan were lifted to national celebrity, becoming as well known throughout the country as they were in the cities in which they worked and resided. By the early twentieth century these celebrities overshadowed the small-town businessmen, civic leaders, and society figures who had dominated the columns of provincial newspapers since the era of the penny press. More important, the new visibility of national celebrities fueled public interest in the national realm which had spawned them, reinforcing the tendency of journalists to focus on them at the expense of local notables. Indeed, the emergence of national celebrities reflected broader nationalizing trends in American society as a whole: the consolidation and increasingly national scope of business enterprises, including those in the burgeoning culture industries; the heightened importance of national politics and the federal government; and improvements in communication and transportation that were undermining regional distinctions and bridging the gap between the city and the countryside.[6]

National celebrities, in short, arose in tandem with a nationalization of the public sphere—and the broader overlapping that occurred around the turn of the century as national spheres coalesced into an extensive transatlantic sphere. The emergence of this transatlantic sphere allowed figures as diverse as Sarah Bernhardt, Kaiser Wilhelm II, Emile Zola, Theodore Roosevelt, Andrew Carnegie, George Bernard Shaw, Sigmund Freud, and Charlie Chaplin to become well known throughout the industrialized West. Thanks to the miracle of modern mass media, readers of newspapers and magazines in the United States were able to acquire information—often seemingly intimate information—about people who lived far away, men and women of wealth, power, and influence whom they would never actually see in the flesh. In a sense, human-interest journalism about these figures was meant to obliterate the physical and social distance that separated readers from the movers and shakers of the world. But this was not all. As the spread of the market economy, industrialization, and new modes of transportation and communication created vast new social and economic networks extending throughout Europe, the United States, and beyond, the mass-circulation press played a vital role in enabling ordinary people to apprehend this new world, mitigating its bewildering complexity and impersonality by offering stories that stressed the continued importance of individual agency. Like other forms of human-interest reporting, celebrity journalism sought to make the remote and impersonal seem familiar and human, a project that was central to the global expansion of Western civilization and efforts to make citizens of the West recognize their place in a larger, unfolding drama—the rise of modernity and secular "progress."

* * *

The growth of the new media institutions that made possible a national mass culture was an important influence on the production of celebrity journalism. By the 1890s most of the writers responsible for lifting public figures to the status of national celebrities were part of a relatively small elite of reporters and feature writers who enjoyed access to them by virtue of their positions with prominent newspapers, magazines, wire services, and feature syndicates. Envied and admired by many of their colleagues, these journalists were among the most successful members of their profession, earning lucrative salaries and commissions and enjoying considerable liberties as writers and autonomy in their choice of assignments. Some of them—Alva Johnston, for instance—were acknowledged stars of the profession, winners of its most coveted prizes and honors. Others, like William Allen White, Grantland Rice, and Adela Rogers St. Johns, were very popular with readers, a status they had gained from their skill as writers and the intimacy they enjoyed with the famous. A handful of them were celebrities themselves, the subjects of gossip and profiles written by their peers.

There was no single career path that allowed journalists to become members of this exclusive group. Many were from solid middle-class and upper-middle-class backgrounds, often the sons and daughters of lawyers, businessmen, or small-town editors who had kindled their interest in journalism. A majority were college educated as well; at the very least, they had taken a few courses before turning to journalism as a career. With far greater opportunities to apprentice themselves to editors and publishers, men were more likely to have entered the profession without benefit of college, usually in their teens, or come to it from another field. Virtually all of them, however, served as newspaper reporters before graduating to the more lucrative field of feature writing. Newspaper work was widely regarded as essential preparation for any kind of advanced journalism, endowing a young man or woman with a keen analytic vision. "A few years of reporting in a big city makes him mentally alert . . . and teaches him the ways of the world as nothing else does," the veteran editor Chester S. Lord argued in 1922 in a short primer on the profession. "He is taught to search for facts, to seek for causes and to foresee results. He gets broadness of vision, expanse of comprehension, and rugged contact with the world." As Lord's gendered language suggests, such an apprenticeship was more common among male reporters. Though some women also came to feature writing and celebrity journalism through this route, most, as Ishbel Ross revealed in her important history of women in journalism, *Ladies of the Press* (1936), began their careers as society reporters or other specialists on the "women's page," a trajectory that influenced the kinds of features they later wrote and the publications they eventually worked for.[7]

Once they made the leap to feature writing, most of these journalists wrote for a variety of publications, capitalizing on their access to get work as freelancers. But many also retained an institutional home that provided them with a regular salary and a platform for their work, which often included straight news stories as well as celebrity journalism. For example, after a distinguished career as a top reporter for Joseph Pulitzer's *New York World*, Samuel G. Blythe became a staff correspondent for the *Saturday Evening Post*, a position that made him one of the most widely read journalists in the country yet also allowed him to contribute occasional pieces to other periodicals. Because staff positions at major magazines were relatively lucrative, many magazine reporters were content to write for their employer alone. Mary B. Mullett, for instance, was the resident profile writer for the *American Magazine* from the late teens to the mid-twenties; John B. Kennedy was her counterpart at *Collier's*. By the early 1930s these writers had moved on and new figures were responsible for producing this popular form.

At the *American Magazine,* celebrity profiles were the domain of two experienced writers: Jerome Beatty, who usually wrote about show-business celebrities, and Beverly Smith, a former reporter for the *New York Herald-Tribune* who was the journalist most often assigned to profile politicians and other more "serious" figures. A similar division of labor prevailed at *Collier's.* Henry F. Pringle, a freelancer who taught journalism at Columbia and whose serious works included a biography of Theodore Roosevelt that won a Pulitzer Prize, was the writer who profiled most entertainers, while Walter Davenport covered celebrities from politics and business.

As these assignments suggest, most writers who produced celebrity journalism were also specialists. Blythe's forte was profiles of politicians, a field he shared in the teens and twenties with William Allen White, whose work often appeared in *Collier's.* Edwin Lefevre, Ida M. Tarbell, and Issac F. Marcosson, meanwhile, specialized in writing about businessmen for magazines like *McClure's,* the *American Magazine,* and the *Saturday Evening Post.* Profiles of sports celebrities, which became increasingly common in the teens and especially the twenties, were the specialty of Hugh Fullerton, Grantland Rice, and Paul Gallico, sportswriters who made their reputations through their work as syndicated newspaper columnists. Early in the century entertainers were profiled by dramatic critics like Gustav Kobbé or "dramatic paragraphers" such as Alan Dale of the Hearst syndicate, who pioneered the intimate style of writing that would later be refined by his successor, Adela Rogers St. Johns. Beginning in the late teens, St. Johns's work appeared in Hearst newspapers, mass-circulation magazines like *Liberty,* and *Photoplay,* one of the most popular movie-fan magazines of the 1920s and 1930s.

By the late 1930s, however, the most widely published authors of celebrity profiles—journalists such as Pringle, Alva Johnston, Margaret Case Harriman, and Geoffrey Hellman—were adept at writing about figures from many different fields—and from a variety of perspectives, depending on the kind of publication in which their work was to appear. Pringle's profiles, for example, were published not only in *Collier's* and *Ladies' Home Journal* but also in the *American Mercury* and in the *New Yorker,* for which he wrote articles notable for their sophistication: their standing in the profession was acknowledged when they were republished in book form. Harriman also was a regular contributor of profiles to the *New Yorker* and like Pringle was able to secure republication of her best work. Yet she too wrote for several mainstream publications like *Ladies' Home Journal* and the *Saturday Evening Post*. Writers like Pringle, Harriman, Johnston, and Hellman were masters of their craft, expertly deploying techniques and rhetorical strategies developed over the years to maximum effect. Moreover, as urbane, well-educated members of the larger New York literary establishment, which by the 1920s included journalists, playwrights, novelists, and critics, they brought a new, more sophisticated outlook to the genre, particularly when writing for magazines associated with the "higher journalism."[8]

The varied backgrounds and careers of these journalists can perhaps best be appreciated by looking at several representative figures. Ray Stannard Baker was one of the pioneers of the field. Born in 1870 in Lansing, Michigan, to a comfortable middle-class family, Baker attended Michigan Agricultural College, where he was editor of the school newspaper and an active fraternity man, and graduated with a B.S. After a brief, disillusioning stint in law school, he moved to Chicago in 1892 and secured a job as a reporter on the *News-Record*. In 1898, having reported extensively on labor unrest and social reform, an experience that altered his view of politics, Baker was hired as a staff writer at *McClure's*. Though now remembered for contributing articles that were central to the rise of muckraking, Baker specialized in writing celebrity profiles and "personalized" features focusing on prominent businessmen, politicians, and inventors. In 1906, in the wake of a disagreement with S. S. McClure, Baker and several of his associates resigned and took over the ailing *American Magazine*. It was for this magazine that Baker wrote some of his most important pieces, including a collection of essays on race relations and the Social Gospel that redefined the genre of personalized news. Though Baker continued writing fiction and philosophical ruminations well into the 1930s, his career as journalist largely ended in 1915, when his support for progressive reform led him join President Wilson's staff, a position that enabled him to become a close confidante of Wilson, the editor of his papers, and the author of his authorized biography.[9]

If Baker's specialty was personalized news, Issac F. Marcosson's was the interview. The son of a traveling salesman, Marcosson was born in Kentucky in 1876 and after high school landed a job as a reporter for the *Louisville Times*. While rising to the position of assistant city editor, Marcosson began to contribute stories to national magazines, and in 1903 he made use of these contacts when he moved to New York City to get a staff writer's job at Walter Hines Page's magazine the

World's Work. It was here that he began his career as an interviewer of prominent politicians and businessmen. His interest in business increased when he moved over to the *Saturday Evening Post* in 1907 and took charge of a personal finance column, a job that led him to develop close contacts with financiers like J. P. Morgan and Thomas F. Ryan. His heyday as an interviewer, however, began with the First World War, when he was able to interview a number of important yet notoriously taciturn political and military leaders, including Prime Minister David Lloyd George of Britain. Marcosson continued producing interviews for the *Post* in the 1920s and 1930s, specializing in European leaders such as Benito Mussolini and Leon Trotsky. After leaving George Horace Lorimer's publication in the mid-1930s, Marcosson devoted much of the rest of his career to producing corporate biographies.[10]

While Marcosson and Baker represented the serious side of celebrity journalism, Adela Rogers St. Johns represented the "soft" side. St. Johns was born in Los Angeles in 1894. Her father, Earl Rogers, was a prominent lawyer, her grandfather a Methodist minister and college president. Encouraged to be a writer by these men, St. Johns began selling short fiction to the *Los Angeles Times* at the age of nine, and when she dropped out of Hollywood High School her father introduced her to William Randolph Hearst, who hired her as a reporter for the *San Francisco Examiner.* In 1914 she moved back to Los Angeles to work for Hearst's *Herald,* a job that allowed her to cover city hall, the police beat, sports events, and Los Angeles society. After marrying William St. Johns, copy editor for the *Herald,* in 1918, St. Johns retired from newspaper work to raise their children, but she continued to produce short stories and human-interest features as a freelancer for magazines like the *Saturday Evening Post, Ladies' Home Journal,* and *Harper's Bazaar.* During these years she also began writing profiles of movie stars for *Photoplay.* In 1925 she went back to newspaper work as a regular staff writer for Hearst's International News Service (INS), covering sporting events like the Rose Bowl and the Kentucky Derby as well as sensational trials and scandals. She also continued writing intimate celebrity profiles and "inside" stories about the divorce of Mary Pickford and Douglas Fairbanks, the abdication of Edward VIII, and the travails of the Woolworth heiress Barbara Hutton. In the 1930s and 1940s St. Johns began to cover politics and other more serious subjects, a shift that culminated in her last assignment for the INS, a series on the Indian leader

Mohandas Gandhi shortly before his death. She then turned to writing books and teaching journalism at UCLA.[11]

Paul Gallico was also born in 1897, but a continent away, in New York City. The son of a classical pianist, Gallico grew up in a highly cultured home and went on to Columbia University, where he rowed crew and was a popular campus figure. After college he married the Radcliffe-educated daughter of a prominent columnist for the *Chicago Tribune*, and through family connections was hired as a movie critic at Joseph Medill Patterson's new tabloid, the *New York Daily News*. When he failed to distinguish himself at this task, Gallico was transferred to the sports department, where he worked his way up from copywriting to producing unusual features. Tall and athletic, Gallico made his reputation at the *Daily News* by engaging in a series of sensational stunts that inspired a new kind of chatty human-interest feature—accounts of him sparring with Jack Dempsey, swimming with the Olympic star Johnny Weismuller, golfing with Bobby Jones, and playing tennis with the amateur champion Helen Wills. The success of these features during the early 1920s allowed Gallico to become one of the most popular sports columnists in New York, a position that gave him considerable national influence and brought him into intimate contact not only with athletes but with fellow sportswriters, a cast that in the 1920s included Grantland Rice, Damon Runyon, W. O. McGeehan, and Westbrook Pegler. Exploiting the opportunities available to well-connected sportswriters, Gallico began writing freelance articles, including profiles of sports celebrities, for a number of publications—from the relatively lowbrow *Liberty* to the cheeky, sophisticated *Vanity Fair*. In the late 1930s, embittered by his experiences, Gallico abruptly quit sportswriting and produced an important memoir, *Farewell to Sport*, that cast a cynical light on the business. He then turned to writing fiction, eventually producing scores of novels, including the best-seller *The Poseidon Adventure*.[12]

Alva Johnston never enjoyed the financial success and notoriety of a Gallico or St. Johns. But he was perhaps the most widely respected profile writer of the interwar period, a journalist of extraordinary skill whose work appeared in many publications. Born in Sacramento, California, in 1888, Johnston left high school to take a job as a cub reporter with the *Sacramento Bee*. He moved to New York in 1911 and joined the staff of Adolph Ochs's *New York Times*, where he remained until

1923, covering all sorts of stories and becoming a specialist in longer personalized features. After he won a Pulitzer Prize for reporting in 1923, Johnston's star within the profession continued to rise, enabling him to join the staff of the *New York Herald-Tribune* in 1928, for which he contributed special features. He greatly impressed the city editor Stanley Walker, who later praised Johnston as the best all-around reporter he had ever known. During these years Johnston also began to write profiles for the *New Yorker.* His remarkable ability to produce the articles, which by the early 1930s had become a signature feature of the magazine, led the editor Harold Ross to hire him as a staff writer in 1932. Throughout the 1930s and 1940s, however, Johnston continued to write celebrity profiles for other magazines, including *Woman's Home Companion* and the *Saturday Evening Post,* endowing them with the unique style that he had perfected in the pieces he wrote for the *New Yorker*—a style that influenced many other writers. "All good Profiles, and copies of Profiles that you see in *Collier's* and the *Saturday Evening Post,* are modeled after the Johnston originals," the writer John O'Hara suggested in 1950. Indeed, it was widely believed that Johnston's influence on celebrity journalism was a major reason for Issac Marcosson's departure from the *Post* in the mid-1930s. Thanks to Johnston, the conventional interviews that Marcosson specialized in had become passé.[13]

By far the most famous producer of celebrity journalism, however, was Walter Winchell, born in 1897 to a family of impoverished Russian immigrants. Hating school, he dropped out at the age of twelve and began working in vaudeville, reveling in the chaotic, fast-paced life of show business. He was fascinated with backstage gossip and began submitting items about vaudeville entertainers to *Variety* and other trade publications in the early 1920s, soon becoming a regular columnist for the *Vaudeville News.* In 1925 he was hired by Bernarr Macfadden to write a column and feature stories for the sensational *New York Evening Graphic.* In 1929, after repeated conflicts with his editor, Winchell went over to Hearst's *Daily Mirror* and became a contributor to his King Features Syndicate. Finally, in 1932 he was hired to do a radio program that became a stunning success and encouraged him to branch out beyond show business and society gossip to political commentary. Winchell's high profile in the press and radio gave him enormous power over celebrities eager for favorable publicity. More important, he was a pivotal figure in the triumph of "story journalism," establishing a new benchmark for sensationalism and the revelation of private affairs. It was in his guise as "town gossip" that he attracted the attention of fellow journalists and himself became the subject of profiles in newspapers and magazines, some of which questioned his obsession with revealing information that had long been regarded as private. These critical jabs by his fellow journalists culminated in 1940 in a long, highly unflattering profile of Winchell in the *New Yorker* that explicitly revealed the anxiety he had aroused among social elites and many well-connected journalists.[14]

Despite their many differences, writers who specialized in celebrity journalism shared an important trait. They were insiders, a fact that allowed them access to celebrities and enabled some to interact with their subjects regularly. Winchell's stature was such that celebrities literally came to him, appearing at his home base, a well-situated table at Sherman Billingsley's Stork Club in midtown Manhattan, for conversation and photo opportunities. Journalists often advertised that they enjoyed having intimate access to figures far removed from the everyday lives of their readers. St. Johns, for example, never missed an opportunity to note that she and her subjects were "real friends." The only exception was the reclusive Greta Garbo, about whom she confessed: "I do not know Garbo. It would be dishonest to pretend that I do. Other writers have done that, to her indignation." Yet this unusual admission did not stop St. Johns from providing as intimate a profile of Garbo as she could without being able to resort to the rhetorical strategies that were her stock-in-trade. The result was a flattering portrait depicting Garbo's obsession with privacy in a highly sympathetic light. One cannot help wondering whether St. Johns's aim was to win Garbo's trust and goodwill, so that eventually she could gain access to her and produce the kind of chatty, in-depth profile that readers expected under her byline.[15]

St. Johns was not the only writer who recognized that access to celebrities depended on more than a writer's institutional affiliation, depending also on the degree to which the writer sympathized with her subjects. To maintain their status as insiders, the authors of celebrity profiles could not publish whatever they wished. They were expected to produce articles that were sympathetic or flattering, that contributed to the subject's effort to gain favorable publicity. As we shall see, refusing do so could cause a journalist to be denied access—and for a writer who specialized in celebrity journalism, this was devastating. But for most writers, conforming to the wishes of their subjects was not much of a problem. Regular access to celebrities and immersion in the exclusive circles that they traveled in led many journalists to sympathize and sometimes even identify with their subjects. As Paul Gallico observed, "It is not easy to break bread with a person, play golf with him, be received in his home as a friend and sometimes a trusted advisor, and then go down to the office and write a signed story critical of the man." Writers of celebrity profiles could be drawn into the promotional campaigns of their subjects, in some cases serving as little more than flacks.[16]

* * *

Of course, this had been true since the era of James Gordon Bennett and the penny press. As we have seen, public figures and ordinary people alike were quick to seize opportunities for self-promotion created by the mass-circulation press, with its expansive understanding of news. Politicians, ministers, reformers, entrepreneurs, showmen—all used the press to attract attention, garner support, or make potential customers aware of their products. In the years before the Civil War, the undisputed master of using "free publicity" in the press to advance his own aims was the show-business entrepreneur P. T. Barnum. As Barnum explained in his autobiography, "If a man says, or does, or proposes something which is noteworthy enough to get into the newspapers as news—something worth reading, hearing, and telling—at once the thing and the man . . . are talked about all through the country and, if of sufficient importance, all over the world." Barnum's innovations, which he employed to promote attractions from the notorious "Feejee Mermaid" to the opera singer Jenny Lind, included planting anonymous stories in newspapers and staging pseudo-events to draw reporters. Unlike many other public figures, Barnum recognized the value of negative publicity: in the modern city, simply being noticed and written about, even if the notice was bad, was the most important thing. To draw attention to his promotions, for example, he often placed newspaper stories that questioned their authenticity, inciting controversies that prompted wide discussion and increased box-office receipts.[17]

Barnum's innovations were soon adopted by other public figures, becoming quite common by the 1880s. These efforts were given a tremendous boost by the press's growing emphasis on human-interest stories and the development of celebrity journalism in the 1890s. The eagerness of newspapers to publish material of this kind made it even easier for promoters and aspiring celebrities to create news or beguile reporters—

particularly if, like Chauncey Depew, they could make themselves appear interesting. Reviewing the various means by which individuals in the late nineteenth century used the press to advance their interests, the journalist Julian Ralph observed that "a shrewd man, who recognizes the place the press has taken and the power it has, will easily manage to make it serve him to some extent while he is serving it." The latter was crucial. The key to getting free publicity, as Ralph and his fellow journalists conceded, was to provide reporters with something of genuine news value, and by the early twentieth century this feature of newsgathering was widely recognized by would-be celebrities as well as reporters. "Those who really have something worth reading will never get the reputation of seeking publicity, however often they are in print," the former journalist H. S. McCauley advised readers in *Getting Your Name in Print,* a handbook published in 1922 that offered advice on using the press to advance one's career or favorite cause.[18]

One celebrity who was extraordinarily good at this game was Theodore Roosevelt. From the outset of his career in politics, as a twenty-five-year-old New York state assemblyman, Roosevelt assiduously cultivated relationships with reporters like Ralph of the *New York Sun.* Conscious of the widespread belief that politicians from his background were priggish and ineffectual in the rough-and-tumble world of politics, Roosevelt went out of his way to convince reporters that he was cut from a different cloth—manly, convivial, and willing to stand apart from other "silk stockings" who refused to sully their hands to get results. Having made these connections, Roosevelt kept reporters abreast of his activities when he moved to the Dakota Territory and took up ranching, and he continued his deft handling of the press when he served as police commissioner of New York during the 1890s, giving frequent interviews and allowing reporters such as Lincoln Steffens and Jacob Riis to accompany him on his rounds. Thus Roosevelt was already well known and regarded as a terrific source of copy by the time he became a national celebrity during the Spanish-American War. It was this fact that encouraged so many reporters to travel to Montauk at the end of the war, where he and his regiment, the Rough Riders, disembarked. The resulting flurry of reports on his exploits and personality was crucial in catapulting him to the governorship and a position of power in the national Republican Party. As governor of New York, Roosevelt brought journalists like Steffens into his inner circle of informal confidantes and advisors, allowing them a highly prized vantage point from which to report on his administration. "[H]e let me in on his most private political plannings, conferences, hesitations, and decisions," Steffens recalled in his autobiography. But central to this arrangement was an implicit agreement. Certain information was confidential, and reporters who published it would be punished by banishment to what came to be called the "Ananias Club." By establishing an etiquette that governed access, Roosevelt was able to use the press to his advantage and keep his political opponents at bay.[19]

The ability of public figures to use the press to promote themselves reached a new level with the appearance of press agents and publicists. The first press agents were employed by big-city theater owners in the mid-nineteenth century to kindle public interest in their plays and the performers appearing in them, but the practice quickly spread to other forms of show business. For example, in the 1850s Barnum hired Rufus Wilmot Griswold to publicize his American Museum; Griswold may have also been the ghostwriter of Barnum's best-selling autobiography. After the Civil War, press agents were also employed by traveling stock companies and circuses, often serving as "advance men." Richard F. "Toby" Hamilton was the press agent for the circus that Barnum and James A. Bailey established in 1880, while Dexter Fellows worked for William F. Cody's famous Wild West Show. By the turn of the century press agentry had become a fixture of show business, with men like Charles Emerson Cook and Channing Pollock commanding large salaries for their services. Cook, a Harvard graduate with experience as a drama critic, was hired as a press agent by the Broadway producer David Belasco in the 1890s and played a key role in making Belasco a highly visible figure in the American theater during the early twentieth century, as much a celebrity as his stars. Like Cook, Pollock was also a former journalist and drama critic. But after an unseemly display of independence, when he insisted on panning the productions of a big advertiser, he was fired and promptly responded to this indignity by going to work for Florenz Ziegfeld and his lieutenant, William A. Brady; in this position he was able to mastermind the celebrity of Anna Held, the first "Ziegfeld girl" and Ziegfeld's common-law wife.[20]

But it was not only in show business that press agentry had established a foothold. "Press agents are now employed by public men, insurance, railway, and telegraph companies, by wholesale and retail dry goods houses, by young cities, summer and winter resorts, lecturers and entertainers, racing associations, hotels and athletic clubs," a writer for a press trade journal noted in 1898. Indeed, by the turn of the century public figures in many fields, including many social and economic elites, had begun to see the wisdom of employing publicists who could better manage their relations with the press.[21] To make themselves more appealing to this clientele, ex-journalists like George Parker, Ivy L. Lee, and Joseph I. C. Clarke cultivated a more sober, professional image as "public relations counselors" and argued that their in-depth understanding of journalism and connections to former colleagues who still worked for the press could be a tremendous benefit to clients. Swayed by these claims, which explicitly distinguished between press agents (presumed to be inveterate liars) and authoritative public relations men, an increasing number of businessmen and public officials began to hire publicists. And as the public relations industry grew, it became attractive to journalists looking for a more stable and financially rewarding career—much to the dismay of newspaper editors who lamented seeing some of their most talented reporters go into the field. Public relations work "in its more intelligent forms" was very attractive to journalists, the editor Stanley Walker admitted in 1934. Unlike newspaper work, it offered them "Easy Work, Short Hours, and Big Pay."[22]

Besides managing relations with the press, public relations counselors like Lee and Edward L. Bernays, who became the most articulate spokesman for the profession in the 1920s, also served as advisors, counseling clients on the publicity implications of different courses of action, a responsibility they were qualified to assume by virtue of their experience as "students" of public opinion and the "mass mind." As Bernays explained in *Crystallizing Public Opinion,*

> The public relations counsel is the lineal descendant, to be sure, of the circus advance-man. . . . The economic conditions which have produced him, however, and made his profession the important one it is to-day, have in themselves materially changed the character of his work. His function now is not to bring his clients by chance to the public's attention, not to extricate them from difficulties into which they have already drifted, but to advise clients how positive results can be accomplished in the field of public relations and to keep them from drifting inadvertently into unfortunate or harmful situations.

These "positive results" included establishing a favorable public profile that would make it more difficult for a client's critics or rivals to disseminate negative material about him. In other words, much of a publicist's work was preventive. Ben Sonnenberg, one of the most successful press agents of 1930s and 1940s, agreed. Given the power of the media to make or break a person's reputation in the "court of public opinion," Sonnenberg noted, it was often necessary for publicists to "practice preventative medicine," rather than simply respond to criticism. But maintaining an assertive profile was not always enough, especially when a celebrity gave his critics ammunition by misbehaving. "Sometimes you have to make your client change, so that the charges which may have been true at one time cease to be." [23]

By the 1920s a wide range of individuals employed press agents or publicists, and the insights developed by these new professionals were available to aspiring celebrities in advice columns and books such as *Getting Your Name in Print*. Over the years, as publicists like Pollock, Lee, and Bernays learned how best to handle reporters and get the most out of them, they developed a set of rules for establishing a fruitful relationship with the press. These rules were outlined in textbooks written for courses in public relations that began to be offered by some colleges during the 1920s, though they could also be gleaned from theoretical treatises like Bernays's *Crystallizing Public Opinion* or the memoirs of such legendary press agents as Dexter Fellows and Harry Reichenbach.[24] By far the most important rule was to allow access and opportunities for frequent interaction between the client and reporters. "No one can hope to obtain favorable publicity for either himself or the organization he represents who feels that he cannot be bothered with talking to representatives of the press, who resents their intrusion into his privacy, or who does not care to answer their questions," Glenn C. Quiett and Ralph D. Casey, the authors of *Principles of Publicity*, wrote in 1926. Publicists urged clients to treat reporters courteously and provide them with regular interviews and photo opportunities. They also advised clients to make sure that any material they provided was genuinely newsworthy and interesting, something that the press could use —rather than material that was blatantly self-promotional. Reporters looked favorably on sources who made their job easier and gave them stories that had real "news value." It was also important not to play favorites, to treat the representatives of all publications identically. This would ensure that no reporters or editors felt left out or angry—keeping them from seeking vengeance by "going after" the client.[25]

Following these rules was no guarantee of good publicity, the authors of these books insisted. But it was an effective strategy for developing a mutually beneficial relationship with reporters and eliciting their sympathy. The best course was to be open, to take the initiative, to concentrate on getting favorable publicity rather than trying to stay out of sight or suppress information. It was a mistake, for example, to ask for special treatment or demand that an unflattering story be squelched. "It is better . . . to tell the reporter the essential facts and request him not to publish them than to adopt a policy of concealment," argued Quiett and Casey. By doing so, clients could help reporters understand their predicament while not making them feel as though they were compromising their independence.[26] A close, trusting relationship with reporters could be a great asset. As H. S. McCauley noted, reporters were sometimes able "to manipulate news stories . . . to the advantage or disadvantage of the chief characters." Here was an opportunity for the client who had earned the goodwill of the press. "By failing to report information he stumbles across [the reporter] is able to suppress incidents unfavorable to his friends. By reporting the same sort of information he is frequently able to highly embarrass those who have gained his enmity, even though his editor does not specifically assign him to 'go after' them." Thus clients could gain a measure of protection by developing a good relationship with reporters; to do so, however, they had to avoid making reporters feel as though their integrity was being compromised—avoid making them feel like flacks, even when, in the end, they performed the essentially same function.[27]

* * *

The determination that many individuals displayed to get favorable notice in the press was not lost on reporters and editors. Even in the era of the penny press, journalists were wary of allowing the columns of their newspapers to become venues for self-promotion. A major source of the famous feud between James Gordon Bennett and P. T. Barnum was the chagrin that Bennett came to feel about the way that Barnum, through his knowledge of the conventions of newsgathering, routinely used the *Herald* for free publicity. Anxious to retain their independence and credibility with readers, journalists were obliged to incorporate a skeptical, even cynical, outlook into their work, particularly when seeking out sources, interviewing prominent public figures, or dealing with people who seemed eager for attention.

It was a wariness of being duped, for example, that inspired reporters to become more aggressive and manipulative in their pursuit and questioning of sources during the second half of the nineteenth century. The new aggressiveness was evident in the lengths to which reporters like Julian Ralph would go to gain access to a source and have their questions directly answered. Recalling his pursuit of a wealthy "Lumber King" who was thought to have information about the Beecher-Tilton scandal, Ralph confessed that he followed the man for days. "I sat on his doorstep until midnight. I was at his house before breakfast. I sent my card wherever he called on business or his social rounds. At last, at one o'clock in the night, he bade me come in." Getting to the man, however, was only the beginning. A journalist also had to make sure that he answered all his questions truthfully—a far more difficult proposition, considering the propensity of sources to lie to the press. As Theodore Dreiser revealed in his memoir of his days as a reporter in St. Louis and Chicago, this was where the manipulation came into play. "One had to approach all . . . as a friend and pretend an interest, perhaps even a sympathy one did not feel. . . . To appear wise when you were ignorant, dull when you were not, disinterested when you were interested, brutal or severe when you might be just the reverse—these were the essential tricks of the trade." To improve their chances of catching a source with his or her guard down, reporters in the late nineteenth century began haunting train stations and other places where public figures might appear and be approached without having time to prepare. While effective at eliciting more spontaneous responses, this strategy inspired the retort of "no comment" and made many celebrities hesitant to make public appearances, a development that led reporters to redouble their efforts at gaining access to their homes.[58]

Journalists brought essentially the same attitude to interviews, especially when the subject—John D. Rockefeller, for example—was known for his reluctance to reveal himself or address serious issues. The conventional wisdom among journalists was that interview subjects were hiding something—or, in the case of publicity hounds like Barnum and Roosevelt, likely to use reporters as conduits for "free publicity." The aim of the interview was to get the subject to reveal something that he would have preferred to conceal, to turn the tables and make him the reporter's "victim." Once the reporter achieved this objective, however, he had to leave without prompting the subject to retract his remarks. As the editor John L. Given warned in 1907, it was not wise to make "a mad dash for the door." "Instead . . . the reporter should change the subject, play the admirer himself, and make his exit gracefully, leaving the other man to wake up when he sees what he has said staring at him in print."[29] Needless to say, these tactics were not very popular with celebrities, and the press's growing reliance on them in the 1880s and 1890s led some prominent men and women to curtail their contact with journalists. Many others, as we have seen, hired press agents and publicists who established conventions for contact between their clients and reporters, thus limiting the random assaults that many clients regarded as intrusive and as damaging their efforts to present a calculated, consistent image to the public.

To deal with these new obstacles, journalists in the early twentieth century developed more refined—though in some cases no less manipulative—techniques for persuading public figures to speak for attribution. The most effective of these, as the profession's premier interviewer, Issac Marcosson, suggested in *Adventures in Interviewing* (1919), was persuasion. "One almost unfailing argument in favour of an interview with a public man is that it will be of some benefit to the interviewee or aid the cause with which he is allied." To win over a recalcitrant source or his publicist, a reporter had to exude confidence and goodwill—he had to "sell [the subject] on the proposition of being interviewed." In these instances, reporters harped on the advantages that a celebrity could gain by submitting to an interview. Another effective technique was exploiting a celebrity's vanity, the "vulnerable point" in the "armour" that celebrities donned to protect themselves from unwanted publicity. Marcosson advised journalists to learn as much as they could about the person they were to interview, especially his or her personal interests and hobbies. By appealing to these interests in an interview, the reporter could "disarm prejudice and even sterilize opposition" to his or her purpose. Through skillful questioning that made frequent reference to personal interests and hobbies, Marcosson suggested, a subject could be directed toward topics of interest to the reporter. "A man may not be interested in the specific proposition you are trying to make to him. He is interested in some other, however. Get him going on it and almost invariably he soon becomes receptive to what you really have in mind." Ironically, as conceived by reporters like Ralph and Marcosson, the art of interviewing bore more than a passing resemblance to the art of the confidence man—a game in which reporters were compelled to engage in deceit in order to get to the truth. This practice was part of a larger trend within the field of mass-circulation journalism in the early twentieth century, a growing emphasis on "faking" and "stunts" by reporters determined to please editors and publishers fixated on circulation figures and the bottom line.[30]

By highlighting the duplicity of their subjects and contrasting this to their own commitment to revealing the truth, journalists like Ralph and Marcosson sought to put some distance between themselves and the reality that much of their profession had succumbed to the same promotional ethos as the men and women they were assigned to cover. For some journalists, press agents and publicists became even more attractive bogeymen. In the 1890s articles critical of press agents began to appear in genteel magazines, and after the turn of the century the mainstream press was filled with stories about the chicanery and guile of these sinister new figures. Yet most of the pieces focused on show-business advance men and had relatively kind words for the new breed of public-relations counselors who were appearing on the scene—a testament to the success of the new men in cultivating a more respectable image. According to a writer for the *Saturday Evening Post*, for example, the new breed of PR men were honest and well educated, and newspaper editors were happy to get their accurate, well-prepared articles. They had developed such a reputation for truth and accuracy that "the average editor has quite as much faith in their stories as though they were written by men regularly on his staff." However, such fulsome praise failed to extinguish the suspicion that many journalists continued to feel toward publicists—even luminaries like Ivy L. Lee and Edward L. Bernays—and criticism of them persisted into the 1920s and 1930s. "Whatever these men and women may choose to call themselves . . . they seek approximately the same thing," Stanley Walker asserted in 1934. "They are paid for using their ability and ingenuity to the end that the interests they represent, whether it be a transit corporation or a visiting magician, appear before the public in a light which is favorable and pleasant, or at least in a guise as friendly as the circumstances will permit." This mission, Walker noted, made relations between publicists and the press intrinsically antagonistic.[31]

But as Walker and other journalists recognized, publicists were not going away, and editors and reporters had no choice but to accommodate themselves to their presence. Indeed, as the scope of news coverage had grown, press agents and publicists had become essential sources of information and prepared articles on a wide range of subjects. "They are part of the news machine," Walker conceded. "The hand of the publicity man, often carefully disguised, may be found in perhaps one-third of the news items in many issues of a New York newspaper." The situation for reporters specializing in writing about celebrities was even more perilous. Needing access to sources who now used publicists to manage their relations with the press, they could not afford to be frozen out of the circle of journalists who abided by the rules. Yet such rules impinged on the autonomy of reporters, keeping them from getting the material they really wanted and making them acutely aware of their complicity in the publicity machine. According to Gallico, though journalists who wrote about celebrities were privy to much inside dope, they were "handcuffed" by their status as insiders and their desire to remain part of the club.[32]

By the 1930s, in the wake of considerable conflict and mutual animosity, journalists and publicists had reached a compromise that allowed them to work together to perform their appointed jobs. In exchange for following the rules set by publicists, reporters were granted access to public figures; publicists and their clients, in turn, received favorable publicity and developed close working relationships with many of the reporters who covered them. In some cases, these reporters could be counted on for protection, downplaying or even suppressing unflattering information about a client. To remain on good terms with key sources, Leo C. Rosten revealed in his pathbreaking sociological study of Washington correspondents, reporters paid them "in the currency of journalism," with copy that served their interests. But a reporter could not go too far in his efforts to protect a celebrity without impairing his reputation as an independent insider and reducing his value as a source of free publicity for the client—the fate that befell Jacob Riis, for example, when he became too closely identified with Theodore Roosevelt. The need for journalists to maintain a modicum of independence—or at least the appearance of it—limited the demands that publicists and their clients could place on reporters, and gave publicists like Sonnenberg some leverage in their efforts to get clients to conform to the images established by publicists and allies in the press.[33]

The press's incorporation into this system made possible the intimate style of reportage developed by writers like Marcosson, Gallico, and St. Johns. Yet it also fueled the doubts that had always clung to the public personas of celebrities. One reason for this was that to establish their credentials as independent insiders, the authors of many celebrity profiles often contrasted their accounts with the "inaccurate" portraits produced by other journalists—including other insiders. Recall that from the turn of the century on, the opening gambit of the typical profile was an insistence that the subject was "misunderstood"—a plight attributable to laziness or a lack of integrity on the part of the press—and that the account that followed was the first "real" glimpse of her. In a profile of Helen Hayes in 1934, for example, St. Johns opened by insisting that Hayes's image as a wholesome "mid-Victorian angel" failed to capture her complexity. To be sure, Hayes was not only a great actress but also "a true daughter, wife, and mother," just as other journalists had maintained. The image they had conjured from this, however, obscured that Hayes was a "red-blooded," even "reckless" person who lived her life with gusto and abandon. Though St. Johns was vague about the reasons for the misrepresentation of Hayes, it would not have taken a leap of imagination for readers to see the hand of Broadway producers and the show-business press apparatus at work here, creating an image of Hayes that expressly downplayed any potentially controversial features of her life. Yet for St. Johns, it was precisely the combination of wholesomeness and recklessness that made Hayes interesting, a worthy subject for a profile. Distinguishing their work from static, one-dimensional portraits, writers like St. Johns made readers aware of the possibility that celebrity images disseminated by the press were of dubious veracity. And while this rhetorical strategy of the writers may have been effective in arousing interest in their articles and endowing them with an aura of authenticity, it may also have made some readers pause and question the authority of all celebrity journalism.[34]

By the 1930s these efforts to establish authenticity by debunking the work of other journalists had devolved into the open acknowledgment of self-promotion, press agentry, and media bias in many articles about celebrities. This angle was especially common in the *New Yorker*, which took great delight in debunking the images of celebrities by offering complex profiles, often revolving around the subject's efforts to manufacture an image through publicity and the aid of the press. Harold Ross's iconoclastic magazine also featured profiles of leading press agents and publicists, offering readers a unique window on the profession and its role in staging pseudo-events and promoting celebrities. One of the most penetrating was a four-part profile of the publicist Russell Birdwell, written by Alva Johnston and published in 1944. As Johnston made clear, Birdwell's profession was firmly ensconced in modern America and integral to the business of newsgathering. Newspapers and magazines published reams of material provided to them by men like

Birdwell, much of it "semi-fictitious" yet virtually all carefully crafted for specific effect. "Birdwell's clients lead, to some extent, the lives of characters in novels," Johnston noted mordantly. "They are partly real, partly literary creations." Some of them lived entirely according to scripts developed for them by Birdwell. "It is a curious art form in which character and incident are grafted upon flesh-and-blood heroes and heroines and in which the finished work is serialized in radio, newsreels, newspapers, magazines, and three-color posters." Of course, Birdwell's characters were real people, and as such could do things that were not in the script. "Young characters are particularly hard to control when the printer's ink runs hot in their veins. They make dates with the wrong individuals and get tangled up in incidents that spoil months of hard work by the author." But Birdwell's reputation for keeping celebrities in the limelight was so great that most of his clients eagerly conformed to his regimen.[35]

Though profiles that harped on the ways in which the images of celebrities were manufactured were most common in the *New Yorker* and other "smart" magazines, in the 1920s and 1930s articles about celebrities in mainstream publications also began to note the activities of publicists. Some of these publicists became well-known to readers, regular characters in stories about their clients. Christy Walsh, for example, was often mentioned in articles about Babe Ruth and figured prominently in press coverage of the most serious crisis in the baseball star's career, his suspension in 1925. The flamboyant Steve Hannagan, publicist for the Indianapolis Speedway and Miami Beach as well as for celebrities such as Gene Tunney, Jock Whitney, and the notorious utilities magnate Samuel Insull, was even more visible to readers of newspapers and magazines. Through his association with the Madison Square Garden promoter Mike Jacobs, Hannagan was also a vital player in generating the initial groundswell of publicity for Joe Louis—a campaign that sought to link the black prizefighter to the racial uplift ideology of the black bourgeoisie by highlighting the idealism and respectability of his "college-educated" managers. In doing so, however, Hannagan, Jacobs, and Louis's allies in the press angered elite African Americans like the journalist Earl Brown, who expressed his disdain in *Life* for Louis's managers and the press "build-up" of the fighter.[36]

With their activities regularly exposed, reporters and editors remained sensitive about their relationship to celebrities and their publicists. They were willing to go along when a celebrity behaved in a manner that did not make them look like liars. Yet if he or she strayed from this path, they sometimes attacked with a vengeance, as if to remind other public figures of the punishment that awaited those who undermined the press's credibility with readers. Reporters and editors for the highly competitive tabloid press were especially likely to display such independence. The system of cooperation that developed between the press and publicists was designed in part to ensure that a celebrity's image was relatively uniform across publications. Reporters interviewed celebrities in "squads," Silas Bent noted in his account of journalistic conventions in the 1920s. And the same information and posed photographs appeared in all newspapers and magazines that chose to publish them. This created a tremendous incentive for each paper to deviate from the others and offer a different perspective—one that was not so much unflattering as unofficial and truly spontaneous. Accordingly, reporters for the major tabloids often paid servants and lackeys for unauthorized inside information, and photographers stalked celebrities to get pictures that were not posed. Some papers—the Hearst press, in particular—enthusiastically printed rumor and innuendo. Embroiled in fierce circulation wars, the tabloid press had much to gain from engaging in these activities. Not only were they guaranteed to sell more papers, but they allowed editors to appeal to the injured celebrity for an exclusive interview that would repair the damage and set the record straight. Though some celebrities, like Charles Lindbergh, responded to these tactics by refusing to have anything to do with tabloid journalists, most forgave them and succumbed to their entreaties for a flattering, fence-mending exclusive.[37]

Indeed, by the 1920s different types of publications played distinct roles in what amounted to a cycle of celebrity journalism. Conservative newspapers and slick mass-circulation magazines were usually the conduits for "official" revelations that celebrities and their publicists wished the public to know. These were often conveyed in the lavish profiles that were regular features in these organs. Because of their willingness to pay for unauthorized information, publish unflattering photographs, and peddle rumor and innuendo, the tabloids were the primary vehicle for unofficial material that diverged from the images cultivated by publicists and sympathetic journalists. These revelations usually inspired a new round of official material designed to answer or accommodate them, usually in-depth profiles that dismissed the charges or put a positive interpretation on them. In some cases, when the tabloids were on the mark, the official response revised a celebrity's persona and recognized past "mistakes"; as Johnston suggested in his profile of Russell Birdwell, the celebrity's character was "rewritten." These efforts at damage control were assisted by the convention of depicting celebrities as "human beings," which allowed journalists to explain, even apologize for their transgressions. Being "only human," who could blame them if they succumbed to the temptations of power, money, and public adulation?

To get a sense of the cycle's operation it is useful to revisit the celebrity Charles Lindbergh. As we have seen, Lindbergh was hesitant to engage in the public appearances, photo opportunities, and interview requests that came with his new celebrity status. He was especially reluctant to consent to chatty profiles and answer questions about his personal life from reporters for the tabloids—questions designed to illuminate his personality. Instead, he made himself available only to a select group of aviation writers, whose access depended on their steering clear, as much as possible, from the subject of his personal life. This flagrant violation of the informal rules governing relations between the press and celebrities drove reporters and editors for the tabloid press crazy, and made them all the more determined to break down his reserve. Their zeal was reinforced by growing evidence, revealed in public appearances, of Lindbergh's haughtiness and seeming contempt for his fans and representatives of the press. The result was a series of sensational and largely unflattering rumors highlighting his arrogance that were published in the tabloid press during the late 1920s and early 1930s and reiterated in a critical profile of Lindbergh in the *New Yorker*. This profile, written by Morris Markey, a staff writer who had formerly worked for the New York *Daily News*, not only rehashed, in extensive detail, rumors that had already been published in the tabloids, making some readers aware of them for the first time. It also took direct aim at the image that Lindbergh and his allies were seeking to project, dismissing him as little more than a stunt pilot, the "Barney Oldfield of aviation," and suggesting that his evasiveness with the press was in fact a calculated ploy to attract publicity.[38]

As Lindbergh's friends in the conservative press reminded him, this would never have occurred if he had followed the rules that allowed other celebrities to develop good relations with reporters. "The newspapers have to follow Lindbergh . . . because of the inordinate public interest in him," noted Julian S. Mason, editor of the conservative *New*

York Evening Post. "It is his fate. He cannot escape it any more than we can escape it." In response to this persistent advice, Lindbergh finally allowed a few trusted reporters to interview him and write the kinds of human-interest profiles he disdained. Published in organs like the *New York Times* and the *Saturday Evening Post,* these accounts sought to answer the charges made by his critics. But they did not entirely satisfy the tabloids, which remained eager for any opportunity to publish information about Lindbergh. It was not until 1932, when his infant son was kidnapped and murdered, that Lindbergh gained the sympathy of reporters, though in later years he remained aloof from them and ultimately moved to England to escape their continual harassment.[39]

* * *

Celebrity journalism was designed to provide readers with authentic inside dope, material that was genuine and spontaneous, that illuminated the subject's "real self." Its business was exposure, and it derived its cachet from the assumption that only through intimate, probing access could the subject really be known. Yet its production was shaped in large part by the interests and ambitions of its subjects. In fact, although explicitly crafted to resemble the fruit of independent journalistic initiative, celebrity journalism in reality was a publicity medium conceived by celebrities, their press agents, and friendly reporters. This was no secret. As we have seen, it was openly discussed in many profiles, becoming a regular angle of reporting by the 1920s and 1930s, even in mainstream publications.

Such revelations made the genre inherently unstable and paradoxical. As readers soon learned, accounts claiming to be authoritative and definitive were anything but. Despite the efforts of journalists, celebrities remained mysterious, elusive, perennially misunderstood. The more that was revealed about them, the less sure one could be that the reported facts were true—since facts that had been promoted as true were habitually revealed to be spurious. This tension within celebrity journalism made things difficult for those seeking to use the press to publicize themselves, since any attempt to do so could never exorcise the doubts that the genre inspired.

The inability of celebrities and their publicists to overcome this problem enables us to see the role of the press in a new light. Though it might seem as if reporters and editors capitulated to celebrities and publicists by allowing themselves to be incorporated into the machinery of self-promotion, in the end it may have been journalists who had the last laugh. After all, the indeterminacy of celebrity journalism worked to their benefit, creating a continual demand for new product, for new information that would finally shed light on the subject's real self. This compelled celebrities to make themselves available to the press— whether they wanted to or not—and encouraged readers to keep buying newspapers and magazines that promised revelations, even when they knew, deep down, that the full disclosure they relished was impossible. Submitting to the press's insatiable demands for interviews, profiles, and photo opportunities could also place celebrities in an awkward position. In the hands of the press they became characters in broader social dramas and morality plays orchestrated by journalists for public consumption, over which they had virtually no control. In short, while the press offered celebrities a vehicle for realizing their ambitions, the ride was not free, and it sometimes involved detours that made the life of celebrities more difficult.

TRUE SUCCESS
THE MASTER PLOT OF
CELEBRITY JOURNALISM

When Charles Lindbergh finally consented to be the subject of a conventional human-interest profile, in early 1931, George Horace Lorimer, the editor of the *Saturday Evening Post*, did not assign the story to a staff writer or one of the well-known journalists who specialized in producing celebrity profiles. Instead, he gave the job to a relatively obscure freelancer, Donald E. Keyhoe, an aviation writer and former Marine pilot who had accompanied Lindbergh on a promotional tour in 1927 and written about him for *Popular Science* and *National Geographic*. The assigning of Keyhoe to the story not only pleased Lindbergh and set the stage for a productive interview. It gave Keyhoe an attractive angle around which to frame the story: the degree to which being a celebrity had changed Lindbergh.

As we have seen, by 1930 press criticism of Lindbergh had steadily escalated, imperiling his image as a serious, self-effacing spokesman for aviation. In the view of some reporters, the once modest "Lindy" had become haughty and arrogant. Keyhoe had been close to Lindbergh during the early stages of his celebrity, but in recent years the two had not had the opportunity to socialize, making Keyhoe seem more objective than the aviation writers who were regarded as Lindbergh's favorites. Better still, the time that had elapsed since their association gave Keyhoe a good vantage point from which to assess the charges being made by the aviator's growing legion of critics.

After tagging along with Lindbergh on a business trip to Manhattan and visiting his rustic home in the New Jersey countryside—the sort of inside access that Lindbergh's critics were denied—Keyhoe was determined to make his readers appreciate the difficulties that Lindbergh had to cope with daily, difficulties that went a long way toward explaining some of his more controversial actions. But he concluded his profile on a positive note. While being a celebrity was arduous, forcing Lindbergh to resort to behavior in public that might be construed as standoffish, the real Lindbergh was "essentially the same" as the young man Keyhoe had known in 1927. This was most apparent after the long drive from New York, when the two arrived at Lindbergh's home and the aviator was warmly received by his wife and small son. Keyhoe wrote: "Never had I seen him so completely free of that tense, on-guard manner which had necessarily grown to be a part of him on his 1927 tour of the forty-eight states, and which had remained with him long afterward. That night he seemed younger, almost boyish, and as he greeted Mrs. Lindbergh I saw more of the old likable Slim in his infectious smile than I had observed for two years in public." For Keyhoe, the appearance of "old likable Slim" was an important revelation, proof that Lindbergh had been able to handle the burdens of celebrity and resist the corruption that often occurred when individuals were thrust into the spotlight. That Lindbergh could achieve this in the face of public adulation and the afflictions that accompanied it was truly remarkable, a testament to his sanity, sobriety, and common sense.[1]

Keyhoe's interest in Lindbergh's ability to withstand the ordeals of celebrity was a common theme in human-interest reporting. Many profiles and sketches employed it. Beginning in the 1890s, it became what might be called the master plot of celebrity journalism, a motif that journalists, publicists, and celebrities alike drew upon in their efforts to project images through the mass media—the struggle of celebrities to achieve "true success." True success was not the same as material success. In fact, the notion rested on a critique of material success and the consequences of upward mobility, a critique inspired by deeply rooted residual beliefs that journalists exploited in their quest to reach a mass audience. Sensitive to the ways in which modernization had altered class relations and the opportunities available to most Americans, journalists in the late nineteenth century and the early twentieth crafted the ideal of true success as a modern alternative to standards of achievement inherited from the mid-nineteenth century, which had encouraged Americans to view ownership of a small farm or shop and fidelity to Victorian notions of "respectability" as the benchmark of success. By the turn of the century, in the wake of industrialization, corporate consolidation, and changes in the workplace that led most Americans to place a greater emotional investment in their leisure time, many of these standards appeared outmoded. Equally important, they lacked appeal among an increasing number of readers or potential readers. Because it was appealing to a wider range of Americans, the ideal of true success served a larger ideological program, promoting the notion that success, happiness, and self-fulfillment had little to do with material goods or social status—a comforting thought for people to embrace in a society increasingly characterized by stark inequalities of wealth and power.[2]

The ideal of true success was most clearly articulated in profiles and sketches, perhaps the most important form of celebrity journalism that emerged in the years after 1890. More than any other type of journalism, celebrity profiles resembled advice and inspirational literature. In many ways, they were direct descendants of the older, hagiographic biographies that were staples of nineteenth-century popular culture. This was especially true of articles that appeared in newspapers and magazines directed at working-class and lower-middle-class readers—the Sunday supplements in the Hearst press, popular weeklies like *Collier's* and *Liberty,* and the publication with the richest trove of such material, the *American Magazine.* Well into the 1930s these organs published celebrity profiles with a distinctly didactic flavor, even while middlebrow magazines, influenced by the *New Yorker,* were moving in the opposite direction.

The differences between these two streams, however, were not as great as they might have seemed. Though contemptuous of didacticism, publications specializing in sophisticated profiles regularly employed the same angles and themes as their "lowbrow" rivals and were just as complicit in promoting the ideal of true success. The major difference was that the subjects in sophisticated profiles, like those in tabloid exposés, were more likely to have "failed," making them no less important in the project of marking the ideal's boundaries. Writing in *Life* in 1938, for example, a journalist chided the Republican politician Thomas Dewey for being conceited and self-righteous, traits he had developed during his widely publicized career as a racket-busting district attorney. In effect, Dewey had come to believe his own press clippings and the B-grade movies that had been inspired by his work, which portrayed him as "a Galahad in shining armor, doing battle against the forces of the underworld." While this article contradicted the puff pieces about Dewey that portrayed him as a paragon of selfless virtue, it addressed the same issue that had framed reporting about Lindbergh: the degree to which public accomplishment and the laurels that it offered could lead celebrities to become conceited.[3]

Many didactic profiles were designed to encourage readers to emulate the behavior and values of their subjects, with bold headlines or sidebars advertising the "lessons" that a celebrity's career revealed. "ARE YOU USING ALL THE POWER YOU'VE GOT?" asked the editors of the *American Magazine* in 1919 in a sidebar accompanying a profile of the actor John Barrymore, which demonstrated the rewards that could be gained by tapping the "hidden reservoirs of power and of ability" that most people were unaware they possessed. Usually these lessons were embedded in the text, often near the beginning though sometimes at the end, in the form of an illustrative anecdote. For example, at the conclusion of a profile of Carole Lombard published in *Liberty* in 1938, the journalist Howard Sharpe described a scene he had witnessed in a studio projection room, where the fun-loving Lombard and her beau, Clark Gable, were on their knees "shooting craps for buttons." This bout of spontaneous play was typical of Lombard, something she regularly did to keep in good spirits. But this "medicine" was not just good for Lombard. It was good, Sharpe insisted, "for *any* girl!"[4]

Other articles allowed readers to derive vicarious enjoyment from the lives of celebrities, often through the use of illustrations and photographs. A profile of George and Edith Gould by Elizabeth Meriwether Gilmer, published in 1909 in *Cosmopolitan*, for instance, allowed readers a seemingly intimate glimpse of their home life and young family, utilizing techniques that remain standard in contemporary magazines like *In Style* and *Vanity Fair*. Yet illustrations were not always necessary to make a profile effective as a showcase for a celebrity's privileged style of life, as Ralph Wallace revealed in an article on the philanthropist Jock Whitney that appeared in the *American Magazine* in 1940. In the course of discussing his interests as an investor and theatrical "angel," Wallace provided readers with a vivid description of Whitney's sumptuous office at Rockefeller Center and a catalogue of some of his extraordinary possessions. Among these were two country homes and a custom-built, eighty-foot yacht.[5]

A substantial number of profiles were concerned with how celebrities became successful and stressed the opportunities for self-expression and professional accomplishment offered by their jobs. According to these articles, the work performed by celebrities was important, interesting, and fulfilling, a theme that was surely attractive to readers who toiled at jobs transformed by scientific management and the broader changes that business historians have called the "organizational revolution." This was true regardless of their occupation or field of expertise—true of baseball players and entertainers as well as of businessmen and government bureaucrats. Reviewing the career of the New York public-works potentate Robert Moses in the *American Magazine* in 1934, Beverly Smith suggested that Moses, voted the most successful member of his Yale class at a recent reunion, deserved another honor as well: that of having had, in his career as a reformer, government expert, adviser to politicians, and developer of parks and parkways, "the most fun." [6]

Celebrity profiles also emphasized the wealth and influence that their subjects had gained, which enabled them to move in circles that were utterly foreign—and probably fascinating—to people of modest means. Articles about Mary Pickford and Douglas Fairbanks, for example, regularly mentioned the small group of writers and movie folk who often gathered in the evenings at their home for dinner, sports, or parlor games, while many profiles of businessmen made note of the exclusive communities and private clubs to which they belonged. According to journalists, the maverick businessman Howard Hughes—who had parlayed the fortune he inherited from his wealthy father into a stake in the motion picture industry—inhabited both the business and entertainment worlds, which allowed him to profit from investments in the machine-tool and aircraft industries while he devoted most of his time to making movies and dating Hollywood starlets. Hughes was not the only celebrity who moved between different yet equally rarefied social and occupational realms. So did the songwriter Irving Berlin. Indeed, it was Berlin's status as perhaps the best-known and successful songwriter in America, journalists suggested, that had enabled this uneducated former song-plugger to meet and eventually marry the heiress Ellin Mackay. Because of their widely disparate backgrounds, their courtship was one of the most widely publicized romances of the 1920s and an important advertisement for the miraculous things that could happen when a person became a celebrity. [7]

The most extraordinary issue that the articles focused on, however, was the public interest and adulation that celebrities often aroused. Rising above the anonymous masses, they achieved a kind of recognition that was exceedingly rare—not least because celebrity status directed public curiosity toward their personalities. This no doubt was a compelling prospect for readers who feared that they would never stand out from the crowd or have their uniqueness widely recognized. Moreover, the kind of public recognition that celebrities enjoyed made it possible for some of them to transcend their particular fields and become cultural icons, the subjects of innumerable conversations, their names a shorthand for well-known subjects or traits—Thomas Edison for invention, John D. Rockefeller for wealth, Jane Addams for social concern, Charlie Chaplin for artistry, Jack Dempsey for swaggering bravado. In a witty and thoughtful profile of Babe Ruth in *Vanity Fair*, Paul Gallico argued that Ruth's tremendous popularity was attributable to the public's extensive knowledge of his background, everyday life, and personality. Coverage of Ruth's every action on and off the field had made him interesting and well known to all kinds of Americans, "a member of every family in the country that cares anything about sport, and a great many that don't."[8]

These features of celebrity profiles, which stressed the positive consequences of being lifted to celebrity status, were accompanied by other features that made the genre unique. For example, unlike much advice literature, celebrity profiles placed considerable emphasis on the role of luck. The wealth, influence, and public recognition that distinguished celebrities from the masses were attributed as much to "breaks" as to their own exertions. A staple of popular literature for centuries, this theme had been central to the wildly popular dime novels of the late nineteenth century, including those written by Horatio Alger. Its increasing use by journalists in the early twentieth century reflected not merely the influence of new intellectual currents that downplayed individual autonomy but a growing reliance on narrative devices borrowed from literature and folklore to make stories interesting to readers.[9]

More important, though the advice offered by celebrity profiles was meant to be applicable to the lives of ordinary people, it was not presented as a formula for achieving the same degree of success and recognition. What it offered was advice on "right living," promising psychic rewards that many journalists regarded as more important than material success or public recognition. Following this advice, they argued, would bring happiness and fulfillment. It was the key to achieving true success, the ideal that informed nearly all celebrity profiles. To achieve true success, people had to make the most of their potential. But this was only the beginning. As we have seen with Lindbergh, the real hallmark of true success was being able to resist the forces that could subvert a person's individual autonomy and cause him to lose touch with his real self.

The novelty of celebrity journalism lay not in its commitment to promoting these principles, however, for journalism was only one of several cultural forms through which they were disseminated. The novelty lay rather in the assertion that celebrities were less likely than ordinary people to realize the ideal of true success. Ironically, this was because of the *degree* of success and recognition that celebrities enjoyed, which lifted them so far above the crowd and enabled them to live so differently. Being a celebrity, as many a profile demonstrated, did not solve all of life's problems; it often created new ones that were even more vexing and difficult to overcome. And while these "burdens" and "trials" only affected celebrities, making their lives unenviable, they bore more than a passing resemblance to problems that plagued virtually everyone— problems that journalists and their readers understood to be central to modernity. For celebrities, achieving true success was therefore a heroic struggle, making their ability to do so all the more impressive—and the rewards that they received all the more deserved. But as framed by journalists, the struggle had a larger meaning, revealing how even lowly, obscure people might navigate the treacherous currents of an urban-industrial society and successfully master the "art of living."

*   *   *

Some of the peculiar features of true success can be discerned in the *American Magazine* profile of John Barrymore mentioned earlier. As the author of the piece, Keene Sumner, observed, by objective standards Barrymore was quite successful well before he began making full use of his "hidden reservoirs of power and of ability." He was a popular and highly paid actor in light comedies and a matinee idol for many young women. Since his performances involved little more than playing a thinly veiled version of himself, Barrymore had no need to work hard or follow the orders of directors. And so he lived a privileged, care-free life, frequently missing rehearsals and immersing himself in the "gay nightlife of New York." Yet according to Sumner, the success that Barrymore enjoyed did not make him happy. Having once aspired to be a painter, deep down Barrymore was frustrated and only continued with the actor's life because it was easy, the course of least resistance. On a hunch, a producer cast him in a more interesting and demanding role, and Barrymore, to even his own surprise, rose to the occasion. From that moment Barrymore directed his once frustrated artistic yearnings into his acting, a process that allowed him to master many difficult roles and become "the greatest living American actor." Sumner reported that this "evolution" was accompanied by changes in Barrymore's personal life: "as a man, he has traveled, too." He stopped frequenting Broadway nightspots and became a more serious and responsible person. The "new" Barrymore was a greater professional success *and* a more contented human being.[10]

As the profile of Barrymore demonstrates, while the ideal of true success belittled materialism, it had no bias against substantive achievement. In fact, many profiles were obsessed with how their subjects had risen to the top of their professions, though, as we have seen, the way that journalists measured achievement was somewhat unusual. By this standard, the "old" Barrymore, despite fame and fortune, was clearly a failure, and the success of the "new" Barrymore was attributable less to his unrivaled position in the profession than to the development of yearnings that had long lain dormant. Interest in achievements was especially common in reportage about newly minted celebrities, which often stressed the distance they had traveled and the obstacles they had overcome in the course of their ascent. For most journalists, the newly gained status of their subjects was richly deserved, a fitting reward for their having made full use of their innate potential, as very few people were able to do. But the program that celebrities followed to harness these powers, reporters noted, was not the classic bourgeois regimen of self-mastery, which built "character" and allowed individuals to achieve a higher level of moral development. In a subtle yet important revision, it was a new modernist program of self-development, suitable for men and women alike, that journalists and many other middle-class Americans regarded as more appropriate for the "machine age." In typical modernist fashion, the rewards that the new program offered were not moral but psychological, the therapeutic ideal of "growth."[11]

At the core of the new regime were values that had been central to the old one—industry, perseverance, and will power. Regardless of their occupation, journalists observed, celebrities worked very hard to achieve success and distinction, and they continued working hard even after reaching the top. Often this involved learning new things and seeking to improve their skills and ability to perform their jobs. For example, by gaining a "thorough knowledge of every intricacy of the foreign business," a young J. P. Morgan had developed the breadth of vision that later allowed him to become the world's most respected and trusted financier, Ray Stannard Baker wrote in 1901. Many celebrities displayed this commitment very early in life, sometimes even as children, ensuring that it became an unconscious habit. Theodore Roosevelt's determination to build up his body as a child, Henry Beach Needham asserted in *McClure's* in 1906, was the same force that had carried him to success as an author, politician, and soldier. The authors of some profiles made industriousness appear integral to their subjects' personalities. Writing about the actress Sarah Bernhardt, for example, a reporter for *Ladies' Home Journal* noted that hard work was her "method of life," her approach to every problem or undertaking. Celebrities were also persistent, continuing their labors despite obstacles and seeming failures. According to journalists, this willingness to persevere often proved to be the key to their rise from obscurity. While others gave up, they soldiered on, demonstrating the enduring value of determination and will power in the "game of life." These values were vital, despite the increasing importance assigned to luck. As Charlie Chaplin explained in *Collier's* in 1922, "Luck provides opportunities, but unless you have some kind of endowment yourself to contribute they will not do you very much good." What distinguished celebrities from ordinary people was their dedication to building up such an endowment, improving themselves, honing their skills and personal resources, so they could be ready if luck arrived—and thus make the most of it.[12]

Yet hard work, perseverance, and will power were more than simply the means to an end. Journalists asserted that these traits—and the work ethic to which they were bound—had an intrinsic value beyond any material success that they might bring. Those who exhibited them were purposeful, self-conscious human beings, people determined to make their mark on the world, engaged with "real life." Such figures plunged enthusiastically into every task that they undertook, regardless of what they stood to gain by performing it. Roosevelt, for example, threw himself "whole-souled" into whatever job needed to be done, William Allen White wrote in 1901, enjoying "the trials, disappointments, the stress of it along with the successes." For Roosevelt and many of the other figures whom journalists portrayed along these lines—from Sarah Bernhardt to Howard Hughes—what mattered was not the material rewards that work might bring but the new experiences and the deep sense of satisfaction that only sincere, engaged activity could provide. Activity of this kind—doing something new, something "a little harder than you ever tackled before"—was essential for personal fulfillment, the actor Douglas Fairbanks advised readers of the *American Magazine* in 1922. Here was an important reworking of the formulation which had linked the work ethic to morality and bourgeois respectability. In the pages of celebrity journalism the work ethic was now yoked to the modernist ideal of "engagement" and the psychic fulfillment that such a commitment was assumed to inspire.[13]

By the early 1920s it was also linked quite openly to self-promotion and "salesmanship." As readers of newspaper and magazine profiles discovered, among the skills that celebrities developed was the ability to sell things—including themselves. Doing so required paying careful attention to public tastes, something that celebrities accomplished through "serious study" and tailoring their "goods" in response to them. As the comedian Harold Lloyd revealed to Mary B. Mullett, "There isn't a harder job in the world than to make people laugh. I work at that job night and day; always thinking and studying it over. No matter where I go, or what I do, it is constantly on my mind." When applied to their own selves, such efforts could inspire fruitful changes in appearance, dress, and demeanor—changes that were now necessary because of the degree to which recognition and success depended on interpersonal relations and the cultivation of pleasing and effective "social selves." But journalists stopped short of completely endorsing this practice. By associating self-promotion with the work ethic and constantly reminding readers of how difficult and time-consuming it was to discern the public's tastes, journalists directed attention away from the possibility that their subjects had succeeded by manipulating images. Whatever misgivings they may have still harbored about self-promotion, by the 1930s journalists regarded "salesmanship" as vital for achievement in virtually every profession or industry, a conclusion that reflected their belief that America had become a mass society inhabited by teeming, anonymous crowds, where more aggressive tactics were required to be noticed. Self-promotion—having the "loudest horn"—now appeared as a legitimate technique that might help a person get a "break," particularly when he or she employed it to trumpet genuine ability that would otherwise go unrecognized. For example, had the playwright William Saroyan not aggressively promoted himself, a journalist suggested in 1940, "he'd still be picking oranges in a California grove, instead of being revered . . . as a sort of literary Lawrence of Arabia." Employing it to make false claims, however, remained beyond the pale.[14]

In most celebrity profiles salesmanship was associated with two important concepts, self-confidence and personality. Self-confidence was invaluable, journalists insisted. It helped people cope with the pressures and potential frustrations that were peculiar to the urban-industrial age and made many individuals feel powerless, insignificant, or degraded. It was especially useful as an antidote to an affliction that the press and the helping professions portrayed as virtually endemic: the "inferiority complex." As the writer Will Irwin explained in 1927 to the readers of *Liberty*, "The young man who starts out with an inferiority complex has generally a hard time getting a start; for the world, on first contact, tends to take you on your own valuation. The man who shows by his attitude that he believes in himself has a much better chance in the early stages of the race of getting to the pole." Profiles of female celebrities made it clear that the same was true of women. "To be thought well of," noted Emma B. Kaufman in a profile of Alice Roosevelt in 1905, "one must first, with honesty, and without too much modesty, think well of oneself." Self-confidence, moreover, was a spur to achievement and growth. It was self-confidence, for example, that swiftly made Katharine Hepburn a movie star, Henry F. Pringle opined in 1933 in *Collier's*. Through a series of bizarre stunts, she made herself noticed and talked about "long before her first picture was released." Yet all of this would have been for naught had she not been talented, "almost as good an actress as she believes herself to be," and keenly interested in further improvement. Thus self-confidence meant not just faith in one's abilities but faith in one's potential—a faith that inspired self-improvement and led some celebrities to become as extraordinary as they claimed to be.[15]

Self-promotion was also linked to the cultivation of personality: the development of traits that enabled a person to distinguish himself from others. Many celebrities were said to possess "vivid" or "magnetic" personalities, and journalists acknowledged the importance of this "gift" in allowing them to be recognized. As a friend of the entertainer George M. Cohan told a writer for *American Magazine*, "There is something electric about him. It isn't just that he is successful and that people defer to him because of that. If he went into a room full of people not one of whom knew who he was, it would be just the same." Among figures like Cohan, Theodore Roosevelt, and Ethel Barrymore, personality was inborn, a quality that radiated out of them without any effort on their part. Writing in *Ladies' Home Journal* in 1911, Barrymore warned readers that personality should not be confused with physical attractiveness. "Many plain people possess it in high degree," she asserted. And while it was impossible to develop the magnetism of a Cohan or a Barrymore, ordinary people could enhance their self-presentation and their chances of attracting favorable notice by adopting the proper techniques. Unfortunately, Barrymore suggested, many people employed the *wrong* techniques. The most widely practiced error was to imitate the idiosyncratic mannerisms and styles of celebrities like herself, which appeared awkward when adopted by others. When a large number of people followed this course, the result was a pathetic spectacle, scores of people acting and dressing in the exactly the same awkward, unnatural ways.[16]

The best way for a person to develop his or her personality, journalists argued, was to look within and identify traits that were unique or interesting, then figure out how these traits might be nurtured, amplified, and expressed. As Henry Ford told the journalist Bruce Barton in 1921, "A young man . . . should look for the single spark of individuality that makes him different from other folks, and develop that for all he's worth." Looking within meant taking stock of one's strengths and weaknesses, and finding ways of shoring up the weaknesses so as to be noticed and appreciated. This argument was especially common in celebrity profiles of women, which continued to stress the importance of learning how to be charming and poised even while they warned readers not to rely excessively on appearances. Eleanor Roosevelt, for example, overcame feelings of inferiority that had plagued her early in life—when she was regarded as an "ugly duckling"—by paying careful attention to how she dressed and comported herself, according to a profile in 1940 by Geoffrey Hellman, a writer for *Life*. Her widely publicized program of self-improvement demonstrated that it was possible to enhance one's personality through "conscious handiwork." But it also reaffirmed the advice that journalists had been peddling since the heyday of Ethel Barrymore. The aim of self-improvement was to make a woman's natural assets more visible—to allow her real self to shine through. In practical terms, this meant adapting manners and fashions to one's individual nature and developing a personal style that expressed the admirable qualities lying within. Thus cultivating personality was not the same as developing a pleasing façade. For men as well as women, it involved developing and learning to display traits that were integral to the self—traits that could be made the essence of the "social selves" universally employed to get along in the world.[17]

The ability of celebrities to display self-confidence and make the most of their innate potential, however, depended in large part on physical health and conditioning. Drawing on new medical and psychological discourses that stressed the connections between health and "states of mind," journalists placed special emphasis on the ways in which celebrities looked after their bodies to keep "running on high." These techniques were surprisingly consistent, followed by men and women alike, and they echoed the formula for achieving optimal health offered by early-twentieth-century advice literature. The first ingredient was rest. Most celebrities were revealed to be fanatical about getting enough sleep and ensuring that they began each day with sufficient energy for the tasks that lay ahead. Their ability to perform these tasks was bolstered by the second ingredient, a well-rounded diet that included a minimum of artificial "stimulants." Displaying admirable moderation, most celebrities were said to avoid heavy foods, alcohol, and other substances assumed to impede good health and undermine the enthusiasm and mental acuity they needed for their work. They were also devotees of regular exercise—everything from horseback riding to golf, tennis, swimming, and tramps in the woods—which strengthened their muscles, restored their nerves, and cleaned the cobwebs from their minds. As important as exercise, journalists noted, were the moments each day that many celebrities set aside for spontaneous play. It was his devotion to play, for example, that made Andrew Carnegie "young in spirit" and "alert in action" at the ostensibly advanced age of seventy, a writer for *Munsey's* suggested in 1908. By following this regimen celebrities not only remained healthy and productive; they also developed self-confidence and the optimism required to make the most of life's opportunities. This, George Creel argued in 1916 in *Everybody's*, was the lesson to be learned from the ascent to fame of Douglas Fairbanks, perhaps the best-known exemplar of physical conditioning, who had gained from it an "indomitable optimism" that was central to his success as an actor and human being. "He has made cheerfulness a habit, and it has paid him in courage, in bubbling energy, and buoyant resolve," Creel asserted, eager to persuade his readers to follow a similar routine.[18]

In short, the success enjoyed by celebrities was ascribed to their ability to make the most of their innate talents and attributes. This meant working hard, displaying the same dedication to the work ethic that had long been a hallmark of successful individuals. It also meant following a program of self-improvement designed to bring out latent traits that might prove useful, paying attention to physical health, and cultivating self-confidence and personality, which were indispensable for rising above the crowd. Together, these imperatives pointed toward a new regimen of self-development, one that replaced the ideal of bourgeois respectability with a new modernist ideal, what the reformer Luther Gulick called "personal efficiency." Profiles of celebrities were potent advertisements for personal efficiency, demonstrating its effectiveness in enabling men and women to achieve distinction in the "machine age," a time when the forces arrayed against the individual led many people to become fatalistic about their chances of making their mark on the world. Celebrities as diverse as Fairbanks, Theodore Roosevelt, Sarah Bernhardt, Ty Cobb, Henry Ford, and Eleanor Roosevelt—who made full use of their inner powers, who worked hard in order to be all they could be—were rebukes to this spirit of resignation. Inspired by the conviction that ordinary people were not living up to their potential, a failure that was eroding faith in individualism and leading some Americans to become depressed or embrace socialism, profiles of celebrities were meant to inspire Americans to regain their faith in the power of the individual.[19]

But not so that they might achieve the same degree of success. As numerous articles made clear, following this new regimen was most likely to enable a man or woman to achieve a relatively modest level of success—not the fame and fortune enjoyed by figures like Carnegie or Fairbanks. This was not only because of the role of luck. It was because some celebrities, though not all, were said to be authentic "geniuses" whose abilities and achievements were far beyond the capacity of ordinary people. Such figures might be profitably emulated, but it was foolish, journalists asserted, to expect that doing so would result in spectacular achievements. In the view of many writers, however, subscribing to the ethos of personal efficiency offered ordinary Americans benefits that were even more valuable than money, power, or social position, benefits that were therapeutic rather than moral. Echoing the psychological theories of William James and his acolytes, they argued that making the most of one's abilities was crucial to achieving happiness and fulfillment—and the "growth" that should be every person's aim.[20]

* * *

But achieving growth required more than personal efficiency. As countless profiles illustrated, relationships with other people were also vital in helping celebrities rise to the top of their fields and grow as individuals. The increasing emphasis on cultivating personality was a reflection of this belief. It stressed the importance of making other people recognize the uniqueness that lay within every individual—uniqueness that might go unacknowledged without the use of assertive techniques expressly meant to attract attention. These techniques required self-confidence, a belief in one's own talents and potential. Yet developing this outlook was not easy, especially if a person faced the world alone. It helped immeasurably if other people were similarly committed and could provide material, moral, and psychological support. Such support allowed celebrities to overcome the hardships and self-doubts that plagued all those who struggled to make the most of themselves. Often this support was provided by family or close friends, though mentors, teachers, and coaches could offer it as well. Regardless of who furnished it, the result was the same: an increase in self-confidence and a greater ability to marshal the inner resources that celebrities needed if they were to achieve and grow.

The role played by parents was especially important. In some cases they served as examples, encouraging their children to carry on the family legacy. Theodore Roosevelt's father, for instance, was often cited as a crucial influence on his son, an "inspiring companion" who sparked his interest in public service. Ethel Barrymore's family had much the same impact, prompting her to follow their example by becoming an actress—a choice that she made voluntarily, not in response to family pressure, Gustav Kobbé suggested in a profile of Barrymore in *Ladies' Home Journal* in 1903. In other cases, parents were instrumental in lighting the "spark" within their child and supporting vocational choices that were risky or seemingly foolhardy. Sympathetic to his daughter's desire to be a movie actress, Clara Bow's father enthusiastically supported her as she learned her craft and steadily achieved success, Jim Tully reported in 1927 in *Pictorial Review*. Without Clara's knowledge, he even submitted her picture to a movie-magazine beauty contest, which resulted in her first break. Of course, some parents were not pleased when their children announced their interest in, say, sports, show business, or politics, and this sometimes led to bitter quarrels and hurt feelings. For example, when Al Jolson's father, a rabbi, objected to his son's early interest in show business and insisted that instead he go to school to learn to be a salesman, Jolson ran away from home and "nearly starved" before getting his first break and beginning his long apprenticeship in vaudeville. But over time these parents were invariably proven wrong—not only by their children's success but by the self-fulfillment that the work they performed so clearly inspired.[21]

Even more illuminating were articles that focused on the childrearing practices of celebrities, which were strikingly consistent—so consistent, in fact, that they can be read as an advertisement for a new "progressive" mode of childrearing. The most widely publicized celebrity parents of the early twentieth century were Theodore Roosevelt and his wife, Edith. The Roosevelts were quite conscious about their childrearing, Jacob Riis noted in a profile of the First Family in *Ladies' Home Journal* in 1902. They were companions and friends to their children, joining them in many kinds of games and encouraging their interest in sports and outdoor exercise. "Perfect equality on the basis of perfect trust between parents and children is a distinguishing trait of the family," Riis wrote. At the same time, however, the Roosevelts were strict about morals and other "serious" subjects, and made it clear who was in charge. Teaching largely through example, the Roosevelts brought up their children to be wholesome and self-reliant. They recognized that each child was different and tailored their approach accordingly. Their goal was to prepare their children to be productive, useful citizens, yet also to help each to fulfill his or her potential. According to journalists, the childrearing regime associated with the Roosevelts— and followed by many other celebrity families—produced children who were productive, patriotic, and sensible in their outlook toward life, who responded to the new freedom that modernity offered by making the right choices. This was a stinging rebuke to the old-style bourgeois family as well as the patriarchal "familialism" practiced by many immigrants. In the view of journalists, both these models of family life failed to appreciate the individuality of children and strained relations between children and parents, producing not responsible citizens but rebels and reprobates.[22]

Ironically, while the new regime emphasized individual differences among children, it downplayed the gender differences that had been central to childrearing for centuries. Riis and other journalists noted, for example, that the Roosevelts encouraged their daughters to be physically active and interested in all sorts of things—even if their proper role, as TR often asserted, was merely to be wives and mothers. Their eldest daughter, Alice, was widely heralded as the "ideal American girl," a young woman whose charm and grace were matched by intelligence, physical vigor, and "intense energy"—traits, Emma B. Kaufman asserted, that made her very much like her father. "She wants to see, to know, to do. She astounds by her capacity for life and living." By the 1920s the feminist implications of the new regime were being more forcefully articulated, as women with careers, usually actresses, assumed the mantle of the "ideal American girl" formerly monopolized by society belles. In 1934, for example, Adela Rogers St. Johns praised Katharine Hepburn as "the finest type of girlhood and womanhood that America produces," and ascribed her many good qualities to a quintessentially progressive upbringing. Like Roosevelt, Hepburn was raised in a home "run entirely for the children." And while she was greatly influenced by her feminist mother, who brought her along to suffrage meetings and imbued her with a belief in women's potential, it was Hepburn's father, a hard-working yet fun-loving surgeon, who encouraged her interest in sports and patiently answered her many questions in a manner that fueled her curiosity and intelligence. With such an upbringing, St. Johns observed, "it was only natural that Katharine should grow up to admire women who *did* things." But intelligence and a yearning for activity did not make Hepburn any less of a woman. Her soul remained "maternal," despite her commitment to individualism. Thus Hepburn's example was reassuring: though progressive childrearing encouraged women to think and behave more like men—as individuals—it could not obliterate their essential difference.[23]

Even more important than parents were the spouses of celebrities, particularly the wives of prominent men. Their duties, journalists reported, were wide ranging, encompassing the old as well as the new. Chauncey Depew's wife, for example, confined herself to domestic responsibilities so that she could keep up their home and maintain the health and mental vigor of her hard-working husband. "Hers is the brain that maps out the routine of his day, hers is the hand that replies to the countless social invitations that inundate him, hers is the verdict that decides on acceptance or regret, hers is the voice that calls a halt and is heeded when tired nature has been crying out unheard." According to reporters, a similar course was followed by the wives of Andrew Carnegie and Henry Ford, whose domestic exertions were portrayed as essential to their husbands' ability to escape from the pressures and worries of business. Carnegie, a writer for *Ladies' Home Journal* suggested, was well aware of the important role that his wife, Louise, played in his life, and "not one husband in a thousand could show a heartier appreciation of such unusual solicitude." But perhaps the most widely publicized helpmeet of the early twentieth century was Edith Wilson, who was credited with saving her husband Woodrow's life after he was felled by a massive stroke. As Charles A. Selden explained,

> In addition to what the country's best medical skill could do, something more and something just as vital was required during the emergency of the President's illness. Mrs. Wilson furnished that indispensable something more. She succeeded so wonderfully in saving the President from anxiety and unhappiness that the doctors had the chance to make their part count. It was she who protected him from the effects of persecution which, in his physical weakness, would have been fatal, but against which the sick-room door would have been no adequate barrier in her absence.[24]

By the 1920s and 1930s the wives of celebrities had assumed additional duties. Besides managing the home and relieving their husbands from having to worry about the children, they also respected their husbands' "idiosyncrasies" and allowed them to grow in their own way. A supportive wife, journalists argued, was one who loved and accepted her husband for who he actually was—and not one who viewed him as some kind of "project" whom she could refine or change. This kind of encouragement was revealed to be important to the success of figures as diverse as Ford, the head of Standard Oil, Walter Teagle, and the entertainer Will Rogers. "There are at least sixty-four kinds of girls that Will Rogers might have chosen for wife," Jerome Beatty noted in the *American Magazine.* "His wife might have turned out to be socially ambitious. She might have dragged Will to parties; she might have bought him a dress suit and forced him to wear it; she might have complained that his name wasn't in big enough type in the advertising; she might have rearranged his routine; she might have quarreled with his managers; she might have been terrifically jealous of his leading women." But this would have "ruined" Rogers, for he was like "an old oak, meant to grow in its own way." Indeed, any attempt to "train" him, Beatty argued, would have undermined the very qualities that made him popular: "His entire success lies in the fact that he is just himself." Fortunately, the woman he did marry, Betty Blake, a fellow Oklahoman, had the good sense not to try to change him and cheerfully tolerated his many eccentricities.[25]

There were times, however, when a more assertive approach was required. Some famous men did not possess the self-confidence and will-power of an Andrew Carnegie or a Henry Ford; nor were they lucky enough to possess the personality of a Will Rogers, which required only that he be allowed to be himself. They needed a wife to do more than orchestrate an anxiety-free domestic life and allow them to grow unimpeded. According to Beatty, Paul Muni, the Oscar-winning movie actor, was just such a man. Fortunately, Muni had a wife, Bella, who could compensate for this and give him the kind of support he required to achieve success and fulfillment. A former actress in the Yiddish theater, where she and Muni met before he became a success, Bella was the most important person in his life. They were "constant companions," on the set as well as at home, and Muni relied heavily on her for advice about parts, performances, and contract negotiations. And for good reason. Bella, the daughter of a well-known theatrical family, knew a great deal about show business. She knew even more about the strengths and potential of her talented but diffident husband. It was Muni's shyness, lack of self-confidence, and quixotic impracticality—seemingly fatal drawbacks—that made his reliance on Bella so crucial. Having given up her own "promising career" to devote herself to his, it was Bella who "led him up the path to the heights, helped to keep his chin up and to make him what he is today." Without his wife to urge him on, Beatty speculated, Muni "might have been a drifter in and out of the theater, never mounting the peak that only a fighter can reach." Here support meant not simply allowing a man to grow in his own way. It meant helping him make the most of himself by focusing his talent and encouraging him to achieve his full potential. As Beatty made clear, Bella was not changing Muni so much as helping him grow by enabling him to gain the roles that would allow the full expression of his gift for acting.[26]

Bella Muni's sublimation of her own talents and ambitions into the career of her husband was hardly unusual. For every wife who supported her famous husband in the more or less traditional fashion, there was another who adopted the more assertive role epitomized by Muni. The women most likely to take the assertive course and have their activities acknowledged by the press were the wives of politicians. One of the first to be portrayed in this light was Mary Bryan, the wife of the perennial Democratic presidential candidate William Jennings Bryan. As Willis J. Abbot revealed in a profile of the Bryans in *Munsey's* in 1907, Mary Bryan was an enterprising, highly intelligent woman who might have gone far had she employed her talents to further her own career. But instead, she had used them—and continued to use them—to further the political career of her husband. "All through their married life," Abbot reported, "she has been studying things that would help Will—shorthand, typewriting, proofreading, the art of editorial expression, and the mysteries . . . of bimetallism." In short, Mary was more than a secretary, more even than a conventional helpmeet. She had a "knowledge of politics . . . as no other woman ever possessed," and early in their married life she had studied law and was admitted to the bar—"not with any expectation of practising" but merely to assist Bryan in his understanding of the issues. Together they put out a weekly newspaper, "The Commoner," which was very much a joint venture. Though overshadowed at the time by the more traditional Edith Roosevelt, Mary Bryan was in fact a harbinger of the future. In subsequent years, journalists would portray the wives of politicians along increasingly Bryanesque lines, stressing their interest and involvement in political issues, and the substantive advice they gave their husbands. This was especially true after the passage of women's suffrage, when the controversy over women's involvement in politics began to wane. The First Ladies Lou Henry Hoover and Eleanor Roosevelt were the most widely publicized of such woman, with Roosevelt acquiring from her political activities the stature of a bona fide political celebrity.[27]

Remarkably, despite devoting themselves to their husband's professional activities, political wives still managed to fulfill all of their responsibilities in the home. Mary Bryan, for example, "for all her intellectual work," was a "thoroughly competent working housewife," and because of this the Bryan home was "a model of neatness and good domestic management." The lack of attention devoted to this theme, however, betrayed an implicit belief that readers were more interested in the unconventional activities that the wives of politicians engaged in. These were far more exciting than their skill at "domestic management." In 1933 Eleanor Roosevelt confessed to a reporter from *Ladies' Home Journal* that she found housekeeping "irksome," a burden she minimized through "systematizing" and "planning," techniques that other women might employ in order to give them more time to do the things they enjoyed—from spending time with their children to helping their husbands with their work to fulfilling their own ambitions through activity outside the home. Far more than the wives of businessmen or entertainers, political wives like Bryan, Hoover, and especially Roosevelt personified the new opportunities available to women in the early twentieth century. Directing their ambitions and interests toward work that supported or was compatible with their husbands' careers as politicians, they expanded the ideal of "partnership" beyond the home. Yet they never forsook their domestic duties, and played crucial roles in providing their husbands with the moral and psychological support that was a hallmark of the new "companionate marriage"—even when, as in Roosevelt's case, their work took them away from their homes and husbands for considerable periods. The publicity given to their activities was a testament to the growing conviction among journalists that politics was an area of interest to women, an area where men and women might work together in common cause. The repeated assertions that political work need not impair domestic life gave this new model of marital relations even greater appeal.[28]

Less common but more significant were couples in which the women as well as the men were devoted to their careers. The most visible of these "modern marriages" were those of entertainers and movie stars. Journalists noted that where husband and wife worked in the same field, common experiences and an understanding of the industry and its pressures allowed them to develop a much stronger bond than would have been possible had each married an "outsider" instead. Yet while offering each other advice and encouragement, these couples knew not to make their work—or the money they earned from it—the focal point of their lives. Mary Pickford and Douglas Fairbanks, for example, devoted most of their time not to "shop talk" but to various forms of play—swimming, horseback riding, travel, intimate dinners, parlor games with close friends—which enabled them to maximize the enjoyment they derived from their time together. George Burns and Gracie Allen also owed the success of their marriage to their ability to keep their work from affecting their happy home life, and, like Pickford and Fairbanks, avoiding lengthy separations that doomed many other show-business marriages. In addition, Fairbanks and Burns were very thoughtful, specializing in small, romantic gestures that made their marriages perpetual honeymoons. According to journalists, the key to the successful marriage of Carole Lombard and Clark Gable was their great love of jokes and games, and the eagerness of Lombard in taking up hunting, skeet shooting, and other masculine sports. "Being a shrewd and pragmatic young lady," Henry F. Pringle observed in a profile of the couple in 1940, "Carole has made herself part of the life which so greatly enchants her husband." Gable, to his credit, welcomed her competitive zeal in all these endeavors, even when she beat him at his own game.[29]

Making "modern marriages" work, in other words, not only required women to take up activities that were commonly regarded as the pastimes of men—and even act more like men, as Lombard did. It also required men to accept women as equals and friends, and support their desire to continue their careers. As Adela Rogers St. Johns suggested, there was much to be gained when wives broadened their horizons and took up activities that brought them into regular contact with their husbands. Writing about the actress Helen Hayes in *Liberty* in 1934, St. Johns revealed that before Hayes met her husband, the playwright Charles MacArthur, she had led a relatively sheltered life, largely among other women. "She got few breaths of reality, never encountered life in the raw." Her affair and subsequent marriage opened up new worlds for her, allowing all the passion, eagerness, and "hunger for life" that had seethed within her to come out and find expression in a whirl of exciting activities. It also inspired her to display more assertiveness in her dealings with theatrical producers and movie executives, and was crucial in enabling her to get the best parts. Fortunately for Hayes, MacArthur fully supported her decision to continue with her career rather than retire and devote herself to him and their young daughter. According to St. Johns, Katharine Hepburn's husband, a Wall Street broker, was equally supportive of his wife's aspirations—even though it meant that she had to spend a lot of time in Los Angeles while he remained in New York. Having met Hepburn when she had already decided on a career in show business, he was "fair enough to see that she must carry out where her restless energy, her ambition, her whole training had led her." Making the most of the opportunities they had to be together, their marriage was the epitome of "perfect understanding and comradeship."[30]

But as St. Johns and other writers acknowledged, the "extraordinary success" enjoyed by such couples was not always conducive to marital bliss. Many "modern marriages" fell apart, including Hepburn's. The reasons that journalists gave for the breakups varied. In some cases, they resulted from a gradual "growing apart," a process more likely to occur when a couple was mismatched or brought divergent expectations to the relationship. This was the lesson that St. Johns drew from the "tragic" separation of Pickford and Fairbanks, for example. From the start, St. Johns insisted with the authority of a true insider, Mary and Doug were "as different as two people could be," and over time "[t]hose traits in each that were most different developed most strongly." In other cases, marriages broke up because commitment to a professional career was time-consuming and mentally draining, encouraging self-centeredness and requiring long separations that led even many well-matched couples to drift apart. Careers distracted couples from each other, and from the means by which relationships had to be continually nurtured. Needless to say, it was virtually always the men who objected to their wives' devoting so much time and attention to their careers. Some men came to resent the success their wives had gained. According to a writer for the *Saturday Evening Post,* this was why the columnist Dorothy Thompson and the novelist Sinclair Lewis had broken up. For several years the two writers had been quite supportive of each other; Lewis had regularly proclaimed himself Thompson's "staunchest fan." But after Lewis won the Nobel Prize he became conceited, and as Thompson's star began to rise in the mid-1930s while his seemed to decline, he "took unkindly to being put in the shade."[31]

The lesson offered by such reporting was clear. One spouse could offer tremendous support and encouragement to the other, including the psychological support that a person needed to grow and fulfill all of his or her potential. But a spouse's ability to provide such support depended in large part on the time and emotional energy that he or she could invest in the relationship, and on the neediness of the other party. People lacking magnetism or self-confidence—the vast majority —needed husbands and wives to be more supportive, to play the essentially therapeutic role that Bella Muni played for her husband Paul. Of course few men were willing to forsake their careers in such a fashion; the best that a woman could hope for was a husband who did not mind if she refused to relinquish hers. As the literature on celebrity divorces demonstrated, however, there were few men who could stand "being put in the shade." As a result, female celebrities often had to go it alone, making their romantic lives a perennial "problem" that could not be resolved unless they retired and assumed a more conventional role— the conclusion of many a popular novel and film, including *Woman of the Year* (1942), in which Katharine Hepburn played a character modeled after Dorothy Thompson. Some celebrity profiles did downplay this issue and instead stressed the fulfillment that women like Thompson and Bette Davis derived from their work. But it remained lurking in the background, the price that women paid for their success and independence.[32]

Thus, like other forms of popular culture in the early twentieth century, celebrity journalism was ambivalent toward women's growing involvement in the public sphere. Particularly in the years after 1920, it supported the professional aspirations and achievements of female celebrities, and endorsed a new companionate marriage in which husbands and wives were "partners," if not exactly equals. Yet by pointing out the difficulties that female celebrities faced in their romantic relationships—and underscoring the importance of these relationships in achieving happiness and personal growth—this endorsement was at best halfhearted. Women could be successful career women or supportive spouses, helping their husbands fulfill their potential and deriving benefits from their success—but unlike men, they could not be both.[33]

* * *

Though achievements and personal growth were a prominent focus of celebrity journalism, there was another equally compelling theme. According to journalists, quite a few celebrities—men as well as women—had problems that prevented them from being happy and fulfilled, in spite of their celebrity status. Some were problems that had troubled them since they were young and obscure, and that becoming a celebrity had not alleviated. For example, many celebrities from impoverished or working-class backgrounds—Charlie Chaplin, Babe Ruth, Clara Bow, among others—had "emotional scars" stemming from parental neglect, material deprivation, or profound feelings of inferiority thought to be common among the poor. These scars were often cited as the underlying causes of their misbehavior. It was, St. Johns wrote, a "fear of life" born during Bow's troubled childhood and adolescence, when her beloved mother became mentally ill, that led her to "live fast and furiously," partying until dawn and engaging in many affairs. But some of the problems that affected celebrities were relatively new and often a direct result of their newly gained status or their struggle to remain at the top. So grave were these problems that many profiles, after encouraging readers to marvel at the subject's accomplishments and style of life, concluded with a sober message: being a celebrity was not so great after all.

One problem that plagued celebrities was a lack of privacy, especially the privacy in public that ordinary people took for granted. Journalists often noted that their subjects could not dine in a restaurant, attend a movie, or even stroll in a park or on a city street without being besieged by gawkers and autograph seekers. Because of this, celebrities avoided public places. When they did leave the secure confines of their homes or workplaces, it was not uncommon for them to wear disguises to keep from being recognized. Of course, once they were recognized, most of them were courteous and obliging. Yet journalists made it clear that the impositions to which many celebrities were subjected were taxing, making their reclusiveness seem understandable, a natural response to pressures that were truly extraordinary. Perhaps the most hounded of all celebrities was Charles Lindbergh, who had naively assumed that he would be allowed to resume a "normal" life after his spectacular solo flight from New York to Paris. "For a year after the transatlantic flight," Donald E. Keyhoe informed readers of the *Saturday Evening Post*, "Lindbergh had no private life at all. He lived under terrific pressure, struggling for every moment of freedom and undergoing an intense physical and mental strain." Writing in 1931, in large part to refurbish the aviator's tarnished public image, Keyhoe suggested that Lindbergh had recently learned to handle these pressures and tolerate "many things which formerly caused him a very natural irritation." But in subsequent years the pressure never completely subsided, and by the mid-1930s, after his son's kidnapping and murder, Lindbergh again became bitter and reclusive, and his friends in the press were again compelled to rise to his defense. "There is nothing wrong with the man personally," his friend the aviation writer Russell Owen wrote in 1939, after Lindbergh had left the United States for England and come under fire for accepting an award from the Nazi government in Germany. "But he has been so badgered, bedeviled, and annoyed that he has what might be called social claustrophobia."[34]

A good deal of this badgering came not from the public but from representatives of the press. As we have seen, beginning in the 1890s, as human-interest reporting became an increasingly important means of attracting readers, reporters began to demand more and more personal information from public figures. And though many public figures were willing to provide it, others were not, inspiring journalists to become more aggressive and celebrities more reclusive. But avoiding the press only created a new series of problems. One was misrepresentation, which occurred when journalists wrote about reclusive figures anyway and their subjects never tried to set the record straight. This, of course, was how Lindbergh was put into the awkward position of having to submit to a gossipy profile, despite his hatred of the genre. Had he opened up to reporters just a bit, the editor Julian S. Mason suggested in an article on Lindbergh's persistent problems with the press, they would have probably left him alone, satisfied with the small morsels he offered them. By strenuously avoiding the press, however, Lindbergh upped the ante and created a bigger problem for himself. Refusing to answer questions from reporters was also the cause of the largely fictitious "legend" that swirled around Katharine Hepburn, Alva Johnston noted in a profile of the actress in *Woman's Home Companion*. "There was sound reason for her caution," but it led to a raft of rumors that were literally "fantastic." But who could blame Lindbergh or Hepburn or Greta Garbo for refusing to have much to do with the press? As the authors of profiles revealed, correcting misperceptions was difficult, time-consuming, and sometimes even degrading, since celebrities often had to answer questions about subjects they regarded as trivial.[35]

Moreover, there was no guarantee that disclosure would be effective in squelching rumors that might be untrue but that made figures appear "colorful." As Hepburn, for example, discovered, "It was futile to give reasonable explanation for anything she did; the mills grinding out the Hollywood chatter were operating on a different principle." Though sympathetic journalists often chided celebrities like Hepburn, Lindbergh, and Garbo for their unwillingness to cooperate with the press, they usually portrayed their behavior not as foolhardy but as a sign of personal integrity—a determination to lead a "normal" life in spite of their celebrity status. "Fighting for a private life" was how Keyhoe described Lindbergh's determination to carve out a space where he could be free from unwarranted intrusion. Johnston, in his profile of Hepburn, adopted nearly the same language, calling Hepburn "a lone crusader for the privacy of private life" and reveling in her "affront to the vast tale-bearing and keyhole-peeping interests of America." Yet even while lauding a celebrity's dedication to preserving a measure of her privacy, journalists revealed quite vividly that the price paid by celebrities for "brief moments of privacy" could be high: the hostility of the press and consistent misrepresentation.[36]

Opening up to the press created another series of unanticipated problems. As Babe Ruth's ghostwriter ruefully noted in a short meditation on fame in the *American Magazine* in 1935, "A famous man always feels as if he were living under false pretenses, that sooner or later he will be found out and showered with pop bottles." The problem in Ruth's case was hyperbole: the press coverage that he had welcomed had lifted him so high, and so obscured his very "human" frailties, that it was inevitable that he should fail to live up to his billing and disappoint his fans. Though much beloved by reporters, who were grateful for his willingness to talk to them and pose for photographs, Ruth was no more effective than Lindbergh in preventing misrepresentation in the press. Depicted as virtually superhuman in his abilities as a ballplayer, he found himself the object of catcalls and criticism during even the briefest slump. This indignity was exacerbated when reporters who had promoted the heroic caricatures of Ruth turned on him as well, blaming his poor performance on the off-the-field activities that they had systematically covered up in their campaign to present him as a wholesome model for young boys. Journalists defended their fickle treatment of celebrities by arguing that they were only responding to public desires. Readers wanted larger-than-life heroes like Lindbergh and Ruth, and yet they also had an "unceasing thirst" for information that revealed the heroes to have feet of clay. This combination of desires, which the press sought to satisfy and subsequently reinforced, was attributed to the American social system, a leveling mechanism that in Russell Owen's words "hoists heroes on pedestals only to throw mud at them later." While superficial, this explanation was not entirely wrongheaded. But it conveniently let the journalists off the hook by making their role seem passive.[37]

An even more disturbing problem was the way in which celebrity status affected personal relationships and made celebrities attractive to people with ulterior motives. Being a celebrity, journalists reported, often brought big money and lucrative business opportunities, and celebrities were inundated with requests for financial assistance and letters seeking to interest them in investment schemes or product endorsements. Most of these requests came through the mail, but some were promoted by people who managed to penetrate the inner circle and pose as "friends" or "advisors." Celebrities always had to be on guard against such self-interested "sharpers," who were eager to exploit their access to line their own pockets. To make matters worse, it was not uncommon for old friends to be corrupted by proximity to the riches and influence that friendship with a celebrity allowed. For example, the prizefighter Jack Dempsey was forced to fire his long-time manager and erstwhile best friend, Jack Kearns, when he discovered that Kearns had begun to exploit him. The most widely publicized victim of sharpers and self-interested sycophants was Charlie Chaplin. According to Jim Tully,

Chaplin's unhappy experiences with people professing to be "friends" had made him lonely, bitter, and suspicious toward others. While dining at the Ambassador Hotel in Los Angeles, for example, Chaplin was showered with smiles and admiring glances from attractive women. But rather than be flattered, he was disturbed: "They know I am Charlie Chaplin. If I came in here an unknown, no one would look at me." Ironically, Tully noted, there was nothing that Chaplin enjoyed more than interacting with people who did not recognize him; they treated him like a regular person. Such encounters, however, were not only infrequent but fleeting. Sooner or later Chaplin would be recognized, and when this occurred his companions would became stiff and awestruck, and the rapport that Chaplin had established with them would be destroyed.[38]

These pressures took their toll on many celebrities. The constant attention they attracted when in public, the unrelenting badgering by the press, the often exaggerated and misleading stories that were published about them even when they cooperated with reporters, the wariness that they were compelled to exercise in their dealings with people, even in private life—all of these encouraged celebrities to feel anxious and self-conscious, as if the press, the public, and even their most intimate comrades were constantly spying on them. This self-consciousness, journalists argued, led many celebrities to "pose" with reporters and in public—and sometimes even at home, since the habit was hard to break. Not surprisingly, posing was most common among actors and movie stars, who were accustomed to playing roles. To one degree or another, however, it affected all celebrities who were recognizable in public and thus vulnerable to the pressures of fame. Indeed, as a writer for the *Saturday Evening Post* observed in 1906, the "acting" that politicians, businessmen, and other civic leaders engaged in was merely an extension of the posing that ordinary people practiced as well: "Everybody is an actor, more or less. The good ones know it. The poor ones do not." Yet because celebrities were recognizable to people who did not know them personally and the subjects of regular coverage in the press, they were more conscious of the pressure to pose, and they yielded to it much more. "When millions of people conspire to make you believe that you are a marvel," noted Mary Pickford and Douglas Fairbanks in 1929, "it is sometimes easy and pleasant to accept this generous verdict and behave as nearly as you can in the way in which you think a marvel would act."[39]

Here lay the biggest problem confronting celebrities and, as journalists made clear, all successful men and women—the danger of developing a "swelled head." Celebrities with swelled heads were aloof, egotistical, affected, and cynical. Few celebrity profiles, to be sure, portrayed their subjects in quite these terms. But the repeated assertions about celebrities who had not succumbed to the affliction certainly made readers aware of it, and perhaps inclined to believe that other celebrities, exposed to the same factors, had proved more vulnerable. This suspicion may have been reinforced by articles revealing the transgressions of celebrities—actions that seemed to run counter to what they claimed to stand for—that implicitly invoked the swelled head as the cause of their behavior. Many reporters covering the presidential campaign of 1912, for example, suggested that a swelled head, and not a commitment to progressive ideals, was behind Theodore Roosevelt's break with the Republican Party and decision to run as a third-party candidate. A similar diagnosis was reached by journalists reporting on the "misbehavior" of Hollywood stars in the early 1920s and by some of the reporters critical of Charles Lindbergh. Lindbergh's swelled head was particularly severe, journalists in the late 1930s and early 1940s suggested in response to his growing commitment to isolationism. As Roger Butterfield argued in a highly critical profile published in 1941 in *Life*, years of living in a fishbowl had made Lindbergh contemptuous of ordinary people and liberal democracy—and easily impressed by the traitorous Cliveden set in England, who encouraged his interest in "strange ideas" like fascism. Haughtiness, arrogance, selfishness, self-indulgence—all were signs of trouble, signs that a celebrity might be developing this disturbing condition.[40]

Informing these stories was an interesting and important assumption—that wealth, power, and social prestige tended to corrupt their possessors. This belief, as numerous scholars have demonstrated, had deep roots in Western culture. But its most potent source of inspiration was the Protestant critique of vanity and worldly achievement that was brought to America during the colonial era, a critique that in the eighteenth century was translated into secular language by republican critics of monarchy and privilege. For much of the nineteenth century, belief in the corrupting influence of wealth, power, and social prestige was confined to the margins of American society, a dim, pessimistic counterpoint to the liberalism that celebrated social mobility and material achievement. In the late nineteenth century, however, the belief was revived by proponents of the Social Gospel and progressive reform as part of a broader attack on class divisions and the materialism brought about by industrialization and the rise of consumerism. And in this secular and progressive guise, it came to influence the mass-circulation press, especially human-interest reportage like celebrity journalism. Employing this theme was an effective rhetorical strategy, giving newspapers and magazines a pseudo-populist editorial voice and making journalism resonate with the complex and often conflicted views of working-class and middle-class readers— Americans disturbed by many of the social and economic changes of the period yet reluctant to consider the possibility that the United States was becoming permanently stratified along class lines.[41]

But the press's use of this discourse was selective and equivocal. While invoking the swelled head as a condition that could easily be contracted by successful people, journalists also demonstrated that it was possible to resist it. The subjects of the great majority of profiles, like Keyhoe's Lindbergh, were living proof of this. They remained modest about their abilities and achievements—even when others extolled them as "geniuses." Their modesty, moreover, extended to their personal demeanor. Celebrities who resisted the swelled head were down-to-earth and unaffected. They did not act like big shots or pose in public, and when they encountered ordinary people they made them feel at ease. This ability to remain natural made it easy for these celebrities to make and keep friends—sincere and loyal friends who appreciated the celebrities for who they really were, not the self-interested types who were drawn to celebrities because of what they could gain from them. And being modest and down-to-earth, the celebrities were resistant to disingenuous flattery and could quickly discern when a person was sidling up to them for the wrong reasons. Along with their families, these friends formed the core of a nurturing inner circle, in which celebrities were treated no differently from anyone else. Finally, celebrities who kept from getting a swelled head retained their optimism. They continued to look at life and the world with the same youthful, energetic spirit they had possessed earlier in life. Though aware of the traps that could ensnare them, they refused to become cynical.[42]

Resisting a case of swelled head took conscious effort, a determination not to be "spoiled" by the rewards and pressures that came with being a celebrity. Drawing on the conventions of nineteenth-century advice literature, journalists likened these efforts to keeping one's "balance." Yet by this they did not mean having the rational and benevolent faculties dominate the baser ones that provoked the selfish behavior associated with a swelled head, an internal struggle in which the goal was self-mastery. Rather, for journalists in the early twentieth century, balance meant maintaining the integrity of the self against outside forces that conspired to undermine individual autonomy and kept a person from growing in his or her own way. Celebrities maintained their balance by recognizing that no matter how hard they tried to improve themselves or how high they rose, it was impossible to completely overcome the weaknesses characteristic of every human being. This allowed the celebrities to take pride in their achievements without feeling as though they were a species apart from ordinary people. Celebrities who kept their balance were able to poke fun at themselves—a powerful antidote to the sense of self-importance to which they were particularly vulnerable. They were also practitioners of positive thinking, refusing to be hardened by events in life that made others cynical or jaded. Regardless of the hand that life dealt them, they continued to have faith—in themselves, in other people, and in the notion, as Henry Ford put it in 1921, that "the world is run on the right principles and is getting better all the time."[43]

The key to preventing a case of swelled head, however, lay in the manner in which celebrities lived their private lives. Surrounded by friends and family who treated them like "normal" people, celebrities ensured that in private they could be themselves, which then made it easier for them to resist the temptation to act "great" in public. According to Jacob Riis, this advantage of a healthy private life was why Theodore Roosevelt was so adamant about spending as much time as possible at his real home in Oyster Bay, New York, and why he and his wife, Edith, insisted on continuing family rituals even when living in the White House. The same commitment, Morris Bacheller noted in *Munsey's*, led Andrew Carnegie to "escape" to his castle in Scotland, where he indulged his fondness for play and where he and his wife regularly fraternized with the locals. The tennis champion Helen Wills was also determined to lead a normal private life, John B. Kennedy revealed in 1926 in *Collier's*. Though besieged with admirers and invitations to parties, which might have enabled her to create a veritable "court," Wills remained a "home girl" committed to her family and her undergraduate studies at Berkeley. As we have seen, in Donald Keyhoe's view Charles Lindbergh shared this determination to enjoy "a quiet, simple, and happy home life" outside the glare of the spotlight, where he could be loved and appreciated not as a great aviator but as "old likable Slim." Carving out an autonomous private life not only allowed celebrities to avoid developing a swelled head. It was also a prerequisite for achieving happiness and fulfillment—perhaps the most important lesson that celebrity journalism offered to readers. By illuminating the struggles of celebrities to remain essentially the same as before—"normal" in the lexicon of celebrity journalism—profiles suggested how ordinary people might cope with some of the same pressures and perhaps achieve happiness as well.[44]

This was certainly the message of an article attributed to Mary Pickford and Douglas Fairbanks that appeared in 1929 in *Liberty*. The key to being happy, they advised readers, was to live exactly as one wished. "We discovered long ago that what we liked best were simple things, ordinary enjoyments, the freedom from all social compulsion, the right to live and act without dictation," Pickford and Fairbanks reported. During their reign as movie stars, however, they had often found it difficult to maintain such an autonomous course. Most people—including some visitors to their home—expected them to be witty and glamorous, as they imagined movie stars should be, and when they discovered Pickford and Fairbanks to be quite ordinary they were disappointed. To prevent this from occurring, Pickford and Fairbanks were often tempted to ham it up, to satisfy their visitors' expectations. But they did not give in to this temptation, recognizing it as the first step to a swelled head. After a hard day's work at the studio, they noted, "we permit ourselves the luxury of being natural and doing exactly what we want to do."[45]

Though these problems were particularly serious for movie stars and other celebrities, Pickford and Fairbanks insisted that they affected ordinary people too. "One of the commonest illusions is that in order to make an impression on other people we must assume qualities we do not possess, adopt airs that sit but poorly upon us, and in general try to sustain the fiction that we are more gifted, important, and splendid than we really are." This, of course, was an extension of the modern emphasis on personality, a project that people felt compelled to undertake in their private life as well as at work, but that Pickford and Fairbanks suggested was alienating. Not only did it inspire a lot of insincere, awkward posing; it also produced anxiety and amplified feelings of inferiority, as people struggled to shape their lives around the expectations of others, not their own preferences. The result was an epidemic of conformity, as Americans from all walks of life looked to others, rather than within themselves, for cues on how to live and act. This "strain of acting up to people's expectations," Pickford and Fairbanks argued, was what prevented celebrities and ordinary people alike from achieving happiness. In their obsession with satisfying the expectations of others, people had lost touch with their real selves. Rediscovering and protecting one's "ordinary self" from these outside pressures, they concluded, was the only sure route to happiness and a "peace of mind that is worth any price."[46]

* * *

The ability to follow one's own course and achieve the "peace of mind" that came from autonomy was the essence of true success, the ideal that shaped virtually all celebrity journalism in the first half of the twentieth century, and still shapes much of it today. Celebrities who embodied the ideal of true success—the vast majority, according to the authors of profiles—made the most of their talents and potential, cultivating personal habits and mental powers that enabled them to achieve *and* grow. They also enjoyed deeply satisfying personal relationships with people who helped them reach their goals by nurturing and respecting their unique personalities. And once they reached the top, they did not allow the pressures of being a celebrity to upset their sense of balance, an even more impressive achievement. Modest, down-to-earth, and optimistic, they were living proof that it was possible to achieve tremendous success and public recognition yet not become corrupted by them—not develop values that separated the successful from the rest of society and encouraged them to think they were better than everyone else. In other words, the celebrity who achieved true success might be rich, powerful, influential, or widely revered. But he or she could not be accused of adopting the outlook or airs that have commonly characterized elites.

This message was not merely ideological but patently fantastic. It was a collective exercise in wishful thinking that ignored the realities of class in twentieth-century America, where new institutions, a vastly enlarged economy, and heightened specialization had empowered a new managerial class while making many Americans feel like little more than cogs in an enormous machine. The discourse of true success acknowledged that successful people might be motivated by mean-spirited ambitions or use unseemly methods to gain material success and public distinction. And it recognized that these successful people might be changed by wealth and status in ways that were undesirable, reinforcing class distinctions that threatened the very foundations of American society. Yet by asserting that their subjects had avoided this fate, the producers of celebrity journalism directed the public's attention away from these disturbing facts and conjured up a more cheerful scenario. Depicting celebrities as paragons of true success—even with the specter of the swelled head hovering in the background—journalists encouraged readers to believe that America's most successful individuals were not very different from themselves. From this point of view, the few celebrities who were different—who had succumbed to a case of swelled head—had "failed." But this was no cause for alarm. That so many celebrities succeeded in the struggle boded well for the vitality of American democracy.

This was only the beginning, however, of the ideological work that the discourse of true success was called upon to perform. As we have seen, embedded in celebrity profiles were briefs in support of personal growth and individual autonomy, goals that journalists regarded as vitally important in the new urban-industrial age. Indeed, during the early twentieth century a wide array of newly empowered professionals and "brain workers"—from physicians and social workers to popular novelists and moving picture screenwriters—offered ordinary Americans much the same advice. This was no coincidence. By promoting these beliefs, journalists and their allies in the professions and the emerging culture industries were engaged in a campaign to transcend divisions of class, ethnicity, and gender and forge a new national community founded on the consensual embrace of "modern" values. At the heart of these values—the nucleus around which they revolved—were growth and autonomy, the sine qua non of true success. Linking celebrities to this new regimen, then, not only encouraged the public to identify with the successful and well-to-do, obscuring the fault lines of class. It also gave the new regimen increased cachet and made palpably clear, through real examples, what could be gained if readers followed it. Moreover, by placing more emphasis on growth and autonomy than on material success, journalists made it clear that the latter, while desirable, was not necessary to being happy and fulfilled. As crafted by journalists and their allies, the ideal of true success was more accessible to ordinary people and peculiarly well suited to women, the lower middle class, the working class, and a large number of immigrants and ethnics—all of whom tended to view private life as more fulfilling than the world of work and public achievement. Promoted by a wide range of institutions, true success became the modern, therapeutic alternative to Victorian respectability.

Of all the institutions peddling it, however, perhaps none was as important as the mass-circulation press. In the early twentieth century newspapers and magazines reached a much larger audience than conventional prescriptive literature, and by the 1920s and 1930s experts in the helping professions had come to recognize the influence of the press and were developing strategies for extending their own influence by making use of it. Also, reports in the press, even human-interest stories, benefited from the aura of objectivity that many newspapers and magazines actively cultivated, perhaps giving the messages that they conveyed more weight than those disseminated by overtly fictional vehicles like motion pictures and popular novels. At the very least, celebrity journalism and the plots of many movies and novels worked in concert, reinforcing themes that were common to all these cultural forms.

The pivotal role of the press in promoting the discourse of true success was also encouraged by its unique position in relation to the popular audience. Like the helping professions, the upper echelons of mass-circulation journalism were dominated by men and women who were well educated, worldly, and deeply committed to serving a useful public function. Yet by virtue of their need to sell their products to a large number of readers, journalists had to be more sensitive to the interests and desires of their target audience. For journalists, being sensitive meant recognizing the new opportunities available to men and women in the modern age, but also recognizing the constraints that dashed their hopes and easily produced feelings of frustration. True success was a perfect solution to this predicament, an ideal, cobbled together from residual as well as emergent materials, that acknowledged the often disturbing new realities of life in an urban-industrial society. But after acknowledging these realities, the ideal of true success then dissolved them in a haze of therapeutic platitudes, directing readers toward a new goal that unlike the old was at once attractive and seemingly within reach.

MR. WEBSTER IN NEW YORK—GOING TO BOSTON. —Mr. Webster, the great statesman of New England, arrived in town on Saturday night, and remained here all day yesterday.

He was called upon, during his brief visit, by many of his sincere admirers and friends, who were happy to find the distinguished Senator in excellent health, considering the fatigue incident to the present painfully severe struggle in Congress. At dinner, in company with two or three friends, the natural elasticity and playfulness of his great mind were displayed, to the enjoyment of his guests, while, occasionally, the topics hinging upon the state of the country, showed that he is deeply impressed with the paramount importance of the admission of California. It is to the settlement of this question that his mind continually reverts; and he has a kind of porental anxiety about it, that, in a measure, absorbes every other feeling.

Mr. Webster will be in Boston, probably, in time to see his friends, in front of the Revere House, at half-past five o'clock this afternoon. Mr. Benjamin R. Curtis, a distinguished gentleman of Boston, supported by the presence of Colonel Perkins, Mr. J. P. Davis, and other citizens, will address the Massachusetts Senator. He will, of course, allude to his recent noble position in the Senate, and the response, on Mr. Webster's part, will follow the spirit and temper of the address. Mr. Webster will speak very briefly—probably not more than fifteen or twenty minutes; but he may be expected to impress upon his hearers, and upon New England, the importance of abandoning the silly agitation in which certain small politicians indulge; of abiding by the constitution, and all the conservative elements of the confederacy; and of coming up manfully and patriotically to the occasion—meeting the difficulty with that self-sacrificing spirit by which alone it can be dispersed. His speech will be an important one to New England, and consequently full of interest here, at the South, and everywhere. Without regard to expense, we have prepared to receive it by telegraph, and shall issue it to-morrow morning.

Mr. Webster will remain in Massachusetts only

An early example of celebrity journalism: a short descriptive account of Daniel Webster's visit to New York City. From James Gordon Bennett's New York Herald, *29 April 1850, 4. (Library of Congress)*

PEOPLE ARE MORE SOBER

Miss Willard, Home from Abroad, Says Even France Is Leaning Temperance-ward.

SUNDAY CLOSING FOR IRELAND.

Calls Roosevelt the Wonder of the Age, and Praises His Work for the Cause.

THE BICYCLE AS A FOE OF ALCOHOL.

The Gifted Reformer Gives to the World a Poem on Anglo-American Friendship.

Miss Frances Elizabeth Willard, the temperance evangelist, landed from the American line steamship New York yesterday overflowing with the milk of human kindness and more than ever convinced that the world is getting soberer. She presided over the great international temperance convention in London, at which a petition for the suppression of the whiskey traffic was shown signed by seven and a half million persons. The fact that she was called to the chair she regards as a great compliment to America. She thinks that it will tend to promote the harmonious relations between the two countries if Lady Henry Somerset presides over the next temperance congress in this country.

Miss Willard was accompanied by Miss Anna Gordon, who goes everywhere with her and whom she described as her guide, counsellor and friend. In her suite were also two stenographers and Miss Charlotte E. Maxwell, founder of St. Botolph's gymnasium in Boston, who puts her through the Lingg system of gymnastics, which is intended to harmoniously develop all the muscles. "She is the head of the heap," said Miss Willard, "and after practising her exercises I feel that I am glad to be in the world."

Those Who Greeted Her.

A number of members of the White Ribbon Army greeted Miss Willard with flowers and enthusiasm. Mrs. Ella A. Boole, of Staten Island, First Vice-President of the Woman's Christian Temperance Union of this State, was there as the delegate from the union's convention, just closed at Rochester, to greet the home-comer. Miss Kate Lunden, a Scandinavian evangelist, was there too. Mrs. W. Jennings Demorest, always the last person Miss Willard sees when she leaves America and the first to greet her when she gets back, overwhelmed her with kisses. Miss Willard's nephew and niece, Mr. and Mrs. Woodward Baldwin, were also on hand.

Mr. Baldwin built up a seat with trunks and rugs for his aunt. She said she wanted to be on a level with her interviewer, as it tired her to look up or down. Then with her large, kindly, gray-blue eyes lighted up with enthusiasm she told her story. She wore a heavy cape coat and a russet-colored straw hat, in which were the white wings of a bird. Some "advanced" women say that the slaughter of birds for material in women's...

You took a drink with him when he was in New York? Well, I guess I'm wrong. Oh, I was thinking of Alphonse Daudet. The President of France, M. Faure, has strong views on temperance.

"I think Mr. Roosevelt is doing a grand work in New York in enforcing the Excise law. The captain of the New York sent me some late copies of The World that he got at Quarantine and I have eagerly read about Mr. Roosevelt's attitude. I am glad that a man of his wealth and prestige is so much of a patriot as to stand up for the laws regardless of attack and insult. He is a wonder of the world and I have been doing nothing but talking him up.

Local Option if Women Voted.

"Local option would be a good thing if women were enfranchised. It is a practical measure, in line with our position. But the only lever with which you can lift whiskey and drop it overboard is prohibition. All devices for limiting it are nets with big meshes in them and holes, too, through which the fish escape.

"It is proper and right that if you have saloons at all they should be closed on Sunday. I do not believe that man should spend his Sabbath in a rum shop, while his wife mopes at home. Men and women should take their amusements together. I do not approve of that style of the separation of the sexes.

"The British Parliament has passed a law giving practical Sunday closing in Ireland, even in the big cities like Dublin. I think the public houses are

anxiously after the latest news as to challenges. She had the English theory that perhaps the Defender won because she is made largely of aluminum and she spoke of "outside weights" and other deep technicalities.

While thinking over the relationship between the two countries Sept. 21, while in London Miss Willard's attention was attracted by the little English flag carried by some of the omnibuses. She sat down and wrote a poem.

"The World has been very kind to me on several occasions," she said to The World reporter, "and I very gladly give you the verses for first publication in your paper."

Here is the poem:

The Flag on the Omnibus.

(By Frances E. Willard, of Chicago.)

The eyes that follow thee, old flag, are fond;
A Western heart leaps up thy folds to greet;
A Saxon's eyes confess the sacred bond,
As England's standard flutters down the street.
With its red for love, and its white for law,
And its blue for the hope that our fathers saw
Of a larger liberty.

Thou art the mother flag of destiny.
Our banner of the spangled star is there;
Cromwell was sire of Washington, and we
Claim the same cross that blazons thy ensign.
With its red for love, &c.

O holy flags, bright with one household glow,
Together light the highway of our God.
Till the dear Cross of Christ to men shall show
That stripes and stars both mark the path he trod
With their red for love, &c.

The long march of the nations shall be led
By these two flags, till war and tumult cease,

him that Lady Henry Somerset and Miss Willard are not as disinterested in the liquor fight as their friends think. Miss Willard said that she gave Mr. Hicks credit for believing that he is properly informed, and that evidently he is a man of education, but that the time which she might devote to joint debates with him would be eaten up by other matters which had engaged her attention before his kind offer reached her.

AUTUMN STYLES AT STERN'S

There Is a Fine Display of New Headgear and Other Novelties.

The autumn display of styles at Stern Brothers in West Twenty-third street reveals some very pretty things in all the departments. Three new hats are the carriage hat, theatre bonnet and the street hat. The former is a very broad affair, short in the back, with point applique lace over the brim and trimmed with ostrich feathers and loops of black satin ribbon. The theatre bonnet is very small and has a frame of sable tails, with loops of white satin ribbon, covered with spangled chiffon, and white ostrich tips in the back, standing and falling on the hair. The street hat is an imported virot with a crown of velvet dressed in silk having an immense bunch of blue poppies on the right side and on the left a bunch of violets.

The prettiest thing in headwear, however, is a sailor of dark green felt

An example of "personalized" news, focusing on the temperance advocate Frances Willard and making extensive use of quotations culled from an interview with her. From Joseph Pulitzer's New York World, *29 September 1895, 4. (Library of Congress)*

MISS VANDERBILT---- OUR NEW DUCHESS.

This Tells All About the Young Heiress Who Will Secure a Foreign Title for the Vanderbilt Millions.

NOT REMARKABLE IN ANY WAY, BUT A GOOD AVERAGE AMERICAN GIRL.

Just How Old She Is, How Big She Is, What She Wears, Her Accomplishments, Her Habits of Life and Her Enormous Fortune.

PERSONAL DESCRIPTION.

AGE—Eighteen years.
HEIGHT—Five feet six inches.
COLOR OF HAIR—Black.
COLOR OF EYES—Dark brown.
EYEBROWS—Delicately arched.
NOSE—Rather slightly retrousse.
WEIGHT—One hundred sixteen and one-half pounds.
FOOT—Slender, with arched instep.
SIZE OF SHOE—Number three, AA last.
LENGTH OF FOOT—Eight and one-half inches.
HAND—Delicate, with tapering fingers.
SIZE OF GLOVE—Five and three-fourths.
LENGTH OF HAND—Six inches.
WAIST MEASURE—Twenty inches.
LENGTH OF SKIRT—Forty-four inches.
FACE—Somewhat oval.
COMPLEXION—Clearest olive, with rosy cheeks.
CHIN—Pointed, indicating vivacity.
MOUTH—Small and without character.
TEETH—White, regular and well kept.
LIPS—Full and describing a Cupid's bow.
ACCOMPLISHMENTS—Music, painting, languages.
CHIEF ACCOMPLISHMENT—None.
MARRIAGE SETTLEMENT—$10,000,000.
ULTIMATE FORTUNE—$25,000,000 (estimated).
EARS—Small and close to the head.
HEAD—Well rounded and well poised.
SPECIAL FAD—None.
FAVORITE COLOR—Pink.
FAVORITE SPORT—Tennis.
FAVORITE RECREATION—Bicycling.
FAVORITE FLOWER—American Beauty rose.

Miss Consuelo Vanderbilt is one of the greatest heiresses in America. The Duke of Marlborough is probably a most eligible peer in Great Britain. The engagement of the young Duke this young heiress is the most notable social event of the year 1895—the most notable in many ways since the great Vanderbilt ball. Their marriage will unite the conspicuously moneyed house of Vanderbilt with the celebrated and historical house of Marlborough. From the standpoint of Fifth avenue it will be the most desirable alliance ever made by an American heiress up to date.

Miss Consuelo Vanderbilt will be the most youthful American Duchess in England. She will be only nineteen on her next birthday. On the day of her marriage she will unquestionably be more than half a million for every year she has lived, to say nothing of what she may ultimately fall heir to at her father's death.

chapeau where any color is introduced. She affects the wearing of large hats, and is never in any but those of the Gainsborough style. Miss Vanderbilt does not discard her muslin frock on cool evenings, but dons a cape of white broadcloth or one of rose-colored silk. She is very partial to capes as outer garments, and of them she has a special array, each fashioned in becoming style and elaborately trimmed.

HER TASTES AND EDUCATION.

Miss Vanderbilt is not a seminary girl or college graduate, but has always received private instruction by a resident governess and visiting tutors. She is of an artistic temperament, loving flowers and pictures. She is wont to roam through the art galleries when abroad, and not a few of the elegant paintings which hang in Marble House are examples of her selecting.

The Future Duchess of Marlborough.

(FROM MR. HARPER PENNINGTON'S OIL PORTRAIT OF MISS CONSUELO VANDERBILT.)

A full-page Sunday supplement feature on Consuelo Vanderbilt, soon to become the Duchess of Marlborough, entirely devoted to personal details that reveal one of the nation's richest young women to be "a good, average American girl." From the New York World, 29 September 1895, 29. (Library of Congress)

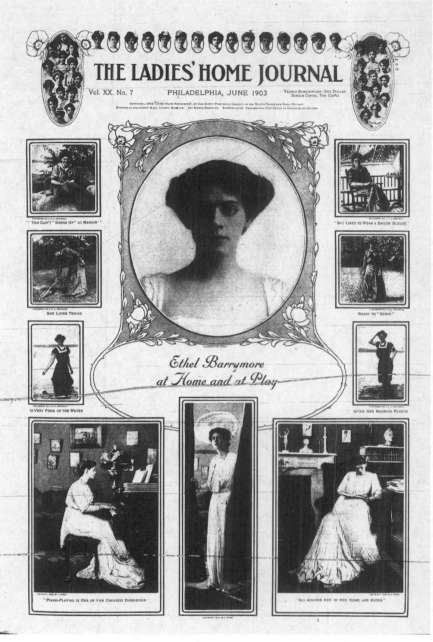

A full-page photo essay that accompanied a feature story on the actress Ethel Barrymore. The use of such photographs was a salient feature of the new-style mass-circulation magazines that began to appear in the 1880s and 1890s. From Ladies' Home Journal, *June 1903, 3. (Library of Congress)*

WILLIAM JENNINGS BRYAN
From his latest photograph by Townsend, Lincoln, Nebraska

THE HOME LIFE OF WILLIAM JENNINGS BRYAN

BY WILLIS J. ABBOT

THE DEMOCRATIC LEADER WITH HIS WIFE AND HIS CHIL-
DREN—THE FINE ESTATE AT FAIRVIEW, NEAR LINCOLN,
NEBRASKA, AND THE BUSY BUT CHEERFUL ROUTINE OF THE
HOUSEHOLD—A PICTURE OF SIMPLE AMERICAN DOMESTICITY

ONE must concede a certain humorous side to any description of the
" home life " of a gentleman who, having just completed a tour of the world
occupying some eighteen months, remains
at home twenty-four hours and then
starts off cn a political pilgrimage
through the Southern States by way of
rest from the rigors of foreign travel.
Few men in this country have traveled

A human-interest profile of the politician William Jennings Bryan focusing on
his "home life" and marriage. Such articles were quite common in newspapers
and magazines in the early twentieth century, giving the men who dominated the
realm of politics a more domestic aura. From Munsey's, *February 1907, 588–92.*
(Library of Congress)

MR. FORD IN HIS FIRST CAR

HENRY FORD'S
Experiment in Good-Will

by
GARET GARRETT

WHEN a meddler drops the S wrench into the wonderful mechanism of supply and demand, there is work for the engineers. They denounce his unintelligence, repair the damage, and wearily note another instance to prove the unexceptional working of the governing principle. But fancy a mechanical genius himself doing it deliberately!

Most unexpectedly and at an exceptional time, when the supply of a certain elemental commodity, in Detroit as elsewhere, so greatly exceeded the demand that unemployment was an acute municipal problem, the Ford Motor Company broke the rules with the amazing announcement that it would pay double the market price for labor.

Nothing like that had happened before, in all the history of modern industrialism. An unnatural commotion immediately followed. Unemployed rushed to Detroit from other cities. Thousands clamored in vain at the Ford Plant for work, and had at last to be wetted down with a fire hose. And at all of the big hotels, promoters, contractors for automobile parts, economists, newspaper correspondents, efficiency engineers, pension-plan specialists, profit-sharing experts, students of eugenics, seekers of money for worthy purposes, magazine writers, and others stood in line from 8 A. M. till midnight, waiting for rooms and bath at five dollars a day and up.

Opinions of the Ford Experiment begin violently to differ at the point of first intentions. The announcement was made in a manner to be regarded either as unimaginably naive or so intentionally theatrical as to produce the maximum quantity of advertising. The employees first read of it in

462

A celebrity profile of a businessman, Henry Ford, emphasizing his role as an "industrial statesman." Note that the language employed in the title evokes pragmatism as well as religious ideals associated with the reformist Social Gospel movement. From Everybody's, *April 1914, 462–74. (Library of Congress)*

The Hidden Talents of "Jack" Barrymore

Nobody thought he "had it in him" to become the great actor he is to-day

By Keene Sumner

THERE are two Barrymores, in one way, of course, there are three: there is Ethel; for, in spite of her being Mrs. Russel Colt, she will keep on being Ethel Barrymore to the end of the chapter. There is Lionel, who, after disappearing into private life for a dozen years, came back to the stage two years ago and has been gathering honors ever since. And, finally, there is John. It is of him I am speaking when I say there are two Barrymores, for the youngest of the trio is not only John, but also Jack.

A few years ago there were no outward and visible signs of John's existence. He was all Jack, then, a clever player of comedy parts, a matinée idol and movie hero; a tall, goodlooking figure in the gay night life of New York. Brilliant? Yes. Talented? Yes. But just Jack Barrymore, with all that the name implies of easy, careless living and working.

No manager wanted to give him "serious parts." All that was asked of him was to go on the stage and act like Jack Barrymore. No one had a more graceful way of handling a wine glass or a cigarette. No one was nicer to the manner born in the rôle of a dashing and dissipated society hero. So that was the kind of part he was usually supplied with.

Even at that, he had his drawbacks, at least, from the manager's point of view. He was as irresponsible as the wind—and far less easy to count on. These were no weather predictions to tell the anxious manager whether Barrymore would be a gale, a zephyr, or even whether he would, figuratively speaking, blow at all. Pretty much like the wine, he blew—or at least, blew in—as he listed.

Of course, in the slang of to-day, he got away with it. Brilliant young actors are not any too plentiful. And, besides, Jack Barrymore had a charming personality, which made people smile over his escapades. There was a quality in him that was partly the spark of genius and partly the unquenchable spirit of Youth; and even his critics were warmed by it.

For all that, however, most of the more or less smiling observers of his career thought that he had, figuratively speaking, bought a through ticket in the gay that it was not going to take him any great height.

And then something happened, something that made a stir on the New York "Rialto," that section of Broadway where the theatre signs blaze by night and all slances and conditions of theatrical folk pass and repass by day. At Woods, the manager, electrified "the profession" by announcing that he was going to give Jack Barrymore a serious part. At least, it was a near-serious one, that of the young crook in "Kick-In," not exactly a Shakespearean rôle, but so radical a departure from the usual type of Barrymore parts that the wiseacres sat up and took notice. He told me about it himself, with a half smile for those who had not believed in him and a wholly sincere note of feeling for the man who did believe.

"People thought Woods was crazy to trust me with the part," he said. "His friends—perhaps they thought they were my friends, too—remonstrated with him; told him he was a fool himself and would make a fool of me. They said I couldn't play anything except comedy rôles.

They flourished the usual theatrical measuring stick of 'personal limitations.' According to them, mine were marked out by my previous parts: from the young good-for-nothing who gayly and facetiously wins out in The Fortune Hunter down to Anatol of the lively Parisian adventures. These, it appeared, were the limit for me, and Woods was besought to let well enough alone, and not try to make a poor character actor out of a fairly good comedian. That he did not yield to their protests showed a confidence in me for which I shall always be grateful."

In the few years since that experiment Barrymore has traveled far and fast, both as an actor and as a man. For even then, at first, he was still the gay, mercurial being who was the despair of managers. And the most significant aspect of the change from "Jack" to "John" Barrymore is something which is not peculiar to his career alone. It happens to thousands of other men in other callings.

This is what I mean: There are, in all of us, hidden reservoirs of power and of ability whose existence other people do not suspect. Perhaps we ourselves do not know that they are there. Perhaps we do know that we have them, but we go along very comfortably without using them. We don't want to be bothered to dig down and find them. We hate to make the effort. Oh, what's the use! We're having a jolly good time as it is. Being bigger, or doing something that the world calls better, takes effort; even if it is only the effort of being different.

Then, perhaps *(Continued on page 140)*

Are You Using All the Power You've Got?

"THERE are, in all of us, hidden reservoirs of power and of ability whose existence other people do not suspect. Perhaps we ourselves do not know that they are there. Perhaps we do know that we have them, but we go along very comfortably without using them. We don't want to be bothered to dig down and find them. We hate to make the effort. Oh, what's the use! We're having a jolly good time as it is. Being bigger, or doing something that the world calls better, takes effort, even if it is only the effort of being different.

"Then, perhaps just out of pique, just to show that you *can* do what somebody says you can't, you *make* the effort. And the surprising result is this: you discover that the real satisfaction is not in showing somebody else that you can do a thing but in showing *yourself* what you can do."

White Studio

John Barrymore

1. IN "PETER IBBETSON."   2. IN JOHN GALSWORTHY'S "JUSTICE."   3. IN TOLSTOY'S "REDEMPTION."

A FEW YEARS ago, "Jack" Barrymore was merely a clever actor in light comedies, a matinée idol, and a movie favorite. To-day he is acclaimed as a great artist, as the greatest living American actor. His wonderful power of characterization is shown in these four pictures: the weak little English clerk in Galsworthy's "Justice," the poetic dreamer in Du Maurier's "Peter Ibbetson," and the two strongly contrasted types he portrays in Tolstoy's "Redemption."

Barrymore comes of a famous family of actors: Mrs. John Drew, the elder, was his grandmother. John Drew is his uncle; Maurice Barrymore was his father; Ethel Barrymore is his sister, and Lionel Barrymore is his brother. He is 37 years old. His wonderful story is told in the article beginning on the opposite page.

By the late 1910s, American Magazine *had become the most important forum for inspirational celebrity profiles, like this one of the actor John Barrymore. Such pieces often included sidebars where the article's "lessons" were summarized. From* American Magazine, *June 1919, 36–37. (General Research Division, The New York Public Library, Astor, Lenox and Tilden Foundations)*

BABE RUTH, BASEBALL SUPERMAN, EXCELS, TOO, IN MINOR SPORTS

The Home-Run Hero Is Good With Driver, Putter, Steering Wheel And Shotgun, and Fairly Good With Saxophone and Hoe

By RICHARDS VIDMER

GEORGE HERMAN RUTH has no private life, that is, none to speak of. Any one who has seen the behemothian Babe readily realizes that his is not a figure easily overlooked, even in a crowd. When so much glamour surrounds him, it naturally follows that he is besieged and beset, wherever he goes, from dawn until dusk, by hero worshipers, autograph hunters and those miscellaneous masses who rush in wherever crowds gather. Besides, he is on public display almost every afternoon between the hours of 2 and 5.

Yet there are many sides to the babbling Babe which even those who pay a dollar-ten to get into the Yankee Stadium are unable to see with the naked eye from the vantage point of a grand stand seat.

To most of those who visit the house that "Jack" built—Colonel Jake Ruppert's "jack"—Babe Ruth is the greatest home-run hitter that the world of baseball has ever produced. They are absolutely right. But they don't go far enough. He is much more than that; his ability to hit home runs further and more frequently than any one else is only the most remarkable thing about this person who does many remarkable things.

Before delving into his non-public performances it may be well to correct a few impressions in regard to his business life. If Ruth hit no more than five home runs a year instead of sixty, and if his batting average over the span of a season was around .200 instead of .300, he would still be one of the greatest baseball players the world has ever seen.

Most spectators in their wonder at the number of home runs he hits, lose sight of the fact that he throws strikes from the outfield with that powerful left arm that once led the American League in pitching; that he runs bases like a man who weighed something less than 175 pounds instead of one who weighs something more than 220; that he makes more spectacular catches of fly balls than any other outfielder in the league, and that never in all his career has he been known to make a bonehead play.

In explaining why the Yankees have been making another parade of what was advertised to be the American League race this year, Manager Miller Huggins pointed to the club's reserve material as the main reason.

"Lazzari was out with a strained back when the season started," the mighty mite argued, "but Durocher took his place and hit .440 while Tony was recovering. A couple of regular pitchers developed sore arms, but Al Shealey, a recruit, filled in and won six straight games while they were resting. Joe Dugan got in the

the man, though there is a very good one of the name, much to the relief of Mr. Ruth himself.

Did you ever stop to consider how many baseballs Babe Ruth autographs in the course of a year? Well, he doesn't. The vast majority of souvenirs that bear the flowing autograph of Babe Ruth were inscribed by the good right hand of Doc Woods, the Yankees' trainer. After a close study of two baseballs, one signed by Ruth and the other by Woods, one shud-

The Superman of Baseball.

Above—Babe Ruth Is Also a Golfer.

Left—The Home-Run King in Action.

Photograph by Times Wide World.

on which the Yankees are traveling through the provinces stops for fuel, freight, mail or passengers, it is surrounded by the citizens. They all want to see Babe Ruth.

He will quit a card game, abandon an argument, lay aside his saxophone or cease whatever he may be doing at the moment and go out on the platform to make a public appearance. His grin makes friends where before there were only awed admirers. Usually he makes a brief speech, consisting of some such remark as:

"Why don't you folks go to bed? Don't you ever sleep around here?"

Ruth dodges the fuss and the furor as much as possible, but when it is unavoidable he secretly revels in it.

He has a strange sense of pride. In a very close game in last year's pennant race the players of the opposing team were trying to get him cross. The Babe merely laughed at the taunts they threw his way. He was called everything in the dictionary and many things not included in that work. Finally one of the tormentors yelled:

"Hey, you big busher, you're dead and don't know it!"

Thereupon the Babe flared up. He turned on the player who had called him a busher. His eyes flashed. His fists clenched, and he advanced threateningly.

"Look here, you!" he said, "call me a bonehead or a bum if you want to, but don't get personal."

way of a pitched ball when he was in the midst of a batting streak, but Gene Robertson went to third base and hit even better than Dugan."

Mr. Huggins might have continued in this strain indefinitely, except for an interruption.

"What about an understudy for Ruth?" he was asked. "If the Babe got hurt who would take his place?"

There was no answer to that. Probably there never will be an answer. No one can take Ruth's place either on the field or in the box office. He is the superman of baseball. There are no imitations. At least, there are no imitations of

ders to think what Doc could do with the Babe's check-book and a well-filled fountain pen.

But Ruth isn't worrying about that. He is merely relieved that Woods can imitate his famous signature so perfectly, for autograph hounds have always been the bane of the Babe's existence. As a matter of fact, they still are.

It would be pure folly for Ruth to leave the Yankee Stadium after a ball game through the regular players' exit. That is, it would be folly if he expected to reach home in time for dinner. The autograph hunters congregate there in droves and hold up the other Yankees until patience is tried, but the Babe would be blocked indefinitely.

So he uses a secret passage, then peeking out to see that no one is watching and then making a wild dash for his car, which is parked at the curb guarded by a policeman. Wary and watchful, as are the urchins of the Bronx, they have not been able to discover the Babe's departing point yet. Far be it from this article to divulge it.

In other cities, Ruth has to leave the park through the same exit as the other players and take his chances. He has lightened his labors abroad by making an iron-

clad rule in regard to autographs. As he steps out of the clubhouse door and the rush starts, he pauses and with a gesture halts the deluge that threatens to submerge him.

"Wait a minute; wa-alt a minute!" he bellows, and the advance falls back in awe at the sound of the great man's voice. "I'll sign for anybody who has a baseball and a fountain pen. No books, no papers, no score cards."

MOST of the idolaters drop back in disappointment, baffled. A few come forward smiling, armed with the stipulated supplies. Some have baseballs but no fountain pens. Some have fountain pens but no baseball. Without both they are eliminated. No matter how heavy the traffic around him, the Babe never loses his temper. In fact, he is one of the most obliging of the world's famous men. He laughs his way out of crowds.

Ruth's popularity with the public around the major league circuit is great, but in the towns and villages where the Yankees never play it is even greater. A crowd stood in the rain at midnight for a train that was an hour late, just for a glimpse of the mighty mauler, and the Babe obliged them. Whenever the train

MOST of the idolaters drop back in disappointment, baffled. A few come forward smiling, armed with the stipulated supplies. Some have baseballs but no fountain pens. Some have fountain pens but no baseball. Without both they are eliminated. No matter how heavy the traffic around him, the Babe never loses his temper. In fact, he is one of the most obliging of the world's famous men. He laughs his way out of crowds.

The Babe is fond of a number of things; horses, practical jokes, children, music, dancing, and all kinds of card games, poker and pinochle in particular; but his real pets are his bats. He calls them by name. Black Betsy, a distinct brunette, was his first love. Betsy was the bat with which he set the world agog by hitting fifty-nine home runs in the course of one season. Then Betsy was broken, and the Babe all but wept. He acquired Big Bertha, however, an ash blend, and did very well. Then he added Beautiful Bella, a Titian type, to his family, and between Bertha and Bella he broke his own record with sixty home runs last season.

Besides poker and pinochle, the Babe plays a great deal of bridge, and plays it rather well, unless

(Continued on Page 22)

George Herman Ruth, Lieutenant of Police Reserves in New York.

Photograph by Times Wide World.

A celebrity profile of a sports figure from the New York Times's Sunday magazine, demonstrating that human-interest journalism was as common to the august Times as it was to the sensational tabloids. From the New York Times Magazine, 1 June 1928, 9. (Library of Congress)

The *Inside* of the *Bowl*

Doug and Mary in the act of being happy to get back from Europe.

Wide World photo

Or, How to Be Happy Though Famous

By

MARY PICKFORD
and
DOUGLAS FAIRBANKS

THE editor of this magazine asked us if this could be advertised as the first article which we have ever written together. We feel tempted to answer that he can go further than that and say that it will be the last one.

In other words, there have been difficulties. We first tried dictating it in relays, one taking up the burden when the other had lost his breath. We got along all right until it developed that we were writing on totally different subjects. As a piece of writing it possessed distinct originality, but it lacked the kind of clarity that magazines and readers demand.

The procession of " I's," which is bad enough in any personal narrative, becomes particularly awkward when it is impossible to tell to which co-author the pronoun refers. So we started using " we," but when we had written this sentence: " We spent the afternoon in having our hair dressed and exercising on the parallel bars," we decided that this method, too, had its weaknesses.

We offer the result, therefore, with misgivings and with a blanket apology to cover its shortcomings. It furnishes conclusive proof that in some things, at least, two heads are not better than one.

Our decision to write this article together was the result of a discovery that without knowing it we were bent on the same errand. The discovery was not a remarkable one, since the errand is the same on which every mortal is busily engaged from birth till death: the quest of happiness.

The reader will please not infer, simply because we have chosen to indulge in this innocent speculation, that we take ourselves to be authorities on the subject of success and happiness, or that we hope with a few deft words to settle the question once for all.

It is our belief that no one upon whom fortune has heaped a full measure of success has really the slightest idea of how it all happened. One can always, when pressed for reasons, dig back into one's early life and discover sterling traits of character, fine habits, and indomitable perseverance that pointed like arrows to future achievement. But we would be great hypocrites if we did not acknowledge that luck has played a leading part in our lives. So, if we were writing one of those little homilies to youth that are so popular these days and wished to be logical, we should have to say, " Be as lucky as possible and nothing can prevent your ultimate success."

To be slightly more serious, there is something, of course, in knowing how to handle and extract full advantage from luck when it arrives. Otherwise luck will be something that happens to somebody else.

Without the sudden (and for us very lucky) growth of the motion picture as a popular medium of expression, where would we be today? The reader can guess this as well as we can. Our guess is that we would not now be asked by magazines to account for our success.

If there is one thing that exceeds the futility of telling people how to be successful it is telling them how to be happy. By following the usual rules, and by unusual

[CONTINUED ON PAGE EIGHTEEN]

A seminal rumination on "true success" attributed to Mary Pickford and Douglas Fairbanks, though probably written by their publicists. Note that being happy and famous is assumed to be difficult. From Liberty, *9 November 1929, 14. (Library of Congress)*

PEOPLE

"Names make news." Last week these names made this news:

From his huge ranch at Larkspur, Colo. **Robert Patterson Lamont Jr.,** son of the U. S. Secretary of Commerce, started for Moscow. He had been offered the job of straightening out Red Russia's cattle industry, at $50,000 a year. Rich, "Bob" Lamont was not tempted by the salary. But the problem of rehabilitating Russia's livestock (which has suffered because peasants slaughtered their beasts rather than turn them over to the collective farms) "is so tremendous that any stockman could not help but be interested."

In Washington's zoo a six-year old gorilla named **N'Gi*** lay ill of a severe chest cold. Because no gorilla had ever lived to maturity in captivity doctors gave

up hope as N'Gi grew weaker. Rich, kind-hearted, publicity-loving Editrix **Eleanor Patterson** of Hearst's Washington *Herald* wired to New York for an oxygen tent. In it, N'Gi continued alive. He took a drink of whiskey, a hot toddy compounded of port wine sent him by German Ambassador **Friedrich W. von Prittwitz und Gaffron,** felt better.

Edith Rockefeller McCormick, daughter of **John Davison Rockefeller,** explained the Depression in terms of astrology for North American Newspaper Alliance and the Chicago *Daily News:* "Every 2,000 years, when we come into a new astrological house, such a crisis takes place. I am sure that those living at the time of the birth of Christ must have experienced relatively the same problems which we are experiencing today. . . . Each one of us is being uprooted. Uprooted so that we face in the opposite direction to that which has been the direction for 2,000 years. This change is inevitable and no one can escape it. Its

*Pronounced *Enjee*.

great purpose is the control of the balance of the universes. . . ."

The $10,000 **Edward W. Bok** award, given annually to a Philadelphia benefactor, was awarded for 1932 to "The Unknown Citizen of Philadelphia." given the unemployed.

"Villa Lewaro," the palatial home built at Irvington-On-Hudson, N. Y. by the late **"Madame"** **Sarah J. Walker,** Negro, who made a fortune from the sale of hair-straightener, was bought by Companions of the Forest of America. The fraternity plans to make the estate a retreat "for tired mothers and their dependents."

At the emergency relief depot in Fond du Lac, Wis. an aged applicant for help gave his name as William Stanton, 107, said he was a brother of **Edward McMasters Stanton,** Secretary of War in Lincoln's cabinet. He wanted a job trimming trees.

In the presence of his mother, **William Randolph Hearst Jr.,** 24, was sworn in by Manhattan's Mayor Walker as a commissioner of local school board No. 9.

Exulted film Actress **Gloria Swanson** in London: "I am going to have another baby! Isn't it wonderful!" Now married to Michael Farmer, Miss Swanson has a daughter Gloria, 12, by her second husband Herbert Somborn; also an adopted son Joseph, 8.

Cartoonist Fontaine Fox (*Toonerville Folks*) tried to get an injunction in a Los Angeles court to restrain **Mickey McGuire,** 12, from using that name in motion pictures. The boy, whose name formerly was Joe Yule Jr., had played the title rôle of *Mickey ("Himself") McGuire* (Cartoonist Fox's famed tough-boy character) in a series of films adapted from the cartoons. Allegedly without Cartoonist Fox's knowledge, Joe had his name legally changed to Mickey McGuire, signed a contract with another picture company.

In her apartment in Manhattan's celebrity-infested Hotel Algonquin **Dorothy Parker,** famed writer of pessimistic verse, took an overdose of sleeping potion, was taken to a hospital. Poetess Parker once wrote:

> *Razors pain you;*
> *Rivers are damp;*
> *Acids stain you;*
> *And drugs cause cramp.*
> *Guns aren't lawful;*
> *Nooses give;*
> *Gas smells awful;*
> *You might as well live.*

At Rollins College. Winter Park, Fla. President **Hamilton Holt** presented the sixth "volume" of his "Animated Magazine." Contents of the "magazine" were read by their respective authors in person, among them Editor **Albert Shaw** of *American Review of Reviews,* Author **Zona Gale, Jane Addams,** Professor **Irving Fisher,** Authors **Rex Beach, Joseph Crosby Lincoln. Opie Read.**

5

. . . .
FROM PARASITES TO
PUBLIC SERVANTS
THE REHABILITATION
OF THE RICH

During the mid-1930s, while the nation was struggling with the hardships produced by the Great Depression, new political and social movements were on the rise, and bitter and sometimes explosive conflicts
were breaking out in many regions of the country, one of the most widely
publicized news stories revolved around the misfortunes of an heiress.
Barbara Hutton was the granddaughter of the dime-store magnate
Frank W. Woolworth, from whom she had inherited a huge fortune at
the age of twelve. In the early 1930s, after a glittering debut, she had
become an object of fascination to the press and many Americans. Her
lavish spending, her struggles to remain thin, her tumultuous and invariably ill-fated romances—all were covered in great detail in newspapers and magazines, and from this coverage there arose an image of
Hutton that became firmly lodged in public discourse: that of the "poor
little rich girl."

According to journalists, great wealth had not made Hutton happy.
Having failed to find true love and personal fulfillment, she was absolutely miserable, a textbook example of a celebrity for whom true success remained elusive, forever beyond her reach. Even Adela Rogers St.
Johns, who in a long, three-part profile of Hutton tried to make the
"5 and 10 princess" appear more sympathetic, was forced to concede
this point, noting at the end that Hutton's recent marriage to a polo-
obsessed Georgian count, which St. Johns had sought to portray as a
"love match," seemed to be in trouble.[1]

At first glance, the press interest in Hutton's personal travails seems like yet another example of gossip mongering. But when we take a closer look, it is possible to see other forces at work. The story of the "poor little rich girl" was in fact a modern incarnation of a much older tale, and the press's use of this motif—and efforts to link it to the discourse of true success—was a contribution to an important debate that had raged since the era of the American Revolution. Was wealth and the influence that it brought deserved? Were the rich forces for good, positive models for their fellow citizens? Were they members of their communities and the nation at large? What was the place of the rich in a democratic society? Could a very rich person like Hutton, with enough wealth to live in a manner totally different from the vast majority, a manner redolent of aristocratic pomp and privilege, retain her democratic sympathies?

These questions, which dogged the rich throughout the nineteenth century, became central to their depiction in the mass-circulation press. As we have seen, journalists made coverage of business and "society" a regular feature of the antebellum penny press, and in the second half of the nineteenth century, as the resources devoted to these beats increased, so did the visibility of businessmen and their families. From the outset, however, press treatment of the wealthy was ambiguous. Extolled for being civic leaders or "captains of industry," they were also the targets of criticism, particularly during economic slumps, when their wealth and power were contrasted with the poverty, insecurity, and relative powerlessness of the majority. To deflect these attacks, businessmen in the mid-nineteenth century cultivated public personas that openly displayed their commitment to "producer" values. Deeply influenced by new strains of humanitarianism, they also stepped up their participation in voluntary associations and civic affairs. Involvement in these activities enabled them to win the respect of newspaper publishers and editors—with whom they often socialized—and ensured that stories about them would be mostly flattering, emphasizing their contributions to the community at large.[2]

By the 1880s this strategy had become less effective. While coverage of businessmen and the well-to-do in provincial newspapers and conservative big city dailies remained essentially unchanged, the appearance of new publications aimed at lower-middle-class and working-class readers encouraged important changes that soon affected virtually all publications. To make their papers appealing and credible to these readers, publishers like Joseph Pulitzer, E. W. Scripps, and William Randolph Hearst were compelled to take a more jaundiced view of the rich, exposing the often unscrupulous methods by which they had gained their fortunes and portraying "society" in a less flattering light. Publication of this material in the newspapers of Pulitzer, Scripps, and Hearst eventually forced more traditional publishers to pay attention to these subjects. The result was a steady increase in stories of financial and personal scandals involving the wealthy, stories that challenged their claims to virtue and prompted some newspapers and magazines to up the ante by reviving the republican-inspired critique of the rich that had not been prominent in the mainstream press since the 1850s.[3]

But it was not only a desire to attract new readers who happened to be hostile to the rich that produced this shift in coverage. Even more important were actual changes in the public and private behavior of businessmen and society figures that began in the 1870s and accelerated for the next two decades—developments that the press could neither ignore nor fit into the discursive categories that had long been employed to portray the wealthy as virtuous. The most momentous of these developments was the emergence of a new economic order dominated by large corporations and investment banks, and the rise to power of a new national elite of businessmen who owned and managed these institutions. These men, who included J. P. Morgan, Jay Gould, William K. Vanderbilt, John D. Rockefeller, and Andrew Carnegie, were fabulously rich, possessing fortunes that dwarfed those of provincial elites. They also enjoyed unprecedented power. Not only did they control enterprises that were national and sometimes even transnational in scope, but they also had political influence, especially among legislators at both the state and federal levels, which enabled them to use the power of the state to protect and enlarge their holdings. Their enormous wealth also allowed many of them to lead a style of life that was unparalleled in American history. Shuttling between their enormous urban mansions and baronial country estates, retreating from the wide array of civic activities that had occupied previous generations in favor of more narrowly defined ones that encouraged class consciousness, immersing themselves in pseudo-aristocratic social rituals designed to forge national connections among America's leading families, the late-nineteenth-century rich showed a new determination to set themselves apart from the rest of society and establish a world of their own.[4]

When accompanied by transformations in the American economy, which undermined the economic security enjoyed by many workers, farmers, and small entrepreneurs, these developments produced an upsurge of hostility toward the wealthy—though not necessarily toward provincial elites or the capitalist system as a whole. Eager to exploit this discontent for political purposes, reformers and radicals began a series of blistering polemical attacks against the "robber barons" and "idle rich" who became the new economic order's most widely publicized icons. By 1900 these attacks had begun to take their toll, inspiring a large number of working-class and middle-class Americans to cast their lot with movements committed to arresting corporate power and bridging divisions of class and ethnicity that appeared to threaten the integrity of the republic. The rhetoric of these movements expressed a profound contempt for the rich, and with an increasing number of Americans drawn to them, it was inevitable that such a view should find its way into the pages of the mass-circulation press, especially newspapers and magazines that sought to appeal to working-class readers. By 1905, in response to a significant surge in anti-corporate and anti-rich sentiment among elements of the public whom publishers were determined to reach, much of the press joined reformers and radicals in denouncing the wealthy, casting them as destructive "parasites" whose values were antithetical to those of a progressive nation.[5]

Yet the press was a reluctant ally in this campaign. Newspaper and magazine publishers, often wealthy men themselves, were extremely wary of angering prominent advertisers, and when necessary they pressured editors to ensure that coverage of business was "balanced" and that calls for reform were moderate and "responsible." As representatives of an emerging professional-managerial class largely sympathetic to corporate capitalism, most editors did not need to be pressured to toe the line; support for the architects of the new corporate order flowed naturally from their worldview. Even many reporters, whose backgrounds tended to be less exalted, found it easy to sympathize with businessmen and their families, especially when they opened up to journalists and made it easier for them to see things from the businessmen's perspective. For example, after a spell as a Wall Street reporter, which enabled him to view the activities of big businessmen from the inside, Lincoln Steffens found himself unconsciously identifying with his sources, "imbued with the Wall Street spirit and view of things." Because of these feelings of sympathy and identification, press criticism of the wealthy paled next to that which appeared in socialist organs like the *Appeal to Reason* or in the speeches and writings of left-wing Progressives like Richard Ely, Henry Demarest Lloyd, and Walter Rauschen-busch.[6]

Indeed, the press's determination to be constructive and stem the rising tide of radicalism led editors and reporters to reconfigure the categories of the past and portray some of the rich more favorably, in terms that directly addressed the charges of their critics and made it possible for the public to see them as constructive members of society—not parasites but "public servants." This campaign did not succeed in eliminating public hostility toward the wealthy; in the 1930s, as we shall see, it flared up again. By this time, however, the terms of debate had changed in ways that made it far more difficult to condemn the rich as a class. Though individual businessmen and society figures might come under fire, their transgressions were no longer ascribed to the mere possession of wealth and power. If they were "bad," it was not because they were rich, a fact seemingly confirmed by the large numbers of rich Americans whom the press now portrayed as "good." Unlike Barbara Hutton, these people had found true success—in spite of their wealth and the privileges that it allowed them to enjoy.

* * *

So successful was the press's rehabilitation of the rich that it is now difficult to appreciate how profound and widespread public contempt for them was during the second half of the nineteenth century. Many Americans, raised in a republican- and evangelical-inspired milieu that celebrated the "producer" values of hard work, frugality, and self-control, associated great wealth with aristocratic decadence, a belief that encouraged them to regard the rich as a cancerous growth that threatened the health of the republic. Before the Civil War, as the historian Eric Foner has shown, these beliefs were most often directed at wealthy southern slaveholders, a class that was easy to assail for its aristocratic pretensions. But when the defeat of the South ushered in an era of rapid economic development and dramatically widened the gap between the richest Americans and the rest of the country, northern capitalists and financiers became the objects of public revulsion.[7]

Some Americans, generally middle-class people, admired these figures. Yet as recent work in social and cultural history makes clear, the majority almost certainly did not. Even many middle-class men—businessmen themselves—viewed the emerging class of big capitalists with scorn. This was because the economic transformations of the period threatened an ideal that was sacred to the middle class and working class alike: the ability of white men to achieve their "competence," to become the owners of small farms and shops, to achieve the economic independence that Americans since the era of Jefferson had regarded as a prerequisite for true political independence. By the 1890s a significant number of Americans had concluded that the changes of the past few decades had rendered this ideal obsolete. Believing that it was impossible to recreate a fluid, decentralized economy dominated by small proprietors, they began to develop an interest in collective responses to corporate capitalism, a trend that inspired agrarian radicalism, trade unionism, and the more advanced varieties of progressive reform. Well into the twentieth century, however, many Americans remained committed to petit-bourgeois producerism, and their disdain for the rich was as fierce as that expressed by socialists. Thus it was not envy that led many Americans in the late nineteenth century to denounce the rich. Sermons, advice literature, editorials in many urban as well as provincial newspapers, the labor press, the burgeoning foreign language press—virtually all the organs of middle-class and working-class opinion defined success as economic independence and middle-class "respectability," a modest level of wealth and comfort that by our standards seems almost spartan. From this vantage point, which united middle-class businessmen who remained fervently committed to private enterprise with Progressives and radicals who were hostile to it, the wealthy businessmen who had come to dominate the American economy were symbols of rapacity and excess.[8]

This was the historical context that led many newspapers and mass-circulation magazines to assume a more critical attitude toward the rich. But publishers and editors did more than simply respond to an increase in public revulsion toward these figures. The press was instrumental in encouraging and manipulating this revulsion by casting the wealthy in specific guises that resonated with the beliefs and prejudices of their readers. This practice was motivated in part by a desire to increase circulation, especially among groups who were known to hold such beliefs and were thus more likely to be reached through appeals of this kind. And once journalists adopted it, it easily became a hardened cynicism. As the veteran editor Chester S. Lord noted, many high-minded editors were induced to follow this course quite inadvertently, because it seemed like a good way of "catering to people who like this sort of reading." Over time, though, as editors came to rely on it more and more, "they gradually absorb[ed] the flavor" and lost all their scruples.[9] Among publishers like Pulitzer, Scripps, and Hearst, however, the new editorial stance was also sparked by political ambition, an interest in positioning their publications as the voice of a unified public and transcending the class and ethnic fault lines that ran across the social landscape of industrial America. Creating such a unified public required redrawing the symbolic boundaries that the press and bourgeois ideologues had drawn in the mid-nineteenth century—lines that had united elites with the middle class and members of the working class who shared their commitment to bourgeois "respectability." The new boundaries drawn by the press and various Progressive reformers pointed toward a rapprochement between the middle class and the largely ethnic working class, as both embraced the new role of worker-consumer. More important, the redrawing of these lines encouraged the public to believe that the rich had no place in this emerging "modern" nation.[10]

The archetype that informed press criticism of wealthy capitalists between 1880 and 1910 was of course the robber baron, a figure of awe-inspiring malevolence who personified the trusts, syndicates, and mammoth investment banks now coming to dominate the American economy. In the view of much of the press, the robber baron was a destructive force in American society, a throwback to an earlier era when men, unrestrained by morality or religious faith, freely indulged their desires for wealth and power, creating an environment where chicanery and cutthroat struggle were widespread. Like the railroad tycoon Jay Gould, the robber baron could be a speculator who bought and sold assets solely to line his own pockets, without regard for the goods or services that he might provide the public. Or he could be a crafty, unscrupulous "fixer" like J. P. Morgan or E. H. Harriman, men who obsessively and manipulatively craved dominance over their rivals and autocratic power. Becoming very rich was only the beginning of Harriman's ambitions, Edwin Lefevre observed in *McClure's* in 1907. His real aim was to become "Czar of the railroad empire of the United States." The robber baron could also be an industrialist like Andrew Carnegie or John D. Rockefeller, one who would regularly and remorselessly use unethical and illegal practices—spies, stealing patents, securing secret rebates from shippers—to acquire monopoly power and keep the prices of his goods unnaturally high. In doing so, the monopolist gained a kind of control that journalists often likened to that of feudal landlord. "Every man and woman and child between the oceans is serf to Mr. Carnegie, and directly or indirectly must render him tribute," Alfred Henry Lewis asserted in 1908, noting the high price of steel that had resulted from Carnegie's business practices. The robber baron was no more charitable toward his workers. Like Henry C. Frick and George Pullman, he had no compunction about exploiting his workers, mercilessly cutting their wages and laying them off during slumps, hiring strikebreakers when they walked off the job, employing all sorts of unscrupulous tactics to keep them from asserting themselves collectively. While these practices allowed the robber baron to keep profits high, they were driving workers into the arms of radicals and, journalists noted ominously, increasing the likelihood of violent revolution.[11]

But the domination of the robber baron over his own field was not the only threat that he posed to the republic. Having bested his more ethical, law-abiding rivals, exploited and impoverished his workers, and rigged his operations to keep stock prices and the cost of his products needlessly high, he had then proceeded to bribe and cajole politicians—the putative servants of the people—in the hopes of making them his "hired men" and preventing the public from using the powers of the government to regulate his nefarious activities or curb his ever-expanding power. This was the disturbing message conveyed by David Graham Phillips's muckraking expose in *Cosmopolitan*, "The Treason of the Senate," which sent shock waves throughout much of the country in 1906. According to journalists like Phillips, Alfred Henry Lewis, Lincoln Steffens, and Charles Edward Russell, robber barons from various industries, under the auspices of the sinister Morgan and with the aid of prominent politicians in both parties, had coalesced into a unified plutocratic class, what the editors of *Cosmopolitan* described as the "Owners of America." And from this perch they were determined to protect their wealth and power from the majority who were coming to recognize the dire threat that they posed to democracy, individual opportunity, and social justice. In short, the rise of the robber barons was not just an economic problem. It was a political problem. By blocking forces committed to reform, wealthy businessmen were encouraging frustration and resignation among common people, sapping their faith in the efficacy of the democratic process, and creating conditions that most Americans viewed as characteristic of the autocratic, class-ridden Old World.[12]

This belief was reinforced by newspaper coverage of "high society." For most of the nineteenth century, editors and reporters had confined themselves to covering the activities of local notables, with wire service reporters providing brief items about elites in other cities, particularly Washington and New York. An increasing reliance on wire services and feature syndicates, and a growing awareness of the importance of national figures like Gould, Rockefeller, and Morgan, sparked a tremendous increase in coverage of such figures and in reportage about the social activities of an identifiable national elite that in the 1880s and 1890s began to coalesce in New York. Since the 1870s, when old-stock New York WASPs led by the Astor family had sought to close the doors to arrivistes like the Vanderbilts and the Goulds, the New York press and wire service correspondents had devoted considerable attention to the internecine feud over who constituted "society." And the arrival of even newer money from the provinces in the 1880s and 1890s only made the situation more interesting to the press and much of the public. Eager to display their prodigious wealth, many rich men spent lavish sums to impress established families and gain entry into exclusive circles. Their campaign eventually succeeded but had unintended consequences of decisive importance. The unprecedented orgy of conspicuous consumption that accompanied it was profoundly disquieting to the press and its middle-class and working-class readers—a sign that the very rich had renounced bourgeois respectability in favor of a new creed of ostentation and self-indulgence.[13]

Throughout the 1880s criticism of the very rich escalated in volume, especially after Pulitzer's *New York World* demonstrated the circulation gains that could be made by adopting a more populist tone. And assailing the lifestyles of the rich was more politically expedient than attacking businessmen. It allowed publishers and editors to display populist credentials without necessarily undermining public support for business or capitalism. Thus while relatively few newspapers and magazines published muckraking exposés of big business, many more published critiques of "high society." These critiques multiplied during the depression of the 1890s. Focusing on such events as the notorious Bradley Martin Ball in 1895, newspaper reporters and wire service correspondents portrayed the rich as dissolute and parasitic, a class of Americans who lived amid grotesque opulence and were completely removed from the virtuous mainstream of society. By 1900 journalists and intellectuals had developed a more systematic critique of what David Graham

Phillips called "swollen fortunes." The most widely remembered contribution was Thorstein Veblen's *Theory of the Leisure Class* (1899), but this was only one of many writings in the 1890s and early 1900s depicting the rich as barbaric, decadent, and selfish. For example, writing in the *Saturday Evening Post* in 1907, a pro-business periodical that eschewed muckraking, Phillips vilified the rich and especially the scions of wealthy families who "squander their leisure in more or less degenerating or fatuously trivial ways," aping the manners and lifestyle of European aristocrats, buying rare antiques and *objets d'art* solely for their value as status symbols. "Instead of stimulating the intense American energy toward improvement along really sane and healthful lines," Phillips suggested, "the swollenly rich have stimulated it back toward barbarism."[14]

By 1910 press criticism of wealthy businessmen and high society had increased in volume and bitterness. Moreover, quite a few conservative papers and mass-circulation magazines like *McClure's, Everybody's,* and *Cosmopolitan* had added their voices to the chorus. Yet as more and more publications joined in, the critique became ambiguous. Amid Ida Tarbell's denunciation of Rockefeller in *McClure's,* for example, was praise for the innovative idea of "combination" which he had done so much to pioneer, and hope that the "machine" built by him and other robber barons could be directed toward public ends, a theme eagerly embraced by other writers who were more sympathetic to big businessmen. Amid accounts of their escalating philanthropic gifts was a growing belief that the rich were undergoing a kind of moral awakening that would soon make them full-fledged public servants and restore them to membership in the national community. And amid the often contemptuous coverage of the antics of "high society" was a fascination with their private lives, which were depicted in ways that made the wealthy seem increasingly familiar and "human" to ordinary readers. Scattered among critical pieces, these more optimistic estimates of the rich appeared as early as the 1890s; at this point, however, they were infrequent and often hedged with reservations conceding ground to their critics. After the turn of the century, however, flattering depictions of the wealthy became more common, paving the way for the more assertive defenses of them that came to dominate public discourse by the 1920s and made their rehabilitation complete.[15]

Writing in *Collier's* in 1906, in the wake of Tarbell's widely excerpted and discussed attack on Rockefeller in *McClure's*, the veteran correspondent Frederick Palmer set the tone for the new apologias. After noting how widespread public revulsion of the oil king had become since the 1880s, Palmer made a startling claim: "The truth is that Rockefeller is one of our best millionaires." Unlike the gladhanding and self-promoting Andrew Carnegie, he was frank about his beliefs and commitments. And though Rockefeller had established his trust "by wickedly crushing out small producers," he was nonetheless a "builder," whose highly efficient company advanced American interests in the global struggle for economic supremacy. "If John D. has made countless millions for himself," Palmer noted, "he has also made countless millions for the United States. . . . If he has made himself the richest American, it is something to his credit that he has paid high wages always for the efficiency he insisted on." It was shortsighted for Americans to criticize Rockefeller, when other robber barons were far more worthy of scorn. If we must vilify millionaires, he concluded, "let us abuse the speculators, the vampires, and the worst types, and make reasonable qualifications for the men who, though they build selfishly, are nevertheless creators."[16]

This argument was not entirely new. Journalists in conservative newspapers like the *New York Times* and pro-business magazines like *Munsey's* had been making it since the 1880s. But at a time when anti-business sentiment was increasing, its application to Rockefeller—aside from Jay Gould, the most reviled of all the robber barons—in *Collier's*, a national magazine with Progressive credentials, was an important milestone, revealing a new interest among editors and publishers of similar publications to appear responsible and constructive in their criticism of businessmen. By 1910 they had joined pro-business publications like *Munsey's* and the *Saturday Evening Post* in celebrating "builders" like Rockefeller, leaving criticism of businessmen to the socialist press and a dwindling number of newspapers and magazines who continued, at their own peril, to engage in muckraking.[17] Together, pro-business publications and Progressive ones like *Collier's* and *McClure's* fashioned a new archetype that gradually came to replace the robber baron in public discourse—the "industrial statesman." The outlines of this new figure were sketched as early as the 1890s, when defenders of business sought to portray controversial businessmen like Rockefeller and J. P. Morgan in a more favorable light. Yet the features of the industrial statesman were not fully realized until after the turn of the century, when the rise of anti-business sentiment forced supporters of businessmen to address their critics more boldly. By the teens and especially the twenties the industrial statesmen had become the primary archetype around which press depictions of capitalists, financiers, and corporate executives revolved. And as this occurred, the robber baron was gradually banished to the dustbin of history.

The industrial statesman was not only a builder. According to journalists, he was bold, energetic, even visionary. Possessing an uncanny ability to realize grandiose plans, he made valuable contributions to American society and material "progress." Thomas Edison and George Westinghouse, for example, were inventors as well as promoters, creators of "[n]ew devices for the use of men." Made affordable through expert planning and economics of scale, these devices offered consumers new comforts and conveniences. Westinghouse's contributions to "the material wealth of the world," Robert Mayhew noted in 1905, were "prodigious beyond estimate." The same was true of Rockefeller, whose impressive Standard Oil Company, reporters argued, produced a wide array of petroleum-based goods of high quality at prices far lower than they would be if competitive conditions prevailed. The work of such men heralded a new world of prosperity and widespread abundance. Equally important, however, was the example that they set as employers. Men like Westinghouse, Rockefeller, and P. D. Armour employed thousands of men at high wages. Indeed, they had brought "order" to their industries, reducing the "ruinous competition" that had forced employers to keep wages low and lay off workers during hard times, and making their workers feel more secure. The industrial statesman was also a visionary investor, putting his money into new ventures and industries that would serve as the foundation for future progress. This penchant of the industrial statesman for looking to the future was a big reason why the public misunderstood him. Seeing only the controversial methods that he employed to reach his ends, the public did not appreciate how the results would enrich the lives of every American. As F. N. Doubleday observed in a profile of Rockefeller in 1908, "no new order of things can go into effect without bringing antagonism into being."[18]

Champions of the industrial statesman did not deny that their hero had used unprecedented, sometimes even unscrupulous tactics to build his firm and eventually dominate his industry. However, journalists insisted that these tactics were incidental to the success of his firm, not the primary reason for it, as critics of corporations like Tarbell and Henry Demarest Lloyd argued. The success of men like Rockefeller, Carnegie, and Morgan was attributed instead to their extraordinary talents as builders, organizers, and, most important, "eliminators of waste." Industrial statesmen were not inspired by the profit motive and had little interest in money, except insofar as it enabled them to gain mastery over chaos. Their aim was efficiency, economies of scale, and eliminating the brutal competition that kept wages low, drove many firms into bankruptcy, and made the entire economy susceptible to catastrophic panics and depressions. It was to prevent such problems that Morgan was organizing mammoth combinations like U.S. Steel and International Harvester, Ray Stannard Baker argued in *McClure's*. In doing so, he was simply continuing the "constructive work" that he had been engaged in since the 1870s. "In times of great excitement in Wall Street, when panic and loss threatened the entire economy, Mr. Morgan has been the first to come to the rescue with his money and credit. . . . For many years he has acted as a sort of balance-wheel to the country's finance, wielding his immense power and credit so as to steady the market when panic threatened."[19]

In the view of many journalists, the achievements of industrial statesmen like Rockefeller and Morgan presaged a new era of cooperation among leading businessmen. Impressed by their confidence and vision, rivals had come to trust them, recognizing that all stood to gain from the realization of their plans. By 1910, the profiles of leading businessmen suggested, the high-handed methods that had so appalled Tarbell— and that even apologists like Baker and Palmer had acknowledged— were vestiges of the past, tactics that many industrial statesmen had been forced to adopt because their rivals were using them. Such tactics had been part of virtually every successful man's arsenal, the business writer C. M. Keys asserted in a long paean to Rockefeller's Standard Oil in *World's Work*, a magazine edited by Walter Hines Page that was unusually sympathetic toward business. Kickbacks and bribes, for example, were commonplace. "Every trader and manufacturer expected them." Thus it was not surprising that businessmen who had been too squeamish to use them—or too shortsighted to sell out to trailblazers like Rockefeller—had been driven out of business; on a certain level, for failing to embrace the future, they had deserved to fail. Rather than focus on such figures, the "losers" and embattled independents who were depicted in Tarbell's *History of Standard Oil* as tragic heroes, Keys and other journalists noted how Rockefeller's former rivals had become rich as stockholders of Standard Oil, and that many of them continued to influence company policy as members of its board.[20]

By the second decade of the twentieth century many reporters were suggesting that the rough methods of businessmen in the late nineteenth century reflected an earlier stage of economic development, one that had thankfully passed, allowing the men who had prevailed to conduct their business in a more ethical and public-spirited manner. No less an authority than Ida Tarbell made this claim in "The Golden Rule in Business," an important series of articles in the *American Magazine* published in 1914–15. Writing in 1917 in *Cosmopolitan*, once the fountainhead of muckraking, Herbert Kaufman expanded on this theme, linking John D. Rockefeller to the mysterious mechanism—incomprehensible to the vast majority—that created "progress." "For us," Kaufman noted, "he can never be an idol, but the future will wash the stains from his crushing feet. History will remember what he has done," not "whom he has undone." The argument was further refined in the 1920s, when a new generation of writers, including the journalist B. C. Forbes, who went on establish *Forbes*, began reassessing the legacy of businessmen like Rockefeller, Carnegie, and Morgan and producing even more celebratory accounts of their rise. This view even influenced critics of capitalism like Matthew Josephson, whose book *The Robber Barons* (1934) argued, in classic Marxist fashion, that the predations of Rockefeller and Morgan in particular had been perversely "constructive," preparing the ground for the socialist paradise to come.[21]

The industrial statesman was also a model manager. Rockefeller, Carnegie, Westinghouse, and the meatpacking magnate P. D. Armour, for example, were revealed to be highly skilled in administering their enormous, far-flung enterprises, which were portrayed by journalists as perfectly functioning "systems" or "machines." A profile of Armour in *McClure's* described in laborious detail how he directed his industrial "empire" from a plain desk in the middle of a large room filled with his lieutenants and a small army of clerks. This was the "nerve center" of his operation, the place from which he issued orders and inspired his subordinates. Rockefeller exerted the same kind of influence at 26 Broadway, Standard Oil's headquarters. Writing in 1908, nearly a decade after his retirement, Keys reported that the "spirit" that Rockefeller had put into the business remained. "It is the engine that runs the machinery," he asserted. Industrial statesmen like Armour, Rockefeller, and the automaker Henry Ford had vast knowledge of their firm's operations at every level—knowledge gained, in Ford's case, from walking around his plants and talking to workers. The statesmen excelled at selecting talented, loyal subordinates to whom they could delegate important responsibilities. They also paid their workers high wages and provided them with all sorts of other incentives, including the opportunity for even the lowliest clerk or factory hand to rise into more challenging and better-paying positions. Ford was widely celebrated for his "visionary" profit-sharing plan that nearly doubled the compensation of his factory workers, an "experiment in good-will," the journalist Garet Garrett noted in 1914 in *Everybody's*. Through such innovative policies, the industrial statesman was able to win the respect and loyalty of his employees, reducing the appeal of unionism and resolving the "labor question" that had vexed employers for nearly a century.[22]

The same qualities were displayed by the salaried managers who increasingly became the subjects of profiles between 1910 and 1929. According to journalists, men like Gerard Swope of General Electric and Walter Teagle of Standard Oil were every bit as constructive as the men who had preceded them, bringing to their jobs the same managerial acumen and commitment to maximum efficiency. Swope, an engineer trained at MIT, had worked his way through a variety of positions—including a number of "dirty jobs" that he took strictly for the experience—before becoming president of General Electric, a writer for *American Magazine* noted in 1926. This unique trajectory enabled him to understand the business like no one ever before, and his application of engineering-inspired problem solving to areas like distribution and marketing was crucial to GE's supremacy and Swope's reputation as one of America's premier corporate executives. Teagle's career, Jerome Beatty argued in a profile in 1931, was just as impressive. The son of one of John D. Rockefeller's partners, Teagle had been groomed from birth to assume a position of responsibility in the oil industry. After graduating from Cornell with a degree in engineering, however, he started at the bottom, working for two years at a series of lowly jobs that made him ideally suited to lead the firm in the "new era" of the 1920s. While Rockefeller and Teagle's immediate predecessors as head of the Standard were primarily "Wall Street oil men," Beatty noted, Teagle was much more: "he's a driller's oil man, a tanker captain's oil man, a refiner's oil man." These qualities first became valuable during the First

World War, when Teagle was elevated to the presidency of Standard Oil and had to divert the firm's resources to war production. "At 26 Broadway they needed a giant—not one who understood only financing and the vagaries of Wall Street, but a leader who knew ships and ports and production; a man who could go into the refineries and oil fields and shipyards and give definite, expert orders; a man who could do more than just exhort the workers to speed up production. He had to tell them *how*." Only an executive with vast experience that included engineering and familiarity with manual labor could perform all of these functions, which were essential not just during wartime but afterward, when new challenges facing the oil industry made having such a man at the helm even more vital.[23]

Like their predecessors, men like Swope and Teagle were not motivated by money. As Swope told a reporter, "Money has never been a paramount consideration with me." And journalists suggested that both men could have been much richer if they had followed the main chance rather than dedicate themselves to the ethos of industrial statesmanship. Committed to providing consumers with the products of the highest quality at the lowest possible price, they were true public servants, carrying the values of the industrial statesman into the ranks of the salaried professional-managerial class. As a result, in the view of journalists, these values came to pervade entire organizations and became features of the system, rather than the characteristics of a few individuals with unusual foresight. But for managers like Swope and Teagle, business was also a great game, a romantic adventure that they embraced with tremendous enthusiasm. Teagle asserted that this enthusiasm was the key to success in any line of work and the salient trait of his ideal employee. "I never knew a man to lose a job if he gave it his whole-hearted effort," Teagle informed Beatty, apparently unaware of the mass layoffs that every major firm—including his own—was undertaking during the early years of the Depression. Refuting the widespread belief that the advent of corporate capitalism had taken the romance out of business and reduced even high-level managers to colorless bureaucrats, celebrity profiles of businessmen in the 1920s and early 1930s offered readers a very different picture, one that endowed the industrial statesman with the aura of a virile, swashbuckling adventurer.[24]

By the early 1930s, however, the celebration of the industrial statesmen had ground to a halt, a casualty of the Great Depression. As numerous historians have noted, the Depression sparked a widespread crisis of confidence in the capitalist system, and while most newspapers and magazines remained staunchly pro-business, the number of profiles of businessmen that appeared in their pages sharply decreased. They were replaced by profiles of politicians and government officials like Robert Moses and Harry Hopkins, who represented the realm where the most important innovations now seemed to be made and in whom most of the public appeared more interested. Only Henry Luce's lavish new magazine *Fortune,* which he launched in 1930, continued to portray businessmen as industrial statesmen, extending the themes developed by journalists in the teens and twenties.[25] Yet this high-priced periodical reached far fewer readers than mass-circulation magazines like *American Magazine* and the *Saturday Evening Post,* and its coverage of businessmen seems more likely to have encouraged confidence within elite circles than among the public at large. In the 1940s, inspired in part by the contributions made by businessmen during the Second World War, paeans to the industrial statesman once again flooded the mainstream press, as the new discourse developed by *Fortune* began to influence editors and reporters at other publications and shape the expanding business sections of newspapers and magazines.[26]

In the postwar era, individual businessmen would continue to be accused by journalists of being greedy, arrogant, unscrupulous, and exploitative. But these figures now appeared to be exceptions to the norm of industrial statesmanship that according to the press prevailed throughout American business. This marked a complete reversal of the older point of view. In the 1890s most journalists had regarded the industrial statesman as the exception, a man who stood above the self-aggrandizement and money grubbing that seemed intrinsic to capitalism. By the 1940s, in response to an aggressive public relations offensive conducted by business leaders and the increasingly pro-business orientation of liberals, these unseemly qualities had been effaced from the mainstream media's coverage of business, and leftists who denounced the corporate chieftains of the period as "robber barons" were viewed as woefully out of touch with the times.

* * *

If public service was the mission of the industrial statesman, it was also the aim of another figure whom journalists constructed in response to criticism of the rich: the "progressive philanthropist." Wealthy Americans had been active as philanthropists and leaders of movements devoted to "good works" for generations. These activities, as we have seen, were central to their identities as civic leaders and resulted in the establishment of a wide array of new institutions during the nineteenth century—from almshouses and YMCA missions to art museums and concert halls for opera and classical music. The "new money" interests that emerged in the years after the Civil War continued this tradition, adding their immense fortunes to the contributions of established families. Yet many of these newly rich men—notably Rockefeller and Carnegie—had their own ideas about the most appropriate philanthropic causes, and their money flowed into new areas like libraries, higher education, and medical research as well as more traditional ones. Between 1865 and 1900 reportage about these developments was quite laudatory, emphasizing the benefits that ordinary people stood to gain from the new institutions that these men were endowing. Beginning in the 1890s, however, a few newspapers and magazines began publishing stories critical of this new brand of philanthropy, and the critical notices increased in frequency after the turn of the century. Criticism peaked around 1905, when a gift from Rockefeller to a Baptist charity was refused, igniting what came to known as the "tainted money" controversy.[27]

By this time many journalists had come to view the philanthropy of the very rich with a new skepticism. The most common charge was that Rockefeller and his fellow millionaires gave to charity in the hopes of directing public attention away from their unseemly business practices. According to Ida Tarbell, Rockefeller's gifts were meant to provide him with "a cloak to cover a multitude of sins." Their gifts, moreover, were said to be paltry compared to the size of their fortunes and the lavish lifestyles that most of them led. Many journalists also worried that the philanthropic activities of the very rich were exacerbating the very problems they were meant to relieve. Directed at symptoms rather than the causes of social problems, they reinforced the gulf that separated the giver from the objects of his charity and allowed the rich to revel in their superiority. Carnegie was often accused of giving away money to gratify his ego—a charge inspired by his flair for publicizing his gifts and insisting that the institutions he had endowed bear his name. Though Rockefeller was never accused of egomania, he was attacked for something even more sinister: seeking to control "the very sources of our intellectual and moral inspiration" through his gifts to churches and colleges, including the University of Chicago, which he endowed in 1890. The possibility that the rich might exert this sort of control seemed confirmed when leading progressive academics were dismissed from teaching posts at private universities like Chicago and Stanford for expressing opinions that rankled wealthy trustees.[28]

Just as the "industrial statesman" emerged from the shadow of the robber barons during their heyday, the "progressive philanthropist" began to appear around the turn of the century, as criticism of the charity work of the rich escalated. By 1905, in the wake of the "tainted money" affair, his features were plainly discernable, and in subsequent years he became the more visible archetype informing depictions of rich philanthropists. Not surprisingly, Rockefeller and Carnegie were among the figures who were recast along these lines, a task made easier by the substantial increase that both men made in their gifts to charity between 1905 and 1910.

But the size of his gifts was not the progressive philanthropist's distinguishing feature. It was the spirit in which he gave. The progressive philanthropist, journalists noted, viewed giving as serious business, an activity to which he devoted much time and mental energy. At the same time, however, it was also a "pleasure," the publisher F. N. Doubleday wrote in 1908 in an important profile of Rockefeller that was widely excerpted in newspapers. Businessmen who embraced the role of the progressive philanthropist gave to charity not to distract attention from their business activities or to win public sympathy. They gave because it was a way for them to put their money to good use, providing them with a deep sense of fulfillment. It was an activity they had engaged in for a long time. The large bequests of recent years, reporters argued, were merely the culmination of this commitment, made possible by the huge fortunes earned from business. As Herbert N. Casson noted in a long feature story in *Munsey's* on the creation of the Rockefeller Foundation in 1910, "What [Rockefeller] began as a poor boy in a Cleveland boarding house he is now about to complete on an international scale." Much of this giving over the years, Casson and other writers revealed, had never been publicized, though publicity would have certainly improved the public's estimate of the donors. As for Carnegie's grandstanding, it was excused on the grounds that a penchant for "the romantic and the picturesque," and not a desire to promote himself, had led him to make a spectacle of his giving. More important, journalists asserted that the example set by progressive philanthropists like Rockefeller and Carnegie had inspired other rich Americans to contribute, leading to a massive increase in support for charitable causes. Thanks to the efforts of progressive philanthropists, Casson observed, the impulse to give was becoming "the very motif of American life."[29]

Even more remarkable, however, were the methods they had pioneered to make their giving more effective. Both Rockefeller and Carnegie were praised for being "efficient" givers whose bequests attacked problems at their roots. Doubleday argued that Rockefeller "likes to get at the cause of things and apply his strength and influence in a creative way." He began to investigate the many requests for aid that he received, a function gradually assumed by a "charity bureau" staffed by highly trained "experts." Seeing that this "scientific" brand of giving minimized waste and enabled gifts to have the maximum positive effect, Rockefeller was persuaded to establish the Rockefeller Foundation, which brought him lavish praise and led other wealthy Americans to endow similar institutions. The founding of these institutions, journalists argued, was the logical outcome of the progressive philanthropist's commitment to placing the "charity business" on a rational basis by bringing to it the organizational abilities he had applied to his businesses. While supporters of the approach conceded that it was relatively unemotional, they believed that gifts from the heart needed to be administered by the head.[30]

Here was an important reworking of the conventional understanding of philanthropy. By associating the gifts of men like Rockefeller and Carnegie with the values of scientific expertise and efficiency—values portrayed as antithetical to self-interest and the profit motive as well as to the sentimentality of traditional benevolence—journalists incorporated these men into the pantheon of reformers devoted to creating a better world. The aim of the progressive philanthropist, in this view, was not merely to relieve suffering but to wipe it out entirely, by raising the standard of living of the majority and establishing new means by which ordinary people could be educated, live long and healthy lives, and make the most of their potential. Through these efforts, Casson suggested, "every Dismal Swamp of human misery can some day be drained." In response to fears that rich men were using organizations like the Rockefeller Foundation to expand their power and influence, journalists stressed that the institutions were self-perpetuating and under the control of disinterested experts, not their benefactors. The men Rockefeller had chosen for his boards, a writer for the *Saturday Evening Post* observed in 1925, were those with "the broadest grasp of the situation to be considered," and once he set them to work he did not "meddle further in their activity." The methods of giving developed by the progressive philanthropist signaled a fruitful alliance between wealthy capitalists and the professional-managerial class, one that promised to direct the staggering wealth earned by the rich toward truly progressive ends— and eventually make the need for charity obsolete.[31]

Rich businessmen were not the only figures who were cast as progressive philanthropists. So too were their wives and children, an argument that refuted the widely held belief that wealthy families were decadent and parasitical. Journalists reported that Rockefeller had taught his children the importance of giving to charity from an early age, and that they remained committed to this responsibility throughout their lives. By the 1920s John D. Rockefeller, Jr., and his wife, Abby Aldrich Rockefeller, were more widely known as philanthropists than as members of "society." This was also true of Helen Miller Gould, daughter of the notorious Jay Gould. According to journalists, Gould's activities were varied and extremely important, revealing her commitment to "the serious business of life." They included her endowment of a bucolic retreat for poor, crippled children near her estate in Westchester County, support for sick and wounded soldiers during the Spanish-American War, and involvement in various political causes. Her charity work, a writer for *Everybody's* noted in 1903, occupied nearly eight hours a day, and the voluminous requests for aid that she received required her to employ several secretaries. Despite her strong desire to help others, Gould was shrewd about determining the most worthy causes, displaying abundant "good sense." "She is not a sentimental giver, nor one who gives for the mere gratification of impulse, or the appearance of munificence," J. P. Coughlan wrote in 1901 in *Munsey's*. "On the contrary, she exerts herself to give where it will do good, and looks to it that her benefactions will genuinely benefit those for whom they are intended."[32]

Gould was not alone in her determination to be useful. By 1910 many other wealthy women were being praised for their contributions to philanthropic causes, which seemed to be taking up more and more of their time and left less for the frivolous "social whirl" that according to reporters had dominated the attention of previous generations of wealthy women. Among the most interesting of the society figures was a small yet visible group whose interest in humanitarian causes had led them to become advocates of women's suffrage. The most widely publicized suffragist in high society was Alva Belmont, who regularly wrote articles for women's magazines promoting the cause. But more interesting to journalists was the younger, more glamorous Katharine Duer Mackay, the wife of a communications magnate and the mother of Ellin Mackay, who would later marry Irving Berlin. The influx of rich women like Mackay had "rejuvenated" the movement, an unnamed writer for the *American Magazine* asserted in 1910, bringing to it intelligence, a deep sense of social responsibility, and "superior executive capacity and training" developed in philanthropic activities. Though some Americans might be skeptical about women's suffrage, there was no denying the importance of the contributions that Mackay and her colleagues were making to society at large. As the magazine noted, "Anything that increases the number of things that men or women think about—that increases the number of useful causes to which they turn their hands— is of national benefit." By drawing other rich women to a cause that brought them out of their gilded circles, women like Belmont and Mackay had "distinctly broadened the life of what we call society." [33]

The horizons of high society were further broadened by the First World War, which offered its members numerous opportunities to display their patriotism and commitment to public service. Just as many corporate executives volunteered their services as "dollar-a-year men," society figures like Helen and Vincent Astor joined organizations devoted to contributing to the war effort. The Astors wound up in France, where Vincent served as a naval attaché and Helen worked as an administrator for the YMCA. These experiences had dramatically altered their perspective, Helen told readers of *Ladies' Home Journal* in 1920. And they were not alone. In Astor's view, many other wealthy young men and women—an entire generation—had matured and grown on account of the war, and were devoting even more of their time to charity work and other forms of public service. For example, Astor revealed that she was taking college courses in economics and social science, belonged to a number of important committees, including one responsible for investigating conditions in factories and another devoted to the "Americanization" of immigrants, and was active in the political work of reform groups like the National Consumers' League. These activities, she noted, provided her with real fulfillment and made the "social whirl" seem boring and artificial. "I do not see how a woman, rich or poor, could be altogether alive to-day and not realize that her time and her energy belong, not to an artificial round of social conventions, but to herself and her husband and her family and the world, the real world," Astor concluded. [34]

This interest in the "real world" pointed toward a more expansive understanding of public service, which shaped press coverage of the new kinds of philanthropic activities that rich Americans began to engage in during the 1920s and 1930s. Some of these activities—like Henry Ford's endowment of his museum at Greenfield Village and John D. Rockefeller Jr.'s lavish reconstruction of colonial Williamsburg—were designed to increase the public's appreciation of America's heritage. Projects of this sort were very appealing to journalists, who were often as eager as Ford and Rockefeller to assimilate immigrants and make them aware of the culture that they needed to embrace in order to become full-fledged "Americans." More daring were the activities of rich women like Abby Aldrich Rockefeller and Gertrude Vanderbilt Whitney, who played leading roles in the establishment of museums devoted to modern art. A renowned sculptor herself, Whitney was also heralded for providing extensive financial aid to promising American artists. The support for modern art and living artists that Whitney, Rockefeller, and others like them provided refuted the widely held belief that rich Americans were imitative and philistine in their tastes. In the view of journalists, women like Rockefeller and Whitney were adding to "civilization" and at the forefront of modernity, not slavish devotees of decadent European fashions.[35]

More daring still were the activities of Gertrude Whitney's nephew Jock Whitney, a man whom the *American Magazine* proclaimed "America's Number One Angel." Whitney's specialty was investing in often risky and bizarre ventures, including Broadway plays and motion pictures that experts in the field told him had little promise. During the Depression these seemingly foolhardy investments were seized upon by the press as yet another manifestation of public service by the rich. While other rich Americans withdrew their money from productive activities or spent it frivolously, Whitney continued to look for new areas in which to invest, a crusade that brought "new jobs to thousands and new entertainment to millions." Yet Whitney's motivation was not public service per se. "He is out to enjoy life as much as possible," the journalist Ralph Wallace wrote. This meant funding activities that were interesting to him, like the new Technicolor process and the film recently made from it, David O. Selznick's "Gone with the Wind." To be sure, it also meant making money. According to Wallace, Whitney had actually enlarged his inheritance through his shrewd and often daring investments. The important thing for Whitney, however, was not that he was making money; it was that he was making it "his own way," supporting worthwhile and important projects that would otherwise go unmade. As a cynical "Wall Streeter" told Wallace, "Jock would rather earn a few thousand in some lousy play than a million in stocks and bonds."[36]

Whitney's preference for small gains acquired through the pursuit of his own interests—an activity that happened to redound to the benefit of the public—made him something other than a progressive philanthropist. Nonetheless, he was an heir to this now venerable tradition. Along with the more sedate "Rockefeller Boys"—"Junior" and Abby's five sons—he epitomized the broader field of activity that the press now associated with the ideal of public service, making contributions that were "constructive" in the spirit of the industrial statesmen but also enriched the commonweal in new and unexpected ways. As philanthropists, patrons of the arts, contributors to campaigns promoting American history and culture, and angels supporting all kinds of "new and exciting things," these wealthy Americans were eminently useful, demonstrating that inherited wealth need not have a debilitating effect on its possessors—and could in fact inspire activities that contributed to American life. Moreover, profiles of these figures legitimized new motives for engaging in this work. While journalists in the early twentieth century had noted that John D. Rockefeller derived pleasure from his bequests to worthy causes, they had insisted that he was motivated primarily by a sense of duty arising from religious convictions, and that it was crucial for the rich to display such a sense of duty if they were to be regarded as useful and public-spirited. By the 1930s this sense of duty no longer occupied so prominent a place in profiles of the wealthy. More common were references to the "enthusiasm" and "great fun" that men like Whitney were said to bring to their work as angels, work allowing them to fulfill their personal ambitions and express their individuality.

Despite press coverage of his varied ventures, most Americans probably did not think of Jock Whitney as an "angel." More than likely, they thought of him as a "millionaire playboy," one of many such figures who regularly appeared in the gossip columns and rotogravure sections of metropolitan newspapers and new-breed magazines like Henry Luce's *Time* and *Life*. In these publications he was revealed to be a successful breeder of thoroughbreds and an expert polo player, a suitor of beautiful debutantes and society women, and a leading figure in what Maury Paul, the society columnist for the Hearst syndicate, called "cafe society," an amalgam of society and show business celebrities who regularly appeared together at posh nightclubs, resorts, and parties. Coverage of these figures marked the culmination of a trend that began in the 1890s, when younger members of society from New York, began eschewing the tradition of privacy and exclusiveness established by Caroline Astor, the doyenne of the "New York Four Hundred." Members of this younger generation began gathering in public restaurants and soliciting the company of actors, writers, and society reporters, who eagerly wrote up accounts of their antics. By 1910 the range of their haunts had expanded to include theaters and new nightclubs and cabarets opened expressly for them, and the rise of newspaper chains and feature syndicates made it possible for readers throughout the country to know their names and recognize their faces. In the freewheeling 1920s the ranks of this increasingly visible coterie were swelled by the addition of politicians, prizefighters, movie folk, and other show business celebrities. Their addition to the mix marked the transformation of "high society" to "cafe society," a group noted for the varied backgrounds and occupations of its members and their high profile in the press.[37]

Much of the reportage devoted to those who traveled in these circles was disparaging. Gossip columnists for urban tabloids and the Hearst press delighted in exposing their foibles, and the composite portrait that arose from these stories was largely unattractive, emphasizing a proclivity for divorce, alcoholism, and sexual deviance. In many respects, the press's coverage of cafe society in the 1920s and 1930s was a continuation of the critique of high society developed by journalists and intellectuals at the turn of the century. Yet it was also a departure in ways that were ultimately advantageous for the rich, defusing the significance of their transgressions and making it possible for some of them to be portrayed quite sympathetically. Ironically, the roots of this transformation can be traced to the turn of the century, the very moment when the Progressive critique of the rich was at the peak of its influence, and when their supporters began distinguishing between fops and parasites who deserved condemnation and wealthy Americans who were not merely useful but "wholesome" and "democratic" as well.

The first strategy that journalists employed in their campaign was to associate the rich with the "simple life," an ideal widely celebrated in the media and advice literature between 1900 and 1920. Devotees of

the simple life—who included older businessmen like John D. Rockefeller and J. P. Morgan as well as young figures like Morgan's part-
ner George W. Perkins and the philanthropist Helen Miller Gould—eschewed many of the spoils available to them by virtue of their wealth,
leading a style of life that was the epitome of "moderation" and "common sense." Their diets were plain and nourishing, and they made it
a habit to get plenty of rest. They were firm believers in regular exercise, engaging in activities like golf and horseback riding that took them
out of doors. As Morris Bacheller observed in a profile of Andrew Carnegie in *Munsey's,* recreation and play were vitally important for rich
businessmen like Carnegie, preventing the pursuit of money from becoming "the controlling interest" in their lives. Wealthy Americans who
led the simple life also avoided the parties and rituals of "high society,"
preferring to socialize among small groups of friends and neighbors.
Reporters noted, for example, that Rockefeller's most frequent golfing companions were ordinary citizens who lived near his Westchester
estate—the town minister, the village schoolteacher, the town iceman,
a master carpenter. To such figures, the world's richest man was simply
"Neighbor John." Gould, Juliet Wilbor Tompkins revealed in 1903,
spent her leisure time with the "self-supporting working girls" she had
met through her charity work and whom she regularly invited to her
home. Living the simple life not only allowed the rich to escape from
the pressures and burdens of their work. It made them more productive and helped them to remain at the top of the business world, Issac
Marcosson argued in the *Saturday Evening Post* in 1914. "To be on this
nerve-racking job day and night," Marcosson noted, "requires a clear
brain, a steady hand, and . . . a good digestion," things that the simple
life could readily provide. Yet in the view of most writers, it was not the
simple life's instrumental value that led the rich to adopt it. They did
so because it made them happy and healthy, because, as Bacheller put
it, such a regimen was conducive to "getting out of life all that it has to
give."[38]

This was why the rich were raising their children to lead the simple
life as well. Writing in *Cosmopolitan* in 1909, Elizabeth Meriwether Gilmer marveled at how content and unpretentious the seven children of
George and Edith Gould were turning out to be, despite the wealth and
luxury that had surrounded them since birth. "They are literally old-
fashioned children, who have fewer frills of embroidery on their petti-
coats, and fewer frills of airs and graces on their manners, than those

of the children of the average twenty-dollar-a-week clerk." John Cushman Fistere, in the *Saturday Evening Post* in 1938, made the same observation about the "Rockefeller Boys." The beneficiaries of a childrearing regimen which had prevented them from being "spoiled" by their wealth and privilege, the sons of "Junior" and Abby were decent, useful, and down-to-earth, possessing "sane social viewpoints" that allowed them to maintain their connection to ordinary people and mainstream America. "Today, none of them would think of demanding special privilege because his name was Rockefeller, any more than he would let anyone take advantage of him for the same reason." This was a crucial argument, refuting the long-standing belief that proximity to wealth and luxury were inevitably corrupting. Committed to ensuring that their children were as "normal" as possible, the Goulds and the Rockefellers had been careful to impart appropriate lessons and offer experiences that broadened the children's horizons and made them aware of their responsibilities to the public. Yet at the same time the parents had stressed the importance of good health and wholesome fun, with the result that their children were active, spirited, and unaffected, fitting members of a democratic society.[39]

By the 1930s, however, rich Americans like the Rockefellers were no longer being linked to the relatively abstemious "simple life" that journalists had associated with their elders. The simplicity of the Rockefellers was an attitude, a frame of mind that deeply shaped their style of life but did not keep them from enjoying their wealth and the unique goods and leisure-time experiences that they could afford. To a degree, this had been true as early as the 1890s, when journalists began visiting the mansions and estates of the rich and writing about their visits in great detail, describing with obvious fascination the sumptuous decor and exotic works of art, the vast landscaped gardens, and the many modern conveniences. Writing for a public that was coming to view itself as consumers, reporters after the turn of the century increasingly downplayed the long-standing connection between high levels of consumption and moral corruption, and instead stressed the benefits that the wealthy derived from their goods. In the view of journalists, the rare or expensive goods owned by rich Americans like Chauncey Depew, J. P. Morgan, and Andrew Carnegie revealed a love of beauty, a sincere interest in art, and a determination "to extract the greatest possible amount of enjoyment from [their] money." They filled their homes with precious things because they liked them and could afford to buy them, not to show off their wealth. Acquired out of a sincere interest that was integral to their sense of self, the goods could even be evidence of the owners' "simplicity"—their determination to live in their own way, and not buy things to impress others or conform to conventional notions of taste.[40]

During the 1920s and 1930s this emphasis on self-expression through leisure and consumption became the new norm shaping stories about the rich. For example, a profile in 1938 of Helen and Vincent Astor, now middle-aged and leading figures in cafe society, stressed their many hobbies and revealed them to be fun-loving and a bit eccentric—not unlike characters in a screwball comedy. An accomplished pianist who played solely for her own pleasure, Helen kept "a baby-grand in every one of her four homes," taking "every spare moment . . . to practice," wherever she happened to be. Vincent loved sailing and fishing, spending much of his time on his sailboat or the family yacht. A devoted reader of detective stories and fan of the radio program "Amos 'n' Andy," he owned many "toys," including an extensive miniature railway, capable of carrying twenty people, that traversed his Hudson Valley estate. According to Ralph Wallace, Jock Whitney's style of life was equally "grand." His office, in a Radio City skyscraper, was elegant yet comfortable, with a well-stocked bar, a sparkling kitchen where a chef made him fancy meals, and a book-lined, soundproof inner sanctuary where Whitney could "snooze on a luxurious divan." He commuted to Manhattan from his Long Island estate on his yacht; his parties in New York and Hollywood, where he also kept a residence, were famous for featuring "high-priced and nationally famous orchestras." Like the Rockefellers, though, the Astors and Whitney were also "serious-minded" and down-to-earth. While journalists did not deny that figures like them were part of cafe society and lived amid luxury, they made it clear that their social activities were not the whole of their existence, and that it was possible to be fun-loving and even a bit self-indulgent yet still remain a useful, constructive citizen. More important, many of the avocations of these celebrities were recognizable and probably even attractive to ordinary Americans, making their style of life seem different only in degree.[41]

This was an important argument. For here were figures who seemed, on the surface, to be precisely the kinds of people Franklin D. Roosevelt denounced as "economic royalists" and whom gossip writers like Walter Winchell loved to expose as feckless libertines out of touch with "Mr. and Mrs. America." Rather than cast them in the ascetic, producerist mold that had been used to make earlier generations appear wholesome and part of the national community, journalists acknowledged that these Americans were rich and indulged themselves in ways that were extravagant. But they suggested that this merely made their subjects eccentric, not morally suspect, as many journalists in the early twentieth century would have argued. One cannot overestimate the importance of this shift in emphasis. Though press criticism of the "idle rich" persisted in the 1920s and increased substantially in the 1930s, in response to changes in public sentiment produced by the Depression, it was no longer couched in the morally charged terms of the past. At worst, the rich appeared pathetic and pitiful, like Barbara Hutton or another widely publicized "poor little rich girl," the tobacco heiress Doris Duke. Yet much-criticized figures like Hutton and Duke were exceptions, and their problems were attributed more often to their being "human"—and thus prone to temptations and weaknesses that affected everyone—not to their wealth. Indeed, their flaws stood in marked contrast to the virtues of the "wholesome rich."[42]

* * *

By portraying them as industrial statesmen, progressive philanthropists, and representatives of the "wholesome rich," journalists made a compelling case for readmitting the wealthy to the national community. And by insisting that these figures had chosen their roles, rising above the temptations that accompanied wealth and power, journalists linked the rich to the ideal of true success. Here was an especially vivid example of how the discourse of true success could shape reporting and allow journalists to contribute to a long-standing debate about the relationship between capitalism and democracy. As figures as diverse as John D. Rockefeller, Helen Miller Gould, Gerard Swope, and Jock Whitney revealed, wealthy Americans could be constructive forces for good, connected to their fellow citizens, and genuinely democratic in their manner of life and sympathies. There was no reason, in short, to believe that wealth was inevitably corrupting.

As we have seen, most of the time this message was conveyed implicitly, its power and clarity emerging through the accumulation of examples. But on occasion it received explicit articulation. For instance, in a long feature story in the *American Magazine* about a vacation that Thomas Edison, Henry Ford, the tire magnate Harvey S. Firestone, and the naturalist John Burroughs took together in the summer of 1918—in which they drove through the Appalachian mountains visiting small towns and camping at night—Mary B. Mullett openly addressed the issue at stake in depictions of the rich as exemplars of true success: "Sometimes we wonder if, after all, we are as democratic as we like to say we are," Mullett noted. "But when . . . we can catch a few of our big men off their guard, just being themselves at play, and can find that they are, above everything else, simple and friendly and kind— which is the essence of democracy—we may sit back with a sigh of satisfaction." As Mullett acknowledged, twentieth-century America was a nation that had produced some "big men," whose wealth, power, and influence were unprecedented. But this was nothing to be concerned about, since the "essence of democracy" was far removed from the institutions over which these men presided. No matter how rich or powerful they might be, their "simple and friendly and kind" demeanor when they encountered ordinary folks on their trip meant that America was still a democratic nation.[43]

Yet if celebrity journalism about the wealthy allowed for their readmission to the national community, the terms of the readmission deserve scrutiny. Contrary to the conventional wisdom, it was the press that was largely responsible for constructing the new archetypes and recasting the rich along new lines, with wealthy Americans and their publicists playing a supporting role. The widely heralded public relations initiatives that Ivy Lee and other public relations men undertook on behalf of corporations and the rich began around 1905, after reporters had already established the terms that Lee and his colleagues would exploit in their own efforts. The result of this campaign in the press was a boon for the rich, reducing and subtly altering media criticism of them and, more than likely, improving their reputation among the public at large. The press's rehabilitation of the rich was integral to the legitimation of corporate capitalism and public acceptance of great wealth, an adjunct of the more systematic public relations campaigns undertaken by corporations and trade associations during the first half of the twentieth century.[44]

Achieving legitimacy, however, required associating the rich with values like simplicity, efficiency, cooperation, systematic planning, sympathy for labor, widespread abundance, and the general "uplift" of humanity—values often associated with Progressives and the left. While being cast in this light enabled the wealthy to win public esteem, it also imposed constraints that limited their actions. Press coverage of the rich in the first half of the twentieth century established symbolic boundaries that may well have affected their behavior and made possible such innovations as the postwar social contract between capital and labor. And while these boundaries steadily expanded over time, giving the wealthy more room to operate without arousing the opprobrium of the press, their existence might have made businessmen and society figures more careful about covering up activities when the boundaries were exceeded. Indeed, the values that journalists sought to associate with the rich suggest that public revulsion toward them was great enough to prevent the new economic order from triumphing on its own terms, by exalting the values of self-interest, competition, and class distinction. The new order could triumph only by appropriating the discourse of the left and assuring the public that a society dominated by large corporations, in which a small few possessed huge fortunes, could also be progressive.

Practical Idealism
Political Celebrity in an Age of Reform

In the summer of 1900, as Americans began turning their attention to the upcoming elections, *McClure's* inaugurated a series of articles on "the most conspicuous of our present-day political figures." Written by William Allen White, an up-and-coming Kansan whose byline would appear above political articles in national magazines for the next forty years, the series began with a profile of the Democratic presidential nominee, William Jennings Bryan, that aimed "to show the reader what manner of man this is that is playing so large a part in our public life."

The reason for this focus on the "man" was simple. "The political party is the grandson of the clan," White suggested. From the clan it inherited its "bigotry" and its habit of encouraging members to view politicians through a partisan lens that produced exaggerated caricatures of them. Views of Bryan, White noted, were a case in point. To his supporters in the Democratic party, he was a virtual demigod, the champion of the people; to his Republican detractors, he was "an arrant demagogue, vacillating by nature, consciously dishonest, the malicious soul of error, and the fountainhead of treasonable doctrines which invite anarchy by the attempt to establish socialism." In White's view, both estimates were "incorrect," for neither acknowledged that "[n]ature never made a human being entirely good or bad." His sketch, by contrast, would provide readers with an understanding of the real Bryan, a perspective that transcended partisan stereotypes.[1]

Though *McClure's* suggested that White's approach was unique and pathbreaking, in fact it was not. His profiles of Bryan, Theodore Roosevelt, former president Grover Cleveland, the Tammany boss Richard

Croker, and the Republican leaders Mark Hanna and Thomas C. Platt resembled articles that other writers were producing for wire services, feature syndicates, and national magazines. They were emblematic of a growing trend in mass-circulation journalism, a new method of writing about political figures that sought to present them in a nonpartisan light. This reportage, which emerged in the 1880s and 1890s, rested on an important premise: that partisan depictions were inaccurate and had outlived their usefulness. To make informed decisions about whom to support, journalists now argued, it was necessary to see politicians without partisan blinders, as "real men" whose temperaments, experience, and training were far more important for understanding their actions and assessing their merits as representatives of the public. Made possible by a growing reliance on advertising revenues, which by the 1880s allowed many publishers and editors to eschew the financial support of the major parties and adopt a more independent line, this new trend in political reporting became increasingly common in newspapers and mass-circulation magazines after the turn of the century. By 1910, while some organs continued to support one party at the expense of the other, the preponderance of wire-service reports and features in virtually all publications encouraged readers to view politics—and the men and women engaged in it—from a new perspective that emphasized commitment to the "public interest."[2]

This trend was inspired by several related factors. First, there was a growing interest among publishers and editors in establishing their publications as tribunes of a reunified public, as institutions able to rise above the conflicts that had become more visible and disturbing to civic leaders and middle-class Americans during the late nineteenth century. The interest in restoring social harmony was often accompanied by dissatisfaction with the major political parties, a conviction held by many Americans that both the Democratic and Republican parties were corrupt, inefficient, and outmoded, and that new institutions were required to mobilize voters and assume functions performed by the parties since before the Civil War, like choosing men to fill appointed positions in government and selecting the recipients of public contracts. By 1900 disdain for the major parties among journalists and much of the public was reinforced by a belief that they stood in the way of badly needed reforms. Dominated by corrupt "bosses," the major parties were said to be in league with powerful businesses determined to escape government regulation and other reforms that might create a larger role for the state or challenge their authority. The new trend toward nonpartisan political reporting, in short, was a response to an increase in public sentiment in favor of reform and a widespread assumption that the major parties—and knee-jerk partisanship in general—were part of the problem.[3]

These concerns profoundly influenced White's portrait of Bryan and the mainstream press's depiction of all politicians, reformers, and political activists. They informed stories in the news columns, including the large number of gossipy short items about politicians that were common in newspapers and magazines by the 1890s. They exerted an influence on editorials as well, though editorials were viewed by many publishers and editors as less important than in the past, a belief that had led to their banishment from the front page. They were especially important in shaping lengthy profiles and human-interest stories about political figures that in the early 1900s became a staple of the Sunday supplements and mass-circulation magazines and a major source of public information about politics. As editorials declined in importance, these articles became a crucial medium through which journalists expressed their political views. Indeed, in them one can discern the outlines of a new archetype that political writers crafted in response to the widespread public revulsion toward partisanship and political "bosses" and that all political figures were ultimately measured against: the "practical idealist." The practical idealist, in the view of the press, stood above partisan politics and its inevitable corruption and kept his or her eye steadily fixed on the public interest. Yet this commitment was coupled with a determination to be practical, to work through the system and with regular politicians to achieve tangible, constructive results.

Emerging around the turn of the century, the discourse of practical idealism exerted a powerful influence over depictions of politicians, reformers, and activists for the next two decades, the era of progressive reform. Sympathetic profiles of these figures portrayed them as paragons of practical idealism, living proof that its values were viable and actively shaping public policy. Critical pieces, by contrast, revealed the degree to which subjects failed to live up to its ideals. In the course of portraying political figures along these lines, journalists expanded the range of political reportage, bringing to it the themes and concerns of human-interest journalism. For the politician or reformer who managed to maintain a commitment to practical idealism was the political world's exemplar of true success, his triumph resembling that of the industrial statesman or the progressive philanthropist, and serving as similar inspiration for his countrymen. So potent and effective was this discourse that it remained influential in the 1920s and 1930s, despite significant changes in the nation's political landscape. Beginning in the 1920s, however, amid the press's broader retreat from interest in reform, journalists refashioned the discourse of practical idealism into a bulwark of conservatism, a weapon that they regularly employed not just against bosses but also against new figures who had arisen in tandem with the impulse toward reform.

* * *

According to the press, the boss, the demagogue, and the fanatic were representatives of the same problem that had come to plague American politics since the nation's emergence as an industrialized and increasingly urbanized society, the problem of "corruption." To be sure, newspapers and magazines had covered political skullduggery for many years. But in the 1860s and 1870s, when state and municipal governments and political machines like Tammany Hall in New York began to assume greater control over the distribution of charters, franchises, and subsidies to entrepreneurs and corporations, the frequency and scale of scandals increased, inviting greater press scrutiny and creating a widespread impression among the public that politics had become more corrupt. Over the years, as metropolitan newspapers stepped up coverage of political scandals, and the most egregious of them drew national attention through wire-service reports and coverage in publications like *Harper's Weekly*, public concern about corruption steadily mounted, reaching a peak in the early twentieth century.[4]

Yet it was not simply an increase in press attention to corruption that produced this state of affairs. It was the new tone that many newspapers and magazines employed in their coverage, an increasingly nonpartisan tone—evident in William Allen White's profiles in *McClure's*, for example, and his remark about partisan "bigotry"—that divided the political world into new camps. By 1900 it was painfully clear to Republicans that there were scoundrels in the party of Lincoln, just as it was clear to Democrats that Tammany Hall was not an aberration but the model for Democratic urban machines throughout the country. This growing realization, which was instrumental in eroding party loyalties and creating a more independent brand of voter, reinforced the press's commitment to presenting political news from a nonpartisan perspective. Equally important, however, was the need to cover new political movements that were emerging. These movements included third parties, labor unions, national organizations like the Women's Christian Temperance Union, and myriad local groups that were bringing Democrats and Republicans together in support of reform. Many of these movements were explicitly nonpartisan, and their leaders often asserted that the major parties were impediments to achieving their goals. Coverage of the movements, moreover, brought dissident voices into the mainstream press and forced journalists to develop new ways of thinking about politics and the kinds of men and women who were becoming prominent in the field. In the midst of his series on important male politicians for *McClure's*, for example, White also produced a profile of the saloon wrecker Carrie Nation for the *Saturday Evening Post*, which enabled him to discuss the origins and implications of the new activism in which Nation and other reformers were engaged.[5]

The result was a conceptual watershed in the mass media's depiction of political news, and a new perspective that redirected coverage of politicians, reformers, and activists toward their efforts to serve the public without becoming corrupt or fanatical in pursuit of their goals. Resisting the forces that encouraged corruption and fanaticism was not easy, journalists noted. Yet failure to resist them did not necessarily make a politician or reformer "bad." It just meant that he or she was "human," as White observed in his profile of Bryan, and thus susceptible to all the weaknesses and flaws that were characteristic of the race. Here was a breakthrough every bit as important as the press's growing disdain for partisanship. By attributing corruption to human frailties, not "immorality," White and other political writers were laying the foundation for a distinctly modern understanding of politics, according to which corruption was largely systemic, a matter of institutions and the broader environment in which politicians went about their business. While reforms could reduce corruption, it could never be eliminated as long as politics was conducted by humans rather than angels. This was a sobering conclusion, but it gave journalists a potent new angle to exploit in their coverage of politics and opened the door to the introduction of human-interest themes in political reporting, since it was the very humanity of politicians that was now paramount. Even while drawing attention to corruption, then, political writers were lowering the bar for politicians who were to be considered honest, a strategy that may have encouraged the public to be more "realistic" about politicians but certainly reinforced the cynicism toward them that would increase so markedly in later years.[6]

Though the new perspective developed by journalists eschewed the overtly moralistic tone that had shaped partisan stereotypes in the nineteenth-century press, it did not entirely dispense with villains. Early in the century the most widely visible one was the professional politician, a role that reporters assigned to any number of figures, including the Republican Speaker of the House, Joseph G. Cannon, and another, even more powerful member of the GOP, Senator Nelson W. Aldrich, whom David Graham Phillips accused of being the chief "organizer" of the plutocratic interests who ruled America and plundered the people. But perhaps the quintessential "pols" were the Republican bosses Boies Penrose and Thomas C. Platt, and their minions in the state legislatures who reflexively supported them out of a combination of partisan loyalty and self-interest. These men, journalists insisted, put the interests of their party or machine above those of the public. To attain and keep themselves in power, they accepted campaign contributions and bribes from rich businessmen and then acted as their patrons' "hired men," quashing or diluting legislation that they found offensive. It also allowed some of them to become very wealthy. Aldrich, for example, was "enormously rich," Phillips reported. Even more revealing was that his daughter had married John D. Rockefeller Jr., linking "the chief exploiter of the American people" with "the chief schemer in the service of their exploiters." Reporters noted that professional politicians like Aldrich and Platt worked behind closed doors, in the proverbial smoke-filled room. After years in politics, which dulled their "moral sense," their main concern was maintaining and possibly extending their power —not issues or principles. To gain reelection, the professional politician exerted influence among his supporters or attracted the necessary public support by repeating the same partisan clichés that members of his party had been trumpeting for decades. The "pol" was cynical and duplicitous, tailoring his appeals for particular audiences, obscuring his objectives with cant and rhetoric.[7]

Another figure whom the press cast as a villain was the urban boss. Unlike the professional politician, who only began to be criticized along nonpartisan lines in the 1880s and 1890s, the urban boss had been a target of crusading journalists since the 1860s, when Henry Raymond's *New York Times* exposed the corrupt practices of William Marcy Tweed, the boss of Tammany Hall. Most criticism of urban bosses had been implicitly partisan: bosses and machines, it was suggested, were a problem afflicting the Democrats, the party of immigrants, ethnics, and the urban working class. By 1900 this view remained influential. Journalists continued to portray corrupt Republicans like Platt as professional politicians and Democrats as urban bosses, though by this time evidence of Republican malfeasance made it virtually impossible to depict corruption as a Democratic problem alone.[8]

The most widely publicized urban boss at the turn of the century was the Tammany chieftain Richard Croker, a regular subject of profiles and feature stories during the early 1900s, including one by White in *McClure's*. Strong-willed and virile, urban bosses like Croker wielded dictatorial power over their "subjects" in a fashion, journalists suggested, that was distinctly "feudal." Under Croker, Tammany Hall was a highly disciplined organization devoted to maintaining power over the working-class wards of New York, and leading it required considerable political skills. Croker had learned these skills as a loyal soldier and ward captain, rising in the organization by virtue of "the sheer force of his crude personality and his faithful observance of the physical rules of systematic organization." Yet as White and other writers grudgingly conceded, his power rested on the loyalty and goodwill that many working-class and immigrant New Yorkers felt toward his organization, which Tammany had earned through its generous disbursement of much-needed goods and services. Thus the urban boss provoked more ambivalence than the professional politician did. He maintained a connection to his constituents that middle-class reformers envied and found exceedingly difficult to sever. Journalists attributed this to his tolerance, a trait that, sadly, most bourgeois reformers did not share. "He does not seek the moral betterment of folk; he aims no higher than to feed the hungry, clothe the naked and shelter the homeless, without pausing to inquire whether they are bound for glory or perdition," Alfred Henry Lewis asserted in 1905 in a largely sympathetic profile of Croker's successor, Timothy D. Sullivan, in *Cosmopolitan*.[9]

The prominence of men like Platt, Croker, and Sullivan in American politics was disturbing to many journalists. That they were capable and often quite intelligent was abundantly clear. Through hard work, perseverance, and an eye toward what would help them get ahead, they had succeeded in the game of politics, rising to positions of power and commanding organizations that were influential and important. Their

outlook, however, was essentially amoral. They cared only about results and not about the methods they employed to reach them. One
reason for this, writers suggested, was that many of these men were uneducated and had learned politics in the "streets," where the struggle
for existence had encouraged them to be practical and made them unaware of higher ideals; others, like Platt and the Republican boss Mark
Hanna, had come to politics from business, bringing business values and
a "cash-register conscience" with them. But in the view of many journalists, even highly educated and cultivated politicians like Aldrich,
Henry Cabot Lodge, and Eugene Hale suffered from an erosion of their
"moral sense." The problem was the atmosphere of politics itself, which
tended to frustrate and dispirit even those who were well intentioned
and had entered politics fully intending to serve the public interest.
As White and other writers lamented, over time politicians invariably
came to see things from the perspective of an insider, becoming obsessed
with their own personal fortunes and pleasing elements who could help
them remain in office. They became a distinct "caste" separate from the
people whom they claimed to represent, with an identifiable appearance
and demeanor, and a peculiar form of speech—"a guarded, polite, dull
and dignified jargon that makes the angels weep." In short, politics in
America had become altogether too much like business: overly practical, focused entirely on the winning of elections and the promotion of
policies guaranteed not to challenge the status quo.[10]

This trend was not only evidence of a steep decline in public virtue.
Journalists argued that it was also leading many thoughtful and concerned Americans to become dissatisfied with the major parties and, in
some cases, flirt with radicalism. "Many people believe that society is
not properly adjusted," White observed in his profile of William Jennings Bryan, "that the machinery of industry is not in gear, and too
many people are being ground by it. There is a widespread belief that
repairs are needed."[11] This situation created opportunities for another
villain whom the press regularly lambasted: the demagogue. The demagogue was cynical, unscrupulous, and wily, a figure who exploited public
dissatisfaction to gain power and popularity. He was not a newcomer
to the political scene. Politicians had been accused of demagoguery by
their opponents and journalists in the partisan press since the 1790s,
and such charges remained a staple of partisan discourse throughout the
nineteenth century. In the early twentieth century, however, this line
of argument was redefined along essentially nonpartisan lines, enabling

journalists working for the independent press to direct it at politicians from either of the major parties as well as new figures, like the Socialist leader Eugene V. Debs, who were seeking mass support for radical causes.

The politician most frequently accused of being a demagogue was Theodore Roosevelt. To his conservative critics in the press, Roosevelt was a dangerous figure who threatened to whip up the mob through his irresponsible attacks on "predatory wealth," which were solely designed to increase his support among the public and satisfy his insatiable lust for power. Writing in 1910, when TR had returned to the political scene advocating a more sweeping brand of progressivism, George Harvey, the editor of *Harper's Weekly,* denounced Roosevelt as "an avowed enemy of the Republic . . . a foe of popular government, [and] a virtual traitor to American institutions as they were created and now exist." To radicals and left-wing newspapers like the *Appeal to Reason,* by contrast, Roosevelt's attacks on the wealthy and efforts to style himself a reformer were part of a cynical ploy, concocted with conservative cronies like Lodge, Elihu Root, and representatives of the House of Morgan, to coopt public hostility and arrest the growth of socialism. Despite their differences, both sets of critics were certain that Roosevelt's claim to be serving the public interest was insincere.[12]

Roosevelt was not the only politician cast as a demagogue, nor would he be the last. Indeed, in the 1930s, when traditional fears of demagoguery were exacerbated by the appearance of European dictators and a growing belief among journalists that ordinary people were easily manipulated by ambitious politicians, many of the same charges were directed at figures such as Huey Long, Father Charles Coughlin, even Franklin D. Roosevelt. Long, who briefly gained a national following during the early years of the New Deal, when he became a leading spokesman for income redistribution and massive public works programs, received the most criticism, not least because journalists recognized that behind his bluster lay shrewdness and intelligence. "He has an extraordinary mind and unbelievable perseverance and vitality, and can, if he will, become a mighty force for good in the Senate," Jerome Beatty noted in a profile of Long in 1933 in the *American Magazine.* But as Beatty conceded, Long's record as governor of Louisiana, where he spent prodigious sums on public works and ruled in the manner of an autocrat, was not auspicious. Even worse, his fondness for violent rhetoric had aggravated class antagonism and made him many enemies, particularly among businessmen, who were convinced that he was driving the state into bankruptcy. According to a writer for *Time,* Long had developed a "political technique" that was quite effective in winning him a large following among the uneducated and impressionable. Yet he was "too intelligent" to believe it himself. It was merely the means by which he sought to amass power.[13]

Reporters were more likely to depict politicians or reformers whom they disliked in a somewhat different guise, as fanatics. During an era of reform, when many new movements were on the rise, this was a far more useful archetype. Though political writers in the nineteenth century had used it intermittently to discredit figures like the labor reformer Henry George, it was not widely employed until the late 1890s, when the emergence of Populism and heightened labor unrest increased public support for radicalism and sweeping programs of reform—a development that many journalists thought likely to result in the establishment of a powerful American socialist movement and a reorientation of political conflict along vaguely "European" lines. For many reporters, most of whom were either Republican in background and sympathies or partial toward the more conservative urban wing of the Democratic party, the quintessential fanatic was Bryan, who seemed determined to transform the party of Jackson into a vehicle for "socialism" and "anarchy." Journalists acknowledged that fanatics like Bryan were well intentioned, inspired by real injustices that cried out for remedy. And throughout the struggle fanatics remained sincerely committed to the cause, often rejecting strategies that would increase their influence but require compromising their principles. "With [Bryan]," White wrote, "an expeditious compromise would be a dishonorable surrender." But fanatics were easily led astray by their zeal and self-righteousness, becoming irresponsible or destructive in their proposals for reform, and using their formidable oratorical skills and "magnetic" personalities to delude the public into thinking that they had all the answers. Like Bryan, fanatics often lacked "practical experience" in the real world; their approach to problems was theoretical, and they were drawn to crackpot notions peddled by "cranks." If the professional politician was altogether too practical, divorcing morality from the practice of politics, the fanatic, journalists argued, was too idealistic, allowing his commitment to social justice to blind him to the complexity of problems and the necessity of working incrementally to solve them.[14]

Appearing on the stage late—long after the demagogue, the urban boss, and the professional politician had assumed their places—the fanatic quickly emerged as a widely employed political archetype, shaping press coverage of radicals like Debs, Emma Goldman, and William "Big Bill" Haywood. During the more conservative 1920s, the archetype also influenced how many journalists portrayed liberals and progressives like Robert M. La Follette and William A. Borah.[15] By the 1920s most journalists had ceased wringing their hands over the pervasiveness of corruption in American politics, in response to new reforms that reduced the most flagrant abuses and a growing, complacent sense that a measure of corruption was endemic to democratic politics. Press coverage of the Teapot Dome scandal, for example, was notable for the lack of moralistic fervor displayed by most of the writers assigned to the story. While reporters in the 1920s hoped that press scrutiny of politicians would discourage corruption, they were under no illusion that it would inspire a moral awakening or make corruption a thing of the past, in contrast to the belief that had inspired many reformist journalists at the turn of the century.[16] As concern about corruption declined, press interest in demagoguery and fanaticism escalated, particularly during the 1930s, when the Depression sparked a dramatic increase in grassroots activism and led to the emergence of political leaders virtually as radical as Debs yet also vastly more popular. This development terrified most journalists, prompting them to redouble their efforts at undermining the appeal of radicals and even of many reformers by casting them as demagogues or fanatics.[17]

* * *

The press's growing interest in corruption and its disdain for partisanship were quickly noted by politicians and others seeking to make their mark on public affairs. As early as the mid-1880s, for example, Theodore Roosevelt had recognized the possibility of carving out a niche for himself as a "practical reformer"—a man committed to the high ideals of genteel reformers like E. L. Godkin and George W. Curtis yet more willing to work within the Republican party with corrupt bosses and "pols" like Roscoe Conkling, Matthew Quay, and James G. Blaine. His Democratic counterpart was Grover Cleveland, a vocal critic of both Tammany-style corruption and the heresies of Populist-influenced Democrats like Bryan. As more politicians altered their views and personas in response to the increasingly nonpartisan orientation of the press, journalists encouraged this trend by lavishing praise on the men who were leading the way. By the turn of the century, the combined efforts of politicians and reporters had produced a new archetype, the "practical idealist," that the press employed when covering politicians and reformers. This new archetype was a virtuous foil to the professional politician, the demagogue, and the fanatic and enabled journalists to measure politicians by a new yardstick. More important, it spurred many more politicians—including some who had come under fire for corruption or partisanship—to alter their self-promotional strategies so that they might resemble practical idealists as well. Not surprisingly, the first politician extolled as a practical idealist was the canny and insightful Roosevelt, but other "progressives"—La Follette, Charles Evans Hughes, William Howard Taft, and Woodrow Wilson— were also cast in this role. However, practical idealism was not always linked to reform. As we shall see, in the 1920s it began to be defined more conservatively, so as to include figures like Calvin Coolidge, Herbert Hoover, and Al Smith.

Practical idealists were honest and public-spirited. Fired by a powerful sense of duty, they were devoted to public service, a trait that many journalists likened to the patriotism of the Founding Fathers. They were also courageous, willing to fight aggressively for right, regardless of the effect on their careers or personal fortunes. As Ray Stannard Baker noted of TR in 1898 in *McClure's*, "It is characteristic of Mr. Roosevelt that when he sees a duty clearly, no advice, however well meant, nor any question of expediency or profit or future favor will turn him by the width of a hair. His career never for a moment eclipses his sense of responsibility." These were important traits, distinguishing practical idealists from professional politicians, who were reluctant to do anything that might imperil their power or position. Of course the practical idealist's willingness to fight, to antagonize powerful interests in his pursuit of the public interest, often resulted in his being ostracized by professional politicians and the "organization." But at the same time, he attracted new kinds of men, inspired by his example and eager to be his allies—men of intelligence and achievement who had often "succeeded in a practical way outside of politics." Unlike the "pol," the practical idealist chose his lieutenants on the basis of merit, choosing for important posts men whose experience and public-spiritedness made them perfectly suited for their various assignments. By bringing such men into politics—"outsiders" who had not been corrupted by politics and usually embodied not the "cash-register conscience" of business but the disinterested perspective of expertise—the practical idealist was in the vanguard of a new movement that would restore integrity to government.[18]

Just as important as his commitment to public service was the practical idealist's determination to be "constructive." Here was where he departed from genteel reformers, whose overzealous attachment to principle made them averse to engaging the bosses and professional politicians who had come to rule American politics. While "armchair reformers" wrung their hands and lamented the republic's fall from virtue, the practical idealist eagerly dove into the muck of political activity. Journalists noted that this willingness to become engaged meant not only battling the "pols" when they were protecting special "interests" or obstructing much-needed reforms, but also working with them from time to time to achieve results that were truly in the public interest. Indeed, the hallmark of the practical idealist was his willingness to work through the system and with the leaders of his own party, when it was possible to do so without compromising sacred principles. Yet as journalists made clear, when a practical idealist like Roosevelt or Woodrow Wilson worked with the leaders of his party, he kept his distance to ensure that the result of the collaboration was good policy. Assessing Wilson's first year in office, Samuel G. Blythe of the *Saturday Evening Post* placed special emphasis on the president's independence from his party—even though he was its undisputed leader. "He will heed a protest, but considers himself under no obligation to act on it if it is not in accordance with his own conclusions." The key to achieving this balance between being constructive and maintaining one's independence, political writers noted, lay in the spirit in which practical idealists like Roosevelt and Wilson engaged in combat. When they fought the "pols" in their own party or in the opposition, they fought fairly, allowing them to work with their opponents at a later date and maintain a "constructive" relationship. The same was true of practical idealists in Congress. Though treated as a pariah by the corrupt politicians who dominated the Senate, Robert M. La Follette had still found ways of being effective and making "an indelible mark upon its legislation," a writer for *Munsey's* observed in 1907. His fellow senators discovered that La Follette was "one of the most tireless and effective political fighters in American public life," and this realization led some of them to support him and establish a progressive vanguard in one of the nation's most corrupt institutions.[19]

By the 1920s, however, the tone of press coverage had changed, and with that change came a shift in the traits ascribed to practical idealists. As the press came to perceive a decline of public interest in reform, journalists began to place greater emphasis on working through the system in a "constructive" fashion. At the same time, they began to display less sympathy for politicians who continued to harp on progressive themes like the power of "predatory wealth." Old-style progressives like La Follette and William A. Borah, for example, were derided for being excessively naive, independent, and self-righteous. "For [La Follette] all high official Washington is subtly penetrated by the wiles of wealth," the veteran journalist William Hard noted in 1923 with obvious disdain, incredulous that anyone could still believe in that old progressive canard. Meanwhile, relatively conventional politicians were extolled as practical idealists. One of the most widely heralded practical idealists of the 1920s was Calvin Coolidge, whose commitment to the public interest manifested itself as devotion to the traditional values of "self-help" and opposition to reform. Another was the engineer-turned-public-servant Herbert Hoover, who during his tenure as secretary of commerce and the first years of his presidency was commonly linked to the "business" values of organization and efficiency. Even more remarkable was the press's warm embrace of Al Smith, a politician who had risen through the ranks of Tammany Hall and remained a loyal son of the Democratic Party. Making Smith the embodiment of practical idealism, however, required reconciling his partisanship with a broader commitment to the public interest. Writing in *Collier's* in 1928, Frank R. Kent conceded that Smith was a "firm believer in organization and in parties." Yet Smith recognized that the best way for a party to stay in power was to govern honestly and efficiently, that "the best possible government is the smartest possible politics: best not only for the people but best for the party and best for the organization." Sensitive to Republican charges that Smith was a party hack, Kent concluded by insisting on his independence: "The truth is that Smith is not only bigger than Tammany now but always has been in the sense that his allegiance or loyalty always stopped short of sacrificing his self-respect." And now that Smith was governor of New York and had a large popular following, he needed Tammany far less than it needed him, allowing him to defy the bosses and more forcefully assert his independence—just as another New York governor, TR, had defied "Boss" Platt.[20]

Practical idealists from Roosevelt to Smith shared another trait that was integral to their ability to be constructive: an inclination toward pragmatism. They were open-minded, willing to listen and gain information from a wide range of sources—ordinary people as well as highly educated and knowledgeable experts. Journalists often suggested that this openness was temperamental, a habit of mind that distinguished a Roosevelt from a Bryan. Men like Bryan were dogmatic, possessing a simplistic "attitude toward truth." "When he faces an alleged fact," White argued, "his habit is not to search it for truth, but to answer it. He is not seeking the truth; he has it, and is seeking to make converts." Practical idealists approached the truth pragmatically, inspired by common sense and vast personal knowledge about human nature gained from experience in the real world. This experience was often supplemented by book learning, and educated politicians like Roosevelt and Wilson were celebrated for the vast knowledge they had gained from reading and study. But most journalists asserted that book learning alone was insufficient; it had to be coupled with the kind of practical education that a man could only get from experience outside the realm of politics. The precise nature of the experience could vary, ranging from Roosevelt's sojourns in Dakota to Wilson's struggles to administer Princeton to Al Smith's apprenticeship in Tammany Hall to Herbert Hoover's career as an engineer. Whatever the source, experience in the real world enabled the practical idealist to understand human beings and recognize the importance of working from "facts." This commitment to facts separated the practical idealist from "sentimentalists" and "dreamers" and made him a more effective political actor.[21]

It also influenced his approach to the issues and problems that confronted him as an executive or legislator. Being pragmatic, a practical idealist was more likely to be cautious and deliberate when he weighed the pros and cons of an issue, getting information from as many sources as possible, and then filtering this information through his own mind to see which position—or combination of positions—was most likely to further the public interest. Though practical idealists had friends and cronies, these figures exerted no more influence over them than the man on the street did. Practical idealists were in effect impervious to "pull," even when it came from friends and members of their own party. Journalists placed special emphasis on the practical idealist's impartial approach to the conflict between capital and labor. Unlike most "pols," who because of their ties to businessmen reflexively opposed the interests of labor, practical idealists like Roosevelt, Wilson, and Charles

Evans Hughes were sympathetic toward the aspirations of workers. But this did not make them blind partisans of organized labor. As Mark Sullivan revealed in a profile of Roosevelt in 1909, "There is at least one labor leader who . . . will never think without flushing of the mistake he made when he presumed, from Roosevelt's sympathy with the proper demands of labor, entire endorsement of the labor union propaganda, and proposed something which aroused the very depths of Roosevelt's indignation." Rejecting positions that expressed "class feeling," practical idealists steered a middle course, supporting labor early in the century, when capital seemed to have all the advantages, but backing off after the First World War, when the demands of labor unions became "excessive" (which some journalists attributed to the insidious influence of "Bolshevism").[22]

The practical idealist's commitment to cautious, impartial deliberation restrained the potential for radicalism that might have arisen from his devotion to pragmatism. It ensured that whatever flaws he saw in the status quo, he would approach them as a "builder," who would protect the "machine" of industrial civilization and the revered institutions of American democracy from "the mob as well as the marauders." Nevertheless, early in the century quite a few mainstream journalists—Lincoln Steffens, Charles Edward Russell, Ray Stannard Baker, even William Allen White—encouraged politicians to make substantial changes in the nation's economic and political arrangements, arguing that the work of the practical idealist was reform: the framing and support of new laws to curb the power of the "interests" that had assumed the upper hand during the late nineteenth century. This commitment was crucial in providing support for the wide-ranging reforms of the Roosevelt and Wilson era, innovations that were portrayed as necessary because of the country's "evolution" yet also congruent with the principles established by the Founding Fathers. In the 1920s, however, some of the very same journalists who had encouraged and applauded Wilson turned on Progressives like La Follette, claiming that his aims were those of a "dangerous radical." For writers like Samuel G. Blythe, who had been one of Wilson's most vocal champions, practical idealism in the 1920s meant conservatism, protecting the institutions bequeathed to Americans by Washington, Jefferson, and Lincoln. From this perspective, the legislation of the Progressive era had been excessive, "an enormous flood of laws directing and prescribing out every contact with life." In the wake of this deviation from "self-government," the mission of a practical idealist like Coolidge was to return to first principles: "to quit running around in circles and howling for a change, and settle down to work."[23]

The practical idealist's approach to the business of governing also derived from his relationship to the public. Practical idealists were committed to the welfare and interests of ordinary people, whom they recognized not only as individuals but also as members of organized interest groups. The ability to see them as both was very important, journalists suggested. It allowed the practical idealist to perceive problems from a "human" perspective that encouraged sympathy and tolerance, and this outlook enabled him to wean ordinary people away from the bosses who had held them in thrall. Yet it also enabled the practical idealist to recognize the connection between specific problems and larger "forces" that needed to be fully understood before the problems could be effectively attacked and solved. Writers asserted that the practical idealist's understanding of the public and its needs arose from regular contact with ordinary people, which did not end when he became a politician.

The practical idealist found many ways to interact with ordinary citizens and keep himself accessible, not only when he was on the road but also at work. Seeing so many of his constituents was time-consuming, journalists noted, but absolutely crucial, providing men like Roosevelt, Wilson, and Hoover with first-hand knowledge that could complement the more abstract "research" conducted by their aides. When practical idealists met with ordinary citizens, they made them feel instantly at ease, peppering them with questions and eagerly soliciting their views. According to reporters, TR was the most sociable, a man who "surrounded himself with all sorts of persons," but even the taciturn Coolidge was known to open up when he was certain that his visitor had "legitimate business." Such contact was vital in enabling the practical idealist to resist the degrading environment of politics and maintain his integrity. Moreover, it kept him from developing the slick and artificial airs of a "pol." As a result, practical idealists remained humble and modest, well aware that their own political fortunes were not identical to those of the republic.[24]

An intimate connection to the people enabled practical idealists to be not merely servants of the public but true leaders. Appealing to his constituents openly, without the use of mesmerizing rhetoric, the practical idealist was clear about his intentions and where he stood on the issues —unlike obfuscating, duplicitous professional politicians. And though this made some of the people recognize their differences with him, it earned the practical idealist their respect and convinced many that he could be trusted to act in the best interests of the country. As White put it in a flattering assessment of TR, the American people "understood him, loved him, and believed in him," although he had "never taken the trouble to truckle with them" and appeared as no one other than himself. The same was true of Wilson, whose determination to dominate Congress and initiate important new legislation—in a radical departure from precedent that some of his conservative critics greeted with dismay—was inspired by the public's faith in his ability to choose a course that would promote "the welfare of the whole people." This faith allowed Roosevelt, Wilson, and other practical idealists to take the public into uncharted territory, where it might not have recognized the need to go.[25]

But their faith also helped practical idealists to resist the will of the people when it seemed uninformed or prejudiced. "The people will not call Roosevelt to act, no matter how loudly they clamor, unless their wisdom is confirmed by his own conscience and judgement," White noted in a reference to Bryan's weakness for reflexively following the "*vox populi*." Wilson possessed exactly the same attributes, Blythe wrote, siphoning public sentiment through his "detached mind" before settling on a course of action. Thus practical idealists could not only promote reform but also arrest the public's inclination to become irrational and destructive. This trait became increasingly important to journalists in the 1920s and 1930s, after their experience with propaganda-induced wartime hysteria made them more wary of the public and suspicious of politicians who sought to arouse grass-roots support. For example, Blythe reported that Calvin Coolidge was determined to "declare a recess in politics, in the expansion of government," and that this decision would arouse the ire of "reformers," "theorists," and "professional politicians," who viewed legislation as a panacea or promoted it so that they would appear important and productive to their constituents. Yet this did not matter to Coolidge, who intuitively recognized that if the mass of Americans did not share his view, they would come to see its wisdom in hindsight.[26]

* * *

The conservatism inherent in the discourse of practical idealism is even more clear when we turn from the press's depiction of politicians to its treatment of reformers and activists. Often highly skilled at attracting the attention of reporters, figures such as William Lloyd Garrison, Sarah and Angelina Grimké, Horace Mann, and Sylvester Graham were frequently the subjects of news stories during the early days of the mass-circulation press, and press coverage of reform remained a constant throughout the nineteenth century. Around the turn of the century, in response to new social problems created by industrialization and urban growth, new reform movements emerged. attracting significant support among the public. As a result the press was compelled to devote even more attention to reformers, including some whom were unabashedly radical. Indeed, the rise of Populism, socialism, and a more assertive brand of activism embodied by the settlement-house movement and groups like the Women's Trade Union League—and the concomitant visibility of men and women like Eugene V. Debs, Jane Addams, and Florence Kelley—put the press, now a big business with a strong stake in the status quo, in an awkward position.

On the whole, journalists showed considerable sympathy for the reform movements of the Progressive era. often producing fawning profiles of the men and women who led them. Yet in giving more coverage to the forces of reform, journalists also gained a measure of power over them. For with increased coverage came the ability to frame the subjects of reportage in ways that worked to the advantage of the press and diverted public hostility from institutions that most journalists were committed to protecting. Here was a way for the press to achieve the delicate balance required of any institution seeking to represent a deeply divided public: identifying itself with the broad public sentiment for reform yet also placating conservatives who worried that encouraging reform might spur the forces of radicalism. By employing the discourse of practical idealism in their coverage of reformers and political activists, journalists were not simply publicizing reform but attempting to mark out its legitimate boundaries.

Reporters acknowledged that virtually all reformers and activists were well-intentioned people devoted to working for social justice. And they made it clear that most of the causes that reformers had embraced were important and worthy of attention. But writers also noted that the indignation aroused by injustice could very easily drive reformers over the edge, making them excessively passionate and irrational. This was what had happened to the temperance crusader Carrie Nation, William Allen White argued in the *Saturday Evening Post* in 1901. Frustrated by the growing influence of saloon culture in her native Kansas, Nation had become a "frantic, brawling, hysterical woman." According to Lincoln Steffens, a similar transformation had affected Eugene Debs during his imprisonment in the wake of the Pullman strike. Though not yet hysterical like Nation, Debs clearly possessed the ability to do something very rash like his hero John Brown, Steffens observed in 1908 in *Everybody's*. Unlike "scientific" socialists, for whom Steffens had more respect, Debs was a man who "speaks and acts from the heart," whose sincere and courageous love for mankind was admirable but also made him dangerous. "The trouble with Debs," Steffens concluded, "is that he puts the happiness of the race above everything else: business, prosperity, property." Debs's affliction was not unusual. When individuals witnessed injustice, reporters noted, they often developed a "holy zeal" to remake the world, a zeal that could very easily lead them to become "cranks." To be effective, this zeal had to be tempered and directed into constructive action. Reformers had to recognize "realities." As the New Dealer Harry Hopkins learned during his early career as a settlement-house worker, "The world couldn't be remade. All you could do was bite at the loaf of misery and hope that some day enough other people would start biting to eat it all up." This realization need not be dispiriting; in Hopkins's case, it inspired him toward greater efforts to achieve tangible results, a writer for the *American Magazine* wrote in 1936. "Faced with the chance to do something practical about New York's monstrous want and poverty he suddenly grew up." The implication here was that radicalism—the urge to make the world over—was not just unrealistic but childish. In the 1920s and 1930s journalists often invoked this theme in describing a public figure's retreat from radicalism—a trajectory that less sympathetic writers might have attributed to cowardice, opportunism, or a failure of will.[27]

In practical terms, being "constructive" and "mature" in approaching social problems meant being able to forge fruitful alliances with other reformers, civic leaders, and politicians—even corrupt bosses if there was no other recourse. Much of Jane Addams's success in Chicago, a writer for *Everybody's* noted in 1903, could be attributed to her successful cultivation of politicians and businessmen, especially her efforts to make them aware of the magnitude of the problems that afflicted the poor. Her associate Florence Kelley, head of the National Consumers' League, shared this trait. As Paul U. Kellogg observed in a profile in the *American Magazine* in 1910, Kelley possessed a remarkable ability to "size up a fundamental dramatic situation or cause in an idea or a phrase which lays hold of men's minds." This allowed her to win influential allies and was the key to her success as the moving force behind new laws protecting women and children. Lillian Wald, the founder of the Henry Street Settlement in New York, was equally effective at eliciting the support of civic leaders, including rich businessmen like the financier Jacob Schiff, despite her penchant for supporting radical causes. Wald's ability to work with such people, Helen Huntington Smith asserted in an uncharacteristically fawning profile of Wald in the *New Yorker* in 1929, was due to her open-mindedness and disarming personal charm. "Most leaders of the masses, gnawed by a sense of inferiority, hate the capitalists," Smith suggested. "Miss Wald has no sense of inferiority, and she hates no one." Indeed, in her dealings with businessmen and politicians like Al Smith she displayed none of the self-righteousness common among reformers, making it much easier to collaborate with them and get them to see her point of view. "She leaves them, if not endorsing her view of life, at least magnanimously admitted that there is much to be said on both sides." Considering the attitude that such men typically had toward reform, this was quite an achievement.[28]

According to journalists, being constructive also meant adopting "realistic" goals and finding the most appropriate methods for achieving them—in short, displaying the pragmatic cast of mind that was a salient trait of the practical idealist. For example, after a brief and controversial career as a diehard radical, when her advocacy of birth control had been coupled with calls for sexual freedom and proletarian revolution, Margaret Sanger had come to see the merits of developing an alliance with physicians and making appeals in the "cool economic phrases" of scientific expertise. This approach, Mildred Adams concluded in a profile of Sanger in the *Delineator* in 1933, increased her support among influential elements of the public and made it more difficult for her foes to denounce her. "Opinions about Margaret Sanger are much gentler than they used to be." The public's estimate of birth control was also much improved. "Then it was an outlaw which shocked the conservatives and moved the Federal Grand Jury to indictment," noted Adams. "Now it has the formal indorsement of all sorts of thoughtful people." It was also a desire to be more constructive that had led Frances Perkins to move from settlement-house work and the National Consumers' League to a job as labor commissioner of New York State, which led to her appointment as FDR's secretary of labor. The best way to advance the interests of workers, Perkins came to realize, was by demonstrating to businessmen that advocates of labor could understand and appreciate the business point of view. "She has shown all her life that she knows the constituent members of any group . . . are men, not monsters," the journalist Maxine Davis observed in 1935. "Employers know that. . . . Therefore they trust her." This was typical of Perkins's approach to reform. Though inspired by a "profound urgency" to help the down and out, she was "never passionate about it."[29]

Reformers like Perkins, whose commitments and activities could be easily reconciled with the progressive emphasis on serving a transcendent public interest, were well suited to being depicted as practical idealists. Long, successful careers as reformers and public servants had made them aware of the kinds of things that reporters covering them were likely to praise, and they exploited this knowledge in their dealings with the press, providing interviewers, for example, with quotations that they knew would make them appear attractive to readers. Activists in the labor movement found it more difficult to get favorable publicity. As figures like Wald and Perkins had demonstrated, the most effective course for reformers sympathetic to labor—at least the course most likely to garner good press—was for them to position themselves as impartial brokers between capital and labor. But adopting such a position was much easier for reformers from upper-middle-class backgrounds, who sympathized with the labor movement but nonetheless stood outside it, than it was for union activists, who had risen from the ranks of the working class and whose success as organizers depended on promoting class solidarity and convincing workers that employers were their natural antagonists. Building a successful labor movement required eschewing the progressive emphasis on social harmony and the public interest in favor of appeals that purposely sought to divide Americans along class lines.

Needless to say, such an approach did not endear labor leaders like Samuel Gompers to the mainstream press, despite his efforts to distance himself and his trade union movement from radicals. Though journalists applauded Gompers's involvement in the National Civic Federation—an organization composed of progressive businessmen, lawyers, and academics committed to ameliorating class conflict through techniques like arbitration—and his efforts to confine the activities of the American Federation of Labor to bread-and-butter issues like wages, hours, and working conditions, they opposed his promotion of class consciousness and his refusal to condemn strikes. The press's view of him improved during the First World War, when he worked closely with government officials and business executives to ensure that labor conflict did not hobble war production. But his adherence to "un-American" doctrines like the "closed shop" still made him a contradictory figure to most journalists. Writing in 1918, when Gompers's power and influence over the Wilson administration were at their peak, Burton J. Hendrick suggested that Gompers's professions of loyalty to the Allied cause were undercut by his commitment to promoting the interests of trade unions and the working class. For all his seeming moderation, Hendrick argued, Gompers was a "militant fighter for the unionization of American industry," a fighter "who will even take advantage of this unexampled calamity to advance his cause." Because of their controversial views, union leaders like Gompers did not receive nearly the publicity that middle-class reformers active in labor reform did. While the press covered the activities of the unions, it did not produce very many profiles or sketches of their leaders.[30]

In the 1930s this reluctance to publicize labor leaders began to change, as the ranks of organized labor swelled because of new federal legislation that made it easier to organize unions and much harder for employers to refuse to recognize them. Not only were readers of newspapers and magazines now more likely to be union members themselves, but journalists recognized that much of the public was more sympathetic to the cause of labor than ever before, a situation that called for both an increase in reportage and a shift in its tone. This new tone is quite noticeable in the profiles and sketches of labor leaders that began to appear in the press during the mid-1930s, but especially in the press's treatment of the union movement's most visible and controversial figure, John L. Lewis, head of the United Mine Workers and a leader in the movement to organize unskilled workers in the mass-production industries. While many journalists portrayed Lewis as little more than a thug, others sought to present him more favorably, in response to his popularity and the growing appeal of industrial unionism among American workers. Writing in the *American Magazine,* for example, the veteran journalist Beverly Smith conceded that Lewis had a proclivity for rough tactics and showing off, traits that he had developed in the "tough environment" of mine workers. But as the son of a miner who was blacklisted on account of his union activism, Lewis's commitment to the cause was sincere. Possessing abundant intelligence and a fierce desire to succeed, he had worked his way up the only ladder available to young working-class men like himself, the union movement, becoming head of the UMW after bitter fratricidal struggles during the 1920s. It was aggressiveness and opportunism, Smith reported, that had propelled Lewis to the top. He had shown the same qualities in the early 1930s, when he recognized the opportunity created by the New Deal and boldly went about building up his union and championing the organization of workers by industry rather than skill, a course that antagonized the old guard in the AFL and aroused the enmity of employers. Though Smith remained wary of Lewis and disturbed by his "despotic" tendencies, he admired his "gallantry" in being willing to cast aside a cushy life as a union bureaucrat and pursue a potentially noble cause.[31]

Less admirable were radical labor activists such as Harry Bridges, a leader of the Longshoremen's Union and, like Lewis, a major figure in the Congress of Industrial Organizations. In a dual profile of Bridges and the far more conservative Dave Beck, a Teamsters' potentate in Seattle, Richard L. Neuberger asserted that the men represented the two poles of the labor movement in America. To be sure, Bridges was sincere and honest; even his longtime enemies recognized this. "His mission . . . is to improve the lot of labor, and he is determined to let nothing stand in the way of its fulfillment." A staunch believer that the rank and file should control their unions, Bridges denounced labor leaders like Beck as autocratic "racketeers"—a prescient charge considering the conviction that eventually unseated Beck from power in the 1950s. But as a businessman told Neuberger, despite his honesty, Bridges was dangerous. He could see "no good in business," and he inspired workers "to hate and mistrust their employers." "This makes for suspicions and antagonisms that simply don't fit into the American scheme of doing things." Beck, by contrast, was determined to work with business to get the best deal for workers. This approach, Neuberger reported, had won him many supporters, not just among laborers but also among businessmen and professionals in his hometown of Seattle, where he was a leading citizen. Indeed, Beck prided himself on running his union like a business, a big reason, he asserted, that "[b]usiness people have confidence in us." "Capital investment, price stabilization, fair competition, reasonable returns—these are the terms in which Dave Beck speaks." They were terms that endeared him to businessmen, making it easier to reach agreements that while allowing for "closed shops," a key union goal, minimized conflicts and disruptive strikes. By embracing a form of

unionism that recognized the employer's point of view and made partners of labor and business, Beck was the practical idealist committed to
achieving constructive results. This conclusion was confirmed by who
his opponents were: "a combination of extreme conservatives and extreme radicals."[32]

The depiction of Bridges as sincere yet, unlike Beck, overzealous was
typical of the press's portrayal of radicals. Such figures were fanatics;
they had not tempered their "holy zeal." Their attachment to quixotic
doctrines like socialism, which bore little relation to the "realities" of
American life, made them reluctant to engage in the sort of incremental,
coalition-oriented activism that was the keynote of the practical idealist. Some of them, like Debs's successor Norman Thomas, were admirable in their own way, men and women who fought "clean" and "above-
board" for what they believed to be just, even at the cost of political
isolation and public hostility. But others were more dangerous, con-
ducting their campaign for social revolution underground, where they
attempted to "bore from within through violence, intimidation, and
deceit."[33] These figures included the Communist leaders William Z. Foster and Earl Browder, whom journalists regularly lambasted. Writing
in the *New Yorker* in 1930, Alva Johnston depicted Foster as an embittered, deluded neurotic, the "drillmaster of a troop of outpatients from
the psychopathic ward." Another journalist, Hubert Kelley, in a profile
of Browder in the *American Magazine* in 1936, suggested that his lack of
faith in the system could be held only by someone maladjusted or imma-
ture, and he attributed Browder's turn to radical politics to a series of
bad breaks, including a stint in prison during the First World War. After
talking at length with Browder, Kelley was struck by how hard-working
and intelligent he was. "If Browder had devoted to American industry
the persistent energy he has given to Communism," Kelley opined, "a
lot of us might be working for him." But without faith in the system—
without confidence that "the world has been changing for the better
year after year"—Browder's energies were instead directed toward its
destruction. Regardless of their sincerity or the methods by which they
pursued their aims, radicals were outside the American grain.[34]

* * *

The press's marginalization of radicals was not without a purpose. As we
have seen, the early twentieth century witnessed a significant increase
in public support for radical causes, including reform movements that

professed moderate aims but were nonetheless radical by the standards of the day. And while support for such groups declined in the 1920s, it rebounded during the Great Depression, when millions of Americans, including many middle-class people, embraced political causes and movements that openly rejected the incremental, collaborative, and implicitly corporatist approach to reform that the press and most politicians had promoted since the turn of the century. During the mid-1930s the growing appeal of movements like Huey Long's Share-Our-Wealth Society, Father Charles Coughlin's National Union for Social Justice, and the industrial unionism of the fledgling CIO led to a realignment of mainstream politics and new opportunities for reformers and radicals to gain influence—influence that much of the press, in turn, was eager to undermine or at the very least confine. The most important result of this realignment was a shift, in the mid-1930s, in the policies of Franklin D. Roosevelt's administration toward support for new initiatives that historians have called the Second New Deal. Geared toward improving the lives of common people, especially the rural and urban working class, the reforms of the mid-1930s marked an important departure from the more business-friendly approach of the First New Deal, and were accompanied by rhetorical appeals by Roosevelt and some of his leading advisers that encouraged the public to view the political landscape as a battleground between ordinary Americans and well-heeled "economic royalists."[35]

At first glance, these appeals were not very different from those that progressives like Theodore Roosevelt, Woodrow Wilson, and Robert M. La Follette had made earlier in the century. And they were accompanied by sketches of FDR, written by supporters in and out of the administration, that sought to reconcile his administration's new course with the principles of practical idealism. Writing in 1935, amid the political struggles being waged over the reforms that would characterize the Second New Deal, the veteran journalist George Creel wrote a spirited defense of Roosevelt in *Collier's* echoing many of the themes that he and other journalists had sounded in the heyday of the Progressive era, when mainstream politicians had attacked the corrupting influence of "predatory wealth" and the discourse of practical idealism had been used to support reform. But in response to the new political currents of the 1930s, Creel pushed his analysis further, suggesting that FDR was poised to move in new directions, forced to do so by the exigencies of the Depression and the larger process of social and industrial "evolution." "Refusing to dodge realities, he stands like iron in his belief that we have come to a stage in the republic's development when unlimited, unrestricted competition must give way to cooperation, and a planned economy substituted for the haphazard, helter-skelter, dog-eat-dog system under which America has been living." For Creel, the pragmatic course was not caution or respect for precedent—the journalistic conventional wisdom of the 1920s—but an acceptance of the necessity for sweeping change. He reassured readers that Roosevelt had no intention of doing away with the profit motive or private property. FDR was determined, however, to prevent private interests from operating against the general welfare. "Courage, initiative and enterprise are to be preserved as precious heritages, but they must be the *real* article, and not mere masks for rapacity." In response to critics who argued that Roosevelt was deviating from the sacred principles of the Constitution, Creel argued that FDR, like Lincoln, did not believe that the framers meant for the Constitution to be a "dead hand," "chilling human aspiration and blocking humanity's advance." Rather, he saw it as "a living force for the expression of the national will with respect to national needs." In short, Roosevelt remained a devotee of practical idealism—principled yet willing to work with forces within the Democratic Party to achieve important reforms; fired by high ideals and a vision of a "rich, full existence for every citizen" yet also realistic and pragmatic in his approach to reform; determined to create a "new social order" yet respectful of "precious heritages" that were worth preserving.[36]

This argument was echoed by other supporters, particularly administration officials who contributed articles to newspaper syndicates and national magazines. Many of these pieces had a more ambivalent tone than Creel's, acknowledging that the Roosevelt administration had made some notable mistakes but dismissing them by emphasizing the noble intentions that lay behind them—FDR's sincere desire to help "the great inarticulate mass of the American people." For example, Harold L. Ickes, Roosevelt's secretary of the interior, noted in the *Saturday Evening Post* in 1936 that Roosevelt was "neither saint nor devil, archangel nor foul fiend." "A very human individual, he possesses faults as well as virtues." Chief among these was a tendency to be lenient with incompetent or irresponsible underlings—men who had regularly embarrassed the administration. But no one, Ickes insisted, could doubt the president's sincerity, that he has sought "to improve the economic status and make better the living conditions of the average man." Moreover, Ickes, playing on his status as an insider, offered readers abundant information linking Roosevelt the man to the tradition of pragmatic problem solving that journalists had long associated with practical idealism. When confronting a difficult problem, for example, FDR was resourceful and ingenious. "To him there are practically no walls that cannot be scaled or penetrated." Like Creel, administration insiders such as Ickes also suggested that new circumstances demanded more extensive reform than in the past, including "class legislation" like the Wagner Act that empowered working-class people at the expense of employers and the rich—not the more impartial, broker-oriented approach that proponents of practical idealism had been promoting since turn of the century. "He wants people to have enough food to nourish them sufficiently, clothing to keep warm, adequate shelter, a proper amount of recreation to keep body and mind healthy and normal, and an education sufficient for the kind of life that he believes every American should lead." To achieve these goals, it was necessary to enlarge the size and the responsibilities of the federal government.[37]

Despite these efforts, Roosevelt's supporters could not stem the criticism that swamped FDR in the wake of the Second New Deal and his strenuous efforts to protect his reforms from the Supreme Court and conservatives in his own party. Support for Roosevelt and the New Deal in newspapers and magazines declined precipitously between 1936 and 1940, as longtime Republican critics were joined by conservative Democrats like Al Smith and disgruntled ex–New Dealers like Hugh Johnson and Raymond Moley. By lending their voices to the steadily growing cast of Roosevelt's critics, such figures gave the movement opposed to the New Deal a more bipartisan flavor and put FDR and his congressional allies on the defensive. Central to this campaign were caustic profiles of FDR, which rejected the arguments of his supporters and placed blame for the misguided policies of the Second New Deal not on irresponsible aides but squarely on the president's shoulders. From this vantage point, Roosevelt's vices far outweighed his virtues, his "human" frailties paving the way for his corruption.[38]

Perhaps Roosevelt's most influential critic during the late 1930s was a former aide and leading figure in the early "brains trust," the economist Raymond Moley. Exploiting his formerly close relationship with Roosevelt and his role as an important architect of the First New Deal, Moley wrote numerous articles critical of the President and the New Deal for publications like *Newsweek* and the *Saturday Evening Post*. Moley's influence, and his usefulness to periodicals eager to appear above partisan wrangling, derived from his status as an erstwhile insider, a man who had been close to Roosevelt and could offer the public a seemingly more detailed and objective view of him. In an article entitled "A Portrait of FDR," Moley argued in 1939 that Roosevelt had become a disturbing amalgam of the demagogue and the fanatic. His concern for the "submerged third" of the country was sincere, but he lacked "a critical and disciplined intelligence," leading him to embrace crackpot ideas and support policies that were wildly inconsistent and threatened sacred institutions like the separation of powers. Worse, intoxicated by his own exaggerated rhetoric, which had led him to believe that he was the "savior" of the common man, Roosevelt had responded to his critics by becoming increasingly dogmatic and cocksure, dismissing aides who had the temerity to disagree with him and waging war on conservatives in Congress and on the Supreme Court, which had struck down many of his programs. The tragedy of this, Moley concluded, was that Roosevelt had squandered a great opportunity. When he came to power in 1933 progressivism was at its peak, having at last won the support of the majority of the population. "In that sense, he was handed a torch that had been carried by others for generations. He was the trustee of a magnificent tradition." And though his administration had accomplished a great deal, he had alienated thousands of Americans who had asked only that "repair work" be done on the existing system that progressives had built up since the turn of the century. By encouraging class consciousness and class conflict, Moley argued, Roosevelt had divided the nation and betrayed the progressive cause, since "[p]rogressivism depends upon co-operation, not upon conflict."[39]

Yet as Moley noted, Roosevelt's corruption was not surprising. It was the sort of thing that could happen to any man, no matter how well intentioned or highly trained he might be. This was precisely why the Constitution had sought to limit the concentration of power in any man or branch of government, he observed. In the view of other critics, however, Roosevelt was more susceptible to such corruption than other men, particularly men with experience in business and "practical affairs" The critics usually attributed this tendency to Roosevelt's temperament and aristocratic background. According to Hugh Johnson, former administrator of the National Recovery Administration, Roosevelt was a "congenital prima donna," whose "aristocratic reserve" led him to surround himself with sycophants and recoil from interaction

—and conflict—with men who were his intellectual equals. "He seeks complete subservience. He thrives on adulation and submission. He believes he has enough on the ball not to need counsel." Writing in *Collier's*, the advertising executive and GOP kingmaker Bruce Barton was even more dismissive of FDR. Seeking to appear moderate and constructive, Barton began his article by insisting that he and other liberal businessmen had begun with high hopes for Roosevelt and the New Deal, and that his hopes were largely borne out during the first two years, when the predominant influence on the president was his long-time aide Louis McHenry Howe. Howe's death, Barton wrote, was an important turning point. Without a "voice of conscience and experience" by his side, Roosevelt fell under the influence of a younger, more irresponsible set of advisors, men like the progressive economist and conservative whipping-boy Rexford G. Tugwell who lacked the will or ability to check Roosevelt's temperamental inclinations as a reformer. Indeed, for Barton, FDR's impulsiveness, dogmatism, and bitterness toward his opponents were evidence of a reformer's habitual "intolerance" and "self-righteousness," traits that arose from the "inferiority complex" that reformers often felt toward successful businessmen, and that Roosevelt shared with many of his younger aides from similarly privileged backgrounds.[40]

Of all the New Dealers, none came under as much fire as Tugwell, a Columbia University economist who was one of the administration's most vocal advocates of social democratic policies. In the view of many journalists, Tugwell was a sinister influence on Roosevelt and the main reason for the New Deal's sharp turn to the left. "Tugwell's philosophy, his mental operations and his very phrases shine through the speeches and messages of his chief," Alva Johnston asserted in a particularly nasty profile of Tugwell in the *Saturday Evening Post* in 1936. "The great change in the political views of Roosevelt dates from his association with Tugwell. In pre-Tugwell days, Roosevelt was an eloquent defender of state rights, and vigorous champion of the Supreme Court, a furious denouncer of extravagance, bureaucracy and centralized government; a prophet who warned the country that taxes must be paid for by the sweat of the workingman." But this was no longer the case. Tugwell, Johnston argued, was an idealist, a dreamer, a crank who entertained fantasies of "making America over into a perfect state in which everybody would be completely regimented and deliriously happy." But though Tugwell posed a threat to the nation, he was unlikely to succeed.

This was because he was arrogant and incapable of cultivating support among politicians who might be able to help him. As Johnston made clear in a long account of Tugwell's checkered career in the Department of Agriculture, he was also a terrible administrator and had thoroughly botched every job that Roosevelt had given him, making him a lightning rod for opponents of the New Deal. For Johnston and many of his other critics, Tugwell's many flaws were attributable to his longtime immersion in left-wing academic circles, where the crackpots and fanatics who had deluded poor William Jennings Bryan had found homes. Though he fancied himself a patriotic American, Tugwell was no less a revolutionary than William Z. Foster. The major difference between them, Johnston concluded, was that while Tugwell was a naive idealist, Foster was a realist who "never indulged . . . in the fancy that a nation could suddenly be made over without plenty of bloodshed."[41]

The late 1930s, as numerous historians have shown, was a pivotal moment in the history of American liberalism and the New Deal, a moment when, for various reasons, the Roosevelt administration and many of its liberal allies gradually backed away from the more aggressive social democratic course suggested by the Second New Deal. As the United States began to mobilize for war, Roosevelt announced that "Dr. New Deal" had been replaced by "Dr. Win-the-War," a new guise that allowed the administration to rebuild bridges to business and regain the goodwill of much of the press. Indeed in the early 1940s Roosevelt was extolled by reporters, in a veritable avalanche of articles depicting him as "commander-in-chief," an angle that much to FDR's relief stressed his role as a national leader and largely obscured the bitter ideological conflicts of the 1930s.[42] Coupled with a new emphasis on using fiscal policy to encourage economic growth and mass consumption, an approach more popular with businessmen, this movement toward the center brought to an end the New Deal's halting efforts to go much beyond the institutional synthesis developed by progressive reformers and liberal businessmen between 1900 and the mid-1930s. It also marked the end of efforts to redefine practical idealism along reformist lines. Having survived the crisis of the 1930s, the conservative version of practical idealism was reenshrined as the prevailing discourse of political reportage, one well-suited to the centrism of mid-century politics, when reformers and liberals—including many former Marxists—went out of their way to appear pragmatic, constructive, and sympathetic to business.

The discourse of practical idealism that the mainstream press employed in its coverage of politics and political celebrities changed considerably between the early twentieth century and the 1930s. In the hands of its original architects, practical idealism was mobilized in support of reform, encouraging the public to believe that the political arena could be reclaimed from the corrupt elements that had commandeered it. Practical idealism inspired readers to believe that some politicians and reformers—who embodied the political version of true success—were sincerely devoted to the public interest, and that through their efforts government could assume important new responsibilities that would make America a more humane and democratic nation. This was a momentous project, offering crucial ideological support to political modernizers from both parties who were eager to create a more centralized and powerful administrative state and convince the public that doing so was compatible with America's republican heritage. By depicting political figures as practical idealists, the press sought to defuse the public's fear of this campaign and reconcile it with revered traditions. As in the press's portrayals of businessmen, the gist of this reporting was that the new institutions of modern American politics were nothing to be concerned about. Manned by practical idealists, they could serve the public interest just as well as older institutions that might appear more responsive to the people's will.

From the start, however, the reformist bent of practical idealism was offset by a residual conservatism, symbolized by the repeated assertion that practical idealists were constructive and understanding of all points of view—including, not coincidentally, the "business point of view." In the 1920s and 1930s these conservative themes came to the fore. Redefined, the discourse of practical idealism was now used by the press to discredit popular movements and the social democratic thrust of the Second New Deal. This was so even though the movements enjoyed widespread public appeal, in fact far wider appeal than some of the movements that journalists in the Progressive era had enthusiastically supported. In short, the mainstream press's waning commitment to reform did not necessarily reflect waning public support for it.

So what accounts for the increasingly conservative uses that the mainstream press made of the discourse of practical idealism? The answer may well lie in the latent ideological mission of mass-circulation journalism. Support for reform came easily to the press during the early twentieth century, when abuses and injustices were grave, and when class and ethnic divisions made it wholly unfeasible for the press to fulfill its intention of serving as the tribune of a unified public. Moreover, at this time many journalists were inspired by new intellectual movements like the Social Gospel, which made reform seem all the more attractive and a natural commitment for members of the emerging professional-managerial class. By the 1920s, however, after much-needed reforms had been enacted and the First World War had chastened most journalists and middle-class Americans, reform no longer seemed necessary or attractive—indeed, the commitments of the progressive generation now appeared naive. Adopting a perspective that effaced class and ethnic divisions prevailing since the mid-nineteenth century and promised to create a new basis for public unity, the editors of most newspapers and magazines viewed their readers primarily as consumers and were reluctant to support or portray favorably movements threatening to divide the cross-class, multiethnic audience that the editors were so laboriously constructing. Nor were they eager to arouse passions among the public and provoke the sort of hysterical outbursts that had occurred during the war, and to which ordinary people were thought to be especially susceptible. Journalists were perfectly willing to acknowledge the often disparate aims of various "interest groups" that composed the body politic. However, with few exceptions, they did not address their readers as members of such groups but as consumer-citizens, members of a single public which the press claimed to serve.[43]

Yet this profession of impartiality was belied by the selective biases that the press regularly betrayed in its coverage of individuals and movements, particularly the undisguised contempt that it expressed for anyone who seemed to threaten business interests. No such contempt—only mild exasperation—was directed at conservatives and reactionaries who zealously opposed organized labor or even the mildest progressive reforms. Thus beneath the lofty rhetoric of objectivity and public service lay a disturbing fact. By the 1920s the mass-circulation press in the United States had become inordinately sympathetic to business interests—not exactly a "business press," as Marxist critics might suggest, but one reflexively inclined toward positions that were either pro-business or reformist in ways acceptable to liberals in the business community. Early in the century this was not yet the case. Uncertain about the outcome of the conflicts that had been sparked by America's emergence as an urban-industrial society and emboldened by a heady sense of independence, many publishers and editors opened their columns to views that were unorthodox and sometimes even radical.

But the powerful incentive to build circulation through appeals to readers as consumers—a strategy handsomely rewarded by advertisers—undercut this openness. Recognizing the importance of retaining the goodwill of advertisers and conservative, upper-middle-class readers, who were not just part of the public but its most influential constituency, editors were forced to make sure that their support for reform was moderate and acknowledged the "business point of view." This strategy was reinforced by the growing professional identity of many editors and reporters, which stressed the importance of being "realistic" in their view of the world. These considerations did not necessarily make the mass-circulation press conservative. Journalists continued to expose injustices and suggest the need for reform, using appeals to "industrial statesmanship," for example, to encourage businessmen to adopt more enlightened policies. These appeals, which gave rise to the myth of the "liberal" press, appalled many businessmen, perhaps the majority. Yet there was an institutional preference for moderation, compelling politicians and reformers to operate within discursive parameters that were hostile to those seeking to change the status quo.

7

THERE'S NO BUSINESS
LIKE SHOW BUSINESS
CELEBRITY AND THE POPULAR
CULTURE INDUSTRIES

In 1938, amid the tumult and recriminations aroused by the policies of the Second New Deal, newspaper readers across the country were informed of an unusual incident. Enraged by the complaints of a well-paid Hollywood director about increases in the income tax, which had "soaked the rich" as promised and made the Roosevelt administration even more unpopular among the well-to-do, the actress Carole Lombard, one of the best-paid women in the movie industry, announced to a United Press reporter, "I gave the Federal Government 65% of my wages last year, and I was glad to do it, too. . . . Income tax money all goes into improvement and protection of the country. . . . I really think I got my money's worth."[1]

Lombard's comments were widely published and inspired reams of commentary among pundits, including a mash note by the mainstream media's leading liberal, Heywood Broun, who cited her as an example of a wealthy American who had come to embrace the new responsibilities of citizenship under the New Deal. Her enthusiastic support for a policy that adversely affected her not only ran against the grain of public expectations about movie stars and the rich in general. It positioned her on the side of the "common people" in the political struggles of the day. Several years later, Alva Johnston suggested that "[p]robably no other news item ever did so much to increase the popularity of a star" and improve Hollywood's standing in the eyes of the public. That standing, Johnston noted, was especially important to Lombard's new employer, the maverick independent producer David O. Selznick, and his press agent, the intrepid Russell Birdwell. It was Birdwell who had had the presence of mind to recognize the publicity value of Lombard's spontaneous outburst, which occurred in the privacy of her dressing room with no reporters present. As Lombard began to rage, Birdwell stopped her and quickly phoned the United Press. A minute later, when he allowed her to continue, a reporter was taking notes on the other end of the line, and within a couple of hours, "an interview was clicking out over the telegraph wires to hundreds of newspapers."[2]

As this incident reveals, Birdwell and Selznick were acutely conscious of the movie industry's reputation and quick to seize any opportunity to improve it. Moreover, they recognized that the best means of doing so lay in associating the industry with populism and "democratic" values —and directing public attention away from the wealth and privileges enjoyed by movie stars and moguls alike. This concern was shared by many other industry leaders and extended to figures in other popular culture industries as well. Nor was it peculiar to the politically charged atmosphere of the 1930s, when public support for economic and cultural populism was at its peak. As we shall see, impresarios of popular culture had shown an interest in improving the reputation of their field as early as the 1850s, and had sought to enlist the press as allies in this campaign. That Birdwell and Selznick were still engaged in it nearly one hundred years later, however, suggests that the campaign had not been entirely successful.

Actors and entertainers first began attracting press coverage in the 1840s, when promoters and theater managers discovered that public interest in an event or performance could be aroused by publicizing the men and women in the cast. This realization gave rise to a "star system" in the theater that by the 1850s made possible the celebrity of performers like Edwin Forrest and Charlotte Cushman. To the delight of promoters and managers, regular press coverage of such popular stars— including accounts of their private lives and personal affairs—could generate a predictable, built-in demand for events in which they appeared. To attract publicity, entrepreneurs cultivated the support of newspaper editors and reporters, rewarding them with everything from lucrative advertising contracts to free tickets and opportunities to hobnob with stars. The result was a surge in advertisements promoting popular culture events as well as "free publicity," newspaper articles about developments in the field that were just as important in making the public aware of upcoming shows and familiar with the fledgling entertainment industry's most compelling personalities.

After the Civil War, press coverage of the popular culture industries increased, as their attractions became more interesting to readers of the mass-circulation press—and thus of greater interest to journalists seeking to make their publications more topical. Growing public interest in theater and vaudeville led newspapers to assign reporters as "dramatic paragraphers," who covered the entertainment beat and produced regular columns and feature stories about show-business celebrities like Edwin Booth, Mary Anderson, and Richard Mansfield. Coverage of foreign actors and entertainers who toured the United States also increased, allowing performers like Sarah Bernhardt and Ellen Terry to become as well known in America as they were in Europe. So great was the appeal of these stories that in the 1880s and 1890s they began to appear in Sunday supplements and new-style mass-circulation magazines like *Munsey's* and *Cosmopolitan.* Indeed, by the turn of the century critics as well as dramatic paragraphers were contributing long features to these publications, and soon feature stories overwhelmed conventional criticism; magazines like *Collier's* and the *Saturday Evening Post* dispensed with reviews altogether.

The triumph of feature stories was complete by the teens, when articles about show-business figures became a staple of newspapers and magazines, and new publications aimed at moving picture "fans" and composed entirely of profiles and features made their first appearance. Though readers with a consuming interest in actors and entertainers became avid readers of specialized publications like *Photoplay* and *Motion Picture,* the attention that newspapers and general-interest magazines devoted to show-business celebrities continued to increase during the 1920s and 1930s, as editors struggled to keep pace with the rising popularity of show business and prevent readers from defecting to their new competitors. A perusal of mass-circulation magazines from the late 1930s reveals that feature stories about the popular culture industries and especially profiles of actors and entertainers were common in the great majority of publications—from *Liberty* and *Collier's* to *Life,* the *Saturday Evening Post,* and the *New Yorker*—making much of the press a virtual adjunct of the publicity departments at the major studios, theatrical syndicates, and radio networks that had come to dominate the production of popular culture.

Yet if press coverage of the popular culture industries served important promotional functions, it often did so indirectly, through rhetorical strategies openly aimed at questions that had long haunted producers—and that press agents had tried for many years to sweep under the rug. These questions cut to the very heart of the enterprise, encouraging public skepticism about the motives of producers and the quality of the products that they peddled. The questions were most forcefully articulated in magazines aimed at a "sophisticated" audience, like the *American Mercury* and the *New Yorker,* whose raison d'être included disdaining popular culture. But they were also raised in mainstream newspapers and magazines, even unabashedly "lowbrow" organs like *Liberty, Photoplay,* and publications of the Hearst press, and consequently the questions were ones that press agents were compelled to acknowledge. As a result, press coverage of show business from the 1890s through the 1930s was tinged with ambivalence, its promotional mission accompanied by an obsession with the unsavory dimensions of the popular culture industries that became a central feature of reportage. This ambivalence was not always on display. Many features, written under the watchful eye of shrewd show-business publicists like Channing Pollock and Russell Birdwell, were relentlessly upbeat. Many others, however, were not. And when coupled with news stories and gossip that openly refuted the more cheery assessments, these articles conjured up a vision of show business that was mixed.

This ambivalence was also expressed in newspaper and magazine profiles of actors and entertainers. These figures played an important symbolic role in their fields, and articles about them, as Alva Johnston observed in his account of Birdwell's career, were often produced to reflect well on the industries in which they were employed. Yet quite a few articles were not so effective as industry propaganda, even when they advanced the interests of individual stars. In their efforts to depict show-business celebrities sympathetically, journalists regularly criticized elements within the popular culture industries and the broader emphasis of the field, suggesting that their subjects, like Carole Lombard, were exemplars of the show-business version of true success, having resisted forces that had compromised a large number of their peers. This argument, which dominated press coverage of popular culture, was integral to the press's efforts to improve the image of show business and make reporting about it resonate with the concerns of readers. By making such invidious distinctions, journalists encouraged public interest in actors and entertainers—but they also perpetuated doubts and suspicions that industry leaders and their publicists were eager to dispel.

*   *   *

Press coverage of popular culture was complicated, from the first, by the efforts of journalists to reach a mass audience at a time when class and ethnic differences in the United States were becoming more pronounced. Following the trail blazed by the entrepreneurs who established the penny press, most newspaper publishers in the mid-nineteenth century were committed to providing working-class and petit-bourgeois readers—a growing majority—with stories that were interesting and informative, and this meant devoting attention to new commercial amusements that were becoming increasingly popular with the same readers. Doing so, however, made editors and publishers vulnerable to attacks by ministers, reformers, and other self-styled arbiters of Victorian morality, who viewed most forms of popular culture as frivolous and potentially dangerous, and accused the press of encouraging immorality through its coverage of the field. To the dismay of publishers, these critics had considerable influence over many middle-class and upper-class Americans, equally important elements of the mass audience that the publishers were intent on serving—perhaps more important given their higher disposable income and greater attractiveness to advertisers. In hopes of satisfying patrons and critics alike, many editors continued to publish stories about popular culture, which they supplemented with moralistic editorials and exposés that allowed the publications to appear respectable to bourgeois readers. For example, in 1869, while reviewers and dramatic paragraphers for the *New York Times* lavished praise on the burlesque performer Lydia Thompson and her troupe the British Blondes, editorials decried the popularity of the same amusements, which pandered to "the base and vulgar elements of human nature."[3]

These editorial appeals were instrumental in encouraging entrepreneurs like P. T. Barnum and Tony Pastor to repackage their amusements, making them more acceptable in the eyes of the press and "respectable" Americans. Though by the 1870s attacks on the popular culture industries had waned after reformers had failed to wean the urban working class and many immigrants and ethnics away from them, Barnum and Pastor recognized that the middle class represented a vast

untapped market. With the assistance of the press, they made significant changes to attract this audience—establishing new rules ban-
ning alcohol and governing conduct within their establishments, hiring
"high-class" performers whom they interspersed among more conventional variety acts, and advertising their shows in ways that made them
seem at once edifying and risqué. At Pastor's enormous, lavishly decorated vaudeville theaters, for example, scantily clad women were billed
as "champion swimmers" or "gymnasts," which made it much easier for
the press to promote them. By the 1890s, in response to these promotional efforts and new imperatives within middle-class culture that encouraged an interest in leisure and intense experience, a large number of
middle-class Americans had become regular patrons of vaudeville and
the theater. To be sure, commercial amusements catering largely to the
working class and immigrants persisted. In the early 1900s, for example,
small, dingy moving picture theaters called "nickelodeons" began to
proliferate in working-class neighborhoods, several years before the first
movie "palaces" were built for middle-class patrons. And the promoters
of these amusements still aroused the ire of bourgeois moralists and elements of the press. But now there was a model that these entrepreneurs
could follow to acquire legitimacy, and by faithfully adhering to it virtually all the major popular culture industries eventually gained substantial middle-class support.[4]

The gentrification of popular culture led the press to tone down its
criticism. In the 1890s self-righteous editorials and fawning interviews
with reformers crusading against the theater and vaudeville faded from
the pages of newspapers and mass-circulation magazines, which thus
became far more effective vehicles for promotion and "free publicity."
Yet editors and reporters did not completely succumb to the blandish-
ments of promoters and press agents. They remained critical of popular culture, especially variety shows and their early-twentieth-century
offspring, the primitive, often ribald moving pictures that immigrant
exhibitors displayed in storefront nickelodeons. At the same time, journalists became vocal champions of high-class vaudeville and the "legitimate" theater—and enthusiastic boosters of producers and performers
in these fields who were committed to "quality" fare. These figures were
contrasted with others who were accused of introducing elements imported from "low" culture and cheapening the industry. For journalists
at the turn of the century, then, popular culture was a sharply bifur-
cated field, composed on the one hand of admirable entrepreneurs who

produced works worthy of public patronage, and on the other hand of hacks and panderers who produced "trash" and whose influence, the press argued, was on the rise. Writing in 1909, Samuel Hopkins Adams asserted that "sensuality" in the legitimate theater had increased markedly since the 1890s, as producers recognized the profits that could be earned by appealing "to the Yahoo that lurks within all of us, to the beast that we hold in leash, out of respect to ourselves and to our fellows."[5]

Among the most influential critics of show business in the early twentieth century were William Winter, Walter Prichard Eaton, and Alan Dale, who reviewed plays for New York newspapers and wrote syndicated feature stories about the state of the theater and its most illustrious stars. Sensitive to their proximity to the sources of theatrical publicity, these critics sought to display their independence by deflating the hype that surrounded many plays and performers. They were also critics of moving pictures and an important influence on movie moguls such as Adolph Zukor, spurring them to produce longer, more serious films. In the teens and twenties, as critics like Winter, Eaton, and Dale began to retire, a new generation of critics and feature writers emerged, including George Jean Nathan, Alexander Woollcott, and Gilbert Seldes. While older critics like Winter and Eaton evaluated popular culture through a vaguely Arnoldian lens, measuring it against works that were said to exemplify "truth" and "beauty," their successors were fundamentally modernist in outlook. From their vantage point, the problem with both popular culture and Arnoldian "high culture" was a lack of creativity, authenticity, and realism. Moreover, like Dale, perhaps the most widely read critic in the nation by virtue of his position as chief dramatic writer for the Hearst press and a pioneer in the production of human-interest features about the theater, younger journalists like Nathan and Woollcott infused their articles with wit and entertaining asides.[6]

Writing for upscale magazines like *Vanity Fair,* the *Smart Set,* and the *New Yorker,* as well as for others closer to the mainstream, these writers exerted a powerful influence on other journalists and the public's view of show business. As committed urbanites. Nathan, Woollcott, and Seldes found much to admire in American popular culture—particularly in the work of such figures as Charlie Chaplin, Al Jolson, and George Herriman, the creator of the comic strip "Krazy Kat." In his pathbreaking book on popular culture, *The Seven Lively Arts* (1924), Seldes expressed dismay that these works were disdained by genteel critics like Winter and Eaton. On the whole, however, these writers reaffirmed the journalistic conventional wisdom that divided the field into artists and hacks. Even Seldes acknowledged the industry's disturbing features as he celebrated figures like Chaplin and Mack Sennett who had been able to surmount them. This not only kept the industry's shortcomings in the public eye; it forced more optimistic writers to acknowledge them as well, establishing a context in which the shortcomings remained a specter always threatening to intrude.[7]

For both sets of critics, the problems with popular culture could be traced to a single source, its slavish devotion to commercialism. Producers were only interested in making money, leading them to rely on hackneyed formulas that were known to attract audiences but kept the field from developing artistically. Cynically exploiting the public's most debased inclinations—the "sensual" and the "animal," in Samuel Hopkins Adams's view—some producers went even further, creating works that were not merely bad but morally offensive. More common, yet equally deplorable, were producers who peddled platitudes and clichés in their lame attempts to make their productions "uplifting." As journalists often noted, commercialization was not confined to vaudeville and musical theater. By the turn of the century it had come to influence producers in the legitimate theater and was epitomized by the rise of David Belasco, whose lavish melodramas set the tone for "serious" Broadway productions in the early 1900s. Though Belasco was the beneficiary of a massive public relations buildup orchestrated by his press agent, Charles Emerson Cook, his productions received mixed reviews from critics, and writers like Alan Dale were of two minds about his success, which was often attributed to gimmicks and special effects. Reporters and critics believed that commercialization was even more pronounced in the fledgling motion picture industry. Indeed, the appearance of the first movies—riotous one- and two-reelers made for working-class audiences—led many writers to express a greater appreciation for the theater, even the works of Belasco and the reigning hacks of musical theater, William A. Brady and Florenz Ziegfeld. Contempt for much of the film industry's fare persisted throughout the 1920s and 1930s, despite the efforts of producers like Zukor and Irving Thalberg to make motion pictures appear more respectable. For example, in an acerbic profile of Thalberg in *Vanity Fair* in 1927, the journalist Jim Tully acknowledged that the movie industry's "boy wonder" had "the beginnings of an artist in his make-up" and, unlike most producers, actually read books. "But as a corporation official, he must give to money the first and last consideration." And this commitment, Tully argued, fatally compromised whatever interest Thalberg had in infusing his films with artistry.[8]

Journalists believed that the commercial imperatives governing the popular culture industries had a profound impact on creative personnel who worked in the field. The demands of producers for simplistic, entertaining plays and scripts encouraged writers to devote themselves to creating such works rather than the more edifying or serious ones that they were capable of producing. The screenwriter Frances Marion, for example, might have been a fine novelist, "far greater than Willa Cather," Tully suggested. But the easy money and comfortable life of a Hollywood hack led her to give up serious fiction for material that she herself recognized as "bunk." The restrictions imposed on actors, reporters noted, were just as severe. Exploiting the public's preference for superficiality, many producers preferred to hire actors who had "personality," and not those with true talent. Once these figures became stars, producers commissioned playwrights and screenwriters to produce vehicles for them that kept their unique attributes in the forefront. This in turn resulted in many actors' being typecast, which allowed them to make a very good living but caused many to become frustrated artistically and ill prepared for moving into different kinds of roles in later years, when the appeal of their personalities had waned. Writing in *Cosmopolitan* in 1906, Dale likened this process to the production of sausage in Chicago, the subject of Upton Sinclair's sensational muckraking novel *The Jungle*. "Every season we drop at least half a dozen meek young people who can neither talk distinctly, act convincingly, nor give any evidence of dramatic fitness, into that fine, open-mouthed machine, and out they come at the other end as 'stars,' full fledged." According to journalists, the frustration felt by moving picture actors was even more acute. Not only was reliance on "personality" and typecasting more common in the film industry, but the nature of production made acting skill largely superfluous. "Real acting of the kind seen in the theatre is seldom in demand in the world of filmdom," a writer for *Woman's Home Companion* argued in 1918. In the view of many journalists, the popular culture industries did not merely waste talent; their commercial bent actually inhibited its development.[9]

Typecasting and preferring actors with "personality" had another baleful effect. Reporters suggested that these trends encouraged many

actors and entertainers to act off stage. This was said to be an occupational hazard for men and women employed in the popular culture
industries, who had a powerful incentive to keep their names and faces
constantly in the public eye. By maintaining a high profile, they made
themselves more attractive to producers and theater managers, and
thus more likely to be employed in their productions. These entertainers
engaged in publicity stunts and made themselves the subjects of gossip and feature stories. They appeared at restaurants, nightclubs, and
premieres, and were frequently seen in other public places, behaving in
a fashion that made them instantly recognizable, often as a version of
the kind of character they regularly played. The actor who was typecast, Alan Dale suggested, could hardly prevent falling victim to this
peculiar aliment. "He has been so busy impersonating other people, his
serious life has been so wrapped up in the pretense that he is somebody else, that when his leisure comes he finds it almost impossible to
sink to the level of his own self." Public expectations made the situation even worse. Afraid of disappointing fans, many actors and entertainers found it almost impossible to be natural. So common was this
practice in the movie industry that journalists in the 1920s and 1930s
gave it a new name: "going Hollywood." Actors so afflicted became the
glamorous characters whom they impersonated, a metamorphosis encouraged by studio publicity and the elaborate lessons that the actors
received to efface all signs of their lowly former selves. Though acting
off stage often brought tangible rewards, journalists insisted that it was
ultimately a dead end for performers, producing unhappiness and con-
fusion. Having been transformed "from one being into another and still
another," Gloria Swanson, for example, did not have the faintest idea of
who the "real Gloria" was, Adela Rogers St. Johns informed readers of
Liberty in 1929.[10]

The commercial nature of the popular culture industries also made
actors and entertainers more susceptible to immorality. Critics of the
theater had assailed the morality of actors since the Elizabethan era,
and during the nineteenth century—as new commercial amusements
like variety and burlesque became fixtures in many American cities, and
a powerful evangelically inspired culture of respectability came to prevail among the urban and provincial middle classes—exposés purport-
ing to reveal the debauchery of actors and entertainers became regular
features in the mass-circulation press. In the early twentieth century, as
the press became increasingly enmeshed in the publicity apparatus of

the popular culture industries, journalists continued to display their independence to readers by exploiting scandals involving people in show business. But in a new twist, they now framed the scandals in ways that made commercialization a major culprit. As Hartley Davis noted in *Munsey's* in 1901, actors and entertainers remained a "clannish lot" who socialized mostly with one another. Flung together on the road for weeks or even months at a time, dressing and undressing in close proximity, men and women often developed immoral relationships that would be frowned upon outside their exclusive world. Yet conventional mores had no influence on them; nor did fear of having their sordid activities revealed. Indeed, being notorious could very easily spark an increase in an entertainer's box office appeal. There were celebrities, observed Davis, who could "measure the value of scandal in dollars and cents." These dangers were amplified when successful actors were typecast. During John Barrymore's early years as a matinee idol on Broadway, the feature writer Keene Sumner reported in 1919, the young actor had little incentive to work on improving his skills, since in play after play he impersonated essentially the same character, "a dashing and dissipated society hero." Lacking motivation and with ample free time, Barrymore became nearly as irresponsible and dissolute as his characters. Rather than reprimand him, however, producers and directors simply looked the other away, since he did his job well enough and was a tremendous box office attraction among young women.[11]

In spite of new opportunities in the moving picture industry that made it possible for actors to enjoy more regular employment and a much higher wage, journalists asserted that the moral climate in Los Angeles, where most movie people settled during the teens, was not much better. Many articles on the inhabitants of "filmdom" portrayed them as spoiled, irresponsible adolescents who partied and spent money with reckless abandon. Reporters explained this by noting that many of the industry's highest-paid stars were not trained actors but ignorant neophytes recently removed from work as deliverymen and telephone operators. During the late teens many feature stories about the emerging movie colony in Hollywood focused on the flood of naive, uneducated young men and women who were moving there in hopes of becoming movie stars—and who, upon arrival, were either ignored or ruthlessly exploited by the crass, often lecherous "aliens" who controlled the industry. The vast majority of these would-be movie stars wound up as bartenders, waitresses, and stenographers—or simply moved back home. If "movie-struck girls" knew the facts about the industry, William A. Page suggested in *Woman's Home Companion*, knew that hundreds of attractive young women were desperately seeking work and that there were "five hundred applicants for every position, even as an extra girl," they would not be so keen on moving to Hollywood and trying to break into the business. Hollywood, Page concluded, was a "rainbow-like illusion which fascinates and attracts, only to bring, in the long run, unhappiness, disappointment, and failure to many thousands of girls every year." [12]

But when serious scandals rocked Hollywood in the early 1920s, the often wry tone of articles like Page's gave way to reporting that expressed outrage and contempt for the industry. The arrest and murder trial of the comedian Roscoe "Fatty" Arbuckle in 1921, for example, led many newspapers and magazines to publish unflattering articles that encouraged the public to view the denizens of Hollywood as wanton libertines. As one report noted in establishing the background for Arbuckle's arrest, which occurred at one of his riotous parties when a woman with whom he was having sex was fatally injured, "All down the glittering gold coast of the Los Angeles motion picture colony, peopled by men and women of humble beginning suddenly possessed of fabulous wealth because of a pretty face, a fat physique, wavy hair or a simpering smile, Fatty Arbuckle is known for the 'parties' he gives. . . . And no guest . . . could go through an Arbuckle affair without finding a new thrill." These thrills, as media coverage of the trial revealed, included massive alcohol consumption, the use of illicit drugs, and perverse sexual practices. Though sympathetic journalists like George Ade, a close friend of the movie industry's new czar, Will Hays, effectively defused the scandals of the early 1920s, the overall impression fostered by reportage about Hollywood remained ambiguous. As portrayed by the press, it was a place of superficiality and self-indulgence, where good looks and personality trumped acting skill, and easy money and commercialism encouraged a style of life that could very easily degenerate into debauchery. [13]

* * *

Thus the triumph of popular culture as a pastime among middle-class Americans did not completely banish criticism of it. Even as the press gave producers reams of "free publicity," many journalists remained dubious of show business, producing articles that depicted the popular culture industries in a less than flattering light. At most, however, these critical pieces formed the outlines of a portrait, for they were accompanied by countless shrewdly placed and expertly crafted feature stories that depicted the business more positively. Among the most important of these were celebrity profiles of producers, composers, and directors. Often written by journalists critical of show business, many of these articles acknowledged the industry's disquieting features. But they did so while asserting that their subjects were far removed from these features, and that exceptions were more common than most people believed. Burying critical commentary in an avalanche of inside dope, the authors of these profiles helped to redefine the conventional wisdom about the popular culture industries, promoting a new view more appealing to middle-class readers. Journalists accomplished this not by overturning the hierarchical categories that had long been employed to dismiss popular culture but by reaffirming them.

Their main argument was that producers of popular culture were motivated by more than money. According to reporters, they were also interested in producing works that were "artistic." The theatrical impresario Daniel Frohman, for example, was a highly cultured man who did not always follow a commercial blueprint, a writer for the *Saturday Evening Post* revealed in 1909. Though Frohman was a businessmen who recognized the importance of the bottom line, "he goes his own way, with much more consideration than you would think for Art and less consideration than you would think for the money side of it." Producers like Frohman and David Belasco were determined to provide something worthwhile to the public—plays that were not just entertaining but thought-provoking and uplifting. This desire, however, ran up against the public's preference for simplistic and superficial productions that featured big stars. As Belasco noted in an interview in 1902 in *Leslie's Weekly,* "One must cater to public taste to a certain extent, you know." Much the same dilemma plagued George M. Cohan, the journalist Peter Clark Macfarlane suggested in a profile of the showman in *Everybody's* in 1914. Early in his career Cohan was an unabashed crowd-pleaser who achieved commercial success by shamelessly pandering to the crowd, an approach that made his plays sentimental and often vulgar. Yet his more recent productions, Macfarlane reported, revealed "ambitions which are worthy of our very high respect." And though his more serious works were not always as successful as his vulgar ones, his interest in moving in this direction was a welcome sign of his awakening "good taste." Macfarlane attributed Cohan's growing seriousness to the influence of critics, and he reported happily that Cohan was eagerly reading Shaw and Shakespeare and preparing himself to write "a big, real moving drama." Whether his audience would follow remained to seen. But in Macfarlane's view, this was much less important than Cohan's determination to grow as an artist.[14]

The same impulses, according to journalists, inspired America's most successful songwriters. Even more than theatrical producers, popular songwriters in the early twentieth century were subjected to terrific abuse by newspaper music critics who deplored their borrowings from the music of African Americans. By the teens, however, a number of writers, in particular the modernist-influenced critics clustered around *Vanity Fair* and the *Smart Set*, began to view popular music more sympathetically—precisely because of its close connection to the seemingly more "authentic" cultures of blacks and Eastern European immigrants. This greater appreciation for popular music was reflected in the growing celebrity of composers like Irving Berlin, who was extolled by journalists for his ability to "catch the rhythm of his land and time." Though Berlin never received a conventional musical education and was proud to write songs for the "mob," his music was also great art, which writers like Alexander Woollcott attributed not to technical sophistication but to simplicity and authenticity. Berlin's songs, Woollcott argued in the *Saturday Evening Post*, were "conversations written to music, and in the best of them there is the true salt of the American language." Even more impressive, in the view of journalists, were the achievements of George Gershwin, who refused to be confined by the genre of popular songwriting yet never lost his belief in the importance of making music that could be appreciated by a wide audience. From the beginning of his career as a Tin Pan Alley songwriter, reporters noted, Gershwin had powerful artistic aspirations, producing hit songs that explicitly eschewed the sentimental. Yet it was not until he wrote *Rhapsody in Blue*, the critic Issac Goldberg contended in 1931 in *Ladies' Home Journal*, that these aspirations were clearly revealed and that Gershwin emerged as a bona fide musical genius, "building upon the rhythms of the jungle a new music compounded of grace, vitality, and dignity." Gershwin's artistry, in short, lay not merely in his invocation of the vernacular, but in his ability to make of it something greater than the sum of its parts. This was a distinguishing feature of all "artists" who plied their trade in the popular culture industries. While looking to blacks, immigrants, or rural people for inspiration, they were able to "repackage" their raw materials into forms that made them appealing to a mass audience and lifted them to the level of art.[15]

Journalists sympathetic to the motion picture industry were also quick to adopt this argument. They reported that most producers and directors were committed to making high-quality films. The problem lay with movie audiences, especially the many working-class people who were regular patrons and preferred pictures that were shallow and mindlessly escapist. As Cecil B. De Mille informed the journalist Karl Kitchen in 1919, "Moving picture plays are made for Lizzie. . . . Lizzie likes plays which she can understand. . . . And she insists on happy endings. Personally, I'm opposed to happy endings, unless they are logical—in keeping with the story. But Lizzie forces us to make the pictures we do." De Mille asserted that he and his colleagues had not given up the idea of making pictures of high quality—despite the financial losses that usually accompanied such experiments. "We are trying to educate Lizzie to appreciate better pictures, but this must be done gradually." As eager partners in this campaign, journalists like Kitchen praised the industry for improving the quality of its product. They also saluted producers and executives who were seeking to make the studios operate more efficiently. Greater efficiency, they suggested, would deter executives from paying actors extravagant salaries that encouraged them to misbehave and gave the entire industry a bad name. It would also make the movie industry more attractive to "business men of culture and larger means." With an influx of these people, Kitchen noted approvingly, "the time will come when the motion picture industry will be entirely Americanized." Finally, by reducing costs and providing studios with a greater margin for error, the trend toward greater efficiency would make it easier for the industry to experiment with better films and survive financial setbacks that might occur if they failed to attract "Lizzie." Of course, the question of what constituted a "quality" film remained unclear. For some journalists, particular those writing for popular newspapers and mass-circulation magazines, such a film was wholesome and morally uplifting, a departure from the sensational and titillating movies that enticed "Lizzie." For others, a quality film was realistic, subtle, and complex, a work of art superior to the moralistic as well as the sensational.[16]

This tension was neatly resolved in profiles of famous directors like Charlie Chaplin and D. W. Griffith, whose work drew plaudits from both camps. These men, writers noted, were sincerely devoted to the art of moviemaking. Despite working in a highly competitive industry, they went to great lengths to ensure that their pictures met their exacting requirements. Chaplin's prodigality and zealousness on the set were legendary, revealing the temperament of a true artistic genius. Indeed, while most movies were "highly social products" created by an array of different people—producers, directors, screenwriters—Chaplin's were "one-man" productions. As Rob Wagner reported in *Ladies' Home Journal* in 1918, Chaplin was the only figure in the industry who wrote his own stories, chose his own cast, directed, acted in the lead role, and edited the final product. Because he was his own boss, Chaplin could take as long as he wished to make a picture, and he labored over scenes again and again until they were perfect. "Chaplin does not allow a single foot of film to leave his studio until it is 'right,'" Karl Kitchen noted in 1919. The fruits of this herculean effort, as a result of which 95 percent of the footage was often cut, were comedies that were hugely popular as well as significant artistic statements, allowing Chaplin the financial security to continue in the same vein. It took many months of work for Chaplin to produce such films, and, as Kitchen pointed out in conversation with him, he could have made more movies, and more money, if he had been less of a perfectionist. Chaplin retorted: "But I am not interested in merely making a lot of pictures, as I used to do. I want to make good pictures, and you can't make good ones if you make them hurriedly or if you have to have them completed at a certain date. I work on my pictures until I have them just the way I want them and I am willing to spend months making a two-reel comedy, if at the end of that time I have something worth while." Making quality films—this was the bottom line for Chaplin.[17]

D. W. Griffith also managed to produce high-quality films that were commercially successful. Unlike Chaplin, whose metier was comedy, Griffith specialized in spectacular, thought-provoking dramas that brought the best features of the legitimate theater, particularly its "realism," to the big screen. The key to Griffith's commercial and artistic success, journalists argued, was his use of innovative new techniques like the "close-up" to dramatize "elemental" human emotions—an approach that revealed how the new medium of moving pictures could fulfill the larger purposes of art. When Griffith developed these techniques, Mary B. Mullett noted in the *American Magazine* in 1921, he encountered considerable opposition among his superiors at Biograph and many of the actors in his company, who failed to recognize how the techniques would improve movie-making. Those first years were "a constant struggle against criticism and ridicule." But Griffith persisted until the skeptics saw the merits of his innovations and became willing collaborators. Like other great artists, Griffith was also familiar with controversy. A former novelist and playwright whose ambition early in life was to be a "great writer," he aroused the ire of some reformers when he released his first full-length feature, the unabashedly racist *The Birth of a Nation*. "Griffith received scores of letters—the vast majority of them from people who had not seen the picture at all—protesting and even threatening," Mullett reported. "He spent three hundred thousand dollars in attorneys' fees, and days and nights of anxiety and worry, because of the unreasoning attacks on what many persons consider the greatest picture ever made." [18]

By focusing on figures like Chaplin, Griffith, and Cecil B. De Mille, rather than directors of more ordinary fare, journalists endowed the movie industry with a cultural patina it had previously lacked. As Robert E. Sherwood conceded in an otherwise jaundiced profile of De Mille in the *New Yorker*, for all his excesses as a director of lavish yet fatuous society melodramas, De Mille had also contributed legitimately to the field. "Where he has failed to engage the intelligence, he has given the eye some of its primest thrills. He has demonstrated, in almost every production that he has ever made, a pictorial sense that amounts to genius." It was vitally important, however, that "artists" like Chaplin, Griffith, and De Mille have mass appeal, for it was their ability to achieve commercial *and* artistic success that made them poster boys for an industry that could never disguise its commercialism—only graft artistic commitments on to it and promote the hybrid as a species of art. [19]

For the most part, though, journalists did not devote much attention to producers, directors, or screenwriters, especially after the mid-1920s, when actors emerged as the movie industry's most widely publicized figures. One reason for this may have been the emergence of the highly bureaucratic studio system, which reduced the individual autonomy of many creative personnel and transformed producers into managers responsible for supervising productions and budgets. During the 1930s and 1940s the only producers and directors who attracted much publicity were iconoclastic independent operators like Walt Disney and David O. Selznick. Disney burst into the public eye during the early 1930s, when his cartoon shorts became popular with moviegoers and attracted the attention of the press. For several years, Jack Jamison noted in a profile in *Liberty* in 1933, Disney had tried without success to interest studio executives in his ideas. Finally, a daring independent producer agreed to back him, and Disney's belief in himself was confirmed. His Mickey Mouse became "the most popular film star in the world," and Disney used his earnings to build a well-appointed studio where he and his devoted staff continued to make cartoons and were developing exciting new projects, including animated feature films. Leaving the business end of their work to his brother, Disney spent all his time on his cartoons, lavishing on them the kind of attention that was characteristic of a true artist. His highest priority, Jamison wrote, was not making money but having fun, something he clearly derived from his constant "inventing," a practice that had seemed unproductive to his bosses at Universal, where he had been briefly and unhappily employed during the 1920s. Ironically, Disney had become rich from work that closely resembled play and that the Hollywood establishment could not appreciate. "He is one of the lucky ones who can make a fortune out of the work they love," Gilbert Seldes wrote admiringly in a 1931 issue of the *New Yorker.* Here again was the combination of commercial success and artistic achievement—now produced not by the confining, rigidly organized studio system but by an independent producer who did things his own way.[20]

Disney's iconoclasm, however, paled next to that of Orson Welles, the flamboyant playwright, producer, and actor who in the late 1930s parlayed success as a theatrical and radio personality into a lucrative contract with a big Hollywood studio. Welles, in the view of the press, was the archetypal eccentric genius, a former child prodigy who had "never grown up." Rather than conform to the ways of Hollywood, the mercurial wunderkind flouted the industry's every convention, arousing the hatred of his superiors at RKO and angering other actors, writers, and directors who envied and resented him. "He hates authority and in his RKO contract made careful provision that none would be imposed on him," a reporter for *Life* noted. Yet Welles was not content with such a formal arrangement; he made sure that RKO lived up to its spirit. For example, when studio executives came by the lot to check on the progress of *Citizen Kane,* Welles stopped production and instructed his company to start a baseball game. He resumed shooting only when "the prowlers were back at the head office screaming that Orson Welles was a mad man squandering company funds." But as the finished product made clear, there was no denying Welles's skills as a writer and cinematic innovator, one of Hollywood's "few creative minds." And though many journalists were appalled by Welles's seemingly insatiable penchant for self-promotion, they conceded that it served his larger purpose, attracting patrons to his "somber, often high-brow products." Reporters observed that *Kane*, despite its complexity, was doing very well at the box office, demonstrating that the public could be lured to artistically ambitious films under the right circumstances. Like Disney, Welles derived great enjoyment from his work and retained the informal, even slovenly air of a true eccentric. "What he looks like is the youngest young man you ever saw having the best time a young man ever had," Frederick L. Collins informed readers of *Liberty* in 1940. His commitment to the cause of art, however, was deadly serious—so serious, in fact, that it completely transcended politics. As Collins explained, "Orson has no leftist ideas about the theater or about life." Brazenly adapting and rewriting the classics, developing innovative projects in a variety of media, and bringing his vision and vitality to the largely moribund world of motion pictures—no other figure, journalists suggested, was so adept at infusing popular culture with the values of art.[21]

* * *

Efforts to link popular culture to the realm of art were not confined to profiles of producers, composers, and directors—figures whose work most clearly resembled that of serious writers and artists. They also shaped profiles of actors and performers, the men and women who appeared in their productions and were far more interesting to the public. From the vantage point of industry publicists and their allies in the press, the tremendous interest that much of the public had in theatrical, moving picture, and radio stars made them ideal subjects for flattering depictions of show business. Once again, however, when this mission was put into practice the results were ambiguous. For in the course of lifting their subjects to a position worthy of public respect, journalists regularly compared them to unnamed figures who embodied the industry's worst features. The result was the perpetuation of negative stereotypes about actors and entertainers that publicists, at the same moment, were seeking to erase.

Profiles of actors and entertainers were usually crafted in response to the widely held notion that they were lazy and lacking in motivation. Journalists asserted that their subjects worked extremely hard, displaying a commitment to the work ethic equal to that of people in other professions. Being an actor was strenuous work, requiring patience, physical stamina, and vast knowledge of the craft, Gustav Kobbé informed readers of *Ladies' Home Journal* in a series on theatrical stars that he wrote shortly after the turn of the century. For example, Kobbé reported that Maude Adams was an "indefatigable worker" who "would play a matinee every day" if her manager let her. Rather than rest between plays, Adams busied herself reading and exercising, and when preparing for a role, she immersed herself in her many books for information about the period and setting. As profiles of movie stars like Mary Pickford and Theda Bara made clear, working in the nascent film industry was equally arduous. Hours were long, and actors were compelled to follow orders and repeat scenes over and over until they met with their directors' approval. The heavy reliance on stunts made physical fitness even more important than in the theater. And reporters noted that the work did not end when filming ceased at the end of the day. To be their best, actors in the movies or the theater had to be constantly studying. Besides going over their lines, they were always reading new scripts and contemporary books and magazines that might give them a deeper understanding of "modern life" and improve their ability to impersonate its myriad characters. As Ethel Barrymore explained in 1911 to readers of *Ladies' Home Journal*, if an actress wants her work to be distinguished, "her knowledge of the world must be vital and broad. She must keep in touch with every part of it. . . . What is interesting the minds of her time must interest her. For only in this way can she understand either the character which the dramatist gives her to portray, or the audience for which she acts." This was true even of those —like Barrymore or Douglas Fairbanks—whose early success was attributable to "personality." Recognizing that the basis for their quick stardom was ephemeral, these actors were even more intent on developing their skills and broadening their repertoire.[22]

This imperative, journalists often suggested, was reinforced by anxiety, the fear of being replaced by more ambitious and hard-working upstarts that haunted even the most successful movie stars. If anything, "keeping at the top" was even more difficult than becoming a star, demanding that actors work even harder and, more important, avoid developing the "temperament" that made some stars difficult for producers and directors to manage. To have a long and successful career in the popular culture industries, reporters argued, actors—even the biggest stars—had be good team players, deferring to those with more expertise and setting a good example for rank-and-file employees. "The higher you rise, the more is expected of you," Joan Crawford observed in 1933 in the *Saturday Evening Post*. "Mistakes are less readily overlooked or forgiven, even though your work depends largely on the cooperation of others, such as studio executives, directors, editors, writers and the rest." When failure occurred, it was important to accept responsibility and avoid pointing a finger at others. It was also wise, Crawford noted, not to anger studio chiefs. "Differences must be arbitrated if the star, right or wrong, wishes to survive." The skater and movie star Sonja Henie certainly learned this lesson when she tried to break into films. Foolishly assuming that making a skating picture was no different than staging an exhibition, something at which she was an expert, Henie chafed at taking orders from producers and directors and responded with "bursts of temperament," Jerome Beatty revealed in a profile of Henie in the *American Magazine*. But as she learned more about making pictures, she came to recognize that the studio people knew what they were doing, and if she followed their orders, the result would be a better film. She gradually acquiesced in their demands, performing stunts repeatedly until they satisfied the director. "When the picture ended," Beatty suggested, "she was as good a trouper as they ever saw on the lot."[23]

Like producers and directors, however, actors also had laudable aspirations to "grow" as artists by seeking challenging roles, and this often put them at odds with the demands of the industry. Early in the century, journalists suggested that the artistic ambitions of their subjects revolved around performing the "classics" and playing difficult, transgressive roles that were "thousands of miles" from their "uninterestingly comfortable and well-fed" lives. By the 1920s profiles of actors emphasized their interest in "sophisticated" dramas and comedies in which the characters were "complex." This remained the ideal throughout the 1930s and 1940s, though as most reporters conceded, relatively few plays and films of this sort were churned out by the popular culture industries, making competition for plum roles particularly intense. The desire to get these roles was nearly always linked to yearnings for self-expression—the struggle to find work that was challenging and creative, that required an actor to develop new skills or emotional depths. Writing in *Liberty* in 1933, for example, Clara Beranger described Wallace Beery's ascent from character actor specializing in "heavies" to leading man as a fight "for good parts, for true expression of himself." Implicit here was the suggestion that the widespread practice of casting on the basis of looks or personality was superficial, based on a refusal to recognize the deeper qualities that made actors, like all people, unique. Well aware that the most eager readers of stories about show-business figures were women, reporters invoked this theme most often in profiles of actresses, who, writers implied, were far more likely than men to be frustrated by typecasting and roles in which they were required to be little more than fashion plates. In a long profile of Joan Crawford in 1938, for example, Katherine Albert wrote that the actress's entire career had been a struggle to grow as an artist and a person—a struggle which pitted her against studio executives more interested in exploiting her sex appeal and ability as a dancer. When Crawford first went to her bosses at MGM and begged for dramatic work, Albert noted, she was rebuffed. "Executives laughed at her. . . . As Joan Crawford her films, cheaply made, brought in money. When they had in her a valuable property, why should they take chances?" But Crawford persisted, putting her career in jeopardy until she was finally given the sort of vehicles her "fantastic, limitless ambition" deserved.[24]

To succeed in this quest for self-expression and artistic growth, actors like Crawford had to be shrewd, assertive, and persistent. The most successful ones, journalists suggested, made sure that they knew as much as possible about the business end of the industry, including the vagaries of public taste. Armed with this knowledge, they were less likely to be duped by producers and studio executives. Reporters marveled at the "business sense" of movie stars like Mary Pickford and Harold Lloyd, who in the late teens and early twenties shrewdly capitalized on their popularity to drive hard bargains with industry chieftains. Do not mistake Pickford for another "pretty little thing," Karl Kitchen warned his readers in 1919, after "America's Sweetheart" had signed the most lucrative deal in the business. "Years of dealing with so-called motion picture magnates have developed Mary Pickford . . . into the cleverest, best posted, keenest minded film maker in the country." In the 1930s, when changes in the movie industry as in the rest of the country made employment prospects for actors increasingly insecure, journalists were even more impressed when stars like James Cagney and Katharine Hepburn stood up for themselves. For example, by threatening to quit the business and thus deprive the studios of the profits that could be generated from his films, Cagney had negotiated a contract that was the envy of his fellow actors, Henry F. Pringle reported in 1932 in *Collier's*. Perhaps the most assertive movie star, however, was Bette Davis, who shocked the Hollywood establishment by trying to break her contract with Warner Brothers and sign with a British studio because of her lack of interest in the roles offered to her. Though studio flacks accused her of being greedy, it was "something much more important" that inspired this drastic act, the writer Noel F. Busch asserted in a highly sympathetic profile of Davis in *Life*. She wanted good roles that would allow her to display her formidable talents, honed on the stage and unappreciated in Hollywood, where producers valued "personality" and many actors with talent had been known to "conceal it more carefully than a craving for cocaine." Davis's revolt challenged the industry truism that "producers are better judges of what stars should do than the stars themselves," and though she failed to gain her "freedom," it forced producers to accommodate her demands and advanced the cause of actors in Hollywood.[25]

Bette Davis was not only star whose battles with the studio system were depicted sympathetically. While most journalists were hostile to Greta Garbo, Adela Rogers St. Johns leaped to her defense, suggesting the deeper reasons for her reclusiveness. Garbo, St. Johns wrote, had no use for Hollywood and the publicity that was necessary to achieve stardom. She remained there only because acting in movies offered her the best means for acquiring the creative autonomy and financial independence she craved. "She is saving every nickel that she may insure those who belong to her against want, and that she herself may some day lead her life undisturbed by any other human being." When Garbo negotiated with studio executives, they were haunted by the knowledge that she would happily give up her career and return to Sweden. Katharine Hepburn enjoyed similar leverage. Even more than other stars, Alva Johnston reported, Hepburn was quite shrewd in her campaign to propel herself to the front rank of movie actresses. But her determination to succeed was tempered by an aloofness from the industry and the pressures that it imposed on other actors. Possessing intelligence and a wide array of interests, Hepburn never let her quest for movie stardom become the sole object of her life, and, as with Garbo, this actually improved her position in her struggles with studio brass. Carole Lombard was another Hollywood "rebel." After years of being typecast as a "glamour girl," Lombard "went on strike" until she persuaded producers to cast her in more interesting roles. When her shrewdness was confirmed by the success of her new vehicles, studio executives were forced to accept her terms, and she signed a contract that paid her a whopping $150,000 per picture and gave her unprecedented control over roles and publicity. Control over these, a writer for *Liberty* noted, allowed Lombard to "preserve and accentuate her own vivid personality instead of yielding to the Hollywood tendency toward standardization." At issue, then, was not simply the power to select roles that were interesting and fulfilled yearnings for artistic growth. What Garbo, Hepburn, and especially Lombard were after, reporters argued, was autonomy, the power to resist a regime that in its efforts to make all actresses appear similarly glamorous, effaced their individuality and potentially imperiled their box-office appeal.[26]

For actors like Lombard, the object of acquiring more money was achieving financial independence. This enabled them to stand up to producers and gain more control over their roles. Barring the ability to establish their own production companies—the route that successful actors like Mary Pickford and Douglas Fairbanks had taken in the teens and twenties, before the industry had become dominated by the studio system—securing a contract that paid well and allowed for a measure of personal autonomy was the most feasible strategy for resisting the alienating impact of typecasting and "standardization." To turn a lucrative salary into financial independence, however, actors had to save their money, not spend it wantonly. The most successful stars, journalists reported, were deeply devoted to saving and investment. More important, unlike actors in the nineteenth century, who often squandered their earnings on foolhardy productions that left them broke, modern celebrities put the bulk of their money in "secure" investments outside of show business, usually real estate. Lombard, for example, owned property in San Francisco and the San Fernando Valley and had numerous "trust funds." This not only gave her leverage in negotiations with studio executives; it gave her an ample nest egg. "She can afford to settle back and live on it whenever she feels that she must give up her superstrenuous professional career," the journalist Howard Sharpe wrote. Though the most talented and savvy stars had a knack for figuring out ways of keeping themselves at the top of their profession, they still recognized the "ephemeral quality of success" and were prepared for the day when their appeal would wane. As George Burns explained to Clara Beranger, "I've got sense enough to know that Gracie [Allen] and I are lucky because we happen to be able to entertain the public at the moment. But they're apt to get tired of us at any time. . . . When they do, we're ready to quit." Journalists suggested that the new interest displayed by successful actors and entertainers like Burns and Allen in saving for the future was one of the most important developments in the field of show business, a sign that a group long noted for its profligacy had adopted the prudent outlook characteristic of the professions.[27]

This commitment to financial security was accompanied by an equally powerful desire to entertain the public. Drawing on the growing conviction that the pleasures provided by leisure and entertainment were essential if one was to lead a happy and fulfilled life, journalists praised actors like Douglas Fairbanks, Mary Pickford, and Harold Lloyd for their contributions to public happiness—contributions that also recognized the need for entertainment to be "wholesome" and thus distinguished their work from that of "foreign-minded" movie producers. In the *American Magazine*, Mary B. Mullett wrote that no one begrudged Lloyd the huge fortune that he earned from his films, since "he has given us in return something we all need and want—a lot of good wholesome laughs." In the 1930s, as the motion picture industry sought to appear even more responsive to the interests of consumers, the emphasis that journalists placed on this angle increased. Actors were now portrayed as deeply committed to pleasing their audience, movie fans as open-minded and supportive of the quest for self-expression that was said to inspire their favorites. Rejecting the claims of critics and studio executives that the glut of formula pictures and the practice of typecasting were responses to the public's bad taste, journalists asserted that stars and their fans were united in their opposition to the overt commercialism of the studios. Indeed, grateful for their support, stars felt a deep sense of obligation to the people who attended their films. When Clark Gable first went into the movie business, Adela Rogers St. Johns reported, his aim was to earn enough money to quit and then fulfill his ambition to travel the world. "Now it's different," he told her. "I owe so much to the people that have enjoyed what I want to give." Rather than quit as he had planned, Gable continued to make movies, providing his fans with thrills and adventure they could never experience in their own lives. "That's what I mean to them. That's why I'm important," Gable asserted. "Not for myself. Not for what I might do if I kicked the whole thing over and went out to shoot tigers or something. What would that mean to any one but myself?"[28]

Thus the peculiarly individualistic desire for growth and autonomy, which fueled the careers of many actors and entertainers was offset by a powerful sense of responsibility toward their fans that made their work resemble a form of public service. This argument obscured the public's role in encouraging industry practices that thwarted the aspirations of actors, pinning most of the blame on the short-sightedness of producers and men whom later generations would call "suits." It also subtly encouraged readers to identify with and support the ambitions of stars. By making it seem as though so much was invested in their efforts to break out of type and play varied, challenging roles, and describing this project in terms that expressly linked it to individuality and personal growth, celebrity profiles were vital to the larger ambitions of actors. But they were not so helpful to the popular culture industries as a whole. While acknowledging that a significant number of actors and entertainers were hard-working, ambitious, and responsible, celebrity profiles continued to lament the field's rampant commercialism, said to be the single greatest obstacle to the professional aspirations of stars.

* * *

According to journalists, the impulses that drove the most admirable actors and entertainers in their careers extended to their private lives. Unlike previous generations of show-business people and a disturbing number of their peers, who continued their acting off stage and spent much of their time engaged in disreputable activities, the subjects of most profiles were natural and down-to-earth, and they devoted their leisure time to wholesome pastimes that helped them relax and escape the pressures of stardom. Originally crafted in the 1890s as part of a campaign to improve the image of Broadway stars, this angle was appropriated by journalists who covered the popular culture industries, becoming one of the most widely invoked narrative motifs of the era. It was especially useful to reporters sympathetic to the motion picture industry, who employed it to counteract negative publicity arising from scandals like that surrounding Fatty Arbuckle. The persistence of scandals, however, made it necessary for journalists to concede that Hollywood—and show business in general—contained more than its share of "featherheads and fools." Unfortunately, as George Ade observed in the wake of the Arbuckle scandal, the public heard altogether too much about these figures and not enough about "the hundreds of thousands of level-headed and sensible people connected with the picture industry who have their own homes and who lead the average and normal lives of respectable citizens." The "respectable citizens" Ade was referring to were not merely to the myriad clerks, accountants, and makeup artists employed by the studios but also the movie industry's biggest stars.[29]

The most remarkable trait exhibited by these stars, journalists argued, was their ability to remain "natural" and resist the forces that led many of their fellows to act off stage. As we have seen, this was a trait common to all celebrities who embodied the ideal of true success. But with show-business celebrities it served a more immediate purpose, refuting the widely held belief that acting and appearing on stage—more than any another profession—had a corrosive influence on the self, encouraging vanity, self-consciousness, and artificiality. Accordingly, flattering profiles of actors and entertainers never failed to mention that their subjects were down-to-earth, while critical stories nearly always suggested the opposite.

In some articles this claim was made in the course of a backstage interview. More often, however, it was made when a reporter visited an actor's home and was able to get a glimpse of his or her domestic life. After visiting Ethel Barrymore, for example, Gustav Kobbé noted, "She is, practically, the same 'off' as 'on' the boards." Clara E. Laughlin, another writer for *Ladies' Home Journal,* concurred, adding that Barrymore possessed "the unaffected, wholesome ways of the outdoor girl" and was the antithesis of "the sinuous women who are at their best when languidly draped on a divan or disposed in the recesses of an easy-chair." The same naturalness was exhibited by movie stars—despite pressure from the public and even others in the movie business to put on airs. Mary B. Mullett reported in 1920 that Theda Bara was "absolutely unaffected and unassuming in manner," a far cry from the "vampires" she played on screen. Indeed, encountering Bara at home was something of shock. Expecting her to live in a dimly lit, exotically decorated apartment and to be every bit the vamp off camera as she was on, Mullett was surprised to find Bara's home comfortable and "flooded with sunshine and fresh air" and Bara herself a "sensible girl" in unpretentious clothing who "evinced a decided preference for discussing literature and philosophy rather than the habits of vampires in general and of herself in particular." Though actors who were unaffected tended to get along better with their fellows, they could also encounter problems, especially in Hollywood, where the forces conspiring to make a person act in his or her private life were especially strong. It was her unwillingness to pose and satisfy such demands, Adela Rogers St. Johns argued, that made

Greta Garbo so unpopular and misunderstood in Hollywood. At parties many of her fellow actors expected her to at least resemble "the woman of the screen." Instead, they encountered "a shy girl who scorns the usual social graces, who speaks only what she thinks, and who shows a contempt for the superficial things in life." Needless to say, they were disappointed. This made Garbo even more reclusive and determined not to become "someone different from her real self."[30]

Visits to the homes of actors and entertainers also revealed them to be wholesome in their choice of leisure activities. Theatrical stars like Barrymore, John Drew, William Gillette, and Julia Marlowe were extolled for rejecting the "bohemianism" that had been common among show-business people in the nineteenth century. Marlowe's private life, for example, was "a busy, cheerful, sensible round of exercise, reading, visiting, modest hospitality, and unaffected good cheer," Kobbé reported in 1903. Reporters wrote of show-business celebrities occupying themselves with activities that were acceptable and quite familiar to ordinary Americans—especially middle-class Americans, the group that many journalists were most eager to convert into fans of the popular culture industries. Of course, the exact nature of these activities changed over time, as journalists responded to broader changes within middle-class culture that deemed a wider range of activities "wholesome." Early in the century, for example, reporters emphasized the keen interest that many actors and entertainers displayed in art, literature, and classical music—traditional bourgeois pursuits associated with the ideal of "refinement." Actors were also portrayed as devotees of sports, exercise, and outdoor activities like gardening, which by the early 1900s had become equally important to the growing suburban middle class. Kobbé's profile of Barrymore opened with a photo gallery showing the actress engaged in her favorite leisure activities, which included tennis and swimming as well as reading and playing the piano. By the 1920s actors were associated with "simple pleasures" that made them appear increasingly easygoing and informal—parlor games, casual dinner parties, listening to the radio, watching movies at home. As Karl Kitchen noted in a syndicated feature entitled "Week-Ending with Doug and Mary," an evening with Hollywood's premier couple was "decidedly intimate and homelike." After a relatively casual dinner, "like any one of a thousand others served in well appointed American homes," the small group in attendance retired to the living room, which Doug and Mary had transformed into "a private picture theater," and watched the latest movies.

Then it was off to bed in preparation for a vigorous day of swimming and horseback riding in the mountains behind their home.[31]

A private life devoted to "simple pleasures" complemented the demands of a strenuous career. Such demands, writers asserted, made it virtually impossible for theatrical and movie stars to engage in the dissipations that had been widespread among players years ago. "Anybody who knows the game from the inside will tell you that the big stars cannot and do not work like dogs all day in the studios, and then raise Cain all night," wrote George Ade in 1922 in the *American Magazine*. "It can't be done." In Hollywood, as in the theater, the only time available for raising Cain was between productions. Yet as reporters often noted, to be successful in show business an actor could not allow too much time to elapse between projects or public interest in him or her would wane. Many stars used their time off between plays or films to "recuperate" at rustic summer homes, where they engaged in the "simple life" and escaped from the relentless scrutiny to which they were subjected most of the year. Maude Adams's summer home in Long Island, Kobbé reported, was a one-hundred-acre farm where the Broadway star kept dogs, horses, and pigs and could "roam around at will" without worrying about being spied on. Pickfair, the palatial home of Mary Pickford and Douglas Fairbanks, served a similar purpose, offering the couple a refuge from their work as well as the crowds that invariably gathered when they ventured into Los Angeles for dinner or a movie. Complete with a tennis court, a gymnasium, a huge swimming pool, a stable full of horses, facilities for ping pong, billiards, and other games—not to mention the home theater that so impressed Karl Kitchen—Pickfair provided the best of country living, only a few minutes from the studios where Pickford and Fairbanks worked. Other movie stars preferred to venture farther from Hollywood in their quest for privacy and freedom. For example, Clark Gable and Carole Lombard spent as much time as possible at their modest "ranch" in a remote area of the San Fernando Valley, Henry F. Pringle noted in a profile of the couple in *Ladies' Home Journal* in 1940. There they worked in the garden and the orchards, hunted, rode horses, and spent quiet afternoons and evenings on their "wide back porch" or in Gable's beloved gun room. One of the best features of the place was that the locals paid "small attention to them," and that the two could shop in the general store without prompting stares.[32]

Yet even when they were in New York or Hollywood, the most widely praised actors and entertainers still avoided the seemingly endless round of parties, premieres, and nightclub appearances that made up the show-business version of the "social whirl." They did so, journalists revealed, not by becoming recluses like Garbo but by being selective about the events they chose to attend. For example, though Ethel Barrymore was regularly invited to lavish parties given by society figures eager to bask in the company of famous actors, she wisely resisted many of the invitations, accepting only those which seemed likely to bring her into contact with people who were really interesting and accomplished in their own right and thus more likely to accept her as herself. "When you leave a dinner-table after meeting such people," Barrymore told Kobbé, "they have given you new views of life to think over, and have said lots of things worth remembering. That is the kind of society I like to move in." Many successful movie stars were just as determined to keep themselves at arm's length from the frivolities that a small yet highly visible number of their colleagues engaged in. According to reporters, the masters of being in but not of Hollywood were Fairbanks and Pickford. This was ironic, since during the 1920s they were regarded as the movie colony's "king" and "queen." To be sure, Doug and Mary appeared at important social functions in Los Angeles and elsewhere, fulfilling their duty as the industry's "ambassadors," and they gave elegant parties in honor of notable visitors to Hollywood. But writers insisted that they kept these social engagements to a minimum, and spent most of their time at home alone or with close friends like Charlie Chaplin and Frances Marion. "They are in no way impregnated by the restlessness of the age," Adela Rogers St. Johns informed readers of *Photoplay* in 1927. Refusing to be swept into the social whirl, Fairbanks and Pickford enjoyed a life that was distinctly "old-fashioned." This was an interesting choice of words. While their preference for quiet evenings at home harkened back to small-town life in the nineteenth century, before the advent of nightlife drew many Americans out on the town, their sumptuous, convenience-filled home and many of the pastimes that they enjoyed were thoroughly modern. From this perspective, Fairbanks and Pickford were avatars of a domestically oriented consumerism that with the help of the press would sweep the nation in the 1940s and 1950s.[33]

Indeed, in the 1920s, when the tabloids provided readers with column after column revealing the extravagant and often reckless ways of Hollywood stars, journalists like St. Johns and Ade had no choice but to cast figures such as Fairbanks and Pickford as exceptions, models of sobriety and "good taste" in a town notable for its garishness and vulgarity. In an article expressly designed to burnish the image of the movie industry, Ade admitted that "some of the picture stars have been spoiled by their sudden prosperity," and had responded by engaging in an unseemly bout of conspicuous consumption and frivolous partying. Instead of saving their money or using it to buy tasteful goods, they spent it on "automobiles and jewels and showy gimcracks." Of course, Fairbanks and Pickford also lived in luxury. Yet reporters argued that their consumption and social life were inspired by a different spirit, an essential decency that separated them from many of their fellows and gave them more in common with ordinary Americans. As Pickford revealed in an interview with Mary B. Mullett, "when I came to New York last winter I intended to buy myself a chinchilla coat. I thought I wanted it very much! But I went home without it. I decided that I didn't need it, and that it would be foolish for me to spend all that money for something I could easily get along without." What interested Pickford was "comfort," not luxury. Pickford's decency and ordinariness were confirmed when a journalist, "looking for thrills," spent a rather dull weekend with her and Fairbanks. Before he left he announced indignantly, "Why, you are just like other people—just like others, only more so! You do the ordinary things in the ordinary manner. There is nothing in the least extraordinary about you." Jerome Beatty discovered that the same was true of Will Rogers. Visiting the star's modest, homey bungalow, he found that Rogers and his wife, Betty, did not attend many openings and parties, and were proud of their "simple existence in the midst of jazzed-up Hollywood." This dogged refusal to conform, Beatty noted, had raised eyebrows among many of Rogers's coworkers, who reflexively followed the crowd along the "party circuit." But it would not baffle ordinary Americans: "any person who has children, or who has lived in a small town and has never lost the calm, sane viewpoint of ordinary folks, any person like that—*he* can understand."[34]

From time to time journalists were confronted with the task of writing sympathetically about stars who could not be portrayed in the mold of Pickford, Fairbanks, or Rogers. One such figure was Mary's and Doug's good friend, Charlie Chaplin. Chaplin's stature as Hollywood's reigning genius allowed him considerable leeway in his activities as a filmmaker, explaining his perfectionism, profligacy, and often harsh treatment of underlings. It was not so useful, however, as a defense against charges of immorality, which dogged him throughout the 1920s. Leaping on every opportunity to expose his marital difficulties and fondness for teenage girls, tabloid reporters made it impossible for his supporters to cast him as a representative of wholesome Hollywood. Instead, sympathetic journalists like Karl Kitchen and Jim Tully redirected the spotlight to Chaplin's past and the deep psychological scars that inspired his misbehavior. Embittered by the hardships of his youth, Chaplin was deeply insecure and "suspicious of mankind." "There is rebellion in his soul," Tully noted in 1927 in a multipart profile of Chaplin in *Pictorial Review*. "It is the rebellion of self-pity, the bitterness of remembered youth." These traits were reinforced by Chaplin's celebrity, which made him all the more dubious of people who sought to be close to him and capricious in his dealings with friends and associates. "Always it should be recalled in Chaplin's favor that he has been wounded as often as he has wounded." Carrying around such baggage, it was not surprising that this "magnificent and brilliant young cynic" sought solace with innocents who seemed to adore him—and then felt betrayed when they turned out to be no different from anyone else. According to Adela Rogers St. Johns, a similar psychological dynamic fueled the frenetic partying of Clara Bow, whose casual sexual liaisons were widely reported in the tabloids. Reared by a deranged mother who envied her beauty and constantly belittled her ambition to become a movie actress, Bow turned for support to her father, but even with his help she could not overcome "the terrible scars of her childhood and adolescent years." But Bow's fervent efforts to "seek forgetfulness in mad gaiety" had not made her happy. After a nightlong conversation with Bow, when the actress opened herself up completely, St. Johns could not help feeling sorry for her. In her determination to wrest from life "every moment of fun and feeling" that she could, Bow was unlikely to grow intellectually or spiritually. There was "no pattern, no purpose to her life." Moreover, she refused to listen to those who urged her to settle down. "And so," St. Johns concluded, "you go on loving her, feeling sorry for her, and praying that she won't get into any real trouble."[35]

By the mid-1930s the image of Hollywood promoted by journalists had changed. In response to the populist currents unleashed by the Depression, which encouraged the press and other mass media to demonize the excesses of the "jazz age," wholesome figures like Pickford, Rogers, and Wallace Beery were portrayed as the norm, representatives of a widespread commitment among movie stars to middle-class propriety. By forcing studio executives to slash salaries and lay off deadwood, W. E. Woodward reported in 1932 in *Collier's*, the Depression had prompted the great majority of actors and entertainers to abandon their carefree ways and adopt a more sober and conventional lifestyle—one that bore striking resemblance to that of the suburban upper-middle class. "It is a land of married couples, twin beds, flowered silk pajamas, kitchen aprons, smoking jackets, child-raising, weak cocktails, ping-pong, dieting, knitted sweaters, tennis-playing, cake-baking, three-car-garages and long telephone conversations. Everybody goes to bed early." Even the erstwhile playgirl Bow, now married and a mother, had graduated to "domesticity and dishwashing." Like many ordinary Americans, quite a few stars were also embracing religion. Religion had never been absent in Hollywood, Clara Beranger remarked in 1935. But, like "the rest of the world," movie stars had been mesmerized by the "materialism" of the teens and twenties. The broad spiritual awakening inspired by the Depression had made them recognize its bankruptcy. "Now the stars are no longer ashamed to say that they believe in God, nor to admit that religion helps them in their life and work." Among those who openly professed a commitment to religion, Beranger reported, were Pickford, Norma Shearer, the director Cecil B. De Mille, and the up-and-coming young actress Barbara Stanwyck. Indeed, Beranger suggested that the movie industry could play a vital role in spreading religious faith throughout the nation and the world. "Hollywood could use its tremendous energy, so often misapplied, to help the churches in their work of giving a weary world new hope, new courage, and a new spiritual impulse. Through its limitless resources for making and distributing drama it could help bridge the gulf of social and national differences and spread over the world the ideal of all religions—love and the brotherhood of man."[36]

Hollywood's new media image was largely—though not entirely—hyperbole. In real life, actors continued to misbehave and occasionally became embroiled in scandals. But the widespread inclusion of morals clauses in contracts, which became de rigueur by the early 1930s, gave producers and studio executives more leverage, and there is evidence that this encouraged actors to tone down or conceal some of their behavior. As a result, there were fewer incidents that the press was compelled to report to maintain its credibility with readers. And smoother relations between the press and industry publicists allowed actors who were well regarded by reporters a modicum of protection from embarrassing stories, though not carte blanche. This arrangement, which collapsed along with the studio system in the late 1940s, enabled the movie industry to rely almost exclusively on actors to display a wholesome façade to the public—a publicity stratagem that created a fruitful counterpoint to the glamour and sensuality that the same figures often exuded in their films.[37]

* * *

More than any other medium, newspapers and magazines played a pivotal role in the growing appeal of popular culture in America. They not only directed public attention toward the products of the expanding popular culture industries, but they lifted its stars to unprecedented heights of celebrity. To increase popular culture's appeal—especially among middle-class readers, who were initially reluctant to patronize new amusements like vaudeville and motion pictures—journalists asserted that show-business celebrities were inspired by many of the same ideals that motivated serious artists and writers. Even actors and entertainers, reporters suggested, were committed to creative autonomy and artistic growth. But profiles also suggested that achieving these lofty and admirable goals was difficult, pitting celebrities against the commercial imperatives of the popular culture industries. Celebrities had to be enterprising, shrewd, and assertive to achieve them. Their artistic inclinations, in short, had to be coupled with values that were distinctly entrepreneurial and linked them symbolically to other professionals and the culture of business. Journalists argued that these commitments also shaped the manner in which actors and entertainers led their private lives, making them more like "ordinary folks" than show-business people had ever been in the past. By fusing art with commerce, and the glamorous world of show business with the evolving norms of middle-class propriety, the authors of celebrity profiles invested the popular culture industries with a new legitimacy.

Yet as we have seen, they accomplished this by continually harping on unattractive, even disreputable features, which elevated some figures at the expense of others and kept alive negative stereotypes that encouraged the public to regard the entire field with skepticism. It should come as no surprise that journalists, eager to make popular culture attractive to the middle class in particular, resorted to such arguments in their attempts to kindle interest in show business. Linking popular culture to art was a sure-fire technique for making it appealing to middle-class readers who liked to think of themselves as "cultured," while associating it with business and especially the professions gave it a patently modern allure. Equally effective were efforts to recast actors and entertainers as respectable yet fun-loving "average Americans," paragons of a new consumerism whose appeal rested on its juxtaposition of the "old-fashioned" and the "modern." Well aware of the prejudices and preferences of their target audience, and determined to assert their independence from industry publicists, journalists were reluctant promoters of popular culture and show-business celebrities—ready to do their part to improve the stature of the field but on their own terms, employing arguments that bolstered their credibility in the eyes of readers.

Displaying independence, however, was not their entire agenda. Journalists were also committed to making reportage about show-business celebrities relevant to a wide range of readers, including many who did not share the prejudices of the middle class. Here is where the focus on personal autonomy was especially useful. In their work as well as in their private lives, the most widely praised show-business celebrities—those who embodied the ideal of true success—were portrayed as icons of autonomy and personal integrity, men and women who were able to follow their own course and achieve professional success and personal fulfillment. To make this point, journalists set them in opposition to institutions within the popular culture industries and larger forces in American society that threatened their autonomy. As people whose work was intimately bound up with self-expression, actors and entertainers were better suited than any other kind of celebrity for central roles in this journalistic morality play, providing ordinary readers with vivid examples of how people might cope with the potentially alienating demands and expectations of employers, authorities, and peer groups. These examples were heartening, even utopian, reaffirming the belief that individualism remained viable in a "mass society" dominated by powerful institutions and the pressures of conformity.

But as journalists discovered, this reassuring message only acquired resonance when it was placed within stories directing attention to the constraints that show-business celebrities had overcome. These constraints still hampered most readers and made the variety of true success enjoyed by actors and entertainers exceedingly difficult for ordinary people to achieve. Recognition of this may well have encouraged many readers to resent as well as envy the stars of stage and screen. And it may have created a market for stories in which these celebrities received their comeuppance.

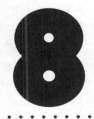

8

HEROES AND PRETENDERS
ATHLETIC CELEBRITY AND THE COMMERCIALIZATION OF SPORTS

On a cool, rainy fall evening in 1926 dozens of prominent celebrities from show business, the arts, politics, business, and "society" assembled in a stadium in Philadelphia, along with approximately 120,000 other hardy souls, to attend a much-anticipated prizefight between the reigning heavyweight champion, Jack Dempsey, and a highly touted contender, Gene Tunney. Celebrities from Hollywood included Charlie Chaplin, Norma Talmadge, and Tom Mix. Broadway was represented by a number of entertainers and producers, including Al Jolson and the star of the Ziegfeld Follies, the comedian Will Rogers. From the world of politics had come three members of President Coolidge's cabinet as well as several governors, congressmen, and big-city mayors.[1]

This extraordinary cast of patrons was not the only remarkable feature of the Dempsey-Tunney fight. Orchestrated by the promoter George "Tex" Rickard, a former prospector who had begun his career staging prizefights on the Western frontier, the bout revealed the widespread popularity that prizefighting and spectator sports in general had achieved since the mid-nineteenth century. The distinguished public figures in attendance; the much larger group of respectable, well-heeled men and women who occupied the best seats; the record-setting box-office receipts and huge sums paid to the fighters; the tremendous interest in the bout exhibited by millions of Americans who were eagerly listening to radios or waiting for the first accounts to appear in the press—all were unprecedented, evidence that sports had indeed entered a "golden age" in the United States. Yet as Rickard could readily attest, these milestones were the product of years of hard work and the culmination of trends that had begun much earlier and in which the press had played a pivotal role. In fact, newspapers and magazines had made it possible for promoters like Rickard to kindle massive public interest in sporting events—and for Dempsey and Tunney to become as well-known as any of the celebrities in attendance.[2]

Like their counterparts in show business, sports celebrities emerged when the press began devoting extensive attention to athletic events and found that public interest in them could be increased by directing the spotlight at figures whom readers were likely to find interesting. But coverage of sports was relatively slow to develop. Metropolitan newspapers in the mid-nineteenth century published only intermittent reports of selected events, usually prizefights or horse races, a practice reinforced by haphazard scheduling and a lack of organization among promoters. By the 1870s press coverage of sports had become more regular, offering readers a steady diet of information about the growing number of events that promoters, athletic clubs, and college teams were staging in the hopes of attracting spectators. A major breakthrough occurred in the 1880s and 1890s, when many large urban dailies gathered reportage about all these sports on a discrete "sports page" and, on Sundays, in a whole section. With more space now available to writers assigned to the sports beat, coverage of all sports expanded dramatically. Accounts of games became longer and more colorful, a form of entertainment in their own right. And they were accompanied by a host of new features designed to whet the public's appetite for upcoming contests, including detailed reports from training camps, columns and "expert" analyses by well-known commentators, and long sketches profiling the most illustrious stars.[3]

This expansion in coverage was inspired by recognition that sports was a circulation booster, attracting male readers from varied backgrounds. One of the virtues of the sports page, editors in the 1890s soon discovered, was that it brought stories about many different sports together, making it easier to turn partisans of one sport into more general enthusiasts. In their broad coverage, which extended from college regattas and lawn tennis tournaments to professional baseball games and boisterous, often controversial prizefights, big-city newspapers like Joseph Pulitzer's *New York World* enlarged the audience for all sports. They also subtly challenged the association of specific sports with distinct classes or groups. Press coverage of college football, for example, made it possible for immigrant workers to think of themselves as fans of Princeton football, just as coverage of prizefights aroused elite and middle-class interest in a sport that had long been linked to the nefarious "sporting fraternity." To encourage this broadening, journalists repackaged various sports to make them more attractive to the wide cross-class audience that most newspaper publishers at the turn of the century were committed to serving, a project requiring top-notch writing skills and an acute sensitivity to the beliefs and prejudices of particular groups of readers: "gentleman" amateurs, the urban middle class, immigrants and ethnics, members of the "respectable" working class, even the young toughs who made up the sporting fraternity. The challenge of sportswriting lay in reconciling the often conflicting values of these readers and fashioning an ideology of sport—a way of thinking about athletic competition—that a majority of them could endorse.[4]

Because of the importance of sports to the economic fortunes of many newspapers, in the early 1900s editors began funneling many of their best writers to the sports department, where they were handsomely paid and given extensive artistic license. In the 1920s, when star reporters at New York papers earned approximately $100 a week, Grantland Rice earned $1,000 a week for producing a syndicated column filled with overblown, sentimental doggerel. By this time the most highly regarded sportswriters—men like Rice, the Chicago-based columnist Hugh Fullerton, the Hearst syndicate's Damon Runyon, Rice's comrade on the *New York Herald-Tribune*, W. O. McGeehan, and Paul Gallico of the *New York Daily News*—wrote feature stories, columns, and reams of commentary for newspapers and feature syndicates, allowing their opinions to reach far into the hinterlands. They also wrote frequent articles for magazines like *Collier's*, the *American Magazine*, *Vanity Fair*, and the *New Yorker*, which began to pay attention to sports in the teens and twenties, as more and more middle-class Americans, including many women, became interested in them. Though some of the articles were written for sports fans, others were directed at a more general audience presumed to be less knowledgeable, but no less curious, about the field's most-heralded stars. All of the reporting was quite effective at weaving together disparate clusters of values—once associated with particular kinds of sports and the class cultures which had supported them—into a coherent outlook that gradually came to shape coverage and influence the views of sports fans and provincial journalists. In this fashion, ideals crafted by a cadre of elite sportswriters became conventional wisdom, displacing the more diverse, class-based currents of opinion that had prevailed during the nineteenth century.[5]

As one might expect, expanded press coverage of sports gave athletes, promoters, and the managers and owners of teams a great boost. By making readers aware of and deeply interested in sporting events, newspapers increased demand for tickets and thus had a direct impact on the "gate." Following the lead of entertainment impresarios, sports promoters in the 1890s and early 1900s developed a number of techniques for attracting "free publicity," including cultivating close relations with beat reporters and leading columnists. With the number of interested readers far exceeding the number of customers who could possibly be accommodated at sporting venues, sportswriters recognized that heightened public interest in sports was good for them too, creating a huge audience of people who had no choice but to turn to the daily press for coverage of events that they were unable to attend in person. Accordingly, many journalists joined forces with athletes and promoters, producing articles that were vital to the fortunes of the industry. As Paul Gallico noted in his memoir of his career as a sportswriter, journalists had to be close to the athletes about whom they wrote if they were "to present the intimate, colorful, personal stories that sell papers." The incorporation of sportswriters into the promotional activities of promoters and athletes sometimes placed them in an uncomfortable position—a predicament familiar to their colleagues who covered the entertainment beat. While some of the events that they publicized were worthy of a "build-up," many others were not, and to kindle public interest in them reporters were compelled to exaggerate and mislead readers—to engage in "ballyhoo." Most promoters, primarily interested in the size of the gate, had no problem with such duplicity. But when a contest that had been touted as evenly matched turned out to be blatantly one-sided and boring to spectators, the credibility of sportswriters who had promoted the event could be tarnished.[6]

This problem inspired journalists to develop a critique of ballyhoo that allowed them to publicize athletic events and sports celebrities yet also distance themselves from the often unseemly excesses of promoters. The architects of this critique were prominent columnists and feature writers like Rice, Fullerton, McGeehan, and Gallico. Rather than dismiss charges that the world of sports was corrupted by cynical and misleading promotional campaigns, they made these charges a recurring theme of their columns and feature stories, just as show-business writers had done with criticism of the popular culture industries. Their articles became venues for speculation, prediction, and exhaustive post-mortems—for distinguishing between authentic "heroes" who deserved their reputations and overrated "pretenders." At the heart of the sports-writers' campaign was their claim to be promoters not of commercial-ized spectacle but of "sport," an ideal far removed from the grubby realities of promoters and box-office receipts. Embodied by the most admirable athletes, the sporting world's exemplars of true success, the ideal of sport celebrated values that contributed to victory in competi-tive struggle—that made men and women "winners." Yet it also encour-aged readers to believe, in Rice's immortal words, that winning was less important than "how you played the Game." Thus journalists recon-ciled themselves to their role within the promotional machinery of the burgeoning sports industry by embracing a larger mission, the promo-tion of values that were more noble than those prevailing in the "real world" and that might ultimately redeem it.[7]

* * *

The ideal of sport championed by sportswriters in the early twentieth century arose from the welter of conflicting imperatives that accompa-nied the press's growing attention to competitive athletics. In the late nineteenth century, as more newspapers made sports coverage a regu-lar feature, journalists assigned to the sports department developed a series of themes that shaped their depiction of notable athletes. From these emerged an archetype that many reporters were reflexively drawn toward when they described a sports figure or assessed his merits. This archetype embodied the "respectable" values that the press and other important institutions had been promoting since the mid-nineteenth century. As numerous scholars have noted, these values were essen-tially bourgeois and were first embraced by the middle classes. But they were also appealing to a substantial number of working-class Ameri-cans, blacks, immigrants, and ethnics, the core of a "culture of respect-ability" to which perhaps a majority of Americans adhered during the second half of the nineteenth century, in spite of the often bitter inter-class conflicts of the era.

Commitment to the culture of respectability encouraged sports-writers to portray athletes as embodiments of courage, honesty, and self-discipline—traits that were likely to make them appealing to the working-class readers of dime novels as well as to middle-class men raised on the homilies of Oliver Wendell Holmes, one of America's best-known writers and physicians and an early spokesman for the character-building virtues of sports. In the early 1900s efforts to depict sports stars as icons of respectability intensified, as journalists and promoters struggled to attract more middle-class patrons to sports like professional baseball and prizefighting. It reached its zenith, however, in newspaper coverage of college football, a sport that was especially well suited to packaging as a middle-class pastime. By 1910 sportswriters had recast a wide range of sports, including baseball and prizefighting, as rituals affirming values like hard work, sobriety, and delayed gratification. They had also begun to stress the importance of teamwork and following the orders of managers and coaches, new values that many journalists viewed as increasingly important in the corporate age.[8]

But these were not the only themes. Determined to wean working-class men from periodicals like Richard Kyle Fox's *National Police Gazette,* a sensational weekly that covered scandals and show business as well as sports and never fully embraced the respectable archetype of athletic celebrity promoted by the metropolitan press, sportswriters for sensational newspapers like those of the Hearst press began in the early 1900s to focus on the extraordinary and the heroic, on feats of physical prowess that lifted athletes above the realm of mere mortals and the constraints that invariably accompanied working for the good of a team. By the teens and twenties, in response to changes within middle-class and working-class culture that enlarged the audience for such fare, mainstream sportswriting had been thoroughly affected by this important trend, making the press's depiction of sports celebrities more ambiguous, but also making it possible for some athletes—notably Jack Dempsey, Babe Ruth, and Red Grange—to enjoy a more widespread appeal, to become "mass idols" on a par with movie stars. The press's new interest in the extraordinary and the heroic added a new dimension to the emerging ideal of sport. By appropriating values that had circulated largely within the disreputable sporting fraternity, sportswriters found a way to make their reportage attractive to a younger generation of immigrants, ethnics, and working-class Americans not so keen on articles and columns written from a narrowly "respectable" point of view. Focusing on the extraordinary and the heroic enabled sportswriters to reach beyond middle-class readers and endow the ideal of sport with potent compensatory appeal.[9]

These developments occurred at a time when spectator sports were undergoing dramatic change. Owing in large part to the expansion of press coverage, between the 1870s and the early 1900s many sports became highly profitable commercial enterprises. The possibility of attracting paying customers to their games through newspaper publicity, and the greater willingness of customers to pay to see a winner, led to a new competitiveness. The managers of baseball teams, for example, signed only the best players and paid them salaries. The same incentives were also at work in prizefighting, leading promoters and publishers like Fox to raise larger and larger purses that would induce the most talented fighters to enter the ring, a process that culminated in the 1880s in the establishment of weight divisions and the crowning of "world champions." Even college football was influenced by this trend, as captains sought to improve their teams by hiring coaches and talented "ringers" who were not matriculated students. By the turn of the century most big-time sports were dominated by professionals—or athletes whose devotion to training and preparing for competition made them amateurs only in name. Not surprisingly, the commercialization of baseball and prizefighting attracted more poor, uneducated working-class men eager to be paid good money to play ball or engage in fisticuffs. For them, professional sports was a chance to escape the poverty and tedium of working-class life while steering clear of conventional channels, which required them to submit to bourgeois authority figures and embrace respectable values. A "job" in sports offered an opportunity to enjoy success on one's own terms, to enjoy a reasonably comfortable life yet remain on the margins of respectable society. Indeed, for professional athletes, one of the great attractions of a career in sports was the relative freedom that it allowed. While sportswriters and promoters struggled to portray athletes as icons of respectability, many followed their own course, behaving in ways that wantonly violated the values held dear by most sportswriters.[10]

Journalists in the early twentieth century responded to these developments by redoubling their efforts to construct a symbolic alternative to them. To accomplish this task, however, they were forced to address the issue of commercialization head on. Like show-business writers, they produced a litany of complaints, identifying the field's biggest problems and singling out figures who embodied them. Perhaps the most disturbing was what many journalists called an excess of "professionalism." For many athletes, winning was the only thing that mattered; they pursued victory with such zeal that they bent and even broke rules to gain advantage over their opponents. In the early 1900s the athlete most often linked to this trend was the baseball star Ty Cobb, who was infamous for spiking opposing players, intimidating umpires, and playing the game with a ferocity that made him unpopular with fellow players and fans. "Sometimes [fans] get so mad at him that you think they're going to tear him to pieces," Ring Lardner noted in a profile of Cobb in the *American Magazine* in 1915. But as numerous sportswriters lamented, such overzealousness was not confined to professional sports like baseball. It pervaded college football and putatively amateur sports like tennis and golf; it even affected women in sports. Cobb's counterpart in the world of amateur athletics, reporters argued, was the French tennis star Suzanne Lenglen, who dominated the women's game during the 1920s. Lenglen was a prime example of an athlete who took her sport too seriously, viewing it as "a rather disagreeable and irksome business, not a game." Journalists conceded that this businesslike approach made her the best player on the women's circuit, just as Cobb was without peer on the baseball diamond. Yet like Cobb, Lenglen was lacking in "sportsmanship," gloating in victory and openly displaying chagrin in defeat, making her highly unpopular even among sportswriters and fans who admired her talent. As Grantland Rice observed in 1926, on the eve of Lenglen's highly publicized matches with Helen Wills, "There has never been another contestant in sport who apparently so dreaded the thought of defeat." Accordingly, many journalists openly expressed relief when Lenglen abandoned amateur tennis for professional exhibitions. Since she had never regarded tennis "as sport for its own sake," the former player Mary K. Browne wrote in *Vanity Fair,* "it is in no way incongruous or extraordinary that she has turned professional. . . . [S]he is now working for herself, instead of for the tournament committees." [11]

Another widely acknowledged problem was the obsession of many athletes and promoters with the size of the gate. Boxing promoters like Tex Rickard were notorious for inducing prizefighters to help them arouse interest in upcoming bouts by staging trumped up "feuds" with rivals. Rickard's most shameless promotional gambit took place in 1910, when he persuaded the former champion Jim Jeffries to come out of retirement to challenge Jack Johnson and reclaim the heavyweight title for the white race. The angle was very effective at whipping up interest in their fight but had disastrous consequences when Johnson trounced the overhyped Jeffries and angry whites throughout the United States retaliated with violent attacks on African Americans. Baseball players and managers engaged in similar shenanigans to draw patrons to ball-parks. Many journalists were dismayed when the owners of professional baseball teams introduced a "livelier" ball and moved outfield fences closer to home plate to capitalize on the public's desire to see more home runs. While most approved of the home run and the new style of play that it encouraged, they worried about blatant efforts to make the game more dramatic and spectacular to casual fans unfamiliar with the intricacies of the "old" baseball. Similar misgivings greeted the adoption of the forward pass and a more open, spectacular style of play in college football. In the view of journalists, too many innovations seemed to have been inspired by a desire to sell more tickets and transform sports into a variety of show business. Perhaps the most disturbing manifestation of this trend were "fixes": persistent efforts to manipulate the outcomes of baseball games and prizefights to exploit betting odds, increase the market value of a fighter, or make contests seem less one-sided than they actually were.[12]

Unfortunately, the obsession with money did not end there. Prize-fighters complained to reporters of being cheated and exploited by promoters and managers. Jack Dempsey's row with his long-time manager Jack Kearns, for example, was one of the most highly publicized events of the mid-1920s, revealing the poisonous impact that big money could have on relations between friends. As the writer John B. Kennedy noted in an interview with Dempsey in *Collier's* in 1925, virtually all sports were filled with "parasites" and "crooks" seeking to take advantage of athletes. Given this state of affairs, who could blame athletes if they became cynical and self-interested as well? Among the most cynical, journalists suggested, were professional baseball players, who chafed under regulations limiting their ability to switch teams and earn the highest possible salaries. Conflicts between team owners and the biggest "drawing cards" were particularly intense, driving some players toward short-lived alternative leagues that appeared from time to time. Failing to break the collective power of team owners, these players augmented their salaries by engaging in barnstorming tours during the off season. The opportunities increased substantially in the teens and twenties, when star athletes also found it possible to make cameo appearances in vaudeville shows and motion pictures. Well aware of their importance to the team, baseball stars such as Cobb, Tris Speaker, and Babe Ruth fully exploited their leverage with owners and managers, "holding out" for higher salaries and winning privileges that often made them resented by ordinary players. Early in his career, Ruth was the most rebellious of these drawing cards, openly defying his manager, team owners, and the new commissioner of baseball, on the assumption that he was "bigger than the game." [13]

To make matters worse, the baleful influence of money on drawing cards like Ruth extended to their off-the-field behavior. Exempted from curfews and other regulations affecting their fellow players, many star athletes, sportswriters reported, were dissolute and profligate, spending vast sums on the "high life" after games and especially during the off season. This phenomenon was not peculiar to the highly commercialized sports scene of the early twentieth century. The prizefighter John L. Sullivan virtually lived in bars and saloons between fights during his reign as heavyweight champion in the 1880s, drinking, brawling, and buying rounds for the house—to the chagrin of sportswriters who longed for a more respectable titleholder. And the passage of time did not dim the appeal of such a lifestyle. Barred from most of the fashionable saloons in his native Chicago, Jack Johnson used his winnings from the prize ring to buy one of his own, the infamous Cafe de Champion, which gained a reputation for interracial mingling and was alleged to be the staging grounds for Johnson's activities as a "white slaver." In the 1920s the most widely publicized bon vivants were Jack Dempsey and Babe Ruth; both were fixtures at nightclubs and speakeasies in Manhattan and regular guests at parties given by society figures eager to fraternize with celebrities. Ruth, in particular, was acclaimed as the sporting world's most renowned "playboy," and though sportswriters were loath to reveal the full extent of his extracurricular activities, their innuendo was so blatant that the truth must have been clear to most adult readers. According to journalists, big stars were also more likely to become contemptuous of fans, refusing to sign autographs and avoiding public appearances—or, even worse, staging cynical publicity stunts that gave them an undeserved reputation for being down-to-earth. The worse offender, W. O. McGeehan asserted, was the seemingly natural Dempsey, whose "considerable guile" led him to act in ways that he knew would "pay dividends" in the form of good publicity. [14]

Thus journalists admitted that the world of sports was plagued with serious problems, which sportswriters, like show-business reporters, attributed to the malevolent influence of money and commercialism. Publicizing these disturbing facts was not usually in the best interests of promoters, team owners, and athletes, who often sought to persuade journalists to cover them up. And on some occasions the journalists would do so, usually out of loyalty to a particular athlete or to the image of the sport that he or she represented. "The sportswriter has few if any heroes," Gallico suggested. "We create many because it is our business to do so, but we do not believe in them. We know them too well. We are concerned as often . . . with keeping them and their weaknesses and peccadillos out of the papers as we are with putting them in." But the incentives for sportswriters to protect sports celebrities were offset by other incentives that were nearly as powerful. Revealing the seamy side of sports—the aim of Gallico's memoir-cum-exposé— worked to the advantage of the press, allowing sportswriters to separate themselves from the public relations machinery with which their work was intimately bound up. Indeed, crafting such an unflattering portrait was a prerequisite for acknowledging and celebrating positive developments—for making the invidious distinctions that were central to the larger mission of promoting the ideal of sport.

* * *

Yet in an environment where commercialization was becoming increasingly pervasive, this was not as easy as it seemed. Because of the growing popularity of sports—including sports that were thoroughly compromised by big money and the cult of winning at any cost—a hard line against commercialization was an impractical strategy, unlikely to attract many readers. The great majority of sportswriters, moreover, approved of many developments that had accompanied the transformation of sports. For example, the level of competition in virtually all sports had increased substantially since the late nineteenth century, providing fans with more for their money. Even more important, Grantland Rice noted in 1928, thanks to press coverage of prominent athletes, "the physical and mental benefits of play and sport have gone out to more millions than the world ever knew before." [15]

The task that lay before sportswriters in the early twentieth century was to incorporate these positive trends into a portrait of sport that was upbeat, that lifted athletic competition to a level far above the real world and allowed journalists to inspire readers with useful and uplifting lessons applicable to the "game of life." This project—the promotion of the ideal of sport—directly influenced the press's treatment of athletes. By the teens and twenties, when commercialization had become pervasive and newspapers and many magazines had come to rely on sports coverage to boost circulation, promoting sport no longer meant extolling athletes who stood entirely apart from commercialization, for such figures were few. Rather, it meant refashioning the personas of the most popular stars—even those who were targets of criticism—in ways that downplayed their relationship to the overtly commercial and endowed them with traits that were the hallmarks of true heroes.

The first order of business was redeeming the work ethic and the value of competition from the moral wilderness of "professionalism." Sportswriters conceded that virtually all champion athletes possessed natural attributes separating them from ordinary people and allowing them to attract the attention of coaches, managers, and promoters who sought promising "raw material." As a class, these athletes were bigger, stronger, and quicker on their feet. They had sharper reflexes, coordination, and eyesight. Many of them also had intuitive "brains" for the sport in which they happened to excel, a trait that was inborn and usually discovered by accident. These "gifts" were a subject of great fascination in the press, the most common explanation for extraordinary athletic achievement and a basis for comparing rival stars. Illustrations and charts provided readers with the "tale of the tape" on prizefighters and football players, while columnists ruminated on the physical "equipment" that made Walter Johnson such a dominant pitcher or Babe Ruth such a terror at the plate.

But sportswriters asserted that true heroes were not content to rely on natural talent alone. From an early age, they had worked hard to improve their game, to make the most of their abilities. And this commitment had not ceased once they reached the top. For example, by incessantly practicing his fielding, hitting, and baserunning, Honus Wagner had made himself the "greatest baseball player in the world," Hugh Fullerton asserted in 1910 in a fawning profile in the *American Magazine*. According to his supporters in the press, Jack Dempsey possessed the same trait. Derided as one-dimensional "slugger" by many reporters and columnists, Dempsey was now interested in expanding his knowledge of boxing "science" to compensate for any decline in the power of his punches that might occur over the years, a writer for *Collier's* reported in 1925. A "passion for improvement" also inspired the golfer Bobby Jones and the tennis champion Bill Tilden, although both were blessed with such extraordinary innate abilities that others might not have seen the need to improve at all. "Shots that would have satisfied most champions," noted Grantland Rice, "failed to satisfy Jones. He was never willing to stand pat on what he had with the feeling that he had done well enough." Even Babe Ruth, perhaps the most widely heralded "natural" in sports, was praised by sportswriters for his efforts to improve his fielding and baserunning and hit for average as well as power. The aim of these efforts, journalists noted, was to eliminate weaknesses and make the athlete a great "all-around" performer, the best strategy for fending off upstarts and ensuring the longevity of a sports career. While extraordinary ability might allow an athlete like Ruth, Tilden, or Jones to achieve stardom, if he did not continue working on his game his spell at the top would be short-lived.[16]

The "passion for improvement" of such figures had a direct impact on their approach to conditioning. Rather than follow the time-honored method of dissipating between matches or during the off-season—the method followed by most professional athletes in the nineteenth century, including the legendary John L. Sullivan—heroes who embodied the ideal of sport never let themselves get out of shape. This made the task of preparing for competition much easier and minimized the inexorable physical decay that occurred over time. "It's the player who takes care of himself that lasts the longest on the pay-roll," the Hearst sportswriter Charles E. Van Loan suggested in a feature on professional baseball players in *Munsey's* in 1912. Ty Cobb, nearing the end of his career, agreed. "The best way to get in condition," he informed Hugh Fullerton in 1924, "is to keep in condition. I never permit myself to get out of shape, or get fat." Prizefighters also followed this regimen. Journalists reported that Dempsey was a "fanatic" about health and conditioning, spending many hours in the gym, while Tunney, nearly ten years after his reign as boxing champion of the American Expeditionary Force, was in better shape than ever, thanks to his vigorous, thoroughly modern training routine, which he followed even when he was not preparing for a fight. Sportswriters acknowledged that there were exceptions to this rule. A "freak" like Babe Ruth, for example, seemed to perform better when he "ran wild" and trained in the irregular manner popularized by Sullivan. But journalists argued that Ruth's widely publicized "collapse" and dismal showing in the 1925 season demonstrated that the "rules" of conditioning applied to everyone. Though Ruth had enough natural talent to enjoy a few years of glory, if he wanted to make baseball a long-term career he had to change his ways and stay in shape year round. "They told me about John L. and what happened to him, but I just laughed to myself," Ruth told a reporter for *Collier's* at the end of 1925. "I was going to be the exception, the popular hero who could do as he pleased. But all those people were right. . . . Now . . . I know that if I am to wind up sitting pretty . . . I've got to face the facts and admit I've been the sappiest of saps." [17]

Physical conditioning only provided the foundation for excellence in sports, however. Equally important, sportswriters suggested, were mental attributes that set the true champion apart from rivals who possessed the same natural abilities and assiduously cultivated skills. First, to break into the upper reaches of competitive sports, athletes had to have self-confidence, faith in their ability to compete at the highest levels. To be the best, to surpass all others, they had to withstand the doubts and fears that arose in the heat of competition, when physical pain made it all too tempting to quit and "pretenders" were revealed to be "yellow." In addition, athletes had to conquer the nervousness to which virtually every human was susceptible in clutch situations. True champions could retain their "mental balance," blocking out everything that might distract them from their game or undermine their will to win. According to Grantland Rice, they possessed "a cool, clear head, a stout heart, a serenity of mind and a concentration on the job." Here, journalists asserted, was the key to Jim Thorpe's record-setting Olympic victories, Jack Dempsey's ability to pummel larger and seemingly stronger opponents, and Babe Ruth's talent for hitting home runs when games were on the line. [18]

The master of the "mental game," in the view of sportswriters, was Bobby Jones. Like many other athletes, Rice noted in *Collier's*, Jones was born with great natural ability, and early lessons allowed him to develop an "almost flawless form." By the time he was a teenager he possessed the physical equipment and skills to be a champion. Yet it took him eight years before he won his first amateur championship, a drought that Rice attributed to Jones's "temperament." During these years, as he struggled against less skilled competitors, Jones was "high-strung, over-keen, boiling inwardly at his own mistakes." It was not until he learned to relax and control his habit of becoming enraged that he developed the mental focus he needed to emerge from the pack and become the game's dominant player. Even more impressive, considering her gender, was the mental concentration of the tennis star Helen Wills. Refuting the conventional wisdom that women were too emotional to be effective in competitive sports, "Little Miss Poker Face" combined well-honed skills with a temperament perfectly suited to the rigors of match play. As Rice observed, "Nothing upsets her mental poise. Nothing seems to affect her serene confidence and determination." This gave Wills a tremendous advantage of her rivals, but it would not have mattered a whit had she not also worked hard to improve her game, for it was the confidence that she gained from this regimen that strengthened her will to win and allowed her to develop her formidable powers of mental concentration. In other words, Wills's mental poise and toughness were traits that she had actively cultivated; they had emerged from her training and from the mental preparation accompanying it.[19]

Athletes with such mental attributes, journalists argued, were also more likely to infuse their play with "science" as a means of achieving victory. For example, it was boxing science—a shrewdly calculated and expertly followed plan of attack—that enabled smaller fighters like Georges Carpentier and Gene Tunney to wear down and defeat larger and more powerful opponents. A similar approach shaped the "inside" baseball practiced by Ty Cobb and John McGraw, the New York Giants' fabled manager. Behind the misunderstood Cobb's competitive zeal, Ring Lardner noted in the *American Magazine* in 1915, was a shrewd mind that understood every dimension of the game and was always seeking tactical advantage over opponents, always seeking a way to steal a base or eke out an extra run. "You can't take no afternoon nap when he's around," Lardner observed about Cobb's skills as a baserunner. "They're lot of other fast guys, but while they're thinkin' about what they're goin' to do he's did it. He's figuring two or three bases ahead all the time." Bobby Jones exhibited similar traits on the golf course, with a brand of play combining efficiency and go-for-broke recklessness, making him not merely successful but the darling of fans. The preeminent strategist in sport, however, was the man who dominated tennis as completely as Jones dominated golf, Bill Tilden. The reason for Tilden's mastery over his rivals, Grantland Rice argued in *Collier's* in 1924, was his ability to upset his opponent's poise by constantly mixing up shots and altering the rhythm of the game. "Being a smart student of competitive psychology, he knew the value of upsetting any defense by keeping an opponent guessing." After several years of losing in the final rounds of tournaments, Tilden had also come to recognize the need to pace himself during early matches to maintain a "reserve force" of energy for the finals. As a result, he was more likely than other top players to lose games and sometimes even sets to inferior players—a habit that led many tennis fans to underrate him. But when the tough matches arrived Tilden was invariably fresher than most of his foes, who in their zeal to annihilate early opponents had not shown the same foresight.[20]

In short, winning in the fiercely competitive world of big-time sports required far more than natural ability, though that was the foundation on which supremacy was built and the subject of innumerable columns and features. Winning also required a commitment to self-improvement and perpetual conditioning, and the cultivation of mental traits that were integral to success in the "game of life," a program that the most admirable athletes—blacks as well as whites, women as well as men—were said to follow. These were values closely associated with the ideal of personal efficiency that had come to pervade advice literature in the early twentieth century, including columns by advice writers for the daily press. As we have seen, the ideal of personal efficiency had an instrumental value that made it appealing to many Americans eager for an edge in the struggle for upward mobility and material success. However, the ideal was also influenced by the modernist discourse of "engagement"—the belief that the experience of committing oneself to an endeavor was its own reward.

Translated into the idiom of sportswriting, this tension was resolved through a kind of fusion. From reading the sports page, or magazine profiles of athletes, or special features in which sportswriters like Hugh Fullerton and Grantland Rice expounded on the lessons that sports offered to ordinary people, Americans could get a very good idea of what it took to succeed in sports and the "game of life." Yet because of sportswriters' contempt for excessive professionalism, these lessons were ambiguous. The most admirable athletes, they insisted, strove to be the best not for the glory or the tangible rewards that came from doing so. Instead, they were inspired by a desire to experience the intrinsic satisfaction that came from fulfilling their potential and mastering a highly demanding and competitive "profession." As Fullerton put it in a feature in the *American Magazine* on the "ten commandments of sport," "Honor the game thou playest, for he who playeth the game straight and hard wins even when he loses." At the core of the ideal of sport, then, lay a professionalism of a rather different and more commendable sort.[21]

* * *

Linking sports celebrities to values associated with the emerging professions—in many ways, the modern equivalent of artisanal culture—
was an effective strategy for rehabilitating competition and the focus
on results that it encouraged. But another theme of sports journalism
in the early twentieth century was even more useful for transforming
athletes into paragons of sport. According to journalists, true heroes
were imbued with the "amateur spirit," an attitude that they brought to
their sport and that distinguished them from many of their peers. This
was not the amateurism of purists like Caspar Whitney, a columnist for
Harper's Weekly and a founder of the magazine *Outing*, who made determined efforts in the 1890s and early 1900s to hold the line against
commercialism. In fact, in the hands of journalists like Fullerton, Rice,
W. O. McGeehan, and Paul Gallico, the meaning of amateurism was revised, making it more amenable to the modern trends that these writers
favored. Aware of the need to attract a wide readership extending beyond the upper-middle class—the constituency most attracted to Whitney's pure amateurism—and sensitive to new cultural currents that
had soured many Americans on the ruthless, self-aggrandizing individualism that had emerged in the wake of industrialization, sportswriters asserted that the amateur spirit was not only compatible with
the commercialization of sports but a perfect antidote to its excesses.
This subtle yet fundamental redefinition of amateurism, which paralleled related efforts to associate business with "public service" and the
entertainment industry with "culture," allowed sportswriters to praise
many professional athletes and join in the promotional activities that
were enlarging the audience for spectator sports. At the same time, it inspired sportswriters to believe that they were engaged in a more serious
enterprise: a critique of the way in which selfishness and acquisitiveness
had come to infect sports and the "game of life" in general.[22]

The salient feature of athletes who possessed the amateur spirit,
sportswriters argued, was their abiding love for the game. "They compete merely for the fun of meeting their brethren," W. O. McGeehan
noted in 1927 in an essay in *Vanity Fair* on the meaning of amateurism.
Of course, they still trained hard to improve their skills, and through
their exertions they acquired the edge they needed to get to the top and
remain there. Yet this training never became drudgery—never became
"work." Not coincidentally, the sports figure whom journalists anointed
as the quintessential new-style amateur was also an amateur in the lit-

eral sense: Bobby Jones. Unlike most golfers of his caliber, sportswriters reported, Jones refused to turn pro and eschewed opportunities to cash in on his fame through product endorsements or by lending his name to business enterprises eager to associate themselves with a champion. As Paul Gallico observed in 1929 in *Liberty*, because he remained an amateur and earned no money from golf, Jones worked as a lawyer in his hometown of Atlanta, leaving him with far less time for golf than other top-flight players had. Eager to make his subject attractive to his predominantly working-class readers, Gallico insisted that Jones did not like having to work and longed for "financial independence from the routine of daily desk slavery." But Jones, unlike nearly all people who shared this longing, could do something about it. If he turned pro or accepted even a few of the many offers that were made to him, Gallico suggested, he could "amass a fortune which would make him independent to the end of his days." Nevertheless, Jones resisted these temptations. He wanted golf to remain a "beloved game," and he feared that the pleasure he derived from it would diminish if he became a professional. According to Gallico, it was precisely because Jones kept his priorities straight and continued, despite his fame, to regard golf as merely a game that he got along so well with his friends and neighbors and was "at heart a quite contented person."[23]

The tennis star Helen Wills, journalists asserted, viewed her sport much the same way. Unlike her chief rival, the notorious Suzanne Lenglen, Wills took up tennis relatively late, at the age of twelve, when she noticed the great fun her father had while playing. Her natural abilities allowed her to make quick progress, and in a month she was far better than he. Yet Wills's father and coaches had never forced her to adopt the tiresome and unrelenting regimen that Lenglen's father had forced on Suzanne—even though Wills's late start made adopting it the logical course if they were serious about making her into a champion. As a result, for Wills even practice was "play," and her great love of the game carried her much farther than anyone would have predicted. Ironically, when Wills lost her highly publicized matches with Lenglen in 1926 she became even more attractive to sportswriters. While conceding Lenglen's superiority on the court, journalists depicted Wills as the more admirable human being—and a better representative of sport. Despite having reached the very pinnacle of women's tennis, Wills still viewed it as a game, and this approach to her sport made it easier for her to accept her losses with grace and dignity. By contrast, a "one-tracker" like Lenglen became distraught when losing and let her professional rivalries affect her relations with other players off the court. Writing in *Vanity Fair*, Mary K. Browne suggested that Lenglen's "early training" was the reason for her poor sportsmanship and lack of contentment. "From the very first, she was made to practice for long, weary hours every day. . . . She has never had a chance to enjoy the game. Tennis, in fact, became her vocation and not her avocation. No wonder, since her life has been dedicated to victory, that she is unable to hide her chagrin when she is losing. Possibly, if she had been trained differently, she might not have been so constantly victorious, but I think she would have been a happier girl."[24]

Depicting literal amateurs like Jones and Wills as embodiments of the amateur spirit was easy. No matter how fiercely they devoted themselves to sports, that they did not play for money and shunned endorsements allowed journalists to endow them with an aura of virtue. Casting professional athletes in this role, however, was more difficult, particularly when they earned a lot or when money figured prominently in reports about their activities. The professional most often linked to the amateur spirit was Babe Ruth. Despite his enormous salary, which made him by far the highest-paid player in baseball, Ruth was an "amateur at heart," sportswriters reported. He played baseball for the sheer love of the game, not for the money. "His attitude and the manner in which he carries himself," W. O. McGeehan asserted, "are the attitude and the manner of the amateur." But making such claims forced journalists to explain the regular contract squabbles with Jacob Ruppert, the owner of the Yankees, that occasionally led Ruth to "hold out" until his demands were met. Most writers defended Ruth by arguing that he was merely seeking his fair share of the profits earned by the team— profits that Ruth had been instrumental in generating. As the man responsible for rekindling fans' interest in baseball after the "Black Sox" scandal, Hugh Fullerton mused in 1926 in *Liberty*, Ruth was "the best investment" that Yankee management had ever made. "He has drawn hundreds of thousands of dollars into their treasury and revived baseball when it was terribly sick." His demands for a salary increase, then, were justified. The Yankees owed him. Ruth's eagerness to endorse products and engage in "personality advertising" posed a different problem. To explain it, sportswriters emphasized his "genial good nature," which made it difficult for him to say no to anyone. Indeed, Ruth's interest in making money was offset by a generosity as prodigious as his abilities with a bat. For example, in a profile of the ballplayer in *Collier's* in 1924, the Hearst sportswriter Arthur Robinson regaled readers with anecdotes about Ruth's proclivity for buying expensive gifts for friends and family, including a luxurious roadster for a priest who had been his mentor as a child. Thus while Ruth was a professional athlete immersed in the money-making opportunities made possible by the commercialization of sports, no one could accuse him of being greedy or even caring very much about money.[25]

The same could not be said of prizefighters, even revered champions, who were rarely associated with the amateur spirit that was alleged to inspire professionals like Ruth. "There is a lot of money in the job of being heavyweight champion," Grantland Rice observed in 1927, "but there doesn't seem to be much fun." Conscious of the mixed feelings that many of their readers continued to hold about this more popular but still disreputable sport, sportswriters employed different arguments to distinguish fighters like Jim Jeffries, Jack Dempsey, Gene Tunney, and Joe Louis from their less admirable peers. They asserted, for example, that such men derived little pleasure from their profession—unlike "roughnecks" who were naturally inclined to fighting and thus well suited to it. Fighters like Jeffries, Dempsey, and Louis simply "drifted" into their sport, discovering that prowess with their fists could provide an alternative to the menial forms of employment that had been their lot. And having reached the top, they were determined to make the best of it. John B. Kennedy revealed to readers of *Collier's* that the former hobo Dempsey was eager to earn as much money as possible from fighting and product endorsements and go into business for himself. "I've learned a good deal about the investment business through my own operations, and . . . I'll make a life's work out of the game," he informed Kennedy. But Dempsey's interest in money did not affect his attitude or style of fighting in the ring. Sportswriters praised his technique of relentlessly attacking opponents and finishing them off as quickly as possible—not so much for the "science" it embodied but because it seemed so sincere and guileless, so antithetical to the practice of easing up in order to extend the length—and manipulate the betting odds—of fights. "The people pay to see fighters do their best," Dempsey explained to another writer for *Collier's*. And though he was frequently approached by gamblers eager to see him "carry" a second-rate fighter, Dempsey always refused. Gene Tunney, journalists reported, was even more disdainful of the "rough stuff" that prevailed in professional boxing and uncomfortable in the role of champion, which required him to engage in cynical publicity stunts and consort with disreputable characters drawn to the "fight game." Having always preferred "nice, respectable people," it was not surprising that he had seized opportunities to socialize with the well-to-do and develop business contacts that might allow him to get out of prizefighting altogether, Robert Ingerley noted in 1927 in a profile of Tunney in *Liberty*.[26]

Athletes who embodied the amateur spirit followed rules and respected traditions. They were good sportsmen who never let their "will to win" get the better of them. This was an especially important theme in articles about professional baseball, enabling sportswriters to distinguish true heroes from arrogant figures like Ty Cobb, whose antics often threatened the sacred aura that sportswriters like Rice and Hugh Fullerton had laboriously constructed around the "national game." Early in his career, Cobb's foils were Christy Mathewson and Honus Wagner, both extolled by journalists for being "team players" and exhibiting qualities of sportsmanship that made them admired by opponents and rival fans. In a profile of Wagner, for example, Fullerton made oblique reference to baseball's premier bad boy when he suggested that though Wagner played to win, he also played fair. "No umpire has ever had occasion to accuse Wagner of rowdyism, and his opponents admire and like him, testifying to his sportsmanship." In the early 1920s, when his slugging diverted public attention from the Black Sox scandal, Babe Ruth was cast as the aging Cobb's new foil, a fun-loving team player who played hard yet accepted the breaks of the game with equanimity. Comparing Cobb and Ruth, W. O. McGeehan argued in 1920 that Cobb was a "prima donna" whose selfish, arrogant behavior was "bad not only for his own team but for the morale of organized baseball." Ruth, on the other hand, set a positive example. "He is big enough to realize that while he is the supreme attraction in baseball at the present time, his teammates and his employers have some rights that must be respected. He is playing the game fairly and earnestly, and the way that he is doing it has earned the regard not only of those who know baseball but of those who seldom see a game."[27]

By 1925, however, after repeated rows with umpires, the Yankees' manager Miller Huggins, the team's owners, and the new commissioner of baseball, it was impossible to depict Ruth in this fashion. Indeed, at the end of the 1925 season he was virtually written off as a has-been, as yet another player who could not withstand the "swelled head" that often afflicted big-time athletic stars. "Too much money and too much applause carried [him] from [his] feet," Grantland Rice opined. The emergence of the "new" Ruth sparked another reversal in his fortunes, however. Returning to the form that made his name in the early 1920s, and shrewdly avoiding conflicts with authority figures, Ruth was again cast as a poster boy for "team play" and graceful deference toward umpires, managers, and the powers that be. "The older and more prominent you get in baseball the closer you've got to follow the rules," Ruth told the sportswriter Bozeman Bulger in an interview that appeared in 1931 in the *Saturday Evening Post*. But the "new" Ruth went even further, serving as a team leader and mentoring younger players like Lou Gehrig. This attitude, Bulger asserted, was quite a departure from that of veterans when Ruth broke into baseball. Rather than see Gehrig as a rival who might upstage him, Ruth saw him as someone who could use his help—and whose contributions could make the Yankees even better as a team. Indeed, Ruth was anything but a prima donna. Though revered by his teammates, he demanded no special privileges. As Bulger noted, "He does not high-hat his associates and probably would not know how to assume a patronizing tone. . . . With his teammates he skylarks, argues, jokes and makes suggestions, all participants on an even footing." [28]

As Ruth's example revealed, getting "drawing cards" to follow rules and accept their role as part of a team was often difficult. Being singled out as an individual star with box-office appeal gave them leverage over managers and coaches, which men like Cobb and the "old" Ruth exploited to maximum advantage. Journalists suggested that the potential for insubordination was especially great among athletes from impoverished backgrounds, who were likely never to have learned the value of self-discipline and were easily mesmerized by the money and acclaim showered on sports celebrities. They lacked the "foundation" and "background" to "face the scenery from the heights without getting dizzy," Rice argued. But Ruth's widely heralded reformation demonstrated that it was possible to turn figures like him into "model citizens." Performing this brand of alchemy required the skills of an "expert manager" like Huggins, whom journalists portrayed as educated and highly intelligent, a "keen and quiet student of temperaments." It took a deft mixture of patience, understanding, and firmness to handle Ruth and turn a motley group of roughnecks into a smoothly running machine, W. O. McGeehan observed in 1929, in the wake of Huggins's death. Paul Gallico agreed, noting that Huggins was the "brains" behind the Yankees, a small man who accomplished the difficult task of winning the respect and loyalty of a group of "thick-headed" athletes, "men whose limited intellect made it hard for them to respect anything that was not their size." Yet Huggins's exertions did not benefit the Yankees alone. By making Ruth recognize his responsibilities to his teammates, Yankee management, and his fans, Huggins had helped the Babe to grow. Thanks to Huggins, Arthur Mann wrote, "Ruth is a man to-day, awake to the responsibility which the passing of years thrust upon us." Unlike other "drawing cards," he now happily signed autographs and mingled with fans, particularly the young boys who looked up to him as an idol. According to sportswriters, it was Ruth's desire not to disappoint them—rather than fear of being fired by the Yanks—that kept him from returning to his rebellious ways. In these accounts, the aim of managers like Huggins and Connie Mack was not simply to extract the best performance from players and direct them in ways most likely to result in victory for the team—and the increased box-office receipts that accrued to winners. It was to enable athletes to fulfill their potential and accept responsibilities incumbent upon every champion—and help to keep sports a game.[29]

The amateur spirit was a complex ideal. It celebrated athletes who followed rules and were team players and responsible idols, traits that subordinated individuals—in this case, highly skilled, exceptional individuals—to the demands and interest of the group. But sportswriters offset the instrumentalism implicit in this theme by suggesting that athletes viewed their profession as "play," and that embracing the commitments and responsibilities of the new-style amateurism was the best strategy for keeping this perspective. Promoting the amateur spirit allowed journalists to condemn the excessive professionalism of "one-trackers," which they likened to the often overzealous pursuit of the main chance that prevailed throughout American society. This argument was central to the efforts of sportswriters to attract readers who shared such concerns—working-class readers committed to ideals of collective solidarity or "moral capitalism" as well as middle-class readers repulsed by the crass boosterism that had overtaken the country after the First World War. Yet in their determination to criticize this phenomenon and depict sport as a realm apart from it, sportswriters were insensitive to the coercive implications of the lessons they conveyed, particularly when discussing the means by which "rebels" like Ruth and the pitching star Dizzy Dean could be transformed into responsible, rule-abiding members of teams. For sportswriters, the natural leaders of teams were not "drawing cards" but managers, and cohesiveness was achieved when players—nearly always from the working class—came to accept the rules laid down by these understanding and insightful bourgeois men. These rules were essential if athletes were to realize their potential.[30]

* * *

The tension was even sharper in accounts of athletes' private lives. Not surprisingly, journalists praised figures who subscribed to respectable values and cooperated with the press's interest in depicting them in this light. The most admirable sports celebrities, reporters in the early twentieth century asserted, were those who were sober or at the very least restrained in their consumption of "stimulants," sincerely committed to education and self-improvement, and devoted to wholesome forms of recreation. Like show-business writers, however, sportswriters in the 1920s and 1930s continually expanded the definition of wholesome activities to include a wider array of casual, informal, even frivolous pastimes that would not have passed muster among their predecessors in the 1890s and early 1900s. In doing so, they substantially revised the ideal of respectability and joined other journalists in fashioning a more relaxed and expressive model of private life that complemented the continued emphasis placed by the press, advice writers, and the helping professions on self-discipline and achieving "personal efficiency." Together, these imperatives became the foundation of the new consumer-oriented way of life that emerged in the 1920s and 1930s and attracted widespread public support after the Second World War.

The easiest figures to portray along these lines were tennis players and golfers, since they were nearly always products of respectable, upper-middle-class families and more likely to embrace in real life values reflecting their backgrounds. The most attractive of these athletes, journalists suggested, were Bill Tilden and Helen Wills. Writing in 1922 in *Collier's*, the columnist Franklin P. Adams praised Tilden for having a rich and interesting life beyond the court. Unlike his rivals, who lived, ate, and breathed tennis, Tilden had many hobbies and enthusiasms, including the theater, about which he was quite knowledgeable and discerning. "He is more an artist than he is anything else," Adams contended. "He is more an artist than nine-tenths of the artists I know." Coming from Adams, a charter member of the Algonquin Round Table and a frequent critic of "boobs," this was high praise. But sportswriters like Grantland Rice concurred, defending Tilden from critics who mistook his "sophisticated" tastes for arrogance. Journalists ascribed the same combination of traits to Wills, the women's amateur champion who mixed tennis with a "heavy art major" at Berkeley and a thoroughly "normal" life. Wills's most impressive quality, however, was her cautious and sensible embrace of "sophisticated" fashions, an approach, Helena Huntington Smith noted in 1927 in the *New Yorker,* that revealed how "a nice, wholesome girl" could make herself beautiful without losing the modesty and "balance" she had gained from her upbringing. Wills's femininity was an important focus of reportage, demonstrating that excellence in sports need not transform female athletes into mannish "muscle molls," Paul Gallico's derisive term for women like the phenomenal multisport star Babe Didrickson. Indeed, press coverage of "Little Miss Poker Face" was vital in shattering stereotypes that had made highly competitive sports seem like masculine endeavors. Yet by placing so much emphasis on Wills's femininity, and contrasting these qualities with the steely resolve and poise that she displayed on the court—neatly symbolized by her nickname—journalists created a new stereotype that could be just as confining for female athletes who did not share Wills's upper-middle-class background or interest in typically feminine pursuits. For example, Didrickson, the product of a working-class family from small-town Texas, was compelled to defend herself against charges of being a "muscle moll" by claiming to have an interest in sewing, knitting, and fashion design. In an issue of the *American Magazine* in 1936 she went further, asserting, "I look forward to having a home and children just like anybody else."[31]

On the whole, it was more difficult for journalists to portray professional athletes as models of bourgeois propriety—especially if they were prizefighters and baseball players, who were usually from rural or working-class backgrounds and often reluctant to adopt values that they regarded as priggish and alien to revered traditions. Nevertheless, beginning in the 1890s sportswriters worked assiduously to depict such figures as James J. Corbett, Honus Wagner, and Christy Mathewson in this guise. Mathewson, for instance, a college-educated star pitcher for the New York Giants, was portrayed as a real-life Frank Merriwell whose off-the-field behavior set a good example for his fellow players. Under his influence, a writer for the *New York Evening World* revealed in 1916, the Giants had become a more sedate and respectable group of men, devoting most of their time on the road to marathon games of checkers. The athlete most fervently promoted as a bourgeois hero during the 1920s was the prizefighter Gene Tunney. Sportswriters like Rice and W. O. McGeehan were delighted when Tunney—at the prodding of Tex Rickard and his press agent, Steve Hannagan—expressed an interest in being cast as a "genteel" alternative to the "pugs" and "roughnecks" who dominated professional boxing, providing a useful angle in their campaign to expand the audience for prizefighting and bring it under the aegis of legitimate sport. Accordingly, they gleefully revealed to readers that this ex-Marine, "a quiet, well-mannered, clean-living young man," was serious, thoughtful, and a devotee of Shakespeare, which he read between bouts of sparring at his training camp. They also made note of Tunney's eagerness to accept invitations to society functions and fraternize with a "higher class" of people than one found in the world of prizefighting. Tunney's supporters maintained that his interest in literature and desire to socialize with "nice people" arose from a long-standing commitment to self-improvement and upward mobility, dating to his upbringing in a respectable working-class family in New York City.[32]

Yet in the view of his critics, a vocal minority of writers that included Paul Gallico and Westbrook Pegler, a columnist for the *Chicago Tribune*, Tunney was a cynical poseur. They argued, not incorrectly, that his persona of "Gene the Genteel" was designed to help Rickard create a dramatic contrast between Tunney and his chief rival, Dempsey. As Gallico explained in 1929 in *Liberty*, "We felt that his bookishness was a prop for ballyhoo; that he was arrogant and overbearing with those who had to write of his doings; and that he was a hypocrite. What contact we had had with him had not lessened these impressions." To be sure, Gallico and Pegler did not question the sincerity of Tunney's disdain for the "fight game," which they found distasteful as well. Nor did they begrudge his desire to cash in on his possession of the championship and go into business with his new friends. But they interpreted these commitments differently, suggesting that they were inspired not by a desire for self-improvement but rather by snobbishness and self-loathing—the familiar motives that lay behind the posturing of many a "swelled head."[33]

That sportswriters would openly criticize an athlete like Tunney was remarkable, a vivid illustration of the degree to which the attitudes of journalists had changed since the era of Christy Mathewson in the early 1900s. The critique of Tunney developed by writers like Gallico and Pegler was deeply influenced by a recognition that some of the formulas relied on by sportswriters since the turn of the century were no longer effective in attracting readers. To the consternation of many writers, athletes who led respectable private lives, and could be fitted into the mold of Merriwell and Mathewson, often lacked widespread appeal. Though embraced by some fans, these athletes were regarded by many others as boring, and public interest in the sports that they dominated would wane. Far more popular, and thus better for sports and the business of sportswriting, were figures like Dempsey and Babe Ruth, who combined extraordinary athletic achievement with "colorful" private lives: rough-hewn pleasure-seekers who simply could not be cast as paragons of self-discipline and bourgeois propriety. As we have seen, such men were relatively easy to find among well-paid professional athletes, particularly during the heyday of Mathewson in the early 1900s, when coaches, managers, and club owners were relatively lax about disciplining their players off the field and many athletes took advantage of this situation by running wild. Before the 1920s, however, misbehaving athletes were usually lambasted or ignored by journalists who insisted that sports celebrities lead "clean" lives off the field. A respectable lifestyle, they argued, went hand-in-hand with perpetual conditioning and was essential to long-term success. This claim was often vindicated when athletes notorious for their debauchery suffered steep declines in their abilities and became "has-beens." Yet as sportswriters in the 1920s were well aware, Dempsey's and Ruth's appeal extended well beyond the predominantly working-class audience that had always looked favorably on "rebels." Their fans included many middle-class Americans and upwardly mobile immigrants who had come to share the contempt that much of the working class had long felt toward Victorian standards of respectability. This cross-class appeal was bolstered in the early 1920s when Dempsey and Ruth dominated their sports in spite of their riotous, self-indulgent private lives.[34]

Dealing with such figures posed a difficult problem for sportswriters, particularly those interested in providing lessons applicable to the "game of life." One response was to portray Dempsey and Ruth as anomalies—athletes so supremely endowed with the traits necessary for success in their sports that conventional "rules" did not apply to them. And since both Dempsey and Ruth were relatively dark-skinned white men from allegedly "inferior" racial stock, these peculiar gifts were often associated with primitivism. In Rice's view, Dempsey was a veritable "caveman" whose physical prowess and slugging ability derived from a "killer instinct" that civilized men had lost long ago. Similar claims were made about Ruth. He was a "freak," a "throwback," a perpetual adolescent whose development had been arrested by the opportunity to make "play" his profession, McGeehan asserted in 1923 in his syndicated column. These were doubled-edged arguments. On the one hand, they allowed sportswriters to support the ideal of "clean living." Since Dempsey and Ruth were not ordinary men, the ideal was one to which they presumably could not be expected to adhere. On the other hand, depicting Dempsey and Ruth in this fashion gave them a vaguely romantic allure that struck a chord among readers increasingly constrained by "civilization"—the same readers who sought release in the "Tarzan" novels of Edgar Rice Burroughs or the exotic rhythms of jazz. For the syndicated columnist Heywood Broun, Dempsey and Ruth were rebukes to a "Puritanism" that was responsible for Prohibition and other misguided efforts to impose an antiquated morality on modern man.[35]

But most sportswriters stopped well short of making such arguments, though there is reason to believe that in private they sympathized with Broun. More concerned about preserving public faith in the ideal of personal efficiency than in exposing the baleful influence of Puritanism, journalists were reluctant to endorse the extracurricular pursuits of Dempsey and Ruth. And in the mid-1920s they leaped at opportunities to chastise both men and reaffirm the "rules" that their behavior had discredited. The attack on Dempsey centered on his seeming unwillingness to fight, a grave offense that rekindled charges of his having avoided serving in the First World War. Defending one's title regularly, against the top contenders, was one of the responsibilities of being champion, sportswriters like Rice reminded readers in 1925, when Dempsey seemed more interested in his budding movie career and his marriage to the actress Estelle Taylor. Some journalists accused him of "going Hollywood" and forsaking old friends and his roots. These charges were reiterated by the writer Jim Tully, who visited Dempsey and his new wife in Hollywood and produced a long feature story in *Liberty* on the champion's lamentable "domestication" at the hands of Taylor, the new "power behind his knuckled throne."

Ruth's fall was even more dramatic: a widely publicized "collapse" during spring training in 1925 that kept him out of the lineup for weeks, an escalating conflict with Miller Huggins that ultimately resulted in his suspension, and a season that saw the Yankees come in seventh and Ruth put up numbers that were mediocre compared to earlier years. Sportswriters attributed Ruth's performance to years of self-indulgence and Yankee management's unwillingness to discipline the game's biggest drawing card. Hugh Fullerton conceded that this approach had worked early on, since Ruth was a "genius" and he erred "so humanly and frankly" that he was hard to punish. But in the end, allowing him such freedom failed to arrest the inevitable decline that occurred when athletes—even supremely talented ones like Ruth—failed to conform to the rules of "clean living."[36]

After 1925 press treatment of both athletes improved dramatically. Dempsey's image benefited from the heroic resolve and boxing prowess that he displayed in his two close defeats by Tunney, fights for which he had trained like never before. Moreover, his widely heralded interest in becoming a businessman put his fondness for nightlife and expensive goods in an entirely different light, as the pastimes of a sophisticated "city boy" and not of a semi-civilized pug. Dempsey benefited as well from the growing revulsion that quite a few sportswriters developed toward Tunney, whose devotion to social climbing seemed so much more intense and pathetic. Next to the pretentious new champion, Dempsey's rough edges and continued fondness for "simple pleasures" like watching movies and playing pool made him appear "natural," a man eager to make the best of his career as a prizefighter yet comfortable in his own skin. Ruth's image, meanwhile, was boosted by his successful effort to honor the vow to "reform" that he made after the disastrous 1925 season. Indeed, when he returned to form and led the Yankees to three straight pennants and two World Series victories, journalists proclaimed the "new" Ruth vastly superior to the "old." Sportswriters continued to portray the "new" Ruth as fun-loving and self-indulgent. But they insisted that baseball's foremost playboy had toned down his wild ways—and that this change in his personal life was one of the keys to the tremendous success he had enjoyed after 1925. Ruth's recreations were now more wholesome and domestic: golf, playing pinochle, reading comics, listening to the radio, going out for an occasional dinner and night on the town. Helping him to maintain this style of life was his new wife, Claire Hodgson, depicted by sportswriters as a genteel and gracious "domestic manager" who, like Miller Huggins, understood her husband's peculiar needs and how best to channel his appetites and energies. Moreover, at the urging of Huggins and his longtime personal manager, Christy Walsh, the "new" Ruth had finally begun to save his money and was "fixed for life." As with Dempsey, these changes had not fundamentally changed the man, nor were they likely to. "The advance of time will never bring Park Avenue elegance or drawing room dignity to Ruth," the sportswriter Joe Williams wrote in 1928 in obvious reference to Tunney, who seemed eager to achieve these goals. Ruth would always remain Ruth—more responsible than in days past but no less "colorful" or down-to-earth.[37]

Here was an ideal strategy for dealing with professional athletes from the wrong side of the tracks who lacked the self-discipline of a true sports hero. As Ruth's reformation demonstrated, these figures did not have to dissipate off the field, as athletes from working-class backgrounds had done for many decades. On the contrary, sportswriters revealed that it was possible to "manage" athletes in their private lives, just as they were managed on the field or in the ring, by directing them toward activities that were enjoyable yet compatible with the quest for personal efficiency. The aim of such a program was to persuade the athlete to embrace not the abstemious regimen associated with Christy Mathewson but a more informal and expressive style of life that offered plenty of opportunities for fun and games, including pastimes that sportswriters in the early 1900s would have surely frowned on. But keeping athletes from straying was only the beginning. Sportswriters noted that personal managers and press agents, who were portrayed as mature and well-intentioned "advisors," could also help athletes to achieve a wide range of goals in their personal and professional lives. Writing in the *Saturday Evening Post*, Larry Snyder, the track coach at Ohio State, recounted how he had steered the Olympic sprinter Jesse Owens, whose mentor he had been, through a maze of endorsement and exhibition offers after Owens's stunning performance at the 1936 Summer Games: the aim was to ensure Owens's refusal of any offers that might "spoil" or "exploit" him and imperil his desire to one day be a coach at a black college.[38]

Though the title of Snyder's article, "My Boy, Jesse," was patently racist, during the 1920s, 1930s, and early 1940s the most important difference between athletes and advisors like Snyder was not race but class. Indeed, the most widely publicized managers of a black athlete were themselves African Americans—John Roxborough and Julian Black,

Joe Louis's "handlers." Many white sportswriters portrayed the two as earnest "college men" intent on molding the ignorant, resolutely low-brow Louis into the sort of man who reflected well on his race and could make whites forget about the "sins" of Jack Johnson. The key to Louis's biracial, cross-class appeal, however, may well have been the way in which most journalists yoked the theme of "racial uplift" to material that revealed Louis to be unpretentious and down-to-earth—thus distancing him from blacks associated with the "colored aristocracy" and the civil-rights movement, whom many whites might regard as "uppity." Under the tutelage of Roxborough and Black, sportswriters like Gallico and Caswell Adams noted, Louis had become more mature and serious about his responsibilities to the public and his race, growing into the role they had crafted for him. Yet as Adams revealed in a glowing profile of Louis in the *Saturday Evening Post* in 1941, Roxborough and Black had failed to cure Louis of his love for popular culture and pastimes like reading comic books that were an affront to the colored aristocracy and pretentious whites alike—but not to working-class and lower-middle-class Americans who embraced the new consumer-oriented model of the "good life." This connection to working-class and lower-middle-class readers was reinforced by reportage focusing on Louis's patriotism, evident from his enlistment in the Army as a "$21 private" shortly after Pearl Harbor. Writing in *Liberty*, Gallico noted that Louis was giving up a lot by joining the Army. At twenty-eight, he was "getting on for a fighter," and when the war was over it was doubtful that he would be able to hold on to his title. But Louis did not care. "You do whatever you can for your country," he told Gallico. "Your country is what made everything possible for you." As portrayed by writers like Gallico and Adams, Louis possessed the unique combination of traits necessary to be a mass idol: a "hunger" for education and personal growth coupled with modesty, simplicity, and a commitment to something larger than the self.[39]

* * *

The emergence of sports celebrities rested on two interrelated developments: a gradual expansion of the audience for spectator sports and the construction of a shared mythology that enabled fans from a variety of backgrounds to make sense of the field and appreciate the achievements of its stars. Admittedly, champion athletes and especially prizefighters had enjoyed large followings in the nineteenth century. But their appeal was narrow compared to that of twentieth-century athletes like Jack Dempsey, Babe Ruth, and Joe Louis. John L. Sullivan was the first sports figure to benefit from expanded press coverage and acquire a fan base extending beyond the core audience of young working-class men. Yet working-class men remained Sullivan's most loyal supporters—as opposed to people who simply found him "interesting" and probably rooted against him when he fought—and coverage of his bouts and activities out of the ring was influenced by the powerful animus that most sportswriters for the metropolitan press felt toward athletes who were unabashedly proletarian in their demeanor and style of life. In short, though Sullivan was the first sports celebrity, he received mostly bad press—even in the otherwise scandalous *National Police Gazette*.[40]

In the early twentieth century, as a new generation of sportswriters struggled to write for a cross-class audience that included many Americans who had soured on the bourgeois prescriptions of the Victorian era, they gradually became more tolerant of athletes who trod their own path, making it possible for figures like Dempsey, Ruth, and Louis to achieve widespread appeal. Indeed, journalists discovered that athletes who possessed "rough edges" and had little interest in covering them up "with a cloak of any polite sort" had the potential to be extremely popular.[41] Of course, their acceptance by the press depended on their willingness to assume the role that journalists had created for sports celebrities—to say the right things and act in a manner befitting a true hero. In other words, the goodwill of the press had to be earned, something that could only be done if athletes cooperated with sportswriters, making it easier for the athletes to be depicted in ways likely to make them appealing to as wide an audience as possible. As we have seen, this role was intimately connected to the ideal of sport, a set of values that journalists in the early twentieth century crafted to insulate themselves from the ballyhoo that was central to the commercialization of sports.

However, the ideal of sport, like other myths constructed by the mass-circulation press, was ambiguous. Its authors were journalists interested in attracting readers from varied backgrounds, and they were careful to include characteristics that would make the myth widely appealing. At the same time, they were eager to appear responsible and connect their work to the serious business that engaged other journalists—and made the press look good to civic leaders and big advertisers. This was the main reason for the emphasis on constructive lessons that readers might apply in the "game of life"—lessons that were helpful but also implicitly conservative, celebrating the virtues of self-discipline, clean living, following rules, playing for the team, and accepting responsibilities that required personal sacrifice. From this perspective, the ideal of sport looks like yet another bourgeois ruse: an effort to promote values that were in the interests of managerial elites and encouraged accommodation to the status quo.

But this is not the only perspective from which to view the ideal of sport. The key to the widespread appeal of the ideal may have been its vaguely progressive features, which can only be appreciated if we discard the post-sixties lens through which many scholars interpret both sports and progressive reform and attempt to view it from the vantage point of ordinary Americans in the early twentieth century. Like other discourses of the era, the ideal of sport was highly critical of excessive competition, rule breaking, acquisitiveness, and self-aggrandizing individualism. In their place, it celebrated values that evoked not the Fordist assembly line but artisanal culture and the world of white-collar professionals: the mastery and pride that could be gained from the assiduous cultivation of skills, love of one's "profession" for its own sake, and the acceptance of rules, responsibilities, and social norms that enabled individuals to live and work together in harmony. These values were attractive to many Americans during the first half of the twentieth century, including workers, immigrants, and racial minorities who joined reform movements or were sympathetic to many, if not all, of their aims. And their appeal, at least in principle, has not waned.[42]

That these values found their way into sportswriting, or that readers of the press embraced them in spite of their seeming conservatism, should come as no surprise. More surprising is that since the 1920s, sportswriters and many of their readers have shown little interest in abandoning them, even as commercialization and the negative features associated with it have strengthened their hold over virtually every form of athletic competition. Sportswriters and most fans still recoil from the notion that sports is just another business in which the competitive, relentlessly instrumental values that prevail in the "real world" hold sway. Is this naiveté and perverseness, as other journalists often suggest when they note the peculiar hold that these beliefs continue to have on their colleagues in the sports department? Or is it an implicit acknowledgment that embedded in the ideal of sport is a better way?

. . . .
EPILOGUE

The master plot of celebrity journalism could take a number of forms, giving reportage about specific kinds of public figures unique emphases. As we have seen, the precise configuration was determined by the concerns of the journalists who covered particular fields or beats. More often than not, the manner in which journalists invoked and adapted the narrative of true success was tied to their efforts to bolster their authority and credibility with readers—to separate themselves from the overtly self-promotional campaigns orchestrated by celebrities and their publicists and foster the illusion of press detachment from the apparatus of publicity.

But journalistic methods were also shaped by interests that inspired the larger journalistic community and, in some cases, other groups within the professional-managerial class. For the authors of celebrity journalism did not work in a vacuum. Often well educated and deeply influenced by an occupational ethic that encouraged worldliness and the seemingly objective outlook of professionals, they were quite familiar with the debates and controversies that occupied the attention of educated Americans. And as human-interest writers for the mass-circulation press, celebrity journalists were in a position to address these issues in a forum where they might have great influence and reach, particularly among the lower-middle class, the working class, immigrants, and white ethnics. Human-interest features, far more than conventional news stories, offered journalists unique opportunities to moralize and promote values and ideological agendas under the guise of "entertainment." Not only were these articles more common in publications read by ordinary Americans; their packaging as "story journalism" and use of tropes and narrative themes derived from vernacular forms may well have made them more subtly influential—and thus more easily converted to conventional wisdom and common sense.[1]

Their position of influence, however, did not give human-interest writers free rein. To make reportage appealing, journalists were compelled to acknowledge the concerns of their readers, a task especially daunting for writers at periodicals aimed toward a lower-class audience. The interests and concerns of these Americans were not always the same as those of educated professionals, and even when they were, lower-class Americans were likely to hold different points of view. These differences were exploited by the most successful editors and publishers of the era— men like Hearst and his savvy lieutenant, Arthur Brisbane—who made them the very starting point of their editorial enterprise. In their efforts to make their work resonate with the hopes and anxieties of the wide assortment of Americans whom they were committed to reaching, the authors of celebrity journalism had no choice but to infuse their stories with what scholars in cultural studies call "popular accents," making them more ambiguous and tension-ridden than the works of other professionals who were also interested in reaching a wide audience but not subject to the same economic imperatives to make their product appealing as a form of popular culture. In short, the proximity that the mass-circulation press enjoyed to the public cut both ways. While it allowed journalists greater access to readers from different classes and ethnic groups and created many opportunities to engage in ideological work, it also complicated their campaigns by requiring them to address issues and adopt positions incompatible with conventional categories and sometimes divergent from the professional-managerial point of view.[2]

Press coverage of the rich, for example, was informed by a recognition that many readers viewed wealthy businessmen and society figures as alien and morally corrupt. As we have seen, this view, one with deep roots in American history, gained new life during the second half of the nineteenth century, when economic development created a new class of fabulously wealthy people who seemed determined to set themselves apart from the mainstream. Some journalists, particularly in the 1890s and early 1900s, shared this view or were sympathetic to it. But many others, probably the majority, did not subscribe to it, even when, like Lincoln Steffens and Ida Tarbell, they recognized and sought to publicize social problems that had arisen alongside industrial capitalism and for which capitalists and financiers were often to blame. Because belief that the rich were corrupt "parasites" was so pervasive, even journalists sympathetic to wealthy Americans were forced to acknowledge this concern before dismissing it. Indeed, as reporters crafted new archetypes through which to portray the rich, the old ones that they sought to banish remained in view, a residual presence that journalists unwittingly evoked every time they asserted that a businessman, philanthropist, or society figure was "productive," "democratic," or "down-to-earth."

A similar dynamic shaped the ways in which journalists framed coverage of political celebrities. Distancing themselves from the conventions of the partisan press, writers like William Allen White established a new yardstick with which to evaluate the performance and commitment of politicians, government officials, and reformers. This project was influenced by the widespread disdain that many Americans had come to feel toward the major political parties, and by a growing belief that new reforms were needed to restore democracy and make more humane the urban-industrial society that the United States had become. Beneath the surface, journalists like White were responding to fears widespread among the middle and lower classes that economic development was transforming the United States into a corrupt plutocracy, in which politicians, beholden to powerful interests, composed a cynical, aloof, self-interested political class. Though sympathetic to the forces of reform, political writers like White were also conscious that many other Americans, including their publishers and the businessmen who paid for advertising, were fearful of some reformers and of what might happen if the public was aroused to support movements that advocated sweeping change. Celebrity journalism about politicians and reformers was meant to allay the fears of both groups, lauding "practical idealists" who were honest, public-spirited, and courageous enough to take on the "interests," yet pragmatic and constructive in their approach to reform.

The press's coverage of show business was also ambiguous. Inclined by their class background to be critical of the popular culture industries, journalists carried these biases with them when they were forced, by the tremendous public appeal of the theater, vaudeville, and moving pictures, to write favorable articles about the field's stars, in some cases becoming indistinguishable from industry flacks. The result was an obsession with the constraints that the popular culture industries imposed on "artists," which journalists like Adela Rogers St. Johns usually blamed on an unseemly devotion to the bottom line. This angle allowed show-business writers to express their preference for "quality" entertainment, a preference that they shared with many middle-class readers. But it also made their reportage interesting to a much wider array of Americans, men and women from a variety of backgrounds who also may have felt that their personal autonomy was being threatened by forces beyond their control, in part because these feelings were being reinforced by novelists, screenwriters, advertisers, and some members of the helping professions. Thus while celebrating the ability of actors and entertainers to follow their own course and fulfill their ambitions, celebrity journalism inadvertently raised public awareness of obstacles they faced, and provided readers with a vivid reminder that in an urban-industrial society, the individualism revered by Americans as their birthright was perpetually under siege.

This tension was even more visible in the press's depiction of sports celebrities. Writing for the broad audience of fans created by the expansion of sports coverage, journalists such as Grantland Rice and Paul Gallico struggled to endow athletic competition with values that made their work useful to readers eager for tips on how to win in the "game of life," advice that encouraged readers to embrace the ethos of personal efficiency and accept a subordinate role within the corporate economy. At the same time, they filled their columns and feature stories with lamentations about the excessive competitiveness and greed of many athletes, which they attributed to the pernicious influence of commercialism. The most admirable athletes, they insisted, were not simply "winners." Rather, they were those able to win while remaining true to values divergent from the win-at-any-cost mentality that pervaded many sports and American society as a whole. This critique of "professionalism," as we have seen, was inspired in part by the middle-class biases of the sportswriters and their desire to display their independence from the machinery of "ballyhoo." Because of their need to reach a wide audience, however, their independence was articulated in ways that gave it tremendous appeal, tapping into popular yearnings to transcend the constraints of "civilization," yet also reaffirming the importance of following rules and sacrificing one's individual interests for the good of a "team." In the 1920s and 1930s these values were quite popular among lower-middle-class and working-class Americans, especially urban ethnics.

Many of these concerns continue to shape celebrity journalism, despite the passage of time, the development of new media like television, and an exponential increase in the number of venues where celebrities appear. Indeed, it is striking how little has changed since the era of John D. Rockefeller and Ethel Barrymore. The obsession of the great majority of celebrity profiles, whether in print or on television, remains the subject's "real self." To be sure, some journalists note that this is an elusive enterprise. But they engage in it all the same, offering their insights and experiences as insiders or first-hand witnesses. Other journalists completely elide the problematic nature of this angle, providing readers or viewers with portraits of celebrities that are virtually identical to those that appeared in the early twentieth century. This is particularly true of interviews and celebrity profiles on television and in mass-circulation magazines aimed at women. To one degree or another, however, it is also true of profiles in magazines that regard themselves as more sophisticated, especially ad-driven publications like the *New York Times Magazine, Vanity Fair,* and Tina Brown's most recent contribution to the field, *Talk.*

Moreover, in nearly all interviews and profiles celebrities are still depicted as interesting, complex "human beings." The aim of the profile remains to illuminate and make sense of these complexities, which are so compelling because readers and viewers can understand or relate to them on some level. And as in the celebrity journalism of the 1920s and 1930s, most profiles portray these complexities in distinctly therapeutic terms. Indeed, since the 1930s this emphasis has steadily increased, as therapeutic discourses have come to replace moralistic and religious ones as the lingua franca of modern America. Writing in *Talk,* for example, the writer Paul Theroux offers readers a vivid, detailed portrait of Elizabeth Taylor, emphasizing the psychic wounds that she sustained as a child star and at the hands of abusive husbands and boyfriends, and concluding with the sort of therapeutic mush that is commonplace in contemporary celebrity journalism: "She expects to be taken on her own terms. . . . It is characteristic of the ball-breaker, the manipulator, the control freak, someone deeply insecure. It is the trait of the bullying man, the coquette, and the cocktease, the person needing reassurance, anyone who wishes to assert control." In such pieces biographical details serve not as inspiration—though they still do in television interviews and downscale publications like *People*—but as the "deeper reason" for the subject's complexities. In response to the superficiality of much celebrity journalism, especially orchestrated television interviews, publications like the *New Yorker* have come to specialize in longer, more speculative profiles, which are said to be the only vehicles adequate to plumbing a subject's complexity. Even Time-Warner, publishers of *People,* have jumped on this bandwagon, with book-length biographical *People Profiles* of celebrities such as Oprah Winfrey and Brad Pitt.[3]

Celebrity journalism is also informed still by the discourse of true success. Like profiles written in the early twentieth century, many contemporary interviews and profiles revel in the achievements of their subjects, especially those that set them apart from ordinary people and as well as other luminaries in their field. This is most common in the business press, which devotes considerable attention to how executives like Bill Gates, Michael Eisner, and Jack Welch run their companies. The reportage about these high achievers also focuses on their private lives, in which they enjoy the rewards of their accomplishments, and in most profiles in general-interest publications and television programs this theme is emphasized far more than the "work" that celebrities perform. Tours of a subject's home are common in Barbara Walters specials and in many magazine spreads. Revealing a celebrity's preferred designers and "taste" in a wide range of commodities—often advertised in the same issue—is the very raison d'être of Time-Warner's vacuous *In Style*, a glossy print version of the popular television program from the 1980s, "Lifestyles of the Rich and Famous." Yet celebrations of achievement and the material riches that it brings are nearly always offset by claims, often made by celebrities themselves, that happiness has nothing to do with wealth and luxury—and by assertions that most celebrities, even such renowned practitioners of conspicuous consumption as Madonna, the software entrepreneur Larry Ellison, and the rap impresario Sean "Puffy" Combs, recognize this and are determined to rearrange their priorities.

For example, after visiting Combs at his lavish home in the Hamptons, Stephanie Tuck, a writer for *In Style*, reports that Puffy's reputation as a "hard-charging player"—an aggressive, materialistic, arrogant bigshot, the persona he often projects in his recordings and business dealings—is misleading. The real Combs, she asserts, is sensitive and human, a modest man committed to improving himself. "I had a problem with arrogance," he confesses to the author, "but I corrected it . . . I mean, I'm *working* on correcting it." More important, he always puts his family before business, an impression confirmed by gushing descriptions of Combs frolicking with his two young children.[4]

A similar message is conveyed by a profile in *Newsweek* of Bill Gates, the richest man in the world. Notorious for his arrogance and combativeness, Gates is now revealed by the technology writer Steven Levy to be more relaxed, frank, and introspective. In part, this is because after years at the helm of Microsoft, he has assumed a new "visionary" role as a promoter of technology and world-class philanthropist, a role that Gates views as "fun." But Levy attributes the change more to Gates's marriage and his being a father, which have encouraged him to lead a "more balanced life." Levy describes Gates's wife, Melinda, as the "point person" in efforts by the couple to maintain "a private space" and develop a "solid family life." To be sure, the real Gates is competitive and a demanding boss—just as the myth suggests. Yet among friends he is also down-to-earth and fun-loving, with a lively sense of humor often directed at himself. As one of his friends tells Levy, "His brain operates different . . . but the rest of him is just like us."[5]

The persistence of these rhetorical strategies and narrative themes is not surprising. After all, the material conditions and cultural currents that sparked the development of celebrity journalism have not disappeared. And a case can be made that in recent years, they have become even more pronounced and ubiquitous. With social and geographic mobility at an all-time high and spreading to new areas of the globe, opportunities for self-aggrandizement and duplicity have also multiplied, inspiring people to be even more wary of the claims of others, who are assumed to be out for themselves, like everyone else in "free agent America." And what are celebrities if not men and women on the make, eager participants in a culture more committed than ever to individual achievement through competition and self-promotion? The continued interest in exposing the "real selves" of celebrities, then, is perfectly understandable, especially when it is almost always the celebrities themselves who set the cycle in motion by plugging the movies, business deals, or political causes in which they are involved. Problems occur when celebrities attempt to draw the line and limit their self-exposure, which only makes the press and public more eager to invade their privacy and reveal them to be frauds. Like it or not, this depressing state of affairs is a direct outgrowth of our commitment as a society to social mobility and the entrepreneurial values of the market. In effect, the price of empowering the free agent within us all is unleashing forces that encourage us to act like confidence men—and making others justifiably suspicious of our motives and plans.

But the most interesting feature of celebrity journalism is not its endorsement of achievement and social mobility but the profound discomfort that it continues to display toward the means by which people succeed and the consequences that are believed to ensue. This discomfort may well be inspired by powerful egalitarian sentiments that remain alive among the many consumers who make up the market for the genre. From this vantage point, the public's obsession with celebrities may appear silly, but it ceases to resemble the medieval idol worship to which some commentators have likened it. This is particularly so when we consider the varied responses that the culture of celebrity elicits among consumers, and that even "true believers" are caught up in a game in which the objects of their interest are not gods or supermen but human beings who are most attractive when they most resemble ordinary people.[6] The real objects of worship in this game may not be celebrities or being rich and famous. What the culture of celebrity may actually celebrate are democratic and collectivist values integral to the ideal of true success— values that are at odds with the atomistic individualism encouraged by the market.

. . . .
NOTES

INTRODUCTION

1. See, for example, Neil Postman, *Amusing Ourselves to Death: Public Discourse in the Age of Show Business* (New York: Penguin, 1986); and Neal Gabler, *Life, the Movie: How Entertainment Conquered Reality* (New York: Alfred A. Knopf, 1999). Both of these works are profoundly indebted to the ur-text of celebrity criticism, Daniel J. Boorstin, *The Image, or What Happened to the American Dream* (New York: Atheneum, 1961).

2. See Richard Dyer, *Stars* (London: British Film Institute, 1979); Christine Gledhill, ed., *Stardom: Industry of Desire* (London: Routledge, 1991).

3. On Whitefield, see Frank Lambert, *Pedlar in Divinity: George Whitefield and the Transatlantic Revivals, 1737–1770* (Princeton, N.J.: Princeton University Press, 1994); on Earhart, see Susan Ware, *Still Missing: Amelia Earhart and the Search for Modern Feminism* (New York: W. W. Norton, 1993).

4. On celebrity in the mid-nineteenth century, see Thomas N. Baker, *Sentiment and Celebrity: Nathaniel Parker Willis and the Trials of Literary Fame* (New York: Oxford University Press, 1999).

5. Joshua Gamson, *Claims to Fame: Celebrity in Contemporary America* (Berkeley: University of California Press, 1993); Janice A. Radway, *Reading the Romance: Women, Patriarchy, and Popular Literature* (Chapel Hill: University of North Carolina Press, 1984). For attempts to study audiences in the past, see Radway, *A Feeling for Books: The Book-of-the-Month Club, Literary Taste, and Middle-Class Desire* (Chapel Hill: University of North Carolina Press, 1997); and Regina Kunzel, "Pulp Fictions and Problem Girls: Reading and Rewriting Single Pregnancy in the Postwar United States," *American Historical Review* 100 (Dec. 1995): 1465–87.

CHAPTER ONE

1. Earl Blackwell and Cleveland Amory, eds., *International Celebrity Register* (New York: Celebrity Register, 1959), v, quoted in Daniel J. Boorstin, *The Image, or What Happened to the American Dream* (New York: Atheneum), 58.

2. Boorstin, *The Image,* 57.

3. For a trenchant analysis of contemporary celebrity, see Joshua Gamson, *Claims to Fame: Celebrity in Contemporary America* (Berkeley: University of

California Press, 1993). See also P. David Marshall, *Celebrity and Power: Fame in Contemporary Culture* (Minneapolis: University of Minnesota Press, 1997); Richard Schickel, *Intimate Strangers: The Culture of Celebrity* (New York: Doubleday, 1986); and James Monaco, ed., *Celebrity: The Media as Image Makers* (New York: Dell, 1978).

4. Leo Braudy, *The Frenzy of Renown: Fame and Its History* (New York: Oxford University Press, 1986).

5. Quoted in Braudy, *Frenzy of Renown*, 355.

6. See Theodore K. Rabb, *The Struggle for Stability in Early Modern Europe* (New York: Oxford University Press, 1975).

7. Robert Darnton, *The Literary Underground of the Old Regime* (Cambridge: Harvard University Press, 1982); quotations on 30, 34. See also Darnton's more recent *The Forbidden Bestsellers of Pre-Revolutionary France* (New York: W. W. Norton, 1996).

8. On the implications of gossip, particularly for women and other marginalized groups, see Patricia Meyer Spacks, *Gossip* (New York: Alfred A. Knopf, 1985). On the predominantly oral culture that sustained gossip, see Peter Burke, *Popular Culture in Early Modern Europe* (New York: Harper and Row, 1978).

9. Jürgen Habermas, *The Structural Transformation of the Public Sphere* (Cambridge: MIT Press, 1989). For a detailed examination of Habermas's concept, see the essays in Craig Calhoun, ed., *Habermas and the Public Sphere* (Cambridge: MIT Press, 1992).

10. See Nancy Fraser, "Rethinking the Public Sphere," and Michael Schudson, "Was There Ever a Public Sphere?," in Calhoun, ed., *Habermas and the Public Sphere*.

11. See Stow Persons, *The Decline of American Gentility* (New York: Columbia University Press, 1973); Joyce Appleby, *Capitalism and a New Social Order: The Republican Vision of the 1790s* (New York: NYU Press, 1984); and especially Gordon S. Wood, *The Radicalism of the American Revolution* (New York: Alfred A. Knopf, 1992). On England, see David Cannadine, *The Decline and Fall of the British Aristocracy* (New Haven: Yale University Press, 1990). Sedgwick quoted in Wood, *Radicalism*, 286.

12. Richard Sennett, *The Fall of Public Man* (New York: Alfred A. Knopf, 1977); Stuart Ewen, *All Consuming Images: The Politics of Style in Contemporary Culture* (New York: Basic Books, 1988); John B. Thompson, *The Media and Modernity: A Social Theory of the Media* (Stanford: Stanford University Press, 1995).

13. Braudy, *Frenzy of Renown*.

14. On the broader implications of this development, see Erving Goffman, *The Presentation of Self in Everyday Life* (Garden City, N.Y.: Doubleday Anchor, 1959).

15. Joyce O. Appleby, *Inheriting the Revolution: The First Generation of Americans* (Cambridge: Harvard University Press, 2000). See also Roy F. Bau-

meister, *Identity: Cultural Change and the Struggle for Self* (New York: Oxford University Press, 1986); and Diane Bjorklund, *Interpreting the Self: Two Hundred Years of American Autobiography* (Chicago: University of Chicago Press, 1998).

16. Benjamin Franklin, *The Autobiography and Other Writings* (New York: Viking Penguin, 1986), 73.

17. On Franklin and Rousseau, see Braudy, *Frenzy of Renown*.

18. Rousseau quoted in Braudy, *Frenzy of Renown*, 375. On biography, see John A. Garraty, *The Nature of Biography* (New York: Alfred A. Knopf, 1957); Reed Whittemore, *Whole Lives: The Shapers of Modern Biography* (Baltimore: Johns Hopkins University Press, 1989); Ira Bruce Nadel, *Biography: Fiction, Fact and Form* (New York: St. Martin's, 1984); and Catherine N. Parke, *Biography: Writing Lives* (New York: Twayne, 1996).

19. William C. Dowling, "Boswell and the Problem of Biography," in *Studies in Biography* (Cambridge: Harvard University Press, 1978); and Dowling, *The Boswellian Hero* (Athens; University of Georgia Press, 1979).

20. Daniel Walker Howe, *Making the American Self: Jonathan Edwards to Abraham Lincoln* (Cambridge: Harvard University Press, 1997); quotation from Channing on 132.

21. On the broader application of the character ideal, see Judy A. Hilkey, *Character Is Capital: Success Manuals and Manhood in Gilded Age America* (Chapel Hill: University of North Carolina Press, 1997). See also Warren I. Susman, "Personality and the Making of Twentieth-Century Culture," in *Culture as History* (New York: Pantheon, 1984), 271–84.

22. Quoted in Nadel, *Biography*, 21.

23. For more on nineteenth-century biography, see Scott E. Casper, *Constructing American Lives: Biography and Culture in Nineteenth-Century America* (Chapel Hill: University of North Carolina Press).

24. The literature on this subject is enormous, but the best staring point remains Karl Polanyi, *The Great Transformation* (Boston: Beacon, 1985).

25. See Eric Hobsbawm, *The Age of Revolution, 1789–1848* (New York: New American Library, 1962); *The Age of Capital, 1848–1875* (New York: New American Library, 1975); *The Age of Empire, 1875–1914* (New York: Pantheon, 1987).

26. See Lewis Mumford, *The City in History* (New York: Harcourt, Brace and World, 1961); Paul M. Hohenberg and Lynn Hollen Lees, *The Making of Urban Europe, 1000–1994* (Cambridge: Harvard University Press, 1995); Gunther Barth, *City People: The Rise of Modern City Culture in Nineteenth-Century America* (New York: Oxford University Press, 1980); and especially Marshall Berman, *All That Is Solid Melts into Air: The Experience of Modernity* (New York: Simon and Schuster, 1982).

27. Jean-Christophe Agnew, *World's Apart: The Market and the Theater in Anglo-American Thought, 1550–1750* (New York: Cambridge University Press, 1986); and C. B. Macpherson, *The Political Theory of Possessive Individualism: Hobbes to Locke* (New York: Oxford University Press, 1962). For an extension

treatment of "market culture" and its implications, see Thomas L. Haskell and Richard F. Teichgraeber III, eds., *The Culture of the Market: Historical Essays* (New York: Cambridge University Press, 1993).

28. Richard L. Bushman, *The Refinement of America: Persons, Houses, Cities* (New York: Alfred A. Knopf, 1992); Stuart Blumin, *The Emergence of the Middle-Class: Social Experience in the American City, 1760–1900* (New York: Cambridge University Press, 1989). For a good discussion of the larger context that produced this trend, see Ewen, *All Consuming Images.*

29. Karen Haltunnen, *Confidence Men and Painted Women: A Study of Middle-Class Culture in America, 1830–1870* (New Haven: Yale University Press, 1982); John F. Kasson, *Rudeness and Civility: Manners in Nineteenth Century America* (New York: Hill and Wang, 1990). Quote from Haltunnen, *Confidence Men and Painted Women,* 66.

30. See especially Mary P. Ryan, *Empire of the Mother: American Writing About Domesticity, 1830–1860* (New York: Harrington Park, 1985).

31. See Stephanie Coontz, *The Social Origins of Private Life: A History of American Families, 1600–1900* (New York: Verso, 1988). Quotation from Nancy Cott, *The Bonds of Womanhood* (New Haven: Yale University Press, 1977), 67.

32. See the later volumes in Philippe Ariès and Georges Duby, eds., *A History of Private Life* (Cambridge: Harvard University Press, 1987–1991). For a provocative account of the role of "home" in the bourgeois worldview, see John R. Gillis, *A World of Their Own Making: Myth, Ritual, and the Quest for Family Values* (New York: Basic Books, 1996).

33. See Baumeister, *Identity;* Charles Taylor, *Sources of the Self* (Cambridge: Harvard University Press, 1991); and Roy Porter, ed., *Rewriting the Self: Histories from the Renaissance to the Present* (London: Routledge, 1997).

34. See Rochelle Gurstein, *The Repeal of Reticence* (New York: Hill and Wang, 1996).

35. Mitchell Stevens, *A History of News* (New York: Viking, 1988); Michael Schudson, *Discovering the News: A Social History of American Newspapers* (New York: Basic Books, 1978); Dan Schiller, *Objectivity and the News: The Public and the Rise of Commercial Journalism* (Philadelphia: Temple University Press, 1981). On the press as a peculiarly urban institution, see Barth, *City People.* Quotations from Barth, 61; and from James L. Crouthamel, *Bennett's New York Herald and the Rise of the Popular Press* (Syracuse, N.Y.: Syracuse University Press, 1993), 22.

36. For a vivid example of this, see Andie Tucher, *Froth and Scum: Truth, Beauty, Goodness, and the Ax Murder in America's First Mass Medium* (Chapel Hill: University of North Carolina Press, 1994).

37. Quoted in Casper, *Constructing American Lives,* 313.

38. David Shi, *Facing Facts: Realism in American Thought and Culture, 1850–1920* (New York: Oxford University Press, 1995); Amy Kaplan, *The Social Construction of American Realism* (Chicago: University of Chicago Press, 1988); Merle Curti, *Human Nature in American Thought* (Madison: University of Wisconsin Press, 1982).

39. On the religious sanction of the new naturalism, see Richard W. Fox, "The Culture of Liberal Protestant Progressivism, 1875–1925," *Journal of Interdisciplinary History* 23 (Winter 1993): 639–60.

40. William Dean Howells, *The Rise of Silas Lapham* (Boston: Ticknor, 1885).

41. Don C. Seitz, *Joseph Pulitzer: His Life and Letters* (New York: Simon and Schuster, 1924), 422. On this trend in newspapers, see Schudson, *The Discovery of the News;* and in magazines, see Christopher P. Wilson, *The Labor of Words: Literary Professionalism in the Progressive Era* (Athens: University of Georgia Press, 1987); Matthew Schneirov, *The Dream of a New Social Order* (New York: Columbia University Press, 1994); and Richard Ohmann, *Selling Culture: Magazines, Markets, and Class at the Turn of the Century* (London: Verso, 1996).

42. See Eli Zaretsky, *Capitalism, the Family, and Personal Life* (New York: Harper and Row, 1976); and, for a case study focusing on working-class people, Roy Rosenzweig, *Eight Hours for What We Will: Workers and Leisure in an Industrial City, 1870–1920* (New York: Cambridge University Press, 1983).

43. Fox, "The Culture of Liberal Protestant Progressivism." Douglass quoted in Howe, *Making the American Self,* 151.

44. Susman, "Personality and the Making of Twentieth-Century Culture." See also T. J. Jackson Lears, "From Salvation to Self-Realization: Advertising and the Therapeutic Roots of the Consumer Culture, 1880–1930," in Richard W. Fox and T. J. Jackson Lears, *The Culture of Consumption* (New York: Pantheon, 1983), 3–38.

45. There is now a vast literature on the growing interest displayed by Americans in leisure-time activities. A good staring point is David Nasaw, *Going Out* (New York: Basic Books, 1993). See also Kathryn Grover, ed., *Hard at Play: Leisure in America, 1840–1940* (Amherst: University of Massachusetts Press, 1992). On the growing interest in leisure among workers, see Rosenzweig, *Eight Hours for What We Will;* and Lawrence Glickman, *A Living Wage: American Workers and the Making of a Consumer Society* (Ithaca, N.Y.: Cornell University Press, 1997); and, among the upper-middle classes, Lewis A. Erenberg, *Steppin' Out: New York Nightlife and the Transformation of American Culture* (Westport, Conn.: Greenwood, 1984).

46. William Leach, *Land of Desire: Merchants, Power, and the Rise of a New American Culture* (New York: Pantheon, 1993). See also T. J. Jackson Lears, *Fables of Abundance: A Cultural History of American Advertising* (New York: Basic Books, 1994). Quotation from Simon Patten, *New Basis of Civilization* (New York: Macmillan, 1907), 137.

47. For an early and influential treatment of this subject, see Leo Lowenthal, "The Triumph of Mass Idols," in *Literature, Popular Culture and Society* (Englewood Cliffs, N.J.: Prentice-Hall, 1961), 109–36.

CHAPTER TWO

1. Chauncey M. Depew, *My Memories of Eighty Years* (New York: Charles Scribner's Sons, 1922), 347. For an account of how public figures like Depew interacted with reporters, see Paul Lancaster, *Gentleman of the Press: The Life and Times of an Early Reporter, Julian Ralph of the Sun* (Syracuse, N.Y.: Syracuse University Press, 1992).

2. Gunther Barth, *City People: The Rise of Modern City Culture in Nineteenth-Century America* (New York: Oxford University Press, 1980.

3. Michael Schudson, *Discovering the News: A Social History of American Newspapers* (New York: Basic Books, 1978).

4. The democratic mission of the American press is the subject of Dan Schiller, *Objectivity and the News: The Public and the Rise of Commercial Journalism* (Philadelphia: Temple University Press, 1981).

5. See Robert Darnton, "Writing News and Telling Stories," *Daedalus* 104 (Spring 1975): 175–94; and Helen MacGill Hughes, *News and the Human Interest Story* (Chicago: University of Chicago Press, 1940).

6. Grant Milnor Hyde, *Newspaper Reporting and Correspondence* (New York: D. Appleton, 1912), 14.

7. See James L. Crouthamel, *Bennett's New York Herald and the Rise of the Popular Press* (Syracuse, N.Y.: Syracuse University Press, 1993); and Andie Tucher, *Froth and Scum: Truth, Beauty, Goodness, and the Ax Murder in America's First Mass Medium* (Chapel Hill: University of North Carolina Press, 1994).

8. See Janet Steele, *The Sun Shines for All: Journalism and Ideology in the Life of Charles A. Dana* (Syracuse, N.Y.: Syracuse University Press, 1993); George Juergens, *Joseph Pulitzer and the New York World* (Princeton, N.J.: Princeton University Press, 1966); David Nasaw, *The Chief: The Life of William Randolph Hearst* (Boston: Houghton Mifflin, 2000).

9. On the roots of the tabloid tradition and its flowering, see John D. Stevens, *Sensationalism and the New York Press* (New York: Columbia University Press, 1991); see also James E. Murphy, "Tabloids as an Urban Response," in Catherine L. Covert and James D. Stevens, eds., *Mass Media between the Wars: Perceptions of Cultural Tension, 1918–1941* (Syracuse, N.Y.: Syracuse University Press, 1984), 55–69.

10. Schudson, *Discovering the News.*

11. *New York Times*, 27 Mar. 1927; Silas Bent, *Ballyhoo: The Voice of the Press* (New York: Boni and Liveright, 1927), 166. See also Stanley Walker, *City Editor* (New York: Frederick A. Stokes, 1934).

12. For a fascinating discussion of the cultural implications of this phenomenon, see Philip Fisher, "Appearing and Disappearing in Public," in Sacvan Bercovitch, ed., *Reconstructing American Literary History* (Cambridge: Harvard University Press, 1986), 155–88.

13. See Tucher, *Froth and Scum;* and Patricia Cline Cohen, *The Murder of Helen Jewett: The Life and Death of a Prostitute in Nineteenth-Century New York* (New York: Alfred A. Knopf, 1998).

14. See Michael M. Mooney, *Evelyn Nesbit and Stanford White: Love and Death in the Gilded Age* (New York: William Morrow, 1976); and Phyllis L. Abramson, *Sob-Sister Journalism* (New York: Greenwood, 1990).

15. Mattie Sheridan, "Home and Home Life of Chauncey M. Depew," *Munsey's* 6 (Jan. 1892): 408–17.

16. *New York Herald,* 28–29 Apr. 1850.

17. *New York World,* 2 Mar. 1890; "In the Public Eye," *Munsey's* 14 (Oct. 1895): 38–46.

18. See Neal Gabler, *Winchell: Gossip, Power and the Culture of Celebrity* (New York: Alfred A. Knopf, 1994).

19. Issac Marcosson, *Adventures in Interviewing* (New York: John Lane, 1919), 83. On the rise of the interview, see Michael Schudson, "Question Authority: A History of the News Interview in American Journalism, 1860s–1930s," *Media, Culture and Society,* Oct. 1994, 565–87.

20. See, for example, "Is Bernard Shaw a Menace to Morals?," *Current Literature* 39 (Nov. 1905): 551–52; and "Einstein Finds the World Narrow," *Literary Digest,* 16 Apr. 1921, 32–34.

21. Quoted in Matthew Schneirov, *The Dream of a New Social Order* (New York: Columbia University Press, 1994), 116. See also Hazel Dicken-Garcia, *Journalistic Standards in Nineteenth-Century America* (Madison: University of Wisconsin Press, 1989).

22. H. F. Harrington, *Chats on Feature Writing* (New York: Harper and Brothers, 1925), 341.

23. *New York World,* 9 Mar. 1890, 19.

24. W. G. Bleyer, *How to Write Special Feature Articles* (Boston: Houghton Mifflin, 1919), 85; "The Unknown Morgan," *Saturday Evening Post,* 10 Jan. 1903, 4.

25. Bleyer, *Feature Articles,* 43; Sheridan, "Home and Home Life of Chauncey M. Depew," 408.

26. See for example, Lindsay Denison, "The Outdoor President," *Ladies' Home Journal* 19 (May 1902): 11–12; W. O. Inglis, "Playing a Round of Golf with John D. Rockefeller," *New York Evening World,* 13 Nov. 1915; Ray Rockman, "Playing Tennis with Sarah Bernhardt," *Ladies' Home Journal* 29 (Feb. 1912): 19, 66.

27. *New York World,* 2 Mar. 1890, 22; *New York American,* 11 Feb. 1910, 1, 5; *New York American,* 13 Feb. 1910, 2CE.

28. Bok quoted in Christopher P. Wilson, *The Labor of Words: Literary Professionalism in the Progressive Era* (Athens: University of Georgia Press), 46.

29. See, for example, Emma B. Kaufman, "The Greatest Living Tenor," *Munsey's* 34 (Mar. 1906), 708–13; Alan Dale, "The Star of the Barrymores," *Cosmopolitan* 52 (Apr. 1912): 693–97; Peter Clark Macfarlane, "George M. Cohan," *Everybody's* 30 (Jan. 1914): 107–20; William Maxwell, "Edison," *American Magazine* 85 (Feb. 1918): 25–27, 80–86; Forrest Crissey, "They Call Him Cal," *Saturday Evening Post,* 25 Oct. 1924, 8–9, 156–69; John K. Winkler, "I'm Tired of Being a Sheik," *Collier's,* 16 Jan. 1926, 28; Adela Rogers St. Johns,

"Clara Bow: The Playgirl of Hollywood," *Liberty,* 3 Aug. 1929, 15–22; Henry F. Pringle, "A Mind of Her Own," *Collier's,* 28 Oct. 1933, 21, 28.

30. St. Johns, "Clara Bow," 15.

31. Angell quoted in Ben Yagoda, *About Town: The New Yorker and the World It Made* (New York: Scribner's, 2000), 133. For examples see "George Jean Nathan: The Victim of an Entirely New Method of Biographical Assault," *Vanity Fair* 9 (Nov. 1917): 65; Grantland Rice, "Ruth Is Stranger Than Fiction," *Vanity Fair* 16 (Apr. 1921): 65, 88; James Kevin McGuiness, "A Symbol in Pugilism," *New Yorker,* 14 Mar. 1925, 15–16; Alva Johnston, "Our Own Lenin," *New Yorker,* 28 June 1930, 19–22; and Henry F. Pringle, "Laird of Woodley," *New Yorker,* 4 Oct. 1930, 30–33.

32. For examples of the *New Yorker*'s influence, see Alva Johnston, "The Hepburn Legend," *Woman's Home Companion* 61 (June 1934): 12–13, 59–62; Walter Davenport, "The Shepherd of Discontent," *Collier's,* 4 May 1935, 12–13, 57–60; Margaret Case Harriman, "He Sells Hope," *Saturday Evening Post,* 14 Aug. 1937, 12–13, 30–34; and Jack Alexander, "Tom Dewey," *Life,* 31 Oct. 1938, 54–61.

33. See, for example, Mary B. Mullett, "Mary Pickford Describes Her Most Thrilling Experiences," *American Magazine* 95 (May 1923): 34–35, 104–14; and W. O. McGeehan, "The Social Life of an Athlete," *Vanity Fair* 29 (Aug. 1927), 63, 94.

34. Mullett, "Mary Pickford Describes Her Most Thrilling Experience," 34; Edwin Lefevre, "Unwritten Interviews," *Saturday Evening Post,* 7 Mar. 1914, 9.

35. On this vitally important development, see Michael L. Carlebach, *American Photojournalism Comes of Age* (Washington: Smithsonian Institution Press, 1997). For a perceptive analysis of the implications of the new visuality made possible by the half-tone process, see Neil Harris, "Iconography and Intellectual History: The Half-Tone Effect," in John Higham and Paul K. Conkin, eds., *New Directions in American Intellectual History* (Baltimore: Johns Hopkins University Press, 1979), 196–211.

36. On Marion's activities as a "ghost" and advisor to Pickford, see Cari Beauchamp, *Without Lying Down: Frances Marion and the Powerful Women of Early Hollywood* (New York: Scribner's, 1997). Tully's role as Chaplin's ghost was revealed in a multipart profile of the filmmaker, "Charlie Chaplin: His Real Life Story," *Pictorial Review* 28 (Jan. 1927): 8–9, 29–34. His many articles on Hollywood include an important series for *Vanity Fair.*

37. On Ford and his ghostwriters see David L. Lewis, *The Public Image of Henry Ford* (Detroit: Wayne State University Press, 1976), 65; Grace Grahn, "My Boss, Wendell Willkie," *American Magazine* 130 (Oct. 1940): 14. For a provocative interpretation of Macfadden's *True Story* as an example of confessional discourse see Ann Fabian, "Making a Commodity of Truth: Speculations on the Career of Bernarr Macfadden," *American Literary History* 5 (Spring 1993): 51–76.

38. In the 1920s the *New York Times Magazine* became one of the preeminent venues for celebrity profiles penned by staff writers or well-connected

freelancers. See for example, Richards Vidmer, "Babe Ruth, Baseball Super-man, Excels, Too, in Minor Sports," *New York Times Magazine,* 10 June 1928, 9, 23; and P. W. Wilson, "How Rockefeller Stays in the Fairway," *New York Times Magazine,* 2 Aug. 1931, 4–5, 20.

39. *New York World,* 2 Mar. 1890, 19; *New York World,* 29 Sept. 1895, 1.

40. Emma B. Kaufman, "Alice Roosevelt," *Munsey's Magazine* 34 (Nov. 1905): 140. See also Gustav Kobbé, "The Girlishness of Ethel Barrymore," *Ladies' Home Journal* 20 (June 1903): 4. Press coverage of the "new woman" is addressed in Jennifer Scanlon, *Inarticulate Longings: The Ladies' Home Journal, Gender, and the Promise of Consumer Culture* (New York: Routledge, 1995); and Ellen Gruber Garvey, *The Adman in the Parlor: Magazines and the Gendering of Consumer Culture, 1880s–1910s* (New York: Oxford University Press, 1996).

41. "A New Leader—Alice Paul—Why She Is," *Everybody's* 35 (July 1915): 127–28. On Sanger see, for example, *New York Times,* 28 Mar. 1917, 11; and Mildred Adams, "Crusader," *Delineator* 123 (Sept. 1933): 15, 46–49.

42. Perkins's reluctance to reveal much about her private life was a key topic in a *New Yorker* profile of her that appeared in 1933. See Russell Lord, "Madame Secretary," *New Yorker,* 2–9 Sept. 1933, 16–19, 20–23. For an example of Roosevelt's deftness in moving from the personal to the political, see Isabel Leighton, "Eleanor Roosevelt—a Recent Portrait," *Ladies' Home Journal* 50 (Mar. 1933): 25, 75–76.

43. Adela Rogers St. Johns, "The Private Life of Katharine Hepburn," *Liberty,* 6 Jan. 1934, 18. See Scanlon, *Inarticulate Longings.*

44. William S. McFeely, *Frederick Douglass* (New York: W. W. Norton, 1990).

45. Louis R. Harlan, *Booker T. Washington: The Making of a Black Leader, 1865–1901* (New York: Oxford University Press, 1972); Harlan, *Booker T. Washington: The Wizard of Tuskegee, 1901–1915* (New York: Oxford University Press, 1983).

46. See, for example, Grace Elizabeth Hale, *Making Whiteness: Segregation and the Culture of the South* (New York: Pantheon, 1997); and Matthew Frye Jacobson, *Whiteness of a Different Color: European Immigrants and the Alchemy of Race* (Cambridge: Harvard University Press, 1998).

47. Walter H. Page, "Booker T. Washington," *Everybody's* 6 (Apr. 1902): 393–98.

48. On Williams see Ann Charters, *Nobody: The Story of Bert Williams* (New York: Macmillan, 1970). The short profile of Williams written by Washington appeared as part of a regular feature, "Interesting People," *American Magazine* 70 (Sept. 1910): 600–604.

49. See Arthur Ashe, *A Hard Road to Glory: A History of the African-American Athlete, 1619–1918* (New York: Warner, 1988).

50. On Johnson, see Randy Roberts, *Papa Jack: Jack Johnson and the Era of White Hopes* (New York: Free Press, 1983).

51. On Johnson's association with the urban demimonde and "race-

mixing," see Kevin J. Mumford, *Interzones: Black/White Sex Districts in Chicago and New York in the Early Twentieth Century* (New York: Columbia University Press, 1997).

52. See Lawrence W. Levine, *Black Culture and Black Consciousness* (New York: Oxford University Press, 1977); and James P. Danky, ed., *African-American Newspapers and Periodicals: A National Bibliography* (Cambridge: Harvard University Press, 1998).

53. See for example, John Erskine, "Dark Nightingale," *Liberty,* 20 Jan. 1940, 39–40.

54. Chris Mead, *Champion—Joe Louis: Black Hero in White America* (New York: Scribner's, 1985).

55. Earl Brown, "Joe Louis," *Life,* 17 June 1940, 48–56. Quotation on 49.

CHAPTER THREE

1. Silas Bent, *Ballyhoo: The Voice of the Press* (New York: Boni and Liveright, 1927), 26.

2. On wire-services, see Richard A. Schwarzlose, *The Nation's Newsbrokers,* vols. 1–2 (Evanston, Ill.: Northwestern University Press, 1989–90). On this emerging journalistic elite, see Paul Lancaster, *Gentleman of the Press: The Life and Times of an Early Reporter, Julian Ralph of the Sun* (Syracuse, N.Y.: Syracuse University Press, 1992).

3. Bent, *Ballyhoo,* 229; H. F. Harrington, *Chats on Feature Writing* (New York: Harper and Brothers, 1925), 560. On syndicates see Elmo Scott Watson, *A History of Newspaper Syndicates in the United States, 1865–1935* (Chicago: Publisher's Auxiliary, 1936).

4. Gerald J. Baldasty, *E. W. Scripps and the Business of Newspapers* (Urbana: University of Illinois Press, 1999); David Nasaw, *The Chief: The Life of William Randolph Hearst* (Boston: Houghton Mifflin, 2000).

5. Ray Stannard Baker, "J. Pierpont Morgan," *McClure's* 17 (Oct. 1901): 507–18. Quotation on 508. See, in particular, Christopher P. Wilson, "The Rhetoric of Consumption: Mass-Market Magazines and the Demise of the Gentle Reader," in Richard Wightman Fox and T. J. Jackson Lears, *The Culture of Consumption: Critical Essays in American History, 1880–1980* (New York: Pantheon, 1983), 39–64.

6. On the shift from diverse urban "commercial cultures" to a national "mass culture," see William R. Taylor, *In Pursuit of Gotham: Culture and Commerce in New York* (New York: Oxford University Press, 1992). On the effects of nationalizing trends on individual communities, see Thomas Bender, *Community and Social Change in America* (New Brunswick, N.J.: Rutgers University Press, 1978). For a perceptive argument about how these trends shaped the modern culture of celebrity, see Richard Schickel, *Intimate Strangers: The Culture of Celebrity* (New York: Doubleday, 1986).

7. Chester S. Lord, *The Young Man and Journalism* (New York: Macmillan, 1922), 155–56; Ishbel Ross, *Ladies of the Press* (New York: Harper, 1936).

8. For evocative renderings of the occupational culture in which these figures operated see Jimmy Breslin, *Damon Runyon* (New York: Ticknor and Fields, 1991); Charles Fountain, *Sportswriter: The Life and Times of Grantland Rice* (New York: Oxford University Press, 1993); and Neal Gabler, *Winchell: Gossip, Power and the Culture of Celebrity* (New York: Alfred A. Knopf, 1994).

9. Robert C. Bannister, *Ray Stannard Baker: The Mind and Thought of a Progressive* (Princeton, N.J.: Princeton University Press, 1966). For examples of Baker's work, see "Theodore Roosevelt," *McClure's* 12 (Nov. 1898): 23–32; "J. Pierpont Morgan" *McClure's* 17 (Oct. 1901): 507–18; and "Marconi's Achievement," *McClure's* 18 (Feb. 1902): 291–99.

10. Issac F. Marcosson, *Adventures in Interviewing* (New York: John Lane, 1919). For examples of Marcosson's work, see "Thomas Fortune Ryan: His Personality and His Point of View," *Saturday Evening Post*, 13 June 1908, 8–9, 21; "Lloyd George," *Everybody's* 36 (Jan. 1917): 1–16; "The President Gets Down to Business," *Saturday Evening Post*, 21 Dec. 1929, 3–4, 78–82.

11. On St. Johns see Jean C. Chance, "Adela Rogers St. Johns," *Dictionary of Literary Biography*, vol. 29, *American Newspaper Journalists, 1926–1950* (Detroit: Gale Research, 1984), 310–12. For examples of her work, see "Why Does the World Love Mary?," *Photoplay* 18 (June 1921): 50, 110–11; "Garbo: The Mystery of Hollywood," *Liberty*, 27 July 1929, 15–22; and "The Private Life of the 5-and-10 Princess," *Liberty*, 16–30 Mar. 1935, 4–9, 32–38, 44–48.

12. See Paul Gallico, *Farewell to Sport* (New York: Alfred A. Knopf, 1938). For examples of his work, see "The Enigma Called Tunney," *Liberty*, 5 Jan. 1929, 46–48; "Jones of Jonesville, Ga.," *Liberty*, 29 Oct. 1929, 50–54; and "The Babe," *Vanity Fair* 38 (May 1932): 38, 73.

13. On Johnston see Stanley Walker, *City Editor* (New York: Frederick A. Stokes, 1934), 309. O'Hara quoted in Ben Yagoda, *About Town: The New Yorker and the World It Made* (New York: Scribner's, 2000), 134. For examples of Johnston's work, see "Scientist and Mob Idol," *New Yorker*, 2–9 Dec. 1933, 23–26, 29–32; "Fiorello H. LaGuardia," *Saturday Evening Post*, 27 June 1934, 5–6, 63–66; and "The Hepburn Legend."

14. Gabler, *Winchell*. For examples of celebrity profiles of Winchell, see John B. Kennedy, "For the Wife and Kiddies," *Collier's*, 5 Oct. 1929, 26; J. P. McEvoy, "He Snoops to Conquer," *Saturday Evening Post*, 13 Aug. 1938, 45; Parker Morrell, "Mr. and Mrs. Walter Winchell," *Ladies Home Journal* 57 (June 1940): 27, 61–63; and St. Clair McKelway, *Gossip: The Life and Times of Walter Winchell* (New York: Viking, 1940), which originally appeared in the *New Yorker*.

15. St. Johns, "Garbo," 17.

16. Gallico, *Farewell to Sport*, 277.

17. Barnum quoted in Scott Cutlip, *Public Relations History: From the 17th Century to the Twentieth Century: The Antecedents* (Hillsdale, N.J.: Erlbaum,

1995), 173. On Barnum see Neil Harris, *Humbug: The Art of P. T. Barnum* (Chicago: University of Chicago Press, 1973); and Bluford Adams, *E Pluribus Barnum: The Great Showman and the Making of U.S. Popular Culture* (Minneapolis: University of Minnesota Press, 1997).

18. Julian Ralph, *The Making of a Journalist* (New York: Harper and Brothers, 1903), 185; H. F. McCauley, *Getting Your Name in Print* (New York: Funk and Wagnalls, 1922), 41.

19. Lincoln Steffens, *The Autobiography of Lincoln Steffens* (New York: Harcourt, Brace, 1931), 350; Edmund Morris, *The Rise of Theodore Roosevelt* (New York: Coward, McCann and Geoghegan, 1979); George Juergens, *News from the White House: the Presidential-Press Relationship in the Progressive Era* (Chicago: University of Chicago Press, 1981).

20. On the early years of press agentry, see Cutlip, *Public Relations History*. On press agents in the theater and show business, see Benjamin McArthur, *Actors and American Culture, 1880–1920* (Philadelphia: Temple University Press, 1984); and Joy S. Kasson, *Buffalo Bill's Wild West* (New York: Hill and Wang, 2000).

21. Quoted in Cutlip, *Public Relations History,* 180.

22. Walker, *City Editor,* 139. For a highly perceptive account of the development of public relations, see Stuart Ewen, *PR!: A Social History of Spin* (New York: Basic Books, 1996).

23. Edward L. Bernays, *Crystallizing Public Opinion* (New York: Horace Liveright, 1923), 56; Sonnenberg quoted in Scott L. Cutlip, *The Unseen Power: Public Relations: A History* (Hillsdale, N.J.: Erlbaum, 1994), 366.

24. See, for example, Glenn C. Quiett and Ralph D. Casey, *Principles of Publicity* (New York: D. Appleton, 1926); Dexter M. Fellows and Andrew Freeman, *This Way to the Big Show* (New York: Halcyon House, 1938); and Harry Reichenbach, as told to David Freedman, *Phantom Fame: The Anatomy of Ballyhoo* (New York: Simon and Schuster, 1931).

25. Quiett and Casey, *Principles of Publicity,* 33.

26. *Ibid.,* 32.

27. McCauley, *Getting Your Name in Print,* 58.

28. Ralph, *Making of a Journalist,* 6; Theodore Dreiser, *A Book about Myself* (New York: Boni and Liveright, 1922), 152–53.

29. John L. Given, *Making a Newspaper* (New York: Henry Holt, 1907), 182.

30. Marcosson, *Adventures in Interviewing,* 47, 69, 76. On the pressure to "fake" and its consequences for reporters, see Christopher P. Wilson, *Labor of Words: Literary Professionalism in the Progressive Era* (Athens: University of Georgia Press, 1987).

31. David Hale, "The Gentle Art of the Publicist," *Saturday Evening Post,* 24 Dec. 1904, 4; Walker, *City Editor,* 135.

32. Walker, *City Editor,* 134; Gallico, *Farewell to Sport,* 281.

33. See Walker, *City Editor;* Gallico, *Farewell to Sport;* and especially Alva Johnston, "Public Relations," *New Yorker,* 19 Aug. 1944, 26–32, 26 Aug. 1944, 26–34, 2 Sept. 1944, 24–28, 9 Sept. 1944. 30–38.

34. Adela Rogers St. Johns, "The Private Life of Helen Hayes," *Liberty*, 10 Nov. 1934, 5.

35. Johnston, "Public Relations," 26 Sept. 1944, 27, 28.

36. On Walsh and Ruth, see John B. Kennedy, "Innocents Aboard," *Collier's*, 14 Apr. 1928, 20, 43–44. For an example of Hannagan's promotional efforts on behalf of Jacobs and Louis, see Steve Hannagan, "Black Gold," *Saturday Evening Post*, 20 June 1936, 14, 74–78. On the *New Yorker* as part of a larger genre of "smart" magazines, see George Douglas, *The Smart Magazines: Fifty Years of Literary Revelry and High Jinks at Vanity Fair, the New Yorker, Life, Esquire, and the Smart Set* (Hamden, Conn.: Archon, 1991).

37. See John D. Stevens, *Sensationalism and the New York Press* (New York: Columbia University Press, 1991); and, on the persistence of photographers, Michael L. Carlebach, *American Photojournalism Comes of Age* (Washington: Smithsonian Institution Press, 1997).

38. Morris Markey, "Young Man of Affairs," *New Yorker*, 20–27 Sept. 1930, 26–29, 30–33; quotation on 33.

39. Julian S. Mason, "Lindbergh and the Press," *Saturday Evening Post*, 3 Aug. 1929, 101. For more on Lindbergh and the press, see my essay "The Man Nobody Knows: Charles A. Lindbergh and the Culture of Celebrity," *Prospects* 21 (1996): 347–72.

CHAPTER FOUR

1. Donald E. Keyhoe, "Lindbergh Four Years After," *Saturday Evening Post*, 30 May 1931, 48.

2. I have borrowed the term "true success" from John C. Cawelti, who uses it to describe the narrative subtext that informed mid-twentieth-century popular novels. See Cawelti, *Adventure, Mystery, and Romance: Formula Stories as Art and Popular Culture* (Chicago: University of Chicago Press, 1976), 260–84.

3. Jack Alexander, "Tom Dewey," *Life*, 31 Oct. 1938, 58.

4. Keene Sumner, "The Hidden Talents of 'Jack' Barrymore," *American Magazine* 87 (June 1919): 36–37, 149–154; Howard Sharpe, "The Mystery of Carole Lombard," *Liberty*, 5 Feb. 1938, 23.

5. Elizabeth Meriwether Gilmer, "The Goulds: A Study of an American Family," *Cosmopolitan* 46 (May 1909): 603–15; Ralph Wallace, "America's No. 1 Angel," *American Magazine* 129 (May 1940): 27, 147–49.

6. Beverly Smith, "Bigger Than Politics," *American Magazine* 118 (Oct. 1934): 55.

7. See, for example, Karl Kitchen, "Week-Ending with Doug and Mary," *New York World Magazine*, 15 May 1922, 3, 13; Jerome Beatty, "The Boy Who Began at the Top," *American Magazine* 113 (Apr. 1932): 34–35, 78–80; *New York Times*, 24 Jan. 1926, 8.

8. Paul Gallico, "The Babe," *Vanity Fair* 38 (May 1932): 73.

9. See Helen MacGill Hughes, *News and the Human Interest Story* (Chicago: University of Chicago Press, 1940).

10. Sumner, "The Hidden Talents of 'Jack' Barrymore," 149.

11. See William James, "The Powers of Men," *American Magazine* 65 (Nov. 1907): 57–65. This is a seminal text that profoundly influenced journalistic discourse on the subject of human potential as well as many works of advice literature. See, for example, Luther Gulick, *The Efficient Life* (New York: Doubleday, Page, 1907); Bruce Barton, *More Power to You* (New York: Century, 1917); and Harry Emerson Fosdick, *On Being a Real Person* (New York: Harper and Brothers, 1943).

12. Ray Stannard Baker, "J. Pierpont Morgan," *McClure's* 17 (Oct. 1901): 509–10; Henry Beach Needham, "Theodore Roosevelt—An Outdoor Man," *McClure's* 26 (Jan. 1906): 238; Ray Rockman, "Playing Tennis with Sarah Bernhardt," *Ladies' Home Journal* 29 (Feb. 1912): 19; Charles Chaplin, "In Defense of Myself," *Collier's*, 11 Nov. 1922, 8.

13. William Allen White, "Roosevelt," *McClure's* 18 (Nov. 1901): 44; Douglas Fairbanks, "How I Keep Running on 'High,'" *American Magazine* 94 (Aug. 1922): 39.

14. Mary B. Mullett, "A Movie Star Who Knows How to Make You Laugh," *American Magazine* 94 (June 1922): 38–39; William A. H. Birnie, "Daring Young Man," *American Magazine* 129 (June 1940): 17. See also Al Jolson, "If I Don't Get Laughs and Don't Get Applause—The Mirror Will Show Who Is to Blame," *American Magazine* 87 (Apr. 1918): 18–19, 154–58; and Mildred (Babe) Didrickson, "I Blow My Own Horn," *American Magazine* 121 (June 1936): 100–104.

15. Will Irwin, "When a Swelled Head Bursts," *Liberty*, 25 July 1925, 25; Emma B. Kaufman, "Alice Roosevelt," *Munsey's* 34 (Nov. 1905): 139; Henry F. Pringle, "A Mind of Her Own," *Collier's*, 28 Oct. 1933, 21.

16. Mary B. Mullett, "George M. Cohan's Definition of One Who Is 'On the Level,'" *American Magazine* 88 (Aug. 1919): 20; Ethel Barrymore, "How Can I Be a Great Actress?," *Ladies' Home Journal*, 15 Mar. 1911, 6.

17. Bruce Barton, "It Would Be Fun to Start Over Again," *American Magazine* 91 (Apr. 1921): 9; Geoffrey T. Hellman, "Mrs. Roosevelt," *Life*, 5 Feb. 1940, 78. On the importance of cultivating an individual style, see Gustav Kobbé, "The Girlishness of Ethel Barrymore," *Ladies' Home Journal* 20 (June 1903): 4. This important theme is addressed in Valerie Steele, *Fashion and Eroticism: Ideals of Feminine Beauty from the Victorian Era to the Jazz Age* (New York: Oxford University Press, 1985); and, more recently, in Kathy Peiss, *Hope in a Jar: The Making of America's Beauty Culture* (New York: Metropolitan, 1998).

18. Morris Bacheller, "Andrew Carnegie and His Home in Scotland, Skibo Castle," *Munsey's* 39 (Sept. 1908): 797; George Creel, "A 'Close-Up' of Douglas Fairbanks," *Everybody's* 35 (Dec. 1916): 729. See also Needham, "Theodore Roosevelt—An Outdoor Man"; Issac F. Marcosson, "Making Men Over," *Munsey's* 48 (Oct. 1912): 65–75; and Fairbanks, "How I Keep Running on 'High.'"

19. For an explicit statement of this, see George Creel, "A 'Close-Up' of Douglas Fairbanks," *Everybody's* 35 (Dec. 1916): 729–38.

20. See Frederick W. Taylor, "Not for the Genius—But for the Average Man," *American Magazine* 85 (Mar. 1918): 16–17, 114–16.

21. Ray Stannard Baker, "Theodore Roosevelt," 23; Kobbé, "The Girlishness of Ethel Barrymore," 3; Jim Tully, "Clara Bow: The Astonishing Life-Story of a Popular Screen Star," *Pictorial Review* 29 (Nov. 1927): 11, 58–62; Jolson, "If I Don't Get Laughs," 158.

22. Jacob Riis, "Mrs. Roosevelt and Her Children," *Ladies' Home Journal* 19 (Aug. 1902): 5–6. See also Gilmer, "The Goulds"; and John Cushman Fistere, "The Rockefeller Boys," *Saturday Evening Post*, 16 July 1938, 8–9, 34–38.

23. Kaufman, "Alice Roosevelt," 140; Adela Rogers St. Johns, "The Private Life of Katharine Hepburn," *Liberty*, 6 Jan. 1934, 18, 21.

24. Mattie Sheridan, "Home and Home Life of Chauncey M. Depew," *Munsey's* 6 (Jan. 1892): 408; Lucy Leffingwell Cable, "The Wife of Andrew Carnegie," *Ladies' Home Journal* 25 (Oct. 1908): 66; Charles A. Selden, "Mrs. Woodrow Wilson," *Ladies' Home Journal* 38 (Oct. 1921): 3.

25. Jerome Beatty, "Betty Holds the Reins," *American Magazine* 110 (Oct. 1930): 62. See also Beatty, "Walter C. Teagle: Giant of Oil," *American Magazine* 112 (Dec. 1931): 18–19, 120–24.

26. Jerome Beatty, "The Man Who Is Always Somebody Else," *American Magazine* 125 (Feb. 1938): 43.

27. Willis J. Abbot, "The Home Life of William Jennings Bryan," *Munsey's* 36 (Feb. 1907): 589; Charlotte Kellogg, "Mrs. Hoover," *Ladies' Home Journal* 47 (Sept. 1930): 24–25, 182–86; Isabel Leighton, "Eleanor Roosevelt—a Recent Portrait," *Ladies' Home Journal* 50 (Mar. 1933): 25, 75–76.

28. Abbot, "Home Life of William Jennings Bryan," 589; Leighton, "Eleanor Roosevelt," 75. See also Hellman, "Mrs. Roosevelt."

29. Adela Rogers St. Johns, "The Married Life of Doug and Mary," *Photoplay* 31 (Feb. 1927): 34–35, 134–36; Clara Beranger, "How Dumb Is Gracie Allen?," *Liberty*, 1 Sept. 1934, 15–17; Henry F. Pringle, "Mr. and Mrs. Clark Gable," *Ladies' Home Journal* 57 (May 1940): 99.

30. Adela Rogers St. Johns, "The Private Life of Helen Hayes," *Liberty*, 10 Nov. 1934, 7; St. Johns, "Private Life of Katharine Hepburn," 21.

31. Adela Rogers St. Johns, "The Real Tragedy of Doug and Mary," *Liberty*, 17 Feb. 1934, 48; Jack Alexander, "Rover Girl in Europe," *Saturday Evening Post*, 25 May 1940, 116.

32. See for example Jack Alexander, "The Girl from Syracuse," *Saturday Evening Post*, 18 May 1940, 9–11, 123–28; and Noel F. Busch, "Bette Davis," *Life*, 23 Jan. 1939, 52–58. For a rare example of an article depicting a husband sacrificing his career for his wife, the poet Edna St. Vincent Millay, see Jerome Beatty, "Best Sellers in Verse," *American Magazine* 113 (Jan. 1932): 36–37, 102–6.

33. This issue is discussed in Jennifer Scanlon, *Inarticulate Longings: The*

Ladies' Home Journal, Gender, and the Promises of Consumer Culture (New York: Routledge, 1995).

34. Keyhoe, "Lindbergh Four Years After," 43; Russell Owen, "What's the Matter with Lindbergh?," *American Magazine* 127 (Apr. 1939): 16.

35. Julian S. Mason, "Lindbergh and the Press," *Saturday Evening Post*, 3 Aug. 1929, 5; Alva Johnston, "The Hepburn Legend," *Woman's Home Companion* 61 (June 1934): 12.

36. Johnston, "The Hepburn Legend," 12, 13; Keyhoe, "Lindbergh Four Years After," 46. See also Adela Rogers St. Johns, "Garbo: The Mystery of Hollywood," *Liberty*, 27 July 1929, 15–22.

37. Babe Ruth, "Fame," *American Magazine* 120 (Aug. 1935): 11; Owen, "What's the Matter with Lindbergh?," 66.

38. Jim Tully, "The Real Life-Story of Charlie Chaplin," *Pictorial Review* 28 (Mar. 1927): 63. See also John B. Kennedy, "They Call Me a Bum," *Collier's*, 12 Sept. 1925, 9; and Kennedy, "The Saddest Young Man in America," *Collier's*, 16 Jan. 1926, 15.

39. "How La Follette Holds On," *Saturday Evening Post*, 17 Feb. 1906, 13; Mary Pickford and Douglas Fairbanks, "The Inside of the Bowl," *Liberty*, 9 Nov. 1929, 22. See also Joan Crawford, "The Job of Keeping at the Top," *Saturday Evening Post*, 17 June 1933, 14–15, 75–76.

40. See Grantland Rice, "The Swelled Head," *American Magazine* 88 (Oct. 1919): 60–61, 202–5. For examples of how journalists invoked the "swelled head" as an explanation of a celebrity's behavior, see A. Maurice Low, "The Greatest of All Issues," *Harper's Weekly*, 14 Sept. 1912, 20; George Ade, "Answering Wild-Eyed Questions about the Movie Stars at Hollywood," *American Magazine* 93 (May 1922): 52–53, 76–82; Morris Markey, "Young Man of Affairs" *New Yorker*, 20 Sept. 1930, 26–29, 27 Sept. 1930, 30–33; and Roger Butterfield, "Lindbergh," *Life*, 11 Aug. 1941, 64.

41. See Richard Weiss, *The American Myth of Success: From Horatio Alger to Norman Vincent Peale* (New York: Basic Books, 1969).

42. See, for example, Sheridan, "Home Life of Depew"; Bacheller, "Andrew Carnegie and His Home in Scotland"; Rockman, "Playing Tennis with Sarah Bernhardt"; Mullett, "George M. Cohan's Definition of One Who Is 'On the Level' "; Paul Gallico, "Jones of Jonesville, Ga.," *Liberty*, 29 Oct. 1929, 50–54; and Keyhoe, "Lindbergh Four Years After."

43. Barton, "It Would Be Fun to Start Over Again," 8. For background on these commitments, see Donald Meyer, *The Positive Thinkers* (New York: Doubleday, 1965); and T. J. Jackson Lears, "From Salvation to Self-Realization: Advertising and the Therapeutic Roots of the Consumer Culture, 1880–1930," in Richard W. Fox and T. J. Jackson Lears, *The Culture of Consumption* (New York: Pantheon, 1983), 3–38.

44. Riis, "Mrs. Roosevelt and Her Children"; Bacheller, "Andrew Carnegie and His Home in Scotland"; John B. Kennedy, "Little Miss Poker Face," *Collier's*, 18 Sept. 1926, 32; Keyhoe, "Lindbergh Four Years After," 48.

45. Pickford and Fairbanks, "The Inside of the Bowl," 20, 18.

46. *Ibid.*, 22.

CHAPTER FIVE

1. Adela Rogers St. Johns, "The Private Life of the 5-and-10 Princess," *Liberty*, 16–30 Mar. 1935, 4–9, 32–38, 44–48.

2. On the tangled relations between gentility and republican- and evangelical-inspired "producer" values in the nineteenth century, see David Shi, *The Simple Life: Plain Living and High Thinking in American Culture* (New York: Oxford University Press, 1985); Richard L. Bushman, *The Refinement of America: Persons, Houses, Cities* (New York: Alfred A. Knopf, 1992); Stow Persons, *The Decline of American Gentility* (New York: Columbia University Press, 1973); and, for a compelling case study, Anthony F. C. Wallace, *Rockdale: The Growth of an American Village in the Early Industrial Revolution* (New York: W. W. Norton, 1978).

3. On the pioneering role of Pulitzer and Hearst in this area, see John D. Stevens, *Sensationalism and the New York Press* (New York: Columbia University Press, 1991).

4. Alan Trachtenberg, *The Incorporation of America: Culture and Society in the Gilded Age* (New York: Hill and Wang, 1982). See also Frederic C. Jaher, *The Urban Establishment: Upper Strata in Boston, New York, Charleston, Chicago, and Los Angeles* (Urbana: University of Illinois Press, 1982)

5. Richard L. McCormick, "The Discovery that Business Corrupts Politics: A Reappraisal of the Origins of Progressivism," *American Historical Review* 86 (Apr. 1981): 247–74.

6. Lincoln Steffens, *The Autobiography of Lincoln Steffens* (New York: Harcourt, Brace, 1931), 194. On press identification with big business, see Christopher P. Wilson, *The Labor of Words: Literary Professionalism in the Progressive Era* (Athens: University of Georgia Press, 1987); Matthew Schneirov, *The Dream of a New Social Order* (New York: Columbia University Press, 1994); Richard Ohmann, *Selling Culture: Magazines, Markets, and Class at the Turn of the Century* (London: Verso, 1996); and Thomas C. Leonard, *The Power of the Press: The Birth of Political Reporting* (New York: Oxford University Press, 1986).

7. See Eric Foner's introductory essay in the 1995 edition of *Free Soil, Free Labor, Free Men: The Ideology of the Republican Party before the Civil War* (New York: Oxford University Press, 1970).

8. See Louis Galambos, *The Public Image of Big Business in America, 1880–1940* (Baltimore: Johns Hopkins University Press, 1975); John L. Thomas, *Alternative America: Henry George, Edward Bellamy, Henry Demarest Lloyd, and the Adversary Tradition* (Cambridge: Harvard University Press, 1983); David P. Thelen, *Paths of Resistance: Tradition and Dignity in Industrializing*

Missouri (New York: Oxford University Press, 1986); and Robert Johnston, *The Radical Middle Class: Populist Democracy and the Question of Capitalism in Progressive Era Portland, Oregon* (forthcoming).

9. Chester L. Lord, *The Young Man and Journalism* (New York: Macmillan), 100.

10. On the political agenda of the mass-circulation press, see George Juergens, *Joseph Pulitzer and the New York World* (Princeton, N.J.: Princeton University Press, 1966); Leonard, *The Power of the Press;* and Ohmann, *Selling Culture.* The centrality of consumerism to progressive reform is discussed in David P. Thelen, *The New Citizenship: The Origins of Progressivism in Wisconsin* (Columbia: University of Missouri Press, 1972); Robert Wiebe, *The Search for Order, 1877–1920* (New York: Hill and Wang, 1967); Lawrence Glickman, *A Living Wage: American Workers and the Making of a Consumer Culture* (Ithaca, N.Y.: Cornell University Press, 1997); and especially Olivier Zunz, *Why the American Century?* (Chicago: University of Chicago Press, 1998).

11. Edwin Lefevre, "Harriman," *American Magazine* 64 (June 1907): 122; Alfred Henry Lewis, "Andrew Carnegie," *Cosmopolitan* 45 (June 1908): 16. See also Murat Halstead and J. Frank Beale, Jr., *Life of Jay Gould: How He Made His Millions* (New York: Edgewood, 1892); Ida M. Tarbell, "John D. Rockefeller: A Character Sketch," *McClure's* 25 (July–Aug. 1905): 227–49, 386–98; and W. T. Stead, *Chicago To-Day; or, The Labour War in America* (London: William Clowes and Sons, 1894).

12. See David Graham Phillips, "The Treason of the Senate," *Cosmopolitan* 41 (Mar.–Nov. 1906); and, from a socialist perspective, W. J. Ghent, *Our Benevolent Feudalism* (New York: Macmillan, 1902). "Owners of America" was the title of a series of profiles of businessmen that appeared in Hearst's *Cosmopolitan* in the wake of Phillips's series on political corruption. See McCormick, "The Discovery That Business Corrupts Politics," for the broader implications of these works.

13. Jaher, *The Urban Establishment.* On the reaction of the New York press to this development, see Juergens, *Joseph Pulitzer;* and Stevens, *Sensationalism and the New York Press.*

14. David Graham Phillips, "Swollen Fortunes," *Saturday Evening Post* 179 (12 Jan. 1907): 11. See also Thorstein Veblen, *The Theory of the Leisure Class* (New York: Macmillan, 1899). The context for this vein of criticism is discussed in Daniel Horowitz, *The Morality of Spending: Attitudes toward the Consumer Society, 1875–1940* (Baltimore: Johns Hopkins University Press, 1985); and Shi, *The Simple Life.*

15. See, for example, Tarbell's chapter on the "legitimate greatness" of the Standard Oil Company in her *History of the Standard Oil Company* (New York: Macmillan, 1904); Alfred Henry Lewis, "Owners of America—J. Pierpont Morgan," *Cosmopolitan* 45 (Aug. 1908); Harold Kellock, "Why Is a Millionaire?," *Everybody's* 23 (July 1910): 56–63; and Elizabeth Meriwether Gilmer, "The Goulds: A Study of an American Family," *Cosmopolitan* 46 (May 1909): 603–15.

16. Frederick Palmer, "One Kind Word for John D.," *Collier's,* 30 June 1906, 14, 24.

17. See Louis Filler, *The Muck-akers* (Stanford: Stanford University Press, 1993).

18. Robert Mayhew, "George Westinghouse," *American Magazine* 60 (Sept. 1905): 582, 578; F. N. Doubleday, "Some Impressions of John D. Rockefeller," *World's Work* 16 (Sept. 1908): 10715. For an early example of a journalist making use of this theme, see Arthur Warren, "Philip D. Armour," *McClure's* 2 (Feb. 1894): 260–80.

19. Ray Stannard Baker, "J. Pierpont Morgan," *McClure's* 17 (Oct. 1901): 515. See also Charles S. Gleed, "Andrew Carnegie," *Cosmopolitan* 33 (July 1902): 297–301; and Julian Ralph, "John Davison Rockefeller," *Cosmopolitan* 33 (June 1902): 160–63.

20. C. M. Keys, "How the Standard Oil Company Does Its Business," *World's Work* 16 (Sept. 1908): 10686.

21. Herbert Kaufman, "Mr. Rockefeller," *Cosmopolitan* 62 (Apr. 1917): 78–79. Ida Tarbell's series, "The Golden Rule in Business," began running in *American Magazine* in October 1914. See also Keys, "How the Standard Oil Company Does Its Business"; Charles J. Woodbury, "Rockefeller and His Standard," *Saturday Evening Post,* 21 Oct. 1911, 8–10, 53; and Gerald Stanley Lee, *Inspired Millionaires: A Forecast* (New York: Kennerley, 1911). Works characteristic of the new mood of the 1920s include B. C. Forbes, *Men Who Are Making America* (New York: B. C. Forbes, 1926); and Burton J. Hendrick, *Life of Andrew Carnegie* (New York: Doubleday, Doran, 1932). See also Matthew Josephson, *The Robber Barons* (New York: Harcourt, Brace, and World, 1934).

22. Warren, "Philip D. Armour," 263; Keys, "How the Standard Oil Company Does Its Business," 10690; Garet Garrett, "Henry Ford's Experiment in Good-Will," *Everybody's* 30 (Apr. 1914): 462–74.

23. Keene Sumner, "Act First and Ask Afterward—If You Are Sure of Your Facts!," *American Magazine* 102 (June 1926): 16–17, 148–53; Jerome Beatty, "Walter Teagle: Giant of Oil," *American Magazine* 112 (Dec. 1931): 19, 122.

24. Sumner, "Act First," 148; Beatty, "Walter Teagle," 124.

25. See, for example, "The Life of Owen D. Young," *Fortune* 3 (Mar. 1931): 89–98; and "Alfred P. Sloan: Chairman," *Fortune* 17 (Apr. 1938): 73–75, 110–14. On Luce and *Fortune,* see James L. Baughman, *Henry R. Luce and the Rise of the American News Media* (Boston: Twayne, 1987).

26. The political context for this is examined in Alan Brinkley, *The End of Reform: New Deal Liberalism in Recession and War* (New York: Alfred A. Knopf, 1995); and Elizabeth Fones-Wolf, *Selling Free Enterprise: The Business Assault on Labor and Liberalism, 1945–1960* (Urbana: University of Illinois Press, 1994).

27. On the varied philanthropic activities of the rich, see Jaher, *The Urban Establishment;* Paul Boyer, *Urban Masses and Moral Order in America, 1820–1920* (Cambridge: Harvard University Press, 1978); Lawrence W. Levine,

Highbrow/Lowbrow: The Emergence of Cultural Hierarchy in America (Cambridge: Harvard University Press, 1989); and Kathleen D. McCarthy, *Women's Culture: American Philanthropy and Art, 1830–1930* (Chicago: University of Chicago Press, 1991).

28. Tarbell, "John D. Rockefeller, Part II," 397; Tarbell, "John D. Rockefeller, Part I," 227. See also Phillips, "Swollen Fortunes"; Palmer, "One Kind Word for John D."; and Lewis, "Andrew Carnegie."

29. Doubleday, "Some Impressions of John D. Rockefeller," 10708; Herbert N. Casson, "The Rockefeller Foundation," *Munsey's* 43 (June 1910): 298; Morris Bacheller, "Andrew Carnegie and His Home in Scotland," *Munsey's* 39 (Sept. 1908): 797; Casson, "Rockefeller Foundation," 304.

30. Doubleday, "Some Impressions of John D. Rockefeller," 10709. See also Casson, "The Rockefeller Foundation"; and Lee, *Inspired Millionaires.*

31. Casson, 303; Aaron Davis, "The Responsibility of Wealth," *Saturday Evening Post,* 23 May 1925, 150. On the faith in scientific expertise see Wiebe, *Search for Order;* John M. Jordan, *Machine-Age Ideology: Social Engineering and American Liberalism, 1911–1939* (Chapel Hill: University of North Carolina Press, 1994); and Daniel T. Rodgers, *Atlantic Crossings: Social Politics in a Progressive Age* (Cambridge: Harvard University Press, 1998).

32. Doubleday, "Some Impressions of John D. Rockefeller," 10711; Albert W. Atwood, "The Rockefeller Fortune," *Saturday Evening Post,* 11 June 1921, 21, 97–98, 101–2; Juliet Wilbor Tompkins, "The Personality of Helen Gould," *Everybody's* 8 (Jan. 1903): 29; J. P. Coughlan, "Helen Miller Gould," *Munsey's* 25 (June 1901): 388, 390.

33. "The Work of Mrs. Mackay," *American Magazine* 70 (Sept. 1910): 610. See also O. H. Dunbar, "Mrs. Mackay at Work," *Harper's Bazaar* 44 (Apr. 1910): 240–41; and Ralph Pulitzer, "New York Society at Work," *Harper's Bazaar* 43 (Dec. 1909): 1188–89. Alva Belmont's articles include "How Can Women Get the Suffrage?," *Independent,* 31 Mar. 1910, 686–89; and "Liberation of a Sex," *Hearst's Magazine* 23 (Apr. 1913): 614–16.

34. Mrs. Vincent Astor, "The World I Live In," *Ladies' Home Journal* 37 (July 1920): 20–21, 105–6; quotation on 105.

35. See, for example, William Lyon Phelps, "Henry Ford: The Most Famous Living American," *Delineator* 120 (May 1932): 9, 74; John B. Kennedy, "My Father Never Said Don't," *Collier's,* 5 May 1927, 14; Frederick L. Collins, "Mrs. John D. Rockefeller, Jr.," *Delineator* 110 (May 1927): 9; and, on Whitney, *New York Times,* 12 Jan. 1930, sec. viii, 11.

36. Ralph Wallace, "America's No. 1 Angel," *American Magazine* 129 (May 1940): 27, 147.

37. See Neal Gabler, *Winchell: Gossip, Power and the Culture of Celebrity* (New York: Alfred A. Knopf, 1994); and, for a more detailed survey, Cleveland Amory, *Who Killed Society?* (New York: Harper and Brothers, 1960).

38. Bacheller, "Andrew Carnegie at His Home in Scotland," 793, 797; *New York Herald,* 26 Dec. 1909, sec. iii, 6; Tompkins, "The Personality of Helen Gould," 30; Issac F. Marcosson, "The Simple Life among the Rich," *Saturday*

Evening Post, 3 Jan. 1914, 8. Henry Ford was a figure whom the press continued to identify with the "simple life" well into the 1930s.

39. Gilmer, "The Goulds," 615; John Cushman Fistere, "The Rockefeller Boys," *Saturday Evening Post,* 16 July 1938, 9, 34.

40. Bacheller, "Andrew Carnegie and His Home in Scotland," 793. See also Mattie Sheridan, "Home and Home Life of Chauncey M. Depew," *Munsey's* 6 (Jan. 1892): 408–17; Baker, "J. Pierpont Morgan"; and R. H. Titherington, "Mr. and Mrs. George J. Gould," *Munsey's* 32 (Mar. 1905): 818–22.

41. Helen Worden, "Mr. and Mrs. Vincent Astor," *Ladies' Home Journal* 55 (Sept. 1938): 29; Wallace, "America's No. 1 Angel," 147.

42. See, for example, Adela Rogers St. Johns, "The Private Life of the 5-and-10 Princess."

43. Mary B. Mullett, "Four Big Men Become Boys Again," *American Magazine* 87 (Feb. 1919): 34.

44. See Stuart Ewen, *PR!: A Social History of Spin* (New York: Basic Books, 1996); and Roland Marchand, *Creating the Corporate Soul: The Rise of Public Relations and Corporate Imagery in American Big Business* (Berkeley: University of California Press, 1998).

CHAPTER SIX

1. William Allen White, "Bryan," *McClure's* 15 (July 1900): 232.

2. See, for example, Ray Stannard Baker, "Theodore Roosevelt," *McClure's* 12 (Nov. 1898): 23–32; Samuel G. Blythe, "Hughes—A Potential President," *Saturday Evening Post,* 16 Mar. 1907, 3–4, 27; Lincoln Steffens, "Roosevelt—Taft—La Follette," *Everybody's* 18 (June 1908): 723–36.

3. Michael McGerr, *The Decline of Popular Politics* (New York: Oxford University Press, 1986).

4. Richard L. McCormick, "The Discovery That Business Corrupts Politics: A Reappraisal of the Origins of Progressivism," *American Historical Review* 86 (Apr. 1981): 247–74; Thomas C. Leonard, *The Power of the Press: The Birth of Political Reporting* (New York: Oxford University Press, 1986).

5. William Allen White, "Carrie Nation and Kansas," *Saturday Evening Post,* 6 Apr. 1901, 2–3. On new forms of political activism, see Steven J. Diner, *A Very Different Age* (New York: Hill and Wang, 1998).

6. See Richard L. McCormick, "The Party Period and Public Policy: An Exploratory Hypothesis," *Journal of American History* 66 (Sept. 1979): 279–98.

7. David Graham Phillips, "Aldrich, Head of It All," *Cosmopolitan* 40 (Apr. 1906): 630; William Allen White, "Platt," *McClure's* 18 (Dec. 1901): 153. See also Mark Sullivan, "The Fight against Cannonism," *Collier's* 43 (27 Mar. 1909): 11.

8. See Leonard, *The Power of the Press,* on coverage of Tammany Hall by *Harper's Weekly.*

9. William Allen White, "Croker," *McClure's* 16 (Feb. 1901): 321; Louis Seibold, "Richard Croker," *Munsey's* 25 (Aug. 1901): 628; Alfred Henry Lewis, "The Modern Robin Hood," *Cosmopolitan* 39 (June 1905): 186–92. This line of argument persisted well into the 1930s, particularly among journalists opposed to Prohibition. See George Creel, "The Boy Friend," *Collier's* 90 (13 Aug. 1932): 11–12, 34.

10. White, "Croker," 322; White, "Hanna," *McClure's* 16 (Nov. 1900): 63. See also David Graham Phillips, "Confusing the People," *Cosmopolitan* 41 (Aug. 1906): 368–77; and White, "Roosevelt: A Force for Righteousness," *McClure's* 28 (Feb. 1907): 386–94.

11. White, "Bryan," 237.

12. "The Issue Autocracy," *Harper's Weekly*, 10 Sept. 1910, 4. See also *New York Times*, 27 June 1904, 8; *New York Herald*, 4 Mar. 1909, 10; A. Maurice Low, "The Greatest of All Issues," *Harper's Weekly*, 14 Sept. 1912, 20.

13. Jerome Beatty, "You Can't Laugh Him Off!," *American Magazine* 115 (Jan. 1933): 32; "Incredible Kingfish," *Time*, 3 Oct. 1932, 11. See also Walter Davenport, "The Shepherd of Discontent," *Collier's*, 4 May 1935, 12–13, 57–60; and A. J. Nock, "Autopsy on the New Deal," *American Mercury* 42 (Sept. 1937): 106–10.

14. White, "Bryan."

15. Lincoln Steffens, "Eugene V. Debs," *Everybody's* 19 (Oct. 1908): 455–69; "Emma Goldman," *American Magazine* 69 (Mar. 1910): 606–8; William Hard, "Fighting Bob—Elder Statesman," *Collier's*, 8 Sept. 1923, 12; Richard Washburn Child, "He Rides Alone," *Saturday Evening Post*, 21 May 1927, 6–7, 187–89. For a dissenting view more favorable to progressives and liberals, see William Allen White, "The Lone Wolf of Idaho," *Collier's*, 12 Sept. 1925, 6, 40. On the context for White's continued interest in reform, see Otis L. Graham, *Encore for Reform: The Old Progressives and the New Deal* (New York: Oxford University Press, 1967).

16. See, for example, "Moral Lessons of the Oil Scandal," *Literary Digest*, 19 Apr. 1924, 32–33.

17. Perhaps the most widely attacked of these figures was Huey Long. See Beatty, "You Can't Laugh Him Off!" Long's place in the populist upheavals of the 1930s is discussed in Alan Brinkley, *Voices of Protest: Huey Long, Father Coughlin, and the Great Depression* (New York: Alfred A. Knopf, 1982).

18. Baker, "Theodore Roosevelt," 23; William Allen White, "One Year of Roosevelt," *Saturday Evening Post*, 4 Oct. 1902, 4.

19. Samuel G. Blythe, "Wilson in Washington," *Saturday Evening Post*, 8 Nov. 1913, 8; Newton Dent, "Senator Robert M. La Follette," *Munsey's* 36 (Feb. 1907): 655.

20. Hard, "Fighting Bob—Elder Statesman," 12; Samuel G. Blythe, "The New President," *Saturday Evening Post*, 20 Oct. 1923, 3–4, 156–58; Issac F. Marcosson, "The President Gets Down to Business," *Saturday Evening Post*, 21 Dec. 1929, 3–4, 78–82; Frank R. Kent, "A Good Look at Al Smith," *Collier's*, 3 Mar. 1928, 9.

21. White, "Bryan," 236.

22. Mark Sullivan, "Roosevelt," *Collier's*, 6 Mar. 1909, 22; "Labor's Attitude toward Red Agitators," *Literary Digest*, 20 Mar. 1920, 21–23.

23. White, "One Year of Roosevelt," 4; George Creel, "The Next Four Years: An Interview with the President," *Everybody's* 36 (Feb. 1917): 129–39; Blythe, "The New President," 4.

24. White, "Roosevelt," 41; Samuel G. Blythe, "W. Wilson—Human Being," *Saturday Evening Post*, 24 May 1913, 3; Kenneth L. Roberts, "Concentrated New England," *Saturday Evening Post*, 31 May 1924, 11; Will Irwin, "Portrait of a President," *Saturday Evening Post*, 17 Jan. 1931, 7.

25. White, "One Year of Roosevelt," 3; Samuel G. Blythe, "Our New President," *Saturday Evening Post*, 1 Mar. 1913, 49.

26. White, "Roosevelt," 45; Blythe, "Our New President," 3; Blythe, "The New President," 4. On the growing concern with popular irrationality among members of the professional-managerial class, see Eugene E. Leach, "Mastering the Crowd," *American Studies* 27 (1986): 99–117; and Stuart Ewen, *PR!: A Social History of Spin* (New York: Basic Books, 1996).

27. William Allen White, "Carrie Nation and Kansas," 3; Steffens, "Eugene V. Debs," 460; Thomas Sugrue, "Hopkins Holds the Bag," *American Magazine* 121 (Mar. 1936): 149, 153. For an example of a largely sympathetic profile of a socialist, see Alfred Henry Lewis, "Joseph Medill Patterson: An Apostle of Hope," *Saturday Evening Post*, 15 Sept. 1906, 3–5. The appearance of this piece in the *Saturday Evening Post* is emblematic of the political open-mindedness displayed by the mainstream press in the early twentieth century.

28. Charlotte Teller, "Miss Jane Addams of Hull House, Chicago," *Everybody's* 8 (Feb. 1903): 168–71; Paul U. Kellogg, "Mrs. Florence Kelley," *American Magazine* 70 (July 1910): 303; Helen Huntington Smith, "Rampant But Respectable," *New Yorker*, 14 Dec. 1929, 32.

29. Mildred Adams, "Crusader," *Delineator* 123 (Sept. 1933): 48, 49; Maxine Davis, "Madame Secretary," *Liberty*, 9 Mar. 1935, 32.

30. Burton J. Hendrick, "The Leadership of Samuel Gompers," *World's Work* 35 (Feb. 1918): 386. See also "Plain Sam Gompers and His Empire," *Literary Digest*, 3 Jan. 1925, 32–36.

31. Beverly Smith, "The Name Is Lewis," *American Magazine* 122 (Sept. 1936): 130.

32. Richard L. Neuberger, "Labor's Overlords," *American Magazine* 125 (Mar. 1938): 169, 167, 170.

33. William A. H. Birnie, "Noble Norman," *American Magazine* 130 (July 1940): 116.

34. Alva Johnston, "Our Own Lenin," *New Yorker*, 28 June 1930, 21; Hubert Kelley, "Our No. 1 Communist," *American Magazine* 121 (Feb. 1936): 29, 115.

35. Alan Dawley, *Struggles for Justice: Social Responsibility and the Liberal State* (Cambridge: Harvard University Press, 1991). See also Michael Denning, *The Cultural Front: The Laboring of American Culture in the Twentieth Century* (London: Verso, 1996).

36. George Creel, "Looking Ahead with Roosevelt," *Collier's,* 17 Sept. 1935, 8, 45, 7.

37. Harold L. Ickes, "Roosevelt as I Know Him," *Saturday Evening Post,* 15 Aug. 1936, 74, 72, 70.

38. See Betty H. Winfield, *FDR and the News Media* (New York: Columbia University Press, 1994).

39. Raymond Moley, "A Portrait of F.D.R.," *Saturday Evening Post,* 16 Sept. 1939, 95, 98. See Graham, *Encore for Reform.*

40. Hugh S. Johnson, "Profile of a President," *Ladies' Home Journal* 55 (Mar. 1938): 103; Bruce Barton, "What's Wrong with Roosevelt," *Collier's,* 5 Nov. 1938, 48. See also Joseph Alsop and Robert Kintner, "We Shall Make America Over," *Saturday Evening Post,* 29 Oct. 1938, 5–7. This is the first of a three-part series that continues on 12 November and concludes the following week.

41. Alva Johnston, "Tugwell, the President's Idea Man," *Saturday Evening Post,* 1 Aug. 1936, 8, 74.

42. See, for example, C. Hurd, "As His Third and Hardest Term Begins," *New York Times Magazine,* 19 Jan. 1941, 3; and F. L. Kluckhohn, "Commander-in-Chief," *New York Times Magazine,* 14 Dec. 1941, 10. On the retreat from the social-democratic emphasis of the Second New Deal, see Brinkley, *End of Reform.*

43. See Gary Gerstle, "The Protean Character of American Liberalism," *American Historical Review* 99 (Oct. 1994): 1043–73.

CHAPTER SEVEN

1. "People," *Time,* 5 Sept. 1938, 22.

2. Alva Johnston, "Public Relations—IV," *New Yorker,* 9 Sept. 1944, 31.

3. Quoted in Robert C. Allen, *Horrible Prettiness: Burlesque and American Culture* (Chapel Hill: University of North Carolina Press, 1991), 127.

4. See Neil Harris, *Humbug: The Art of P. T. Barnum* (Chicago: University of Chicago Press, 1973); David Nasaw, *Going Out: The Rise and Fall of Public Amusements* (New York: Basic Books, 1993); and, for a broader treatment, Jim Cullen, *The Art of Democracy* (New York: Monthly Review Press, 1996).

5. Quoted in Paul R. Gorman, *Left Intellectuals and Popular Culture in Twentieth-Century America* (Chapel Hill: University of North Carolina Press, 1996), 20. For the context that produced this new view of the popular culture industries, see Lawrence W. Levine, *Highbrow/Lowbrow: The Emergence of Cultural Hierarchy in America* (Cambridge: Harvard University Press, 1989); and Jackson Lears, "Mass Culture and Its Critics," in Mary Kupiec Cayton, Elliott J. Gorn, and Peter W. Williams, eds., *Encyclopedia of American Social History* 3:1591–1610 (New York: Scribner's, 1993).

6. On dramatic critics, see Benjamin McArthur, *Actors and American Cul-*

ture, *1880–1920* (Philadelphia: Temple University Press, 1984). For examples of their work, see Alan Dale, "Can a Dramatic Critic Be Quite Honest?," *Cosmopolitan* 41 (Aug. 1906): 397–404; and "Theater's Responsibility," *Cosmopolitan* 43 (July 1907): 294–304; Walter Prichard Eaton, "Canned Drama," *American Magazine* 68 (Sept. 1909): 493–500.

7. On the emerging modernist critique of popular culture, see Gorman, *Left Intellectuals and Popular Culture;* and Michael G. Kammen, *The Lively Arts: Gilbert Seldes and the Transformation of Cultural Criticism in the U.S.* (New York: Oxford University Press, 1996).

8. Alan Dale, "The Success of Belasco," *Cosmopolitan* 44 (Mar. 1908): 395–96; Eaton, "Canned Drama"; Jim Tully, "Irving Thalberg," *Vanity Fair* 29 (Oct. 1927): 98.

9. Jim Tully, "Frances Marion," *Vanity Fair* 27 (Jan. 1927): 63; Alan Dale, "Recipes for Making Stars," *Cosmopolitan* 42 (Dec. 1906): 195; Walter Prichard Eaton, "Personality and the Player," *Collier's,* 22 Oct. 1910, 17, 34; William A. Page, "The Movie-Struck Girl," *Woman's Home Companion* 45 (June 1918): 18.

10. Alan Dale, "Acting Off the Stage," *Cosmopolitan* 45 (July 1908): 172; Adela Rogers St. Johns, "Madame la Marquise," *Liberty,* 30 Nov. 1929, 19.

11. Hartley Davis, "Whom the Stage Demoralizes," *Munsey's* 25 (Apr. 1901): 88; Keene Sumner, "The Hidden Talents of 'Jack' Barrymore," *American Magazine* 87 (June 1919): 37.

12. Page, "Movie-Struck Girl," 18. See Karl Kitchen's widely syndicated series on Hollywood which appeared in the *New York World Magazine* and other periodicals from 6 April to 11 May 1919.

13. Quoted in Richard DeCordova, *Picture Personalities: The Emergence of the Star System in America* (Urbana: University of Illinois Press, 1990), 126. See also Herbert Corey, "They're Funny People," *Everybody's* 41 (Oct. 1919): 52–57, 109–11.

14. "An Intimate Friend of Frohman," *Saturday Evening Post,* 16 Jan. 1909, 15; Eleanor Franklin, "David Belasco and the Belasco Theatre," *Leslie's Weekly,* 16 Oct. 1902, 370; Peter Clark Macfarlane, "George M. Cohan," *Everybody's* 30 (Jan. 1914): 119.

15. Alexander Woollcott, "The Story of Irving Berlin," *Saturday Evening Post,* 24 Jan. 1925, 6; Woollcott, "Story of Irving Berlin," *Saturday Evening Post,* 7 Feb. 1925, 32; Issac Goldberg, "Music By Gershwin," *Ladies' Home Journal* 48 (Feb. 1931): 12. On the relationship between modernist critics and African-American culture, see Ann Douglas, *Terrible Honesty: Mongrel Manhattan in the 1920s* (New York: Hill and Wang, 1994).

16. Karl Kitchen, "Running at Full Blast," *New York World Magazine,* 4 May 1919, 15; Kitchen, "The Comeback of Hollywood," *New York World Magazine,* 11 Mar. 1923, 3. De Mille was cited as an exemplar of both kinds of "quality." See Mary B. Mullet, "How Cecil B. De Mille Works and What He Knows about Us," *American Magazine* 101 (July 1925): 34–35, 131–39; and R. E. Sherwood, "The Hollywood Zeus," *New Yorker,* 28 Nov. 1925, 11–12.

17. Rob Wagner, "Mr. Charles Spencer Chaplin: The Man You Don't Know," *Ladies' Home Journal* 35 (Sept. 1918): 82; Karl Kitchen, "At Work with Charlie Chaplin," *New York World Magazine,* 27 Apr. 1919, 7, 15.

18. Mary B. Mullett, "The Greatest Moving Picture Producer in the World," *American Magazine* 91 (Apr. 1921): 34, 144.

19. Sherwood, "The Hollywood Zeus," 11.

20. Jack Jamison, "He Gave Us Mickey Mouse," *Liberty,* 14 Jan. 1933, 52; Gilbert Seldes, "Mickey-Mouse Maker," *New Yorker,* 19 Dec. 1931, 27.

21. "Orson Welles: Once a Child Prodigy, He Has Never Grown Up," *Life,* 26 May 1941, 108; Frederick L. Collins, "Has Orson Welles Gone Hollywood?," *Liberty,* 20 Jan. 1940, 14, 15.

22. Gustav Kobbé, "Maude Adams and Her Long Island Farm," *Ladies' Home Journal* 20 (Nov. 1903): 10; Frederick James Smith, "Mary Pickford," *American Magazine* 77 (Apr. 1914): 64–66; Mary B. Mullett, "Theda Bara— Queen of the Vampires," *American Magazine* 90 (Sept. 1920): 34–35, 90–100; Ethel Barrymore, "How Can I Be a Great Actress?," 6.

23. Joan Crawford, "The Job of Keeping at the Top," *Saturday Evening Post,* 17 June 1933, 14, 15; Jerome Beatty, "$1,000,000 on Ice," *American Magazine* 124 (Nov. 1937): 114.

24. Kate Jordan, "Our Youngest Leading Lady," *Leslie's Weekly,* 5 Dec. 1895, 366; Clara Beranger, "The Private Life of Wallace Beery," *Liberty,* 15 July 1933, 6; Katherine Albert, "Afraid of Hollywood: The Story of a Star in the Making," *Liberty,* 14 May 1938, 54.

25. Karl Kitchen, "A Day with Mary Pickford," *New York World Magazine,* 11 May 1919, 7; Henry F. Pringle, "Tough—By Request," *Collier's,* 3 Sept. 1932, 45; Noel F. Busch, "Bette Davis," *Life,* 23 Jan. 1939, 53.

26. Adela Rogers St. Johns, "Garbo: The Mystery of Hollywood," *Liberty,* 27 July 1929, 21; Alva Johnston, "The Hepburn Legend," *Woman's Home Companion* 61 (June 1934): 62; Howard Sharpe, "The Mystery of Carole Lombard," *Liberty,* 5 Feb. 1938, 22.

27. Sharpe, "Mystery of Carole Lombard," 23; Clara Beranger, "How Dumb Is Gracie Allen?," *Liberty,* 1 Sept. 1934, 16. See also Edna Ferber, "They Earn Their Millions," *Collier's,* 4 Dec. 1920, 7–8, 24–28.

28. Mullett, "Movie Star Who Knows What Makes You Laugh," 37; Adela Rogers St. Johns, "Is Clark Gable a Changed Man?," *Liberty,* 26 Dec. 1936, 8.

29. George Ade, "Answering Wild-Eyed Questions about the Movie Stars at Hollywood," *American Magazine* 93 (May 1922): 53.

30. Gustav Kobbé, "The Girlishness of Ethel Barrymore," *Ladies' Home Journal* 20 (June 1903): 4; Clara E. Laughlin, "How Ethel Barrymore Thinks a Young Girl Should Dress," *Ladies' Home Journal* 25 (May 1908): 13; Mullett, "Theda Bara—Queen of the Vampires," 100, 34; St. Johns, "Garbo," 15.

31. Gustav Kobbé, "The Actress We Know as Julia Marlowe," *Ladies' Home Journal* 20 (Feb. 1903): 7; Karl Kitchen, "Week-Ending with Doug and Mary," *New York World Magazine,* 14 May 1922, 8. For more on this shift in the leisure-time preferences of the middle class, see the essays in Kathryn Grover, ed.,

Hard at Play: Leisure in America, 1840–1940 (Amherst: University of Massachusetts Press, 1992); and, on the role of actors in encouraging them, Lary May, *Screening Out the Past: The Birth of Mass Culture and the Motion Picture Industry* (New York: Oxford University Press, 1980).

32. Ade, "Answering Wild-Eyed Questions," 52; Gustav Kobbé, "Maude Adams at Her Long Island Farm," 9; Alma Whitaker, "How They Manage Their Homes," *Photoplay* 35 (May 1929): 34; Henry F. Pringle, "Mr. and Mrs. Clark Gable," *Ladies' Home Journal* 57 (May 1940): 99.

33. Kobbé, "The Girlishness of Ethel Barrymore," 4; Adela Rogers St. Johns, "The Married Life of Doug and Mary," *Photoplay* 31 (Feb. 1927): 134.

34. Ade, "Answering Wild-Eyed Questions," 52; Mary B. Mullett, "Mary Pickford Describes Her Most Thrilling Experience," *American Magazine* 95 (May 1923): 113; Mary Pickford and Douglas Fairbanks, "The Inside of the Bowl," *Liberty*, 9 Nov. 1929, 20; Jerome Beatty, "Betty Holds the Reins," *American Magazine* 110 (Oct. 1930): 113.

35. Jim Tully, "The Real Life-Story of Charlie Chaplin," *Pictorial Review* 28 (Apr. 1927): 108; Tully, "Real Life-Story of Charlie Chaplin," *Pictorial Review* 28 (Feb. 1927): 72; Adela Rogers St. Johns, "Clara Bow: The Playgirl of Hollywood," *Liberty*, 3 Aug. 1929, 19, 20. For more information about these figures and their problematic relationship with the press, see Charles J. Maland, *Chaplin and American Culture* (Princeton, N.J.: Princeton University Press, 1989); and David Stenn, *Clara Bow: Runnin' Wild* (New York: Doubleday, 1988).

36. W. E. Woodward, "Nine O'Clock Town," *Collier's*, 30 Apr. 1932, 53; Clara Beranger, "Is Hollywood Getting Religion?," *Liberty*, 19 Jan. 1935, 26, 28. On the social context that produced this new emphasis in reportage, see Terry A. Cooney, *Balancing Acts: American Thought and Culture in the 1930s* (Boston: Twayne, 1995).

37. See Robert Sklar, *Movie-Made America* (New York: Random House, 1975); Thomas Cripps, *Hollywood's High Noon* (Baltimore: Johns Hopkins University Press, 1997); and especially Christine Gledhill, ed., *Stardom: Industry of Desire* (London: Routledge, 1991).

CHAPTER EIGHT

1. For a fascinating behind-the-scenes account of the Dempsey-Tunney fight and its sequel, see Bruce J. Evensen, *When Dempsey Fought Tunney: Heroes, Hokum, and Storytelling in the Jazz Age* (Knoxville: University of Tennessee Press, 1996).

2. See Elliott J. Gorn and Warren Goldstein, *A Brief History of American Sports* (New York: Hill and Wang, 1993).

3. John Rickard Betts, "Sporting Journalism in Nineteenth-Century America," *American Quarterly* 5 (Spring 1953): 39–56.

4. On the role of the press in popularizing college football and the more gen-

eral project of creating "fans," see Michael Oriard, *Reading Football: How the Popular Press Created an American Spectacle* (Chapel Hill: University of North Carolina Press, 1993).

5. The milieu of elite sportswriters is nicely rendered in Charles Fountain, *Sportswriter: The Life and Times of Grantland Rice* (New York: Oxford University Press, 1993).

6. Paul Gallico, *Farewell to Sport* (New York: Alfred A. Knopf), 282. See also Stanley Woodward, *Sports Page* (New York: Simon and Schuster, 1949).

7. For a blatant example of reportage that makes this connection, see Hugh S. Fullerton, "The Ten Commandments of Sport, and of Everything Else," *American Magazine* 92 (Aug. 1921): 54, 78.

8. See Gorn and Goldstein, *Brief History of American Sports.*

9. For an interesting case study of these conflicting values at work, see Elliott J. Gorn, "The Manassa Mauler and the Fighting Marine: An Interpretation of the Dempsey-Tunney Fights," *Journal of American Studies* 19 (1985): 27–47. See also Gail Bederman, *Manliness and Civilization* (Chicago: University of Chicago Press, 1995).

10. On the sporting fraternity, see Elliott J. Gorn, *The Manly Art: Bare-Knuckle Prizefighting in America* (Ithaca, N.Y.: Cornell University Press, 1986). For information on the broader context that inspired this revolt against genteel masculinity, see Mark C. Carnes and Clyde Griffen, eds., *Meanings for Manhood: Constructions of Masculinity in Victorian America* (Chicago: University of Chicago Press, 1990).

11. Ring W. Lardner, "Tyrus: The Greatest of 'Em All," *American Magazine* 79 (June 1915): 23; Grantland Rice, "The Rival Queens," *Collier's*, 30 Jan. 1926, 14; Mary K. Browne, "Suzanne Lenglen," *Vanity Fair* 27 (Oct. 1926): 102. See also "Temperament at the Tennis Net," *Literary Digest*, 27 Feb. 1926, 62–67.

12. See W. O. McGeehan, "How Much Is Ballyhoo?," *Vanity Fair* 29 (Sept. 1928): 76, 114; and Gallico, *Farewell to Sport.*

13. John B. Kennedy, "They Call Me a Bum," *Collier's*, 12 Sept. 1925, 9; Grantland Rice, "The Sportlight," *New York Tribune*, 20 Oct. 1921, 15.

14. Grantland Rice, "The Sportlight," *New York Herald-Tribune*, 8 Sept. 1925; W. O. McGeehan, "The Social Life of an Athlete," *Vanity Fair* 29 (Aug. 1927): 94. On Ruth's relationship with sportswriters, see Ken Sobel, *Babe Ruth and the American Dream* (New York: Random House, 1974).

15. Grantland Rice, "The Sportlight," *New York Herald-Tribune*, 29 Feb. 1928, 26.

16. Hugh Fullerton, "Wagner: The Greatest Baseball Player in the World," *American Magazine* 69 (Jan. 1910): 378; Joseph Mulvaney, "The Dempsey You Don't Know," *Collier's*, 14 Mar. 1926, 8; Grantland Rice, "There's Only One Bobby Jones," *Collier's*, 4 Apr. 1925, 20; Grantland Rice, "Good Anywhere," *Collier's*, 26 May 1928, 15.

17. Charles E. Van Loan, "Big Leaguers in the Spangles and Out," *Munsey's* 47 (July 1912): 535; Hugh Fullerton, "Ty Cobb Says—If Going Stale, Drink!,"

Liberty, 20 Sept. 1924, 42; Mulvaney, "The Dempsey You Don't Know," 8; Joe Winkworth, "I Have Been a Babe and a Boob," *Collier's,* 31 Oct. 1925, 15.

18. Grantland Rice, "Yellow Streak," *American Magazine* 88 (Dec. 1919): 57; Grantland Rice, "The Sportlight," *New York Herald-Tribune,* 1 Apr. 1924, 15.

19. Grantland Rice, "Makings of the Mighty," *Collier's,* 3 Nov. 1928, 17.

20. Lardner, "Tyrus," 22; Rice, "There's Only One Bobby Jones," 20; Rice, "Big Bill Tilden," *Collier's,* 29 Nov. 1924, 17.

21. Fullerton, "The Ten Commandments of Sport," 54.

22. For a thoughtful analysis of the tension between amateurism and professionalism, see S. W. Pope, *Patriotic Games: Sporting Traditions in the American Imagination, 1876–1926* (New York: Oxford University Press, 1997).

23. W. O. McGeehan, "The Amateur Spirit," *Vanity Fair* 27 (Jan. 1927): 104; Paul Gallico, "Jones of Jonesville, Ga.," *Liberty,* 29 Oct. 1929, 54.

24. John B. Kennedy, "Little Miss Poker Face," 10; Browne, "Suzanne Lenglen," 102; Grantland Rice, "Rival Queens," 14. On the Lenglen-Wills matches, see Larry Engelmann, *The Goddess and the American Girl* (New York: Oxford University Press, 1988).

25. McGeehan, "The Amateur Spirit," 104; Fullerton, "Can Babe Ruth Come Back?," Liberty, 1 May 1926, 56; Arthur Robinson, "My Friend Babe Ruth," *Collier's,* 20 Sept. 1924, 7–8, 28.

26. Grantland Rice, "Rocks in the Glory Path," *Collier's,* 5 Mar. 1927, 28; Mulvaney, "The Dempsey You Don't Know," 9; Robert Ingerley, "Gene Tunney: Champion de Luxe," *Liberty,* 14 May 1927, 52. See also McGeehan, "The Social Life of an Athlete," 63, 94.

27. Fullerton, "Wagner," 379; W. O. McGeehan, "In All Fairness," *New York Tribune,* 31 May 1920, 12.

28. Grantland Rice, "The Sportlight," *New York Herald-Tribune,* 8 Sept. 1925, 16; Arthur Mann, "The New Babe Ruth," *New York Evening World,* 28 Apr. 1928; Bozeman Bulger, "And Along Came Ruth," *Saturday Evening Post,* 28 Nov. 1931, 6, 38.

29. Rice, "The Sportlight," 8 Sept. 1925, 15; W. O. McGeehan, "Down the Line," *New York Herald-Tribune,* 27 Sept. 1929; Paul Gallico, "Huggins Was a Little Guy," *New York Daily News,* 50; "Taps for Huggins: A Great Little Bear-Tamer," *Literary Digest,* 12 Oct. 1929, 40. See also Grantland Rice, "King of Diamonds," *Collier's,* 3 May 1930, 24.

30. For a particularly vivid example of this motif, see J. Roy Stockton, "Me and My Public," *Saturday Evening Post,* 12 Sept. 1936, 8–9, 69–73.

31. Franklin P. Adams, "Bill Tilden, the Temperamental," *Collier's,* 28 Oct. 1922, 8, 22; Rice, "Big Bill Tilden," 17; Kennedy, "Little Miss Poker Face," 10; Helena Huntington Smith, "Another Glorified Girl," *New Yorker,* 27 Aug. 1927, 16–18; Mildred (Babe) Didrickson, "I Blow My Own Horn," *American Magazine* 121 (June 1936): 104.

32. "Why Matty Lasts," *Literary Digest,* 23 Aug. 1913, 299; Hugh S. Fullerton, "How the Ball Players of the Big Leagues Live and Act When off the Dia-

mond," *American Magazine* 72 (July 1911): 321–31; Ingerley, "Gene Tunney: Champion de Luxe"; McGeehan, "The Social Life of an Athlete," 63; Kelly Coombs, "Gene the Genteel," *New Yorker,* 20 Aug. 1927, 16–19.

33. Paul Gallico, "The Enigma Called Tunney," *Liberty,* 5 Jan. 1929, 46.

34. See Damon Runyon, "Says Damon Runyon," *New York American,* 24 Feb. 1923; and Grantland Rice, "What Draws the Crowds," *Collier's,* 20 June 1925, 10, 44.

35. Grantland Rice, "Can Dempsey Come Back?," *Collier's,* 12 June 1926, 7; W. O. McGeehan, "Down the Line," *New York Herald,* 20 Feb. 1923; Heywood Broun, "Bambino the Maestro," *Vanity Fair* 18 (May 1922): 79. On the appeal of the primitive in this period, see Marianna Torgovnick, *Gone Primitive: Savage Intellect, Modern Lives* (Chicago: University of Chicago Press, 1990); and Ann Douglas, *Terrible Honesty: Mongrel Manhattan in the 1920s* (New York: Hill and Wang, 1994.

36. Rice, "The Sportlight," *New York Herald-Tribune,* 8 Sept. 1925; Rice, "Can Dempsey Come Back?," 7; Jim Tully, "Can Dempsey Still Fight?," *Liberty,* 22 Aug. 1925, 30; Fullerton, "Can Babe Ruth Come Back?," 53.

37. Grantland Rice, "Iron Handshaker," *Collier's,* 13 Apr. 1929, 20; John Kieran, "Sports of the Times," *New York Times,* 28 Feb. 1927; "Ruth's Record-Breaking Series," *Literary Digest* 99 (27 Oct. 1928): 62; Dick Williams, "The Saga of Swat," *Liberty,* 22 Apr. 1933, 16.

38. See, for example, John B. Kennedy, "Innocents Aboard," *Collier's,* 14 Apr. 1928; Larry Snyder, "My Boy Jesse," *Saturday Evening Post,* 7 Nov. 1936, 14–15, 97–101.

39. Caswell Adams, "Introducing—The New Joe Louis," *Saturday Evening Post,* 10 May 1941, 26–27, 106–11; Paul Gallico, "Citizen Barrow," *Reader's Digest* 40 (June 1942): 24. This article originally appeared in *Liberty* and marked the brief return of Paul Gallico to sports journalism.

40. On Sullivan, see Michael T. Isenberg, *John L. Sullivan and His America* (Urbana: University of Illinois Press, 1988).

41. Grantland Rice, "What Draws the Crowds," *Collier's,* 20 June 1925, 10.

42. Richard Sennett and Jonathan Cobb, *The Hidden Injuries of Class* (New York: Alfred A. Knopf, 1972); Robert Bellah et al., *Habits of the Heart: Individualism and Commitment in American Life* (New York: Harper and Row, 1985); Herbert Gans, *Middle-American Individualism* (New York: Free Press, 1988).

EPILOGUE

1. My thinking here about the ideological power of human-interest journalism has been strongly influenced by the efforts of cultural historians to apply Antonio Gramsci's concept of "hegemony" to the study of popular culture. See, for example, T. J. Jackson Lears, "The Concept of Cultural Hegemony: Problems and Possibilities," *American Historical Review* 90 (June 1985):

567–90; George Lipsitz, "Popular Culture: This Ain't No Sideshow," in *Time Passages: Collective Memory and American Popular Culture* (Minneapolis: University of Minnesota Press, 1990); and, for a more theoretical account, Stuart Hall, "Culture, Media, and the 'Ideological Effect,'" in James Curran, Michael Gurevitch, and Janet Woollocott, eds., *Mass Communication and Society* (London: Edward Arnold, 1977), 315–48.

2. On "popular accents," see Stuart Hall, "Notes on Deconstructing 'the Popular,'" in Raphael Samuel, ed., *People's History and Socialist Theory* (London: Routledge and Kegan Paul, 1981), 227–40; and Michael Denning, *Mechanic Accents: Dime Novels and Working-Class Culture in America* (London: Verso, 1987). For a subtle and important account stressing the ambiguous nature of much popular culture, see Fredric Jameson, "Reification and Utopia in Mass Culture," *Social Text* 1 (1979): 130–48.

3. Paul Theroux, "Ms. Taylor Will See You Now," *Talk* 1 (Oct. 1999): 216.

4. Stephanie Tuck, "Puff and Stuff," *In Style* 6 (Oct. 1999): 395.

5. Steven Levy, "Behind the Gates Myth," *Newsweek*, 30 Aug. 1999, 47.

6. For a fascinating account of how audiences relate to the culture of celebrity, see Joshua Gamson, *Claims to Fame: Celebrity in Contemporary America* (Berkeley: University of California Press, 1993).

INDEX

Hannagan, Steve, 76, 101, 266
Hard, William, 185
Harper's, 56, 80
Harper's Bazaar, 86
Harper's Weekly, 43, 175, 180, 257
Harriman, E. H., 147
Harriman, Margaret Case, 68, 84, 85
Harrington, H. F., 56, 79
Harvey, George, 180
Hayes, Helen, 100, 127
Hayes, Will, 217
Haywood, William (Big Bill), 182
Hearst, William Randolph, 8, 33,
    46, 80, 86, 142, 147, 275
Held, Anna, 92
Hellinger, Mark, 53
Hellman, Geoffrey, 84, 85, 117
Hendrick, Burton J., 194
Henie, Sonja, 226
Henry, Patrick, 18
Hepburn, Katharine, 68, 116, 122,
    127, 128, 131, 227, 228, 229
Herriman, George, 212
History of Standard Oil (Tarbell),
    154
Hodgson, Claire, 269–70
Holmes, Oliver Wendell, 246
Hoover, Herbert, 183, 185, 186, 188
Hoover, Lou Henry, 125
Hopkins, Harry, 157, 191
Howe, Louis McHenry, 201
Howells, William Dean, 35
Huggins, Miller, 261, 262–63, 269,
    270
Hughes, Charles Evans, 183, 187
Hughes, Howard, 110, 114
Human-interest journalism: emer-
    gence of, 30–36; influence of, on
    celebrity, 36–40; and approaches
    for treating celebrities, 42–75
Hume, David, 19
Hutton, Barbara, 86, 141–42, 169

Ickes, Harold L., 198–99
Ingalls, John J., 52

Ingerly, Robert, 261
In Style, 109, 279
International Celebrity Register
    (Blackwell and Amory), 11–12, 73
International News Service, 80, 86
Interviews, 53–55
Irwin, Will, 116

Jacobs, Mike, 74, 76, 101
James, William, 34
Jamison, Jack, 223
Jefferson, Joseph, 57
Jefferson, Thomas, 19
Jeffries, Jim, 72, 248, 260
Jewett, Helen, 49
Johnson, Hugh, 199, 200–201
Johnson, Jack, 71–72, 248, 250, 271
Johnson, Samuel, 20
Johnson, Walter, 252
Johnston, Alva, 61, 82, 84, 85, 87–
    88, 100–101, 103, 131, 196, 201–2,
    206–7, 209, 228
Jolson, Al, 120, 212, 241
Jones, Bobby, 87, 252–53, 254, 255,
    257–58, 259
Josephson, Matthew, 154
Journalists: treatment of public
    figures by, 31–34 35–36, 40, 48;
    as insiders familiar with celeb-
    rities, 64–65, 89; as specialists
    producing celebrity journalism,
    82–90; wariness of, 95–102; and
    criticism of rich, 142–50; and
    "industrial statesmen," 151–57;
    depict wealthy as "progressive
    philanthropists," 157–64; cast
    rich as "wholesome," 164–69;
    new treatment of politicians and
    political activists by, 172–75; por-
    tray political figures as bosses,
    demagogues, and fanatics, 175–
    82; associate political figures
    with "practical idealism," 182–
    96; response of, to New Deal and
    radicalism, 196–202; and popu-

lar culture industries, 207–10; criticize commercialism of popular culture industries, 210–17; and producers of popular culture as "artists," 217–31; depict some actors and entertainers as "wholesome," 231–39; and emerging world of spectator sports, 242–45; and ideal of "sport," 245–47; criticize commercialization and spread of entertainment values in sports, 247–51; link athletes to personal efficiency and ethos of professions, 251–56; promotion of "amateur spirit" by, 257–64; and private lives of athletes, 264–71; and public influence through human-interest journalism, 274–75

Kaufman, Emma B., 67, 116, 122
Kaufman, Herbert, 154
Kearns, Jack, 132, 249
Kelley, Florence, 190, 191
Kelley, Hubert, 196
Kellogg, Paul U., 191
Kennedy, John B., 83, 136, 249, 260
Kent, Frank R., 185
Kerensky, Alexander, 47
Keyhoe, Donald E., 106–7, 130, 131, 135, 136–37
Keys, C. M., 153–54
King Features Syndicate, 88
Kitchen, Karl, 220, 221, 227, 233, 234, 237
Kobbe, Gustav, 84, 120, 225, 232, 233, 234, 35

Labor leaders: as subjects of celebrity journalism, 193–96
Ladies' Home Journal, 58, 59, 60, 64, 84, 85, 86, 114, 116, 120, 121, 122, 125, 162, 219, 221, 225, 234
Ladies of the Press (Ross), 83

La Follette, Robert M., 182, 183, 184, 185, 197
Langtry, Lillie, 51
Lardner, Ring, 248, 255
Laughlin, Clara E., 232
Lee, Ivy L., 93, 94, 98, 170
Lefevre, Edwin, 62, 84, 147
Leggett, William, 22
Lenglen, Suzanne, 248, 258–59
Leslie's Weekly, 218
Levy, Steven, 279–80
Lewis, Alfred Henry, 50, 148, 178
Lewis, John L., 194–95
Lewis, Sinclair, 128
Liberty, 60, 61, 66, 68, 84, 87, 108, 109, 116, 127, 137, 208, 209, 223, 224, 226, 229, 258, 259, 261, 266, 268, 271
Life, 61, 64, 74, 101, 108, 117, 134, 164, 208, 223, 228
Lind, Jenny, 50, 90
Lindbergh, Charles A., 1–3, 13, 65, 102, 103–4, 106–7, 109, 111, 130–31, 132, 134, 135, 136–37
Lloyd, Harold, 115, 227, 230
Lloyd, Henry Demarest, 145, 153
Lodge, Henry Cabot, 179, 180
Lombard, Carole, 109, 126–27, 206–7, 209, 228–29, 234
Long, Huey, 180–81, 197
Loos, Anita, 48
Lord, Chester S., 83, 146
Lorimer, George H., 80, 106
Los Angeles Herald, 86
Los Angeles Times, 86
Louis XIV (king of France), 14
Louis, Joe, 72–73, 74–75, 76, 101, 260, 271, 272
Louisville Times, 85
Luce, Henry, 8, 157

MacArthur, Charles, 127
Macfadden, Bernarr, 64, 88
Macfarlane, Peter Clark, 218–19
Mack, Connie, 263

Robinson, Arthur, 260
Robinson, Bill (Bojangles), 72
Robinson-Jewett murder case, 49
Rockefeller, Abby Aldrich, 161, 163
Rockefeller, John D., 42, 55, 58, 96,
    111, 143, 147, 149, 151, 152, 153–
    54, 155, 158, 159, 160, 161, 164,
    166, 169, 277
Rockefeller, John D. Jr., 161, 163,
    177
Rockefeller family, 164, 167
Rogers, Betty Blake, 123, 236
Rogers, Earl, 86
Rogers, Will, 123, 124, 236, 237, 241
Roosevelt, Alice, 67, 116, 121–22
Roosevelt, Edith, 121, 125, 136
Roosevelt, Eleanor, 68, 117, 119,
    125–12
Roosevelt, Franklin D., 53, 180,
    197–202
Roosevelt, Theodore, 53, 55, 58, 60,
    67, 81, 84, 91–92, 96, 99, 114, 116,
    119, 120, 121, 134, 136, 172, 180,
    182, 183, 184, 185, 186, 187, 188,
    189, 197
Roosevelt, Theodore Jr., 58
Root, Elihu, 180
Ross, Harold, 61, 88
Ross, Ishbel, 83
Rosten, Leo C., 99
Rousseau, Jean-Jacques, 19, 20, 21
Roxborough, John, 270–71
Runyon, Damon, 80, 87, 243
Russell, Charles Edward, 148, 187
Russell, Lillian, 57, 66
Ruth, George Herman (Babe), 48,
    65, 101, 111, 129, 131–32, 246,
    249–50, 252, 253–54, 259–60,
    261–63, 267–70, 272
Ruppert, Jacob, 48, 259
Ryan, Thomas F., 86

Sacramento Bee, 87
St. Johns, Adela Rogers, 59, 60, 61,
    68, 80, 82, 84, 86–87, 89, 99, 100,

122, 127, 129, 141, 215, 228, 230,
    232, 235, 237, 276
St. Johns, William, 86
San Francisco Examiner, 80, 86
Sanger, Margaret, 67, 68, 192
Saroyan, William, 115
Saturday Evening Post, 57, 59, 61,
    62, 65, 74, 80, 83, 84, 85, 86, 88,
    98, 104, 106, 128, 130, 133, 150,
    151, 157, 160, 166, 167, 176, 184,
    190, 198, 199, 201, 208, 218, 219,
    226, 262, 270, 271
Schiff, Jacob, 192
Schudson, Michael, 36
Scriber's, 56, 79, 80
Scripps, E. W., 46, 80, 142, 147
Sedgwick, Theodore, 17
Selden, Charles A., 123
Seldes, Gilbert, 212, 223
Selfhood: and new views influencing
    depiction of celebrities, 36–40
Self-presentation: affected by emer-
    gence of public sphere, 17–20;
    and use of "fronts," 26–28; and
    changes inspired by development
    of press, 33, 90–95
Self-realization: as goal of personal
    growth, 38; and "true success" in
    celebrity profiles, 113–19
Selznick, David O., 207, 222
Sennett, Mack, 213
Seven Lively Arts, The (Seldes),
    212–13
Sharpe, Howard, 109, 229
Shaw, George Bernard, 54, 55, 81
Shearer, Norma, 238
Sheridan, Mattie, 58, 63
Sherwood, Robert E., 222
Smart Set, 212, 219
Smiles, Samuel, 23–24, 35, 41
Smith, Alfred, 183, 185, 186, 192,
    199
Smith, Beverly, 84, 110, 194–95
Smith, Helen Huntington, 192, 265
Snyder, Larry, 270